Also by Variorum:

Bede and his World: The Jarrow Lectures, 1958–1993

In the Collected Studies Series:

HELMUT GNEUSS
Language and History in Early England

HELMUT GNEUSS
Books and Libraries in Early England

URSULA DRONKE
Myth and Fiction in Early Norse Lands

MICHAEL W. HERREN
Latin Letters in Early Christian Ireland

WALLACE MARTIN LINDSAY
ed. Michael Lapidge
Studies in Early Medieval Latin Glossaries

P. SIMS-WILLIAMS
Britain and Early Christian Europe

CHARLES W. JONES
ed. Wesley M. Stevens
Bede, the Schools and the Computus

DAVID N. DUMVILLE
Britons and Anglo-Saxons in the Early Middle Ages

NEIL WRIGHT
History and Literature in Late Antiquity and the
Early Medieval West

SUSAN REYNOLDS
Ideas and Solidarities of the Medieval Laity:
England and Western Europe

ADRIAAN VERHULST
Rural and Urban Aspects of Early Medieval North-West Europe

BENEDICTA WARD
Signs and Wonders: Saints, Miracles and Prayer from the
4th Century to the 14th

COLLECTED STUDIES SERIES

North of the Tees

Professor H.S. Offler
(1913–1991)

H. S. Offler

North of the Tees

Studies in Medieval British History

Edited by
A. J. Piper and A. I. Doyle

LONDON AND NEW YORK

1996

First published 1996 by Variorum, Ashgate Publishing

Published 2017 by Routledge
2 Park Square, Milton Park, Abingdon, Oxon OX14 4RN
52 Vanderbilt Avenue, New York, NY 10017

Routledge is an imprint of the Taylor & Francis Group, an informa business

This edition copyright © 1996 by B.E. Offler

All rights reserved. No part of this book may be reprinted or reproduced or utilised in any form or by any electronic, mechanical, or other means, now known or hereafter invented, including photocopying and recording, or in any information storage or retrieval system, without permission in writing from the publishers.

Notice:
Product or corporate names may be trademarks or registered trademarks, and are used only for identification and explanation without intent to infringe.

British Library CIP Data

    Offler, H.S. (Hilary Seton), 1913–1991
    North of the Tees: Studies in Medieval British History. — (Variorum Collected Studies Series: 547)
    1. Great Britain—History—Medieval, 1066–1485. I. Title. II. Doyle, A.I. (A. Ian). III. Piper, A.J. (Alan J.).
    941'.02

US Library of Congress CIP Data

    Offler, H.S. (Hilary Seton), 1913–1991
    North of the Tees: Studies in Medieval British History / H.S. Offler; edited by A.I. Doyle and A.J. Piper.
      p. cm. — (Variorum Collected Studies Series: CS547)
    Includes indexes (cloth: alk. paper)
    1. England, Northern—History. 2. Great Britain—History—Medieval, 1066–1485. I. Doyle, A.I. (A. Ian). II. Piper, A.J. (Alan J.). III. Title. IV. Series: Collected Studies: CS547.
    DA670.N73O34 1996   96–18604
    942.7–dc20   CIP

ISBN 13: 978-0-86078-599-6 (hbk)

COLLECTED STUDIES SERIES CS547

CONTENTS

Foreword		vii–xi
Acknowledgements		xii
P. D. A. Harvey, Memoir of Hilary Seton Offler, 1913–1991 *1991 Lectures and Memoirs. Proceedings of the British Academy 80, pp. 433–52. Oxford, 1991*		xiii–xxxii
I	Medieval historians of Durham *Inaugural Lecture of the Professor of Medieval History Delivered in the Applebey Lecture Theatre, University of Durham, 14 March 1958*	3–24
II	A note on the last medieval bishops of Hexham *Archaeologia Aeliana, 4th ser., 40. Newcastle upon Tyne, 1962*	163–169
III	The early archdeacons in the diocese of Durham *Transactions of the Architectural and Archaeological Society of Durham and Northumberland 10. Gateshead, 1962*	189–207
IV	The date of Durham (*Carmen de situ Dunelmi*) *Journal of English and Germanic Philology 61. Urbana, Ill., 1962*	591–594
V	William of St Calais, first Norman bishop of Durham *Transactions of the Architectural and Archaeological Society of Durham and Northumberland 10. Gateshead, 1950*	258–279
VI	The tractate *De iniusta vexacione Willelmi episcopi primi* *English Historical Review 66. Harlow, 1951*	321–341
VII	Ranulf Flambard as bishop of Durham (1099–1128) *Durham University Journal 64. Durham, 1971, and Durham Cathedral Lecture. Durham, 1971*	14–25

VIII	A Northumberland charter of King Henry I *Archaeologia Aeliana, 4th ser., 44. Newcastle upon Tyne, 1967*	181–188
IX	A note on the early history of the Priory of Carlisle *Transactions of the Cumberland and Westmorland Antiquarian and Archaeological Society, NS 65. Kendal, 1965*	176–181
X	Hexham and the *Historia Regum* *Transactions of the Architectural and Archaeological Society of Durham and Northumberland, NS 2. Newcastle upon Tyne, 1971*	51–62
XI	A medieval chronicle from Scotland *Co-authored with J. M. Todd* *The Scottish Historical Review 47. Aberdeen, 1968*	151–159
XII	Re-reading Boldon Book *First publication*	1–38
XIII	Fitz Meldred, Neville and Hansard *First publication*	1–17
XIV	Murder on Framwellgate Bridge *Archaeologia Aeliana, 5th ser., 16. Newcastle upon Tyne, 1988*	193–211
XV	A note on the northern Franciscan chronicle *Nottingham Medieval Studies 28. Nottingham, 1984*	45–59
XVI	Reason in politics, 1363–4, a *Quaestio* from Scotland *First publication*	1–26
General Index		1–18
Index of Manuscripts		19–21

This volume contains xxxii + 287 pages

FOREWORD

H. S. Offler died on 24 January 1991, a few days before his seventy-eighth birthday. This volume begins with the fine memoir by Paul Harvey, who succeeded him as professor of history in Durham in 1978. In it he notes HSO's 'profound belief in the importance of local history', and quotes his remark that 'Again and again . . . the ambitions of the synthesist shatter on the recalcitrance of the local facts'.[1] One major expression of these views was the time that HSO gave to the work of the Surtees Society, in publishing original historical materials relating to the area covered by the ancient kingdom of Northumbria: he served as Secretary from 1950 to 1966 and, most fittingly, as President from 1980 until 1987, when it finally proved impossible to rebut his determined insistence that age required him to resign. In the latter rôle he could be relied upon to give meticulous attention whenever his comments on proposed publications were sought, and to provide welcome re-assurance when the present Secretary (AJP) was confronted with manifestations of temperament on the part of contributing editors, which HSO would describe as 'whim-whams'.

As Secretary of the Society he oversaw the preparation of eighteen volumes, 160–177. His strenuous devotion to this task was exemplified by the fact that in 1951 he spent the day and night before leaving for his wedding producing the final typescript of one volume, and then broke his journey to Hertfordshire to deliver it to the printers. In 1968 he crowned these achievements by producing one of the finest volumes to grace the Society's series of publications, *Durham Episcopal Charters 1071–1152*, (Vol. 179). In it HSO deployed to great effect the technical skills required of a medieval historian in dealing with original documents. Two aspects of the material attracted his particular attention: the light that it shed on the development of the baronial structure in Anglo-Norman Durham, and the analysis of the process whereby the monks of Durham made good their lack of foundation charters by an extended sequence of forgeries. These and related themes figure in a significant number of the studies in the present volume.

County Durham was not covered by the great survey of 1086 which produced the Domesday Book. In consequence the Durham episcopal charters for 1071–1152 represent a source of capital importance for

---

[1] See Memoir below, p. 447

reconstructing the way in which tenurial patterns changed in the century after the Norman Conquest; this is amply demonstrated by HSO's extended annotation of each document. His interest in disentangling the intricacies of baronial family relationships is well illustrated in the present volume by discussion of a charter of Henry I shedding light on the barony of Ellingham or Jesmond (VIII), and, much more substantially, by a previously unpublished study that provides surer ground for the early history of the Neville family (XIII). The trajectory of this family, from its roots in pre-Conquest Northumbria to the very apogee of political influence in fifteenth-century England, appealed to HSO's pride in his adopted *patria*, the land 'twixt Tyne and Tees, and one decisive episode in the rise of the Nevilles prompted him to produce an apparently uncharacteristic excursion into sensationalism, 'Murder on Framwellgate Bridge' (XIV). Although this does indeed concern the murder of Sir Richard Marmaduke by Sir Robert Neville in Durham in 1318, the focus is in fact the complex history of the two families involved which led up to the murder; for the welter of contemporary violence that it exemplified HSO expressed a profound distaste, perhaps reflecting his own harsh experience as an artillery officer in World War II.

HSO's distinguished war service sprang from a strong sense of necessary duty and he grew in sympathy for men who took such action as the hour required. In his earliest foray into Durham history, the study of Bishop William of St Calais, 1080–96, (V), he registers a note of disapproval for Bishop William's political ambition. Twenty years later, after considerable experience as head of a university department of history, he was gentler in his treatment of a much more questionable character, Rannulf Flambard, bishop of Durham from 1099 to 1128 (VII). In the cold light of day the explanation for the 'infinitely discreditable' story of Flambard's attempted violation of Christina of Markyate may not ring quite true; heard in the medieval dormitory of the Durham monks from HSO's own lips, when, as if by some providential *coup de théâtre*, the gathering darkness of a winter's evening left only this consummate advocate's face illuminated by the solitary lamp at the reading-desk, it was bewitching and left an abiding impression that he could not withhold a certain measure of admiration from his quick-witted and resilient subject.

The study of Bishop Flambard rests on the solid foundation already laid in the edition of his charters, just as an important part of the ground for this edition had been cleared by the investigations of the early archdeacons of the diocese of Durham (III). It was by such measured steps that HSO commonly stalked his quarry. In contrast the most substantial of the previously unpublished writings, 'Re-reading Boldon Book' (XII), did not spring quite naturally from what had gone before; alone among the studies here, it was conceived in provocation, at the publication in 1982 of a less than adequate edition of Boldon Book, the late twelfth-century survey of the bishop of

Durham's estates, whose particular importance rests on the absence of County Durham from the Domesday survey. The result was a technical *tour de force*, dense in parts perhaps, but masterly in its marshalling of historical detail, its detection of corrupt transmission, and its unravelling of the problems of a document attested by multiple dynamic witnesses of varying codicological integrity. It forms the indispensable foundation for any future edition, although, as HSO stresses, anyone drawn to such a task will have to overcome formidable difficulties in presenting the result of their labours in a comprehensible manner.

HSO balanced his contributions to the study of north-eastern history from documentary sources with work on the literary sources, bringing to this his command of Latin and the experience born of his greatest undertaking, the editing of Ockham's political works. Apart from the pithy study on the date of the *Carmen de situ Dunelmi* (IV), he was primarily concerned with historiographical texts, for, like many historians of his generation, he generally gave a wide berth to hagiographical writers, such as Reginald of Durham. For his inaugural lecture as professor of medieval history he prepared a fine survey, 'Medieval historians of Durham' (I). This was a very deliberate choice, even though he was obliged to confront his audience with the fact that after the earlier twelfth century Durham could not lay claim to an historical school of any great distinction, save perhaps for the mid-fourteenth-century writer, generally taken to be the monk Robert Graystanes, who made effective use of archival materials in his work.

HSO's survey of the medieval historians of Durham did not encompass the so-called *Gesta Dunelmensia*, an incomplete report of events in the monastery during the earlier stages of Bishop Bek's dispute with Prior Hoton that broke out in 1300, splitting the community;[2] as a contemporary account it fell outside what he defined as historiography. Also omitted was an older piece, rather similar in nature, and largely consisting of a detailed account of the trial of Bishop St Calais in the royal court in 1088, the *De iniusta vexacione*. This had, however, attracted HSO's attention soon after he came to Durham, and gave rise to the most controversial study in the present volume (VI), published in 1951.[3] Controversial because it attacked the authenticity of a text prized by others as a unique contemporary eye-witness account of proceedings in William II's court. HSO's attack did not achieve total demolition with one single devastating bombshell; rather, in the manner of an artillery officer, he peppered his target with a stream of well-aimed fire, to the point where parts of it might be judged untenable, or at least unsafe,

---

[2] *Gesta Dunelmensia, A. D. M⁰CCC⁰*, ed. R. K. Richardson, *Camden Miscellany xiii* (Camden 3rd series 34; 1924), pp. iv–xiv and 1–58.

[3] An edition of *De iniusta vexacione* prepared by HSO will be published in the Camden series.

although not all have not felt obliged to abandon it. Here HSO probably underestimated the influence of the new canonical jurisprudence in England in 1088, but he did present a disconcerting accumulation of anomalies surrounding the persons mentioned in the text, comparable to those in the witness-lists of forged episcopal charters to which he subsequently turned his attention. His surmise that the text may have been put into its present form to rebut Eadmer's slurs on Bishop St Calais is strengthened by the fact that Eadmer's work was certainly known in Durham, being used as one of the sources supplementing the *Historia regum*.[4]

HSO maintained a keen interest in the *Historia regum*, much the most complicated, and the most important, historical work connected with Durham, and this led him in several directions. Apart from treatment in his inaugural lecture, his two published studies, Nos II and X, are not, however, concerned with Durham's part in the development and transmission of the text, but with that played by the Augustinian canons of Hexham; this well reflects his view that 'history writing in Durham weakened when it became too exclusively interested in Durham's history',[5] and serves as a reminder that Durham's Benedictines were not always the only competent medieval historians north of the Tees. His investigations involved one manuscript (Paris, Bibliothèque nationale, ms. nouv. acq. lat. 692) containing extracts from the *Historia regum* and John of Hexham's *Historia xxv annorum*; this also contained a little other material, among which he noticed an entry bearing on the beginnings of Carlisle cathedral priory (IX). The contents of the manuscript, and in particular a short inserted supplement, were subsequently afforded fuller consideration in collaboration with Dr John Todd in 'A medieval chronicle from Scotland' (XI).[6] From this there was a natural line of development by way of the Lanercost chronicle to a Latin Brut chronicle discussed in 'A note on the Northern Franciscan chronicle' (XV). Here again HSO showed himself an inveterate collator of texts, as in his work on Ockham; the great strength of his technical historiographical studies was his perseverance in setting a particular text against its possible pre-existing sources, identifing these, and so bringing into the spotlight what was likely to be original and worth closer attention. This study also brought him full circle back to Durham and the possibility of local authorship.

The final study (XVI) may appear to stand somewhat apart from the rest of the volume, in that it concerns a *quaestio* bearing on Scottish history. The

---

[4] M. Brett, 'John of Worcester and his contemporaries', in *The Writing of History in the Middle Ages: essays presented to Richard William Southern*, ed. R. H. C. Davis and J. M. Wallace-Hadrill (Oxford, 1981), pp. 119–21.

[5] Article I below, p. 18.

[6] It would have given HSO particular satisfaction that Dr Todd's fine edition of the Lanercost cartulary will appear in a forthcoming Surtees Society volume.

academic form of the text links well with HSO's interest in Ockham, but the Scottish dimension seems to represent an excursion onto foreign territory. In fact HSO took considerable delight in drawing attention to the possibility that twelfth-century Scottish kings might have succeeded in making the Border between England and Scotland not the Tweed, nor even the Tyne, but the Tees.[7] His allusions to this were especially striking when uttered in the senior common room in Durham Castle, formerly the twelfth-century bishop's hall, with its windows looking northwards to the hills over which King David II led the Scottish forces to defeat and capture at the battle of Neville's Cross in 1346, and so to the predicament from which the *quaestio* sprang.

This final study has had a somewhat chequered history. HSO unsuccessfully submitted it for publication in the *Scottish Historical Review*, but a copy of his text later came into the hands of Professor A. A. M. Duncan, who was urged to prepare an edition and translation, unaware that HSO had put his work on it into a finished state. This came to light only in January 1996, a few weeks before the publication of Professor Duncan's work in *Scottish Historical Society Miscellany* 12. HSO's foray beyond the Border had left its mark, but its full extent had not passed into Scottish memory.

A. J. PIPER

University of Durham
March 1996

Publisher's note: The articles in this volume, as in all others in the Collected Studies Series, have not been given a new, continuous pagination. In order to avoid confusion, and to facilitate their use where these same studies have been referred to elsewhere, the original pagination has been maintained wherever possible.

Each article has been given a Roman number in order of appearance, as listed in the Contents. This number is repeated on each page and cited in index entries.

In his set of offprints Professor Offler marked minor typographical errors, and AID and AJP have noticed a few more; these have been corrected. There were also longer notes, printed here at the end of the articles which they concern; an asterisk in the margin of the original articles indicates the points to which they refer. In a few instances AJP has felt it desirable to add further references or to supply amplifications; these are enclosed in square brackets.

---

[7] See Article XIII below.

ACKNOWLEDGEMENTS

The estate of H.S. Offler, the editors and publisher would like to thank all the original publishers and individuals, who have given permission to reproduce the articles in this volume: The University of Durham (I); The Society of Antiquaries of Newcastle upon Tyne (II, VIII & XIV); Professor A.F. Harding, *The Transactions of the Architectural and Archaeological Society of Durham and Northumberland* (III, V & X); the Board of Trustees of the University of Illinois and the University of Illinois Press (IV); Longman Group Ltd (VI); *Durham University Journal* (VII); Mr B.C. Jones, *The Transactions of the Cumberland and Westmorland Antiquarian and Archaeological Society* (IX); the Trustees of the Scottish Historical Review Trust (XI); *Nottingham Medieval Studies* (XV); and The British Academy for their 1991 *Lectures and Memoirs*.

Hilary Seton Offler
1913–1991

H. S. OFFLER was born on 3 February 1913. His father, Horace Offler, was manager, later general manager and secretary, of King's Acre Nurseries at Hereford. This was a long-established and substantial firm, with a shop in the city and from 120 to 200 men and boys on the pay-roll. The family lived in the city and after attending a 'dame school' (his own phrase) Offler in 1923 entered Hereford High School for Boys, a school of some 250 pupils with a small sixth form. In December 1928, two months before his sixteenth birthday, he won a scholarship to Emmanuel College, Cambridge. Both school and college were disconcerted at this achievement by one so young. His headmaster, R. G. Ruscoe, who had written that he 'would certainly be taken for a boy of 17 or 18 at least', explained that he had been put in for the scholarship 'as a trial shot'; Edward Welbourne, history tutor at Emmanuel, wrote that 'none of us knew . . . that he was so young—and though I ought to have noticed it from his papers I did not feel conscious of it in my talk with him'. It was agreed that the rules should be stretched to allow Offler to spend a further year at school; 'the worst mistake,' wrote Welbourne, advising him how to use this time, 'would be to know too much history and too little else'.

His early success was due to sheer native talent. A near-contemporary describes the school at this time as 'certainly no academic hot-house. . . . It was a happy school and . . . not outstanding in really any other way'. However, the history master, 'Araby' Heal, 'did really encourage us . . . ; one always felt one could do a little bit better after that essay had come back'. Offler himself deeply appreciated his school, looking for no more from it than what it could offer. He wrote, long afterwards, that 'it was a pretty rough world; but for the most part it was also tolerant and kindly. . . . there was little attempt to frustrate the common ambition of us all,

© The British Academy 1993.
Reproduced by permission from *Proceedings of the British Academy* 80, *1991 Lectures and Memoirs*.

H. S. OFFLER *(right)* with Professor Thacker

which was to turn into men as quickly as possible'. He had a special word for the woodwork master: 'On the whole the School understood craftsmanship far better than scholarship, and he was indeed a superb craftsman, teaching . . . —so gently, but quite inflexibly—the lesson that the only satisfactory way of doing any job was to do it in a proper fashion'. Among his schoolfellows, Offler

> had a reputation of being aloof, a very stern and efficient prefect, more feared by the juniors than Ruscoe himself. He must have had an enormous capacity for work. In the prefects' room . . . there were some large volumes of old history books . . . things like Lecky's *History of England*, and Offler had read them and annotated them from cover to cover.

According to another schoolfellow

> He was not just a 'swot', however. I remember a school cricket match at Wyeside when Offler was fielding at forward short-leg. A fast ball . . . was struck savagely in the direction of Offler, who turned to scan the boundary behind him, as did all the spectators. Offler, however, had caught the ball and transferred it to the pocket of his flannels with such speed that almost everyone around had been deceived.

Besides cricket, he played rugger, introduced in the school while he was there, and throughout his life he took keen interest in both games. Indeed, in all this there is much that those who knew him only in later life will recognize: a man who mostly seemed older than his years, stocky and sturdy, a strong personality, self-reliant and ready to accept the world as he found it, with a quick wit and mischievous sense of humour more often concealed than displayed, a prodigious and varied reader of history, a scholar whose work was marked by insistence on a craftsmanship little short of perfectionism. He became, however, sterner with himself than with other people and his aloofness cannot have lasted long, though he remained, in words he occasionally used of others, a very private person.[1]

In 1930 he went up to Emmanuel, aged seventeen. His undergraduate days were clouded by his parents' difficulties. The previous year Horace Offler had been ill and had had one leg amputated; during his unavoidably long absence from work the firm was less efficiently run and in May 1930 it collapsed, depriving him of both work and income. Offler's anxieties, long concealed, that he was adding to his father's financial burdens eventually

---

[1] This account of Offler's schooldays is drawn from the archives of Emmanuel College, Cambridge (henceforth ECA), tutorial file for Offler, letters of Ruscoe (14 Nov., 22 Dec. 1928), Welbourne (two of 18 Dec. 1928), Horace Offler (4 Mar. 1932); recorded recollections by Mr A. G. Gale; *Hereford High School for Boys. An Account of its first Fifty Years*, ed. R. G. Ruscoe (Hereford, 1962), pp.41–5; letter by Mr F. J. Handley in *Hereford Times*, 14 Feb. 1991.

produced short-lived physical symptoms of strain, whereupon Welbourne, now his tutor, went to much trouble to give practical help: he got the College to enhance the scholarship, corresponded with Horace Offler ('a most excellent and very courageous man, who has like Job, been persecuted by fate in a most alarming way'), and arranged for Offler to have a holiday in Paris under the aegis of an Emmanuel man who was in the diplomatic service. This was characteristic of Welbourne, who took a close and kindly interest in all his pupils; as he told Horace Offler, 'We are, as you may perhaps understand, more of a family and less of an institution than in appearance we may seem to be'.[2] Throughout Offler's Cambridge days, and later, Welbourne appears as his friend and guide. Offler, though very much his own man, seems to have had much in common with Welbourne in his wide reading and in his outlook on the world, and also later in the attention he paid to his pupils.[3] Welbourne, on the other hand, had little time for the technical mastery in dealing with historical sources that Offler made his own; whatever Welbourne's influence, Offler did not model himself on him.[4]

Welbourne soon saw Offler as a quite exceptional undergraduate. In June 1933 he wrote that he was 'not only the best historian who has been at this college for at least ten years, but is perhaps, the best I can fairly expect to meet as a pupil'. By then he had been placed in the first class in the first-year intercollegiate examination in history, and in Part I (starred for distinction) and Part II of the Historical Tripos. Early the previous year Welbourne had already envisaged his continuing at Cambridge on graduation, and he himself seems to have had no hesitation; his father wrote of 'his studious nature' and 'his great desire for a scholastic career', remarking that on completing Part II of the Tripos he 'had hardly reached Home ere he resumed his studies'. From his first year it was medieval history that had most attracted him. Welbourne consulted G. T. Lapsley and J. P. Whitney and all were agreed that he should take a fourth undergraduate year to work for Section III of Part II of the Theological Tripos, 'a Section entirely devoted to Church History, where the work is

---

[2] ECA, tutorial file for Offler, especially letters of Welbourne (26 Feb., 2, 5 Mar. 1932), Horace Offler (4 Mar., 15 Apr. 1932).

[3] They were alike too in typing their own letters, but Offler was much the better typist. In quotations, following editorial conventions of which Offler would approve, Welbourne's typing slips have been silently corrected. The correspondence between Welbourne and Offler from 1928 to 1945 in the ECA tutorial file is of more than simply personal interest in their comments on contemporary Cambridge, on European affairs before and during the war and on other matters.

[4] There are interesting memoirs of Welbourne in *Emmanuel College Magazine*, xlviii (1965-6), pp.6-12, and by D. Newsome, 'Two Emmanuel Historians', ibid., pp.21-34 (reprinted in *Emmanuel College Magazine: Quatercentenary Issue* [1984], pp.104-14).

so arranged as to facilitate candidature for the Lightfoot Scholarship, a university scholarship of some value and a good deal of distinction'. As Welbourne put it,

> so young a man as Mr Offler needs a year of undergraduate work, both to broaden his basis of knowledge, and to prevent the harm which would almost certainly be done to a man of the highest promise, by premature work on original sources.

His scholarship was renewed, and a year later he had not only been placed yet again in the first class but had won the Lightfoot Scholarship with work on the pontificate of Boniface VIII and had been elected to a research studentship at Emmanuel. In 1936 he was awarded a research fellowship, also at Emmanuel, which continued until 1940.[5]

Offler took part in few leisure activities at Cambridge. He walked, in and around Cambridge, he may have played some rugger in his first year and he certainly took a keen interest in the college's fortunes in athletics.[6] From his first year onwards he was a member of the college's Pococurante Club (named after the Venetian noble in *Candide*), an essay society of twelve members, to which he read papers 'In his inimitable fashion' on medieval and later topics; in one he used Antonio Magliabecchi, Florentine librarian and book-collector of the seventeenth century, 'as a stalking horse behind which to propound his own peculiar ideas about the necessity of a moratorium on the publication of books'.[7] According to Sir David Pitblado, his college contemporary and friend, 'Offler soon became a central figure in a loosely knit group brought together by mutual liking rather than common studies or political leanings (none of us, if I remember correctly, was a member of a political club, though we were well aware of the time in which we were living)'; though he had already developed the measured style of speech that was so weighty and authoritative when he was older, 'The rest of us were not overawed by his avuncular manner, but enjoyed the quality of his thought and wit'.[8] In his first long vacation he went with Pitblado on his first visit to Germany, walking in the Harz and the Thüringerwald and staying in youth hostels. On another holiday, in 1936, they stayed at a

---

[5] ECA, tutorial file for Offler, letters of Welbourne (10 June 1931, 2 Mar. 1932, 22 June 1933, 16 Jan. 1934), Horace Offler (24 June 1933).

[6] Memoir of Offler by Sir David Pitblado in *Emmanuel College Magazine*, lxxiii (1990–1), p.137; ECA, tutorial file for Offler, letter of Welbourne (30 Sept. 1943) mentions his playing rugger as an undergraduate but his name does not appear in the College Cup Competition teams listed in *Emmanuel College Magazine*.

[7] ECA, SOC 24/1,2 (minute books of the Pococurante Club); the quotations are from minutes respectively of 17 Oct. 1932 and 2 Nov. 1938 (the latter was written by Offler himself as secretary).

[8] Pitblado in *Emmanuel College Magazine*, lxxiii (1990–1), p.137.

country house on the Weser, where a baroness took foreign paying guests to improve their German; then they went to Berlin, full of preparations for the Olympic Games, with the Nazi Party much in evidence. 'My dear Pit,' declared Offler, 'I'm afraid we shall have to fight these people.' His realism and prescience are indisputable.[9]

By 1936, however, work as well as leisure was taking Offler to Germany. In April 1934 Welbourne had introduced him to C. W. Previté-Orton of St John's College, who supervised his research; the topic registered was 'Lewis of Bavaria'. Supervisor and subject were well chosen. After Previté-Orton's death in 1947 Offler referred to him as his 'master and friend', and Previté-Orton early remarked on Offler's 'fresh and original mind . . . following up clues and suggestions with remarkable skill and pertinacity'. This was in February 1936, when he reported that Offler

> seems to have produced an original and sound picture of Lewis, his reign, and Germany in his time. Out of a confused welter of events, persons, dynasties, feuds and political moves, he has made a coherent, purposeful history, and has changed an obscure farrago into an articulated and meaning development.

This much was achieved from printed sources. He now sought to revise and expand his work by research on manuscripts, and much of the following year was spent away from Cambridge: at Paris and Berlin in June and September 1936 for practice in palaeography and diplomatic, at the Public Record Office in the winter of 1936–7, at Marseilles, Avignon and Paris in March and April 1937 and at Munich, other places in Bavaria, Vienna and again Paris in the summer. His mastery of codicology and textual criticism is clear from his doctoral thesis, which includes detailed discussion and edited texts of documents he found on these travels; equally clear is his mastery of languages. Apparently he had already by 1934 taught himself German (only French was taught at his school), but by 1940 Welbourne described him as having 'a very intimate knowledge of Germany, good knowledge of German, some knowledge of French, some knowledge also of Italian, Spanish, Dutch and perhaps a little Czech, and an immense capacity for work'.

The products of this work were impressive, the more so as Offler did much tutorial work at Emmanuel throughout these years of research and in 1937–9 lectured for the Historical Faculty first on late-medieval German history, then on medieval European history in general. The dissertation which won him his research fellowship in 1936 dealt with Lewis's reign in general. His thesis, submitted in 1938 and accepted for a doctorate, was confined to 'The Emperor Lewis IV and the Curia from 1330 to 1347: Canon

---

[9] Ex inf. Sir David Pitblado.

Law and International Relationship in the first half of the Fourteenth Century'. Its aims were first to elucidate the negotiations between Lewis and the papacy, reinterpreting the procurations, documents of authorisation for the emperor's proctors at Avignon, and second to set these negotiations in the wider picture of European politics. His first article, 'England and Germany at the Beginning of the Hundred Years' War', was published in the *English Historical Review* in October 1939; another, 'Kaiser Ludwig IV and die Prokurationenfrage', was to have appeared at the same time in *Deutsches Archiv für Geschichte des Mittelalters* and proofs were sent back in August, 'but,' he later wrote, 'what became of them I do not know; I imagine the article was suppressed for patriotic reasons'. Meanwhile, however, work on fourteenth-century politics led naturally to an interest in the writings on political theory that either underlay or stemmed from them, and he accepted an invitation to join J. G. Sikes and other Cambridge scholars in editing the complete political works of William of Ockham. He collaborated in searching for relevant manuscripts on the Continent, and in the first volume, published by Manchester University Press in 1940, he edited one tract himself, 'Consultatio de Causa Matrimoniali', and completed the work of R. H. Snape on another, 'An Princeps . . . possit recipere Bona Ecclesiarum'. These later works were in no way by-products of his doctoral thesis, sections of it worked up for publication; rather, the thesis was simply one, not especially important, stage in a longer programme of intellectual exploration, which rapidly moved beyond it to further areas of interest and discovery. In fact he never took the Ph.D. degree to which he was entitled, seeing it perhaps as a mere bauble. 'Now you've got this out of the way,' he long after told a younger colleague who had just achieved a doctorate, 'go away and become a learned man—but it may take some years.'[10]

In Offler's case this process, which others might have supposed tolerably complete, was interrupted by war. His research fellowship expired in June 1940 and, perhaps because of what he had seen of Nazi Germany, he felt a strong personal commitment to fight. Welbourne tried to get him a non-combatant post that would put his skills to best use: Offler 'is extremely anxious to get into a combatant unit,' he wrote to the recruiting board, 'but I am anxious that his services should not be wasted'. Offler however, 'calling himself an author when teachers were a reserved occupation', cut the ground from beneath his feet: 'Mr Offler made personal application

---

[10] These two paragraphs on Offler's work from 1934 to 1940 are drawn from papers in the possession of Mrs B. E. Offler (henceforth Offler papers), application for Durham readership; ECA, tutorial file for Offler, letters of Welbourne (27 Apr., 10 Oct. 1934, 15 July 1940), Previté-Orton (26 Feb. 1936); ECA, personal file for Offler, letter of Offler (10 May 1938).

to this Office,' the secretary of the board replied, 'and requested that his calling up for service be expedited'. He joined up on 15 August. Medically he was below Class I because of poor eyesight—he already wore thick glasses—and this restricted the form of his active service.[11] He was placed in the Royal Artillery, in the 111th Heavy Anti-Aircraft Regiment (an attempt to transfer to the RAF was unsuccessful), and spent the following winter more or less uncomfortably in Scotland. In April 1941 he wrote as a Lance-Bombardier to Welbourne from Johnstone, Renfrewshire, where they were under canvas:

> We did our stuff reasonably competently in the Clyde blitz—that is to say we diverted the bombers from their industrial targets on to the tenements of Clydebank. There they killed some thousands, but the shipyards go on almost unaffected. But sometimes I wonder how long the men will fail to realise that this is the purpose of AA. gunnery—and how long I shall be able to refrain from telling them.[12]

For a time his battery was posted in Northern Ireland, but by October he was at Royal Artillery OCTU at Shrivenham. When commissioned he was posted to no.268 Battery of the 40th (Highland) Light Anti-Aircraft Regiment, in which he spent the rest of the war. It was part of the 51st (Highland) Division, heavily involved in the fighting from Egypt to Sicily and from Normandy to Germany, and much of his service was in the front line. He reached the Western Desert in September 1942, just before the battle of El Alamein. From March to August 1943 he was seconded to serve as liaison officer with a Free French flying column in Tunisia (1er Régiment de Marche de Spahis Marocains), which he described in a letter to Welbourne:

> They were Spahis, all ex-horsemen, and some had killed Germans and Italians in this war from horseback with pistol and sabre. Henceforward I shall always walk with my legs a little bowed. But they did teach me for the first time what is really meant by an eye for country and by and large were the most gallant collection of people I have ever met.[13]

What he did not tell Welbourne (or anyone else, perhaps even his own parents) was that he had been awarded the Croix de Guerre—for want of a new one General Leclerc took the cross from his own uniform and pinned it on Offler—and had been cited by Leclerc:

---

[11] ECA, tutorial file for Offler, letters of Welbourne (2 Feb., two of 15 July 1940, 30 Jan. 1941, 30 Sept. 1943), W. G. Brown (20 July 1940); Offler papers include notes, with precise dates, of his principal movements during his war service.

[12] ECA, tutorial file for Offler, letters of Offler (14 Jan. ['1940'], 5, 24 Feb., 18 Apr. 1941), Welbourne (30 Jan., 18 Feb. 1941).

[13] ECA, tutorial file for Offler, letters of Offler (20 Oct. 1941, 29 Aug. 1943).

A parfaitement assuré son service de liaison dans des conditions difficiles et souvent sous le feu violent de l'ennemi . . . . A rendu de réels services au Régiment et a été un bel exemple de courage, de sang-froid et de camaraderie au combat.[14]

When he rejoined his battery it was in Sicily; it returned to England in November, then sailed for Normandy immediately after the landings in June 1944. In August he wrote:

> There is a most peculiar—and in some ways unhappy—difference between being with an Army which knows final victory is certain, and probably soon, and the old desert and even Sicilian days when we lived so much among uncertainties that they ceased to worry us . . . . This has been on the whole a much nastier war than the Mediterranean one—partly because we are always working at much closer quarters, because of the terrain . . .

Whether from events in Normandy or for other reasons, the war affected Offler deeply, and in later life he spoke little of his experiences. By May 1945 his unit was at Bremen. He was released from the army in June 1946.[15]

In his absence on war service attempts had been made to get him a post at Cambridge, but unsuccessfully. As Welbourne put it, 'he has left several of his contemporary rivals still adding to their academic accomplishments', and 'he will have gone to the War like so many other people to his cost'.[16] He was, however, appointed to a lectureship at Bristol University which he took up in October 1946; then, a year later, he was appointed Reader in Medieval History in the Durham Colleges of Durham University. In 1956 he was appointed Professor of Medieval History, the post he held until he retired, and he remained at Durham for the rest of his life. He married, in 1951, his colleague Betty Elfreda Jackson, and from 1952 onwards they lived in an attractively situated house in Old Elvet, in the centre of Durham. This patently happy marriage and their family life—they had two sons—were clearly of the greatest importance to Offler. He joined University College and became a prominent member of its Senior Common Room in Durham Castle. He was soon a keen supporter of the university's rugger club, though his own physical recreation was a daily walk in the outskirts of the city. There was a modestly convivial side to his life: he was a founder member of a college dining club and he enjoyed regular meetings with university and other friends in one or another of the city's pubs. For well over forty years his life was centred on Durham, a city that

---

[14] Ex inf. Mr R. Evans; Offler papers, copy of divisional order of 2 June 1943.
[15] ECA, tutorial file for Offler, letters of Offler (25 June, 29 Aug. 1944), Welbourne (12 May 1945).
[16] ECA, tutorial file for Offler, letters of E. M. W. Tillyard (21 Sept. 1943), Welbourne (30 Sept. 1943, two of 12 May 1945), Previté-Orton (15 May 1945).

strangely blends elements of the two other places most familiar to him, Hereford and Cambridge.

In the army Offler can have had little opportunity for systematic reading, though according to a fellow-officer 'even in the thick of it he had his nose in a book (or books)'.[17] The return to historical work must have been a severe challenge. He met it with an entirely new venture. The Swiss cultural organization Pro Helvetia had initiated the project of publishing, through Oxford University Press, *A Short History of Switzerland*, and Offler joined Edgar Bonjour of Basle and G. R. Potter in writing it. He was working on it at Bristol, when publication was expected in 1948; in the event it appeared in 1952. Offler's contribution, on the period from the Celtic settlement to the end of the fourteenth century, touched only in the last of its five chapters on his earlier work on fourteenth-century politics. Its hundred pages, readable and informative, are the longest piece of his own continuous prose that he ever published. To the end of his days he continued to work steadily on manuscripts and texts, to read, to ponder and to write, but he seems never to have recaptured the pace—or perhaps the intellectual excitement—of those years when at Cambridge and London, Paris and Munich, he was discovering for himself, from first-hand evidence, what was really going on between the imperial and papal courts in the mid-fourteenth century. The interruption and experiences of war may have contributed to this, and of course he was now acquiring new and time-consuming responsibilities, both academic and personal. But rather more it reflects the maturing of his views on the role of publication in historical work. He saw putting work into print as something not to be undertaken lightly, and he would warn younger colleagues against premature publication, in his generation more likely to be damaging to an academic career than it has since become. Publication should rather be the outcome not only of comprehensive research but of long, careful thought that was certain it had found the right answer—or as certain as possible. Already in 1937 he remarked cynically that 'Most historians would admit that to discover "Wie es eigentlich war" is beyond their usual attainment'.[18] He saw no point in writing a second time what had already been written once, or in writing anything at all unless one had something to say that was worth saying, and to publish something that was wrong would be to create error, a disservice to scholarship far worse than keeping silent. The historian should write primarily for other historians: 'historians' history—the only sort that matters', as he put it in 1958.[19] He saw the risk, however: 'If the

[17] Letter from Mr R. Evans to the author, 27 Jan. 1992.
[18] *English Historical Review* (henceforth *EHR*), lii (1937), p.323 (review of E. K. Winter, *Rudolph IV von Österreich*, vol.ii [1936]).
[19] H. S. Offler, *Medieval Historians of Durham* (Durham, 1958), p.5.

professionals are going to concentrate wholly on the puzzles,' he wrote in 1972, 'into what sort of hands will the writing of the narratives fall, and who, save a diminishing band of experts, will soon be interested even in the puzzles?'[20] *A Short History of Switzerland*, with no footnote references and the briefest of bibliographies, is the nearest he himself ever came to writing for a wide public, though later, in 1965, he also contributed a substantial and important section to *Europe in the Late Middle Ages*, edited by J. R. Hale, J. R. L. Highfield and Beryl Smalley.

After he left the army Offler never returned to Germany—indeed, after 1950 at the latest his only travel outside Britain, for work or for pleasure, was when he went to Trinity College, Dublin, as an external examiner. His research on manuscripts abroad was done through photocopies and microfilms. However, he soon resumed contact with German scholars and he published articles in the *Deutsches Archiv für Erforschung des Mittelalters* in 1951 and 1954.[21] The second of these, on the various political views at the court of Lewis the Bavarian in the autumn of 1331, examines the role of certain tracts in reflecting and forming opinion, and henceforward he worked not on the actual politics of the period but exclusively on the political writings these politics produced. 'I shall be most interested to see some up-to-date learning about Lewis the Bavarian and the Curia,' he wrote in 1983; 'It is many years since I have done much serious work on this subject—partly because of the way in which the edition of the *Constitutiones* for Lewis's reign has stuck at 1330; partly because I had little fresh to say about it.'[22] His paper to the Royal Historical Society in 1955, a general analysis of the aims and policies of popes and emperors from the 1320s to the 1340s, was the last he wrote simply on political events. In the words of Professor Jürgen Miethke it 'displays, in small compass, complete mastery of an intractable mass of detailed research, clear grasp, and reflection on the fundamental problems of the period and on historically acceptable solutions'.[23]

For the rest of Offler's life the core of his work in this field was the editing of William of Ockham's political works, continuing the project

---

[20] *EHR*, lxxxvii (1972), p.577 (review of R. W. Southern, *Medieval Humanism and Other Studies* [1970]).
[21] 'Über die Prokuratorien Ludwigs des Bayern für die römische Kurie', viii (1951), pp. 461-87; 'Meinungsverschiedenheiten am Hof Ludwigs des Bayern im Herbst 1331', xi (1954), pp. 191-206.
[22] Letter to J. Miethke, 29 Dec. 1983.
[23] 'Empire and Papacy: the Last Struggle', *Transactions of the Royal Historical Society*, 5th ser., vi (1956), pp.21-47; 'Sein Aufsatz über "The Last Struggle" zeigt in komprimierter Kürze die volle Beherrschung einer unübersichtlichen Detailforschung, klare Begriffe, Nachdenken über die Grundprobleme des Zeitalters, wie über historisch mögliche Lösungswege' (letter to the author, 7 Nov. 1991).

begun before the war under the leadership of J. G. Sikes. Sikes had died, tragically by suicide, in 1941 and had bequeathed all relevant material to Offler and R. F. Bennett, another of the first volume's editors, as his literary executors. Together they took over responsibility for the project. Offler himself edited volume three, containing the 'Tractatus contra Ioannem' and the 'Tractatus contra Benedictum' as well as the short 'Epistola ad Fratres Minores', and this was published in 1956. Volume two, however, presented a problem. It was to consist of the bulk of the long 'Opus Nonaginta Dierum', of which the first six chapters, edited by Bennett and Sikes, had formed the concluding section of volume one. Sikes had prepared the rest of the tract, and on his death it was at once set up in type; it needed, however, very substantial revision. Bennett began this, but in 1958 passed the work over to Offler: Manchester University Press, now having to pay the printer to keep the type standing, was pressing hard for its completion. It was published in 1963. Offler was conscious that Sikes, who had a 'nervous affliction of his hands, which made holding a pen a difficult and exhausting feat for him', had worked extremely hard to complete the text in the face of great personal and physical difficulties—he must, Offler commented to Bennett, 'have been very far from his proper self when he passed the copy for press (if he did so)'—and in the introduction, characteristically, wrote that

> those with experience in handling a work of this length will know that by far the heaviest labour comes at the first stage of establishing the text and verifying the references. That labour Sikes accomplished. If there is any credit to be had from editing a medieval author, let it go to the memory of a good scholar and a brave man. For the volume's deficiencies the responsibility is mine alone.

Those with such experience will in fact be more likely to agree with what C. R. Cheney wrote to him on its publication: 'your first pages of introduction are a model of modesty and generosity, and I hope that they will be widely recognized as such'. In the course of revision Offler had collated anew the three sources of the text and had reassessed their relative importance—in itself a major work. The problems, however, did not end with volume two. Stocks of volume one were exhausted and a reprint was mooted. In 1961 he wrote to Bennett:

> Nothing in the nature of a complete revision of the text can be envisaged (or needs to be): but simply the printing of a supplement correcting things (misprints, etc.) which are obviously wrong. What we all underestimated, I suspect, was the sheer mechanical difficulty Sikes found in communicating his intentions to the printers. Using vol. I over the years I have become more and more conscious of this, and so am unwilling that it should be reissued as a photographic reprint *tel quel* without an appendix of corrections.

He must have soon changed his mind; as he wrote to Cheney in 1972, 'Tinkering with that version would have been useless, particularly as there was a good deal of new ms. stuff to incorporate. So I have done the whole thing anew'. Offler's own annotated copy of the 1940 volume shows the scale of revision needed; in random samples of the sections that Sikes edited there are from forty to seventy notes per page. The revised edition of volume one was published in 1974, by which time he was well advanced with volume four. This he finished before his death, though it has yet to be published. With it he completed the work of editing Ockham's shorter political works, leaving for others only the Dialogus, 'the final towering massif'.[24]

Editing Ockham's political writings was unquestionably Offler's greatest work. Miethke describes his editions as 'models of the art of editing', a comment that, from one well versed in the German tradition of fine historical editing, would have given him especial pleasure.[25] His strength as an editor lay in his care and thoroughness and in his technical skills; he was a superb Latinist and textual critic, and every page of his editions shows the erudition with which he established correct readings and identified sources and parallels. He was discriminating in his references to other scholars' work and his accolade was never given lightly. Professor G. D. Knysh comments that 'I consider his terse "Knysh, *art. cit.*, pp.77–9" . . . to be one of the finest compliments I have ever received'.[26] Offler seems never to have questioned existing editorial conventions, and was in no doubt that an editor's job included standardizing spelling, capital letters and punctuation, to produce not only a text that reproduced the original writer's intention, but also a text easily intelligible to the modern reader. In a letter to Miethke in 1981 he remarked that 'Looking back after 50 years' activity in medieval history, more and more I incline to the view that much of the most genuine progress has occurred in the field of codicology. It would be a pity if it grew too far apart from the art of editing'. He then cited a recent edition, 'the codicology outstandingly good; the editing leaving much to be desired'.[27] Here, as in many other matters, he looked for improved performance within the existing framework rather than for reassessment of basic premises. In working on Ockham at Durham he

---

[24] ECA, tutorial file for Offler, letter of Offler (5 Feb. 1941); *Guillelmi de Ockham Opera Politica*, ed. J. G. Sikes et al. (in progress; Manchester, 1940–), i (2nd edn), p.viii; ii, pp.ix–x; Offler papers, letters of Offler to Bennett (28 Dec. 1957, 2 Dec. 1961), Cheney (14 Nov. 1972), and of Cheney (20 May 1963). Offler's annotated set of the *Opera Politica* is in Durham University Library.
[25] 'Kabinettstücke der Editionskunst' (letter to the author, 7 Nov. 1991).
[26] The reference is in the forthcoming vol. iv of the *Opera Politica* (letter to the author, 7 Nov. 1991).
[27] Letter to Miethke, 19 Jan. 1981.

felt somewhat isolated; in 1972 he told Cheney, *à propos* financing the new edition of volume one, that

> since Jacob's death you are the only scholar in this country who has shown the slightest interest in this project (and abroad they are busy making their own books out of it—which is fair enough, and pleasing in its way, but not immediately helpful to me).

—a remark made without self-pity, a failing wholly alien to Offler, who once described it as 'perhaps intelligence's worst modern vice'.[28] He saw Ockham's political writings simply as a response to particular circumstances, having no significant connection with Ockham's philosophical or theological work; in this he differed from some other scholars. In 1982 he wrote to Professor A. S. McGrade:

> If pushed, I might be willing to admit that it was a loss to western thought that Ockham, by getting caught up in the imbroglio with John XXII and Michael of Cesena and Lewis of Bavaria, was diverted from the school study of theology and philosophy to the polemical activities which so preoccupied (wasted?) the last 25 years of his life.[29]

He thus viewed the texts he edited as historical documents, simply reflecting the events of their own time, rather than as works of political philosophy with wider application.

The work on Ockham produced not only the edited volumes but articles and notes on particular points arising from these and other contemporary texts. On the other hand, it was not only on Ockham that Offler employed his editorial talents. On moving to Durham, besides continuing the work he had already begun at Cambridge he embarked on an entirely new field of study: north-east England in the Middle Ages. He began with work on William of St Calais, Bishop of Durham 1080–96, writing one article on him for the *Transactions* of the local archaeological society and another, on 'The Tractate De Iniusta Vexacione Willelmi Episcopi Primi', in the *English Historical Review*; this discussed the content and date of this little work, showing that it cannot be safely used as a contemporary source of the events it describes and was probably 'a product of the period of brilliant literary activity at Durham in the second quarter of the twelfth century'.[30] Before long he had taken this interest a good

---

[28] Offler papers, letter to Cheney (14 Nov. 1972; 'Jacob' is, of course, E. F. Jacob); *Durham University Journal*, xl (1947–8), p.63 (review of F. M. Powicke, *Three Lectures* [1947]).
[29] Letter to McGrade, 7 May 1982.
[30] 'William of St. Calais, first Norman Bishop of Durham', *Transactions of the Architectural and Archaeological Society of Durham and Northumberland*, x, pt iii (1950), pp. 258–79; 'The Tractate De Iniusta Vexacione Willelmi Episcopi Primi', *EHR*, lxvi, pp.321–41 (quotation from p.341).

deal further. His inaugural lecture as professor, in 1958, on 'Medieval Historians of Durham', showed how familiar he had made himself not only with the medieval chronicles of the area but also with the works of later antiquaries; and from then on he published occasional articles on particular problems of the medieval north-east, showing still wider knowledge of local sources. He served as Secretary (and thus general editor) of the Surtees Society from 1950 to 1966 and as President from 1980 to 1987, and in 1971 he took as his subject for Durham's annual Cathedral Lecture 'Ranulf Flambard as Bishop of Durham (1099–1128)'.[31] All this was no mere *jeu d'esprit*. He had a profound belief in the importance of local history—and a clear sense of the distinction between local history and parochial antiquarianism.[32] Here, if anywhere, one might discover 'Wie es eigentlich war', and he once remarked in a review how 'Again and again . . . the ambitions of the synthesist shatter on the recalcitrance of the local facts'.[33] Very soon after Offler came to Durham he wrote, in reviewing Professor Barlow's *Durham Jurisdictional Peculiars*, that 'A prerequisite to progress is a diplomatic study of the whole corpus of Durham's twelfth century charters, based on a detailed comparative examination of all the originals'.[34] He may already have envisaged meeting this need. His edition of *Durham Episcopal Charters 1071–1152*, published by the Surtees Society in 1968, is the most important of his contributions to north-eastern history. It is an edition of a very different sort of document from Ockham's works but it is a no less impressive witness of Offler's editorial skills, not least in the way it treats problems of authenticity and in the thoroughness of the historical notes on each charter.

There can be few historians whose reviews are so well worth reading as a collection; Offler regarded reviewing as an important part of his work. It began in 1936, when his first review appeared in the *English Historical Review* (Previté-Orton was then its editor),[35] and from then until 1991 he published up to fifteen reviews every year, apart from the gap produced by the war. Besides the *English Historical Review*, where he appeared in nearly every volume, he reviewed particularly for the *Durham University Journal* and, from the 1960s, for *Erasmus* and the *Journal of Theological Studies*. In his reviews he put more of himself than in his other writings and

---

[31] Published in *Durham University Journal*, lxiv (1971–2), pp.14–25 (to which, in one copy in Durham University Library, an unknown annotator has appended 'In your usual tradition, Prof, punchy and sound'); also issued separately by the Dean and Chapter.
[32] Cf. Offler, *Medieval Historians*, p.13.
[33] *EHR*, xciii (1978), p.610 (review of *Die Burgen im deutschen Sprachraum*, ed. H. Patze [1976]).
[34] *Durham University Journal*, xlii (1949–50), p.125.
[35] *EHR*, li (1936), pp.520–3 (review of E. K. Winter, *Rudolph IV von Österreich*, vol.i [1934]).

their occasional asides and comments recall the brilliant choice of words, often epigrammatic, that made his conversation so memorable. Some tell us much about Offler the historian:

> Essays collected together provide a more concentrated distillation of the author's essence than do the chapters of a book; the reader can find himself in the plight of a thirsty man offered nothing more satisfying than repeated thimblefuls of *crème de menthe*.[36]

Others tell us more than he often revealed about Offler the man:

> But the Middle Ages give little comfort to the optimistic liberal reasoning that because persecution ought not to be successful, it never is. Is it indeed a misconception that belief can be enforced? . . . The horrid truth is that the medieval inquisition was very largely a successful institution.[37]

We get here a sudden glimpse of the young man who in 1940 asked that his call-up be expedited. But underlying all his reviewing was his belief that what was offered to the learned world in print should be definitive work of the highest standard. He was sometimes disappointed, and he criticized sternly what seemed to him any failing of judgment, accuracy or Latinity. He lost friends in this process—which was a pity: in his private correspondence with other historians he was just as uncompromising over any ideas or conclusions that he considered in the least slipshod, but his comments were always tempered with a wealth of positive advice and help. He put his own learning at the disposal of other scholars—whether well-established or beginners—with ready generosity. Some of his letters—notably, in latter years, his detailed technical correspondence with Knysh, McGrade and Miethke—are little less than learned articles, of what others would consider publishable quality.

This mixture of generous personal kindness and of uncompromising insistence on the highest standards informed all Offler's life in Durham. His teaching, perhaps especially attuned to the most able and to those who had most difficulties, was appreciated by all his pupils. One wrote, after his death, how his

> massive learning very imperfectly concealed a rich vein of humour. If we used to hang on his every word in tutorial, we eagerly looked forward to his brilliantly performed lectures and avidly collected fresh examples of the Offlerian *mot juste*. His clear and incisive judgements were constantly shot through with a spontaneous and biting wit. He was the first and

---

[36] *EHR*, lxxxvii (1972), p.576 (review of R. W. Southern, *Medieval Humanism and Other Studies* [1970]).

[37] *EHR*, lxxxiv (1969), p.575 (review of G. Leff, *Heresy in the Later Middle Ages* [1967]).

perhaps the only scholar I have encountered who made everything into an intellectual treat.[38]

'You and I,' he told one pupil, 'have something in common—we neither of us know how to spell sheriff but I look it up in the dictionary.'[39] From a lesser personality such a remark might soon be forgotten; Offler's magisterial utterance would be remembered for life. In his room was a copy of Lawrence Durrell's *Esprit de Corps* which he lent, as recommended reading, to those he suspected of overworking before examinations. His interest in those he taught was in no way assumed; he could recall long afterwards every detail of their performance in Finals. The story is told of a colleague driving him (he did not himself drive) to one address after another in the Durham outskirts in search of an errant pupil to whom he considered himself bound to deliver in person a note initiating formal proceedings on her shortcomings. Indeed, to all departmental administration he brought a conscientious thoroughness that secured the best by doing as much as possible himself; he disliked delegating work, even the typing of letters. For many years he and his fellow-professor of modern history personally interviewed all candidates for admission as undergraduates; other colleagues took no part in this chore. Throughout his career he himself always served as representative of history on the boards of studies of other departments. But besides himself shouldering much of his department's administrative work, he showed his generosity to his colleagues in many ways. They discovered only after many occasions that the annual examiners' lunch, assumed to be funded from some official source, was actually paid for on his initiative from professorial pockets. On the other hand he exercised strong personal control of the department and always knew what he wanted for it. It is well remembered in Durham how, when he was on research leave in 1966-7, the department in his absence voted to move from the Faculty of Arts to the Faculty of Social Sciences; breaking his leave, Offler insisted on speaking in Senate (of which he was not then a member), and single-handed secured the reversal of this decision. In Senate, indeed, he was not only a robust defender of his department's interests, but a strong and effective speaker on many matters. He had an instinct for timing his interventions and developed it to perfection; this, combined with his gift of language—he was a master of the telling phrase—and his weighty delivery, gave him unrivalled influence on its decisions.

He was indeed an awe-inspiring figure—as he must have been even when young. In 1941 when a Lance-Bombardier he wrote to Welbourne

---

[38] Letter from Dr J. C. Thewlis to Mrs Offler, 2 Feb. 1991.
[39] Letter from Mrs G. Cole to Mrs Offler, 10 Feb. 1991.

from Scotland 'as the comrade of men who living and working with me for the past 6 months persist in calling me Mr'.[40] In Durham there were few who addressed him as Seton, the forename he had used from childhood (it was the surname of the owner of King's Acre Nurseries), and he was probably always more at ease with the older masculine form of address by surname alone. This was at one with his rather old-fashioned way of life: neither the motor-car nor the television played any part in it, and he had a telephone at home only after his retirement, when it would not be a channel for the intrusion of business. But if he appeared conservative in his outlook and in his policy for the department this reflected pragmatism, not dogma: he always preferred the devil he knew. Certainly Offler was never dismissive of new approaches or techniques in historical work, though their value had to be proved and he scorned the merely pretentious. 'In its early years,' he wrote to Miethke in 1988, '*Annales* served a valuable function in widening horizons, but during the last few decades the pretensions of its school have become ridiculously exaggerated.'[41] He occasionally commented—whether justly or not—that no one in Durham would discuss history with him; and he seldom left Durham. He went each year to his wartime battery's reunion in Edinburgh, but conferences, seminars and other learned gatherings did not attract him. 'Do your utmost to frustrate any motions towards an Ockhamist "celebration" or "occasion",' he wrote to McGrade in 1983, '. . . I feel more and more doubtful about the value of such jamborees, except perhaps for the careers of the participants.'[42] However, he served on the Council of the Royal Historical Society from 1969 to 1972 and this, followed by his election to the Fellowship of the British Academy in 1974, brought him into wider fields of learned activity.

Offler retired from the university in 1978; his colleagues presented him with a printed bibliography of his historical writings, including reviews, an invaluable guide to his intellectual career.[43] He was given a room a few doors away from the history department in North Bailey, he lunched every week in University College and he continued to be a familiar figure in Durham, often to be seen, with stick and pipe, walking at deliberate pace through the streets or chatting to a colleague or other friend. For me, who now met him for the first time, the difficult task of succeeding Offler in the Chair of Medieval History was made infinitely easier by his extreme courtesy and correctness. In the years that followed there were many changes in the history department that he must have disagreed with, even disapproved of—among them, indeed, the department's transfer to

[40] ECA, tutorial file for Offler, letter of Offler (14 Jan. 1941 ['1940']).
[41] Letter to Miethke, 18 Feb. 1988.
[42] Letter to McGrade, 31 Mar. 1983.
[43] *A List of the Historical Writings 1936–1978 of Hilary Seton Offler* (Durham, 1978).

the Faculty of Social Sciences that he had so strenuously resisted. Whenever we met he never made the slightest reference to such matters. He continued to work and to publish on Ockham and related topics; a long article appeared in 1986 in the *Deutsches Archiv für Erforschung des Mittelalters* on the complicated question of the authorship of the tract 'Allegaciones de potestate imperiali', written in support of Lewis the Bavarian in 1338, and therewith on Ockham's part in the ferment of political views at this time.[44] In a note sending me an offprint of the shorter, but still weighty 'Notes on the Text of Marsilius of Padua's "Defensor Minor"', published in 1982, he remarked 'Not, I fear, what one could call a good read, though I am a little proud of the emendation at X.2.11'. He had reason to be:

> *Et rarius*: this interjection into a straightforward quotation of I Tim.1,20 is quite meaningless, though both Vasoli, p.134 and Quillet have managed to translate it. It is to be rejected as the intrusion of a corrupted gloss. Somewhere along the line of tradition to O the name *Alexander* in the scriptural quotation caught a scribe's eye; facetiously he added *et Darius*; after that, downhill all the way.[45]

In 1990 a further article discussed the origin of Ockham's political thought—'Rather sadly one has to admit that valiant efforts to show that Ockham's political and social ideas were determined by his philosophical positions seem to have run into a dead end'—and its effect on other thinkers down to the Council of Basle.[46] However, work continued too on the medieval north-east. An account of the complex politics behind an incident at Durham in 1318 appeared in *Archaeologia Aeliana* in 1988 as 'Murder on Framwellgate Bridge', the closest he ever came to what he would call a 'catchpenny title'. Work completed but still to be published includes not only the fourth volume of Ockham's political works but also an important article on the text of Boldon Book, the survey of the Bishop of Durham's estates made in 1183 or 1184.

Offler died suddenly on 24 January 1991 after four days' illness from which he was fully expected to recover. In a perceptive obituary Dr Margaret Harvey wrote that 'He was a proud man who would have hated to become helpless in old age'.[47] This is true; but we may be sure he would have met this with the same fortitude that he brought to all

---

[44] 'Zum Verfasser der "Allegaciones de potestate imperiali" (1338)', xlii (1986), pp.555–619.
[45] *Mittellateinisches Jahrbuch*, xvii (1982), p.215.
[46] 'The "Influence" of Ockham's Political Thinking: The First Century', in *Die Gegenwart Ockhams*, ed. W. Vossenkuhl and R. Schönberger (Weinheim, 1990), pp.338–65; the quotation is from p.345.
[47] *The Independent*, 31 Jan. 1991, p.29.

life's chances, still permitting himself the occasional flash of mischievous humour.

P. D. A. HARVEY
University of Durham

Note. I have had much help in compiling this memoir, not least from those who have kindly read it in draft, providing useful comments and suggestions. Above all I am grateful to Mrs B. E. Offler, who has generously and readily put at my disposal letters and other papers of her husband, as well as providing much other information; Mrs G. Cole and Dr J. C. Thewlis have kindly allowed me to quote extracts from their letters to her. Professor D. J. A. Matthew has made available to me the information he gathered on Offler's schooldays, and I am also much indebted to Mr A. G. Gale and Mr F. J. Handley for permission to make use of their recollections. The Master and Fellows of Emmanuel College, Cambridge, through their Archivist, Dr A. S. Bendall, very kindly gave me access to their records and permission to quote from them, and I am especially grateful too to Sir David Pitblado and Mr R. Evans, who gave me helpful information respectively on Offler's years at Cambridge and in the army. A particular word of thanks is due to the scholars who responded with much generosity to requests for copies of correspondence and for advice on Offler's contribution to a field of study of which I know little: Dr A. Black, Dr J. Coleman, Fr G. Gál, Professor J. Kilcullen, Professor G. D. Knysh, Dr R. Lambertini, Professor G. Leff, Professor A. S. McGrade, Dr A. E. McGrath, Professor J. Miethke, Professor J. Morrall and Professor B. Tierney. I have been able to draw directly on only a small part of the information and comments they sent me, but all has been of great assistance in building up a picture of Offler and his work. So many of Offler's friends and colleagues in Durham have provided information, suggestions and anecdotes that it is not possible for me to name them individually, but I am much indebted to them all and would particularly mention the help I have had from Professor W. R. Ward.

I

MEDIEVAL HISTORIANS OF DURHAM

AN OCCASION of this kind is often legitimately used to publish programmes and to move freely at lofty levels of generalisation. My hope is, that it will not be taken amiss if I follow a different course. The nature of history, the 'use' of history, the comparative beauties of this and that sort of history: these topics have been very thoroughly pursued of late. No doubt all this debate, heated and incoherent though it may sometimes seem, is gratifying evidence of enthusiasm and, sometimes, of hard thought. But perhaps I am not alone in feeling that it is becoming rather a bore. At any rate, I beg to be excused from adding to it to-day. In a healthy world salesmanship and scholarship are activities which need keeping far apart. As I see it, any particular merit which can be attributed to the study of medieval history depends on its claim to promote the accurate discussion of precise problems. And so my choice has fallen on a limited subject.

My theme is to be the writing of history in Durham during the middle ages. But before I embark upon it, it is proper to recall how long and at times how well medieval history has been studied here. Immediately there comes to mind the distinguished succession of local antiquarians, beginning in the sixteenth century. Perhaps the author of *The Rites of Durham* scarcely qualifies for inclusion: he seems too much part of the medieval tradition itself, looking at it from the inside still, not from without. But Christopher Watson demands a word. His 'History of Duresme', dated 1574, remains fragmentary and unprinted. What speak more directly to us are his scribbles in a manuscript of Durham historical material which he once owned. To some indifferent late fourteenth-century verses about St Cuthbert he appends the comment: 'Hear wants fyve leaves for which I would geve fyve oulde angells'.[1] I doubt whether the verses were worth so much good currency; but clearly this was a man of the right spirit. The various short histories of the Church of Durham produced hereabouts in the early seventeenth century await an expert bibliographer. Unoriginal and summary as they are, they yet show a continuing concern with the story of the see: a concern further stimulated by Bishop Cosin, and pursued, the more keenly perhaps because not wholly in a spirit of disinterested enquiry, by the three Mickletons and the two Spearmans. From the late seventeenth and early eighteenth century come admirable names: John Smith, the first critical editor of Bede, Thomas Rud, librarian to the Dean and Chapter, and Thomas Bedford. Their contemporary, Thomas Baker of Crook Hall, was probably the most learned student of this country's antiquities that county Durham has produced; as great scholars of his time knew, and as Horace Walpole glimpsed (though he chose to misunderstand the situation), Baker's importance and range of knowledge transcended local limits. And so the catalogue goes on: through the physician Christopher Hunter and the two attorneys, George Allan and William Hutchinson, in the eighteenth century, to Surtees, the Raines, William Greenwell and J. T. Fowler in the nineteenth: men inspired to seek out and publish what they could find about Durham's past, and especially about that long past we call the middle ages. They found and printed a very great deal. No doubt some of their work was rough hewn. But though we are entitled to correct their transcriptions when it is necessary, and put questions to the past which they did not think of asking, only a mean spirit would fail to recognise how much we owe to them.

These men were mostly native to or long resident in the Bishopric. Our 'Saxon nymph', Elizabeth Elstob, was born in Newcastle, but her half-heroic, half-pitiful career as a propagandist for Old English studies was played out mainly in the south. Other medieval scholars, of wide horizons, have found their way to Durham from elsewhere. In comparatively recent times the chances of war and persecution brought Alexander Hamilton Thompson and Wilhelm Levison to live and work amongst us, to our immense profit. It was in his official rooms in the Keep of the Castle that Hastings Rashdall continued the studies which were to issue in *The Universities of Medieval Europe*; there, with much help from dictionaries and the German master at Durham School, he first made his way through Denifle's great book.[2] At Durham School under James Raine the elder had studied

Joseph Stevenson, the surgeon's son from Berwick. Intended at one time for the presbyterian ministry, later archivist to the Dean and Chapter, curate of St Giles and honorary M.A. of this University, he died a Jesuit in his eighty-ninth year. Work among the original documents of the middle ages, in the Durham Treasury, in London and at the Vatican, had filled that long lifetime. Stevenson's techniques as editor and as archivist may sometimes cause modern precisians to raise an eyebrow. But he holds no insignificant place in that comparatively small band of men who, for better or worse, saw into print during the nineteenth century nearly all the important narrative sources of English medieval history.

There is a last name on which I wish to dwell for a moment. When this University was very young, it appointed as Reader in History Thomas Greenwood, of St John's College, Cambridge, and of Gray's Inn. His subject lay outside the examination courses of the time, and his pupils, it would seem, were few. All that our printed *History* tells of him is this:

> 'Asked in 1869 why he had not applied for his stipend for the past year, he replied that, as he had not been asked to lecture for some years, he felt some scruple about it. Senate "while appreciating his delicacy of feeling" ordered the stipend to be paid'.[3]

(Perhaps I may be allowed to express the hope that, should like circumstances recur, both parties would behave as well.) History ought to do better by Thomas Greenwood than that anecdote, for he did very much better by her. When the history of historiography progresses (as inevitably it will) from obscure Germans in the eighteenth century to obscure Englishmen in the next, this considerable scholar will be well worth his paragraph. He wrote historians' history — the only sort that matters — at a time when there were not many men in this country with the will or capacity to do so. Between 1856 and 1865 appeared the five volumes of his *Cathedra Petri: a political History of the great Latin Patriarchate*, an historical survey of the papacy down to the death of Innocent III. Overshadowed at the time by the almost simultaneous publication of Dean Milman's *History of Latin Christianity*, Greenwood's book wears the better of the two. He had read the sources hard and had a judicial mind; his account of the early medieval popes, as a wise old teacher, now dead, pointed out to me in Cambridge quarter of a century ago, withstands the tooth of time. In his combination of the long view with a detailed examination of a great subject, Thomas Greenwood offers an example from which we can still profit.

∽ ∽ ∽

History was written at Durham during the middle ages mainly by members of the monastic community settled here by Bishop William of St Calais in 1083. Most things of consequence which the monks wrote have long been in print.[4] But there is still much to be learnt about their methods from the manuscripts. Of these perhaps rather more than thirty of specifically historical interest survive, a few here still, the others scattered in libraries up and down the country, some of them bearing traces of the minds and pens of many Durham monks. Piety should not mislead us into exaggerating the value of these labours. Though Durham did produce much conscientious and some talented history in these centuries, it did not produce a really great historian or commentator on current affairs: no one to rank with William of Malmesbury or with Matthew Paris; no one who calls for or could possibly sustain the sort of minute scrutiny to which German scholars have recently subjected Widukind of Corvei and Ordericus Vitalis. Nevertheless, despite the lack of an outstanding historical genius, there was accomplished here one piece of transmission of capital importance for our understanding of the past, and to that I shall have to return.

The best period of historical activity in Durham begins a bare twenty years after the founding of the monastery with the work of Symeon, who produced between 1104 and 1107 the book which modern editors have called *Historia Dunelmensis Ecclesiae*. It was not so called in the middle ages, and its original title, though seemingly more clumsy, is in fact more informative: 'Libellus de exordio atque procursu istius, hoc est Dunelmensis ecclesie'.[5] His aim, Symeon tells us, has been to put together in ordered fashion whatever can be found about these matters in Bede's history and in other works. When the literary sources fail he has eked out the story by the help of faithful oral tradition and of his own experience. From these materials is constructed the story of St Cuthert's see, successively at Lindisfarne, at Chester-le-Street and at Durham, from its beginnings in seventh-century Northumbria down to the death of William of St Calais in 1096. Symeon's protest that his abilities for the task are small is perhaps no more than a commonplace of modesty. But there is no reason to discount his statement that he had been set to work *maiorum auctoritate*, by the decision, that is to say, of his monastic superiors. Symeon's *Libellus*, then, is a piece of official history.

Why at this date was the need of an official history being felt at Durham? To chase that fine athletic hare would take us much deeper into the early history of the monastery, and especially into its relations with Bishop Rannulf Flambard, than time allows. We need not boggle at the phrase. Official history is not necessarily bad or dishonest history, and we have good cause to feel grateful to Symeon for his pamphlet. Much of the early part is, of course, verbal repetition or close paraphrase of earlier sources. Their range and variety have been brought home to us more fully in recent years. Sir Edmund Craster's reconstruction of the eleventh-century pre-monastic chronicle of Durham; Dr Colgrave's researches into the post-Bedan miracle stories; Professor Dobbie's edition of the letter of Cuthbert to Cuthwine on the death of Bede; Dr Hohler's work on the masses for the deposition and translation of St Cuthbert:[6] studies such as these have thrown fresh light on the extent of Symeon's borrowings. Today we would put much more of the *Libellus* into distinctive type than did its last editor, Thomas Arnold in 1882. That does not mean that we ought to decry Symeon as 'a mere compiler'. Scissors and paste was part of his method, indeed — but can anyone who has the courage to deal in historical narrative expect wholly to escape that imputation? Symeon showed skill in selecting, ordering, sometimes in reconciling his authorities: the scissors were quite deftly wielded; the paste was of good quality. Occasionally he can be caught out on a point of chronology, or failing to understand his source. I wish I understood why he did not mention the tradition, which he knew, of a ninth-century translation of St Cuthbert's body to

Norham. He was a monk of his time, and so would make St Cuthbert guilty of an antifeminism which was not of the seventh century; his taste for relating visions of the other world, which some of us find hard to share, was known and admired by contemporaries, so that as late as 1126 a Yorkshire priest was communicating to him a choice specimen of this kind, recently edited by a Benedictine scholar[7]. What we should not underestimate is the strength and immediacy of Symeon's experience of a living tradition, and his value as a reporter of things heard and seen. He wrote in a Durham which was beginning to build better than it has since known how, prepared as it was to take the risk of leading western Europe in architectural experiment. He had been one of the nine monks who, under Prior Turgot's direction, had opened St Cuthbert's coffin and handled his body in August 1104; to him the Lindisfarne Gospels and the Stonyhurst Gospel were venerable books, indeed, but completely familiar; almost certainly he had seen the place at Jarrow where stood the stone dwelling in which Bede had sat to meditate and read and write. And official historian though he was, Symeon was not servile. He was prepared to remind his prior and his bishop of their duties with decent freedom. That was no small thing, when the prior was Turgot, and the bishop, Flambard.

There need be no hesitation about accepting Symeon as the author of the *Libellus*, though the earliest manuscripts do not mention his name.[8] We are in more doubtful case with another work, the *Historia Regum*, which had been attributed to him before the end of the twelfth century. In contrast to the *Libellus*, with its localised and ecclesiastical interest, the *Historia Regum* has a wider and secular scope. It contains a mass of material, part of which is of prime importance for the history of this country in the early middle ages. The mass has not been shaped into a single whole, and the only manuscript which survives complete has been heavily contaminated by later influences from elsewhere, most manifestly from Hexham, but perhaps not from there alone.[9] Speaking broadly, the *Historia Regum* is composed of two overlapping histories, the earlier one running from 731 to 957 and the later from 848 to 1129. Probably we should be

MEDIEVAL HISTORIANS OF DURHAM

cautious about regarding the first of these histories as a unity.[10] Its great worth comes from its incorporation of contemporary and authentic Northumbrian annals written in the eighth century and the early tenth. Possibly (though this is by no means certain) they were put into something like their present form at a date when forest still covered the peninsula of Durham.[11] At the most, Symeon can have been only the transcriber or editor of this part of the *Historia Regum*. The second history cannot compare in importance with the first, though at times it offers valuable information about northern affairs. That it represents the work of a single compiler seems a reasonable working hypothesis. For most of the way, from 889 to 1119, he is content to transcribe the Latin chronicle of Worcester, with omissions and occasional interpolations. He made some use of an O.E. chronicle very like the E version, as Stubbs and Pauli saw,[12] and also of foreign sources, including the chronicle of the Irish monk Marianus Scottus: Marianus the supreme chamber historian, undertaking as he did to compose a universal history when literally immured in his cell at Mainz.[13] The second history was finished about 1130. Presumably at this time it was joined to the first one, to form the *Historia Regum*, not indeed as we have it today, but as it was before the diocese of York got to work upon it.

There is ancient but not contemporary evidence that in some way Symeon was concerned with this compilation.[14] He was not the author of the first part. Was he directly responsible for all or any of the second? It would be hazardous to determine that question in our present state of knowledge. The *Historia Regum* contains passages which cannot easily be reconciled with Symeon's *Libellus*, nor with the supposition that the same man wrote them both.[15] Still, over a couple of decades, perhaps even an historian may be permitted to have changed his mind. One would like to give Symeon more credit for the *Historia Regum* than as yet seems wholly safe to allow him. Despite its disorders, its borrowings and its problems, this is the most important history book ever put together in Durham. Had the early Northumbrian annals not been incorporated in it, they would not have survived in like fullness elsewhere, and our dark ages would be appreciably darker. Moreover, the *Historia Regum* was the vehicle by which this unique information was conveyed into the mainstream of historical writing in Britain. Though it survives complete in only one manuscript, the derived and related texts are numerous and significant. As Stubbs made clear in that magnificent preface to his edition of Roger of Howden, about the middle of the twelfth century the *Historia* was deflated and tidied up, strengthened in its unsatisfactory treatment of the early ninth century by an injection from Henry of Huntingdon, and given a new conclusion covering the years 1121-1148 from the same author. The resulting *Historia post Bedam* or *Cronica Regum Northumbrie* was preferred to the unrevised *Historia* even in Durham.[16] Almost unaltered, it was adopted by Roger of Howden as the first part of his chronicle; combined with more Henry of Huntingdon in some northern monastery about 1180 it was turned into a history running from Julius Caesar to 1154;[17] much later it was to provide another Yorkshire historian, Walter of Guisborough, with the opening section of his book.[18] The *Historia Regum* itself, throughout its length, was laid heavily under contribution by the authors of the first part of the *Chronicle of Melrose* in the last quarter of the twelfth century.[19] Most important of all, both parts of the *Historia Regum* were drawn upon by the compiler of the *Flores Historiarum*.[20] In this way the Northumbrian material of the conjoint chronicles was carried over into the St Albans tradition — perhaps the most influential school of historical writing in later medieval England. For an appreciable part of the little they have been able to know about their northern history in the eighth century and the early tenth, Englishmen from Henry II's reign to the present have been indebted to the Durham compiler of the *Historia Regum*.

A couple of set-pieces did not exhaust the energy of this period. During the first six or seven decades of the twelfth century Durham also produced a great deal of miscellaneous historical writing. Some of it was lively and tendencious, like the early treatise *De obsessione Dunelmi*, written, it would seem, to justify territorial revindications by the see, or the pamphlet *De iniusta vexacione Willelmi episcopi primi*, confected to defend the dubious reputation of William of St Calais: material to be used with caution, but offering the careful interpreter precious information which he can hardly find elsewhere. Professor Levison was surely right in assigning to this time the compilation of those *Annales Lindisfarnenses et Dunelmenses*, which their discoverer, G. H. Pertz, mistakenly thought to represent contemporary entries from the eighth century onwards.[21] Their importance, consequently, is much reduced, though not quite nullified. It would indeed be dangerous to discount as worthless some very minor historical efforts of these years. In 1131/2 there was made in Durham what at first view seems a completely empty abridgement of part of the *Historia Regum*. It *is* an empty abridgement, except for the year 1101, when it suddenly deviates from its model and offers what I take to be a contribution to our scanty knowledge of the invasion of England in that year by the king's elder brother, Robert Curthose: a contribution the more convincing when one remembers that Robert's chief supporter had been Rannulf bishop of Durham.[22]

Even when they have little by way of new 'fact' to offer, some of these writings do serve to indicate how methods of historical enquiry were developing. There is a short piece which sometimes goes under the name *De primo Saxonum adventu*, an attempt by some monk at Durham to make clear the succession and regnal years of the kings of the Heptarchy: to construct for himself, one might almost say, a little *Handbook of Chronology*. Comparison between the first form of this, made while Henry I was still alive, and a revised version produced here in the late 'sixties is illuminating.[23] A generation has brought not only expansion (the earlier episcopal lists for York and Durham have now been expanded into regular short histories of the sees), but also great improvements in the way in which the materials are grasped and ordered. Above all, there is a new and agreeable element of sophistication. The earlier Durham historians tell us that in 737 the Northumbrian king Ceolwulf resigned his kingdom and became a monk at Lindisfarne. He added Warkworth and other lands to the patrimony of St Cuthbert; he also secured permission for the monks to use wine or beer, whereas before their only drink had been milk or water, according to the tradition of St Aidan. This is what the Durham monk in the 'sixties makes of it:

> '[Ceolwulf] granted such abundance of land to the said church in order that the monks, who up to this time had been wont to drink only water or milk in the hereditary manner of the Scots [he means, of course, the Irish] . . . might henceforth be able to drink beer'.[24]

You will perceive what has happened. Our author has not been content to repeat two disjunct pieces of information; he has tried to establish a causal relation between them. He knows how to put two and two together, just like any modern scholar; and, just as any modern scholar is apt to do, he has made the answer five.

After Symeon we cannot find names for these Durham historians. Their abilities were considerable. The continuation of the *Libellus* composed between 1144 and 1152, which recounts the attempted usurpation of the see by William Cumin after the death of Bishop Geoffrey Rufus, can hold its own as a piece of sustained and vivid narrative with anything which was being written in England at this time. But by the last quarter of the twelfth century inspiration had undoubtedly flagged; a permanent and unhappy change can now be noticed in historical writing at Durham. What seems to have occurred was a voluntary restriction of the range of interest: a turning inwards to almost exclusive concern with the fortunes of the monastery and the see. It is difficult to suggest a wholly satisfactory explanation of this change, and, regret it as we may, we are not entitled to blame it: to write history was not among the reasons why men became monks in the middle ages. Perhaps it was just the lack of a man with the right aptitude at the critical moment, so that a tradition was dropped and neglected. At any rate, creative interest in secular history languished. Symeon's account of the early history of his church had not proliferated, as had the history of Ordericus (which, as Dr Wolter reminds us, in its original intention was even more local and limited than Symeon's),[25] into a general survey of the society of his time. It was at Hexham, not here, that the *Historia Regum* was continued.

MEDIEVAL HISTORIANS OF DURHAM

The tradition of writing history on a national scale was never fully recovered. When towards the end of the thirteenth century a Durham monk tried to put together a *Cronica regum Anglie post Conquestum*, by dint of much borrowing he brought a general history down to 1201, but then he gave up the struggle and his work turned into an almost wholly Durham chronicle.[26] The Richard of Durham whose narrative for the period 1201 to 1297 lies behind what is now known as the Lanercost Chronicle, was not a Durham monk, but a Franciscan friar.[27] Here and there in the manuscripts traces of an individual's interest in national affairs can be found; possibly surprises still await us.[28] But for the present the generalisation seems valid: the monastery of Durham had lost interest in writing general history — even when that came very close indeed. On 17 October 1346 there took place at Neville's Cross, almost on the monastery's doorstep, one of the most important battles of the fourteenth century. A Durham monk fifty years later wishing to read about it would have found almost nothing by domestic authors; instead he would have needed to turn to the *Historia Aurea* of John, vicar of Tynemouth, which lay in three fattish volumes in the cloister library.[29]

History writing at Durham thus tended to parochialism. It took the form of grafting on to the stock of Symeon's *Libellus* a succession of pieces to make a continuing history of the bishops and ultimately of the priors. Symeon's pamphlet had ended with the death of William of St Calais; soon after 1128 a continuation covering the episcopate of Rannulf Flambard was composed; between 1144 and 1152 there was added the account of Bishop Geoffrey Rufus and the struggle between William of St Barbara and William Cumin.[30] A process had begun which was to continue intermittently into the sixteenth century. Already at this stage can be noticed, I think, a change in emphasis foreshadowed in the later parts of Symeon. The career of the individual bishop comes to hold the centre of the story, sometimes treated in a way which offers a faint but unmistakeable echo of the classical manner in biography. And new titles for the joint work of Symeon and his continuators reflect two expectations: that it shall be kept more or less up-to-date, and that it shall recount the deeds of the bishops. As the twelfth century wore on, Symeon's 'pamphlet concerning the origin and onset of this church of ours, that is, the church of Durham' became, together with its later accretions, *Liber de statu Dunelmensis ecclesiae*. That name took root, though just after the middle of the century there was already current at Hexham the alternative title *Gesta episcoporum Dunelmensium*, which was generally used in the later middle ages.[31].

Not until the turn of the twelfth and thirteenth centuries was the next continuation added, to carry the story first perhaps to 1199 and then to 1214.[32] That Geoffrey of Coldingham deserves the credit for it seems reasonably assured. The earliest manuscript does not name him, but later ones do,[33] and there are similarities in style between this continuation and the *Vita* of the hermit Bartholomew which is also attributed to Geoffrey. He is an author who improves on better acquaintance. He was indeed an overconscious stylist, but hard muscle of thought and information underlies his writing. On one occasion we find him referring to the prophecies of Merlin. Even this aberration serves usefully to remind us that though the monks of Durham may not have been brilliant historians, they did not show much appetite for the British History. Perhaps it was their grounding in Anglo-Saxon antiquity which protected them from that deception.

Geoffrey composed with some aid from written sources, but mostly, it must be supposed, from the memories of others and his own experience. The next continuator of the *Gesta episcoporum* stood further away from much that he wrote about, for his segment of the Durham history, from 1214 to 1334, was not completed till 1336. Robert Graystanes belonged to a world in some ways very different from that of the men we have considered up to now. He had benefited from the monastery's foundation of a house of study at Oxford, had become a doctor of theology, and, perhaps even better, a lover and acquirer of books. After serving as subprior he was the monks' choice for succession to the see on the death of Bishop Louis de Beaumont in 1333. Elected bishop by the chapter, though royal consent was lacking he yet managed to secure confirmation by Archbishop Melton of York, consecration and installation. But the pope had already provided the king's candidate, Richard of Bury, and Robert declined a hopeless struggle. More profitably he turned, or returned, to bringing the *Gesta episcoporum* up to date. In this his achievement seems to me more praiseworthy than is sometimes allowed. Admittedly, in his hands the history is largely a house journal, concentrating on the convent of Durham and its possessions, and above all on the defence of its rights against attempted encroachments by diocesan or metropolitan. But within these limitations Graystanes tells an entertaining tale with a good deal more than average competence. He does, of course, perpetrate a howler or two[34] — but that is an occupational risk of historians. Thanks to Professor Barlow's edition of the thirteenth-century Durham annals in the Cottonian manuscript Julius D. IV, we can now better appreciate what Henry Wharton perceived in the seventeenth century:[35] how much Graystanes depended for the early part of his history on the work of other men. But even at this stage, when he is at his weakest, he is something better than a mere paraphraser. In his second chapter he gives a short account of the episcopate of Richard Marsh — no more than seventeen lines of printed text.[36] The first seven are derived in the main from the thirteenth-century annals. Though in one instance Graystanes corrects a mistaken date in his source, he adds to confusion by interpolating from Geoffrey of Coldingham a phrase which he has misunderstood. Then again, what he has to say about the death and burial of Richard Marsh in 1226 is copied literally from the thirteenth-century annals. Were this all, Graystanes would not deserve much of a mark. But in the middle of his borrowings he adds just a couple of sentences which give a glimpse of better things. Bishop Richard, he tells us, interfered in many ways with the rights of the monks. Nevertheless, in his second year he confirmed to the prior and convent their liberties according to the tenor of Bishop St Calais' charter; he appropriated to them the church of Dalton and confirmed the appropriation of the churches of Aycliffe and Pittington. How had Graystanes acquired this circumstantial information? There seems no doubt about the answer. He had been into the archives and turned up the documents; they still survive, readily identifiable, in the Durham Treasury.[37] By the fourteenth century the monastery had accumulated a formidable mass of business and legal records. Graystanes' strength as an historian lay in his use of this material. Narrow as his history might be, it was yet documented much more fully than history written in Durham had been before. A closer study of how Graystanes selected and used these records would be profitable. He calls for reediting as imperatively as any of the Durham historians;[38] and perhaps his is the case in which the effort and expense would be best rewarded.

When Graystanes had finished his chronicle, there were available in Durham all the elements of a continuous history of the church of St Cuthbert from the seventh century down to 1334. Within fifty years they had been turned into a single book: the *Gesta episcoporum* had found their definitive form. The process can be followed in the manuscripts: the smoothing-over of the joints, the making of new chapter divisions and lists of contents, the introduction of some small amount of additional material, even the provision of a not inadequate index.[39] But all this fussing, though it has the fascination of intricacy and tells something of the ways in which medieval men put a book together, had little to do with writing history. Indeed, after Graystanes history at Durham, so far as any creative effort was demanded, fell into a pretty miserable state. Spasmodically the *Gesta* were kept up: perhaps in the last third of the fourteenth century a short biography of Bishop Richard of Bury was added, taken in part from a hanging tablet in the church, in part from the oral reminiscences of a certain William de Chambre who had known him, and rounded off by a list of Richard's benefactions to the cathedral. Somewhat later, it would seem, the story of the priors was brought down to 1391 and an account of Thomas Hatfield's episcopate was written.[40] If the whole of the account belongs to this time, it reveals an historical tradition in full dissolution. The characterisation of Hatfield is most desperately unoriginal. It is no more than a mosaic of literal borrowings from earlier parts of the *Gesta*, attributing to Hatfield qualities which earlier writers had discerned in Bishops Rannulf, St Barbara, du Puiset, Bek and Kellawe, and in Prior Geoffrey Burdon.[41] Clearly, it was time to revivify the Durham chronicle.

The way in which the task was undertaken by that able man John Wessington, probably before he became prior in 1416, was revealed by Sir Edmund Craster thirty years ago in a paper which laid the foundation for the modern study of the Durham historians.[42] Wessington had it in mind to produce a new history of St Cuthbert's church from its beginnings, to be constructed on a much broader basis of narrative and documentary sources than the old *Gesta episcoporum*. It would be foolish to underrate Wessington's achievement, which holds a respectable place among Benedictine historical writings in fifteenth-century England. If he thought of history largely as a means of buttressing the legal claims of his community, he set about compiling it in ways which were more thorough and (if I dare use the term) more scientific than those of his predecessors. He was responsible besides, directly or indirectly, for many shorter historical pieces of more limited scope. One of these has recently received high praise from an American scholar for its 'clear, concise handling of a difficult piece of administrative history',[43] and there are others of which much the same might be said. But it is not unfair to point out also that there were limitations to Wessington's success in reforming the history of St Cuthbert's church. His original plan, which would have brought the new account down to the middle of the fourteenth century at least, seems never to have been carried out in full; the most complete version which survives in a finished state reaches no further than 1195.[44] And the new path indicated by Wessington did not prove permanently attractive; his attempt to lift history writing at Durham out of the rut on to a new level of competence was not in the long run successful. Old intellectual habits were too strong to be swept away by his brisk, businesslike approach. The result was regrettable. For it was the *Gesta episcoporum*, not Wessington's history, which found continuators here until the Reformation and beyond.

Their work down to the account of Thomas Hatfield has been touched on already. Until late in the fifteenth century it amounts to little more than a series of meagre notices about the appointment and decease of bishop and priors. Then it begins to take on body again, giving the impression of a more or less contemporary record. The *Gesta* have some interesting things to say about Prior

Thomas Castell, Bishop Tunstall and Hugh Whitehead, last prior and first dean of Durham. Not till 1574 does this old monastic chronicle, which had started as the story of saints and kings, finally peter out with a tale of misdemeanour by the executor of a suffragan bishop. What hands in succession were concerned in this compilation from 1334 onwards is a question which awaits investigation. The attribution to William de Chambre made by Henry Wharton, though it still persists, will obviously not do. In the last generation or so before the Suppression there were still monks interested in Durham's past. Dr Thomas Swalwell comes to mind — a great reader of Durham histories, as his marginalia in many manuscripts bear witness. From his report, perhaps even from his pen, comes a late pre-Reformation account of a miracle by St Cuthbert: the cure at the saint's shrine of the royal servant Richard Powell in 1502.[45] Then there was Dr William Todd, whose combination of historical and devotional interests Mr Pantin has set in an attractive light, and to whose zeal as a collector we owe the preservation of some unique material.[46] After the Suppression he became first prebendary of the fifth stall on the new foundation, and was not deprived until 1567. The last portion of the Durham chronicle, with its careful but transparent partisanship for the old order and the men of the old order, would, one feels, have been much to his taste.

A good deal remains to be done on the details of this story. But perhaps the outlines are clear enough to justify a couple of reflections. The first is of comfort to the holder of a new chair and therefore of a new responsibility. These Durham historians in the middle ages are shadowy figures. But on the evidence of their works it can fairly be said that they were not men of outstanding ability; if some had talent, others fell to mediocrity or below it. Yet, working within their limits, by their devotion to a useful task they have managed to leave posterity much in their debt and have deserved to escape oblivion. The other reflection is more austere, for it warns us of a danger. History writing in Durham weakened when it became too exclusively interested in Durham's history. The wealth of historical remains and associations which crowd in upon us here must be an inspiration. Possibly it can also be a snare. Provincials we are, and I hope we know how to exploit provincials' strength, untroubled by sick suburban yearnings. That does not mean that we can afford to fall bemused and hypnotised by contemplation of our own riches. Our local studies find their proper proportion only when seen in the light of a far wider experience. Whatever men may make of Europe's future, western Christendom in the middle ages is still a valid field of historical study: a field rich and extensive enough to defeat attempts by even the strongest individuals to comprehend, let alone exhaust it. By nature we here in Durham are rooted in that field. Inescapably the duty lies on us of making all we can of it intelligible to ourselves and our successors.

NOTES

[1] B[ritish] M[useum], Cotton ms. Titus A. II, fo. 151v. That Watson owned this ms. is shown by the note on fo. 162v about the birthdays of himself and his children. I take the hand to be the same in both instances.

[2] cf. P. E. Matheson, *Life of Hastings Rashdall*, Oxford, 1928, p. 46.

[3] C. E. Whiting, *The University of Durham*, London, 1933, p. 94.

[4] The H[istoria] R[egum] and the H[istoria] D[unelmensis] E[cclesiae] with its continuations down to c. 1180 were first edited by Roger Twysden in his *Historiae Anglicanae Scriptores Decem*, 1652. Thomas Bedford's edn. of HDE, based on better ms. authority than Twysden's, came out in 1732. The further continuations, by Geoffrey of Coldingham, Graystanes etc., were printed, with arbitrary omissions, by Henry Wharton in vol. I of *Anglia Sacra*, 1691; they were reedited with a mass of illustrative documents by James Raine the elder, [*Historiae Dunelmensis*] *Scriptores Tres* (Surtees Society, 1839). J. Hodgson Hinde included a new edition of HR together with many shorter pieces of Durham historical writing in his *Symeonis Dunelmensis Opera et Collectanea*, of which only vol. I appeared (Surtees Society, 1868). HDE and HR and many shorter pieces were edited again by Thomas Arnold for the Rolls Series in two volumes, 1882 and 1885. Arnold does not hold a high place among the Rolls Series editors, though his edns. are the most accessible and generally quoted. The thirteenth-century Durham annals in BM. Cotton ms. Julius D. IV have been published by Professor Frank Barlow, *Durham Annals and Documents of the Thirteenth Century* (Surtees Society, 1945).

[5] Durham University Library, Bishop Cosin's ms. V. ii. 6, fo. 11; BM. Cotton ms. Faustina A. V, fo. 25.

[6] H. H. E. Craster, 'The Red Book of Durham', *EHR* xl (1925), 504-32; B. Colgrave, 'The post-Bedan miracles and translations of St Cuthbert', in *The Early Cultures of North West Europe* (H. M. Chadwick Memorial Studies), Cambridge, 1950, pp. 305-32. E. van Kirk Dobbie, *The Manuscripts of Caedmon's Hymn and Bede's Death Song*, New York, 1937, p. 97 suggests that the Latin translation of Bede's death song in HDE i, 15 (ed. Arnold, I, p. 44) is Symeon's work. Traces of the mass for the Translation of St Cuthbert composed c. 1104 and of the older office for the saint which had come north in the tenth century can be noted in HDE i, 10 and 3 (pp. 33 and 22); cf. C. Hohler, 'Durham Services in Honour of St Cuthbert', in *The Relics of St Cuthbert*, ed. by C. F. Battiscombe, Oxford, 1956, pp. 166, 171.

[7] Dom Hugh Farmer, O.S.B., 'The Vision of Orm', *Analecta Bollandiana* lxxv (1957), 72-82.

[8] The earliest to do so is the third in date, Cambridge University Library, ms. Ff. i. 27 (late twelfth century). Symeon's name appears in the heading of HDE in the Holkham Hall ms. 468 (thirteenth century), fo. 3, and seems to have been erased from the heading in York Cathedral ms. XVI. I. 12 (fourteenth century) fo. 99. I am grateful to Lord Leicester for permission to acquire photostats of his manuscript, and to the honorary librarian at Holkham, Dr Hassall, for helping me to obtain them.

[9] Corpus Christi College, Cambridge, ms. 139 (late twelfth century), the source of all the edns. The version of HR to be found in Paris, Bibliothèque nationale, ms. nouv. acq. lat. 692 (late twelfth century), fos. 1-42v is much abbreviated, containing only small extracts from the first and more valuable part. The most complete modern account of HR is by P. Hunter Blair, 'Symeon's History of the Kings', *Archaeologia Aeliana*, fourth series, xvi (1939), 89-100.

[10] cf. W. S. Angus, 'The Annals for the tenth century in Symeon of Durham's *Historia Regum*', *Durham University Journal*, xxxii (1940), 213 sqq.

[11] Arnold's theory that the first part of HR was compiled by a tenth-century 'Cuthbertine' at Chester-le-Street (II, pp. xvii-xxv) is not very firmly based; cf. the remarks by W. H. Stevenson in his edn. of *Asser*, Oxford, 1904, p. lix.

MEDIEVAL HISTORIANS OF DURHAM 21

[12] W. Stubbs, *Chronica Magistri Rogeri de Houedene*, I (Rolls Series, 1868), p. xxx; R. Pauli, M[onumenta] G[ermaniae] H[istorica], SS. XIII (1881), p. 102. Instances can be noted in HR s.aa. 1032, 1053, 1069, 1084, 1088, 1106, 1117, 1118.

[13] HR borrows from Marianus s.aa. 1068, 1073, 1074, 1075, 1080, 1081, 1082, and from the second continuation of Marianus s.aa. 1083, 1084; cf. Marianus' *Chronicon*, ed. G. Waitz, *MGH. SS.* V (1844) pp. 559-63. S.aa. 876, 898, 906 (by error), 941, 994 (conflated with material from 1024) HR used a collection of Norman annals, very similar to, if not identical with that used by the Latin interpolator of Chron. E. In one instance, s.a. 1013, as Arnold pointed out (II, p. xxxiv), HR draws on William of Jumièges.

[14] The Corpus ms. 139, fos. 51v and 131v attributes HR to Symeon at the beginning and end of the work; cf. Arnold, II, pp. 3, 283. No author is named in the Paris ms.

[15] cf. Hodgson Hinde, *op. cit.*, pp. xxvii *sqq*. All Hodgson Hinde's objections are not equally valid, but in sum they are still formidable.

[16] Stubbs, *Howden*, I, pp. xxvi, xxxi-iii. Professor Rothwell has identified a ms. of *Historia post Bedam* not used by Stubbs in Inner Temple Library, Petyt ms. 511.2; cf. *The Chronicle of Walter of Guisborough*, ed. H. Rothwell, *Camden Series*, lxxxix, 1957, p. x. No copy of HR appears in the medieval catalogues of the Durham library, but *Historia post Bedam* was certainly there in 1395; cf. *Catalogi Veteres Librorum Ecclesiae Cathedralis Dunelm.* (Surtees Society, 1838), p. 56. This volume survives as St John's College, Oxford, ms. 97.

[17] cf. T. Arnold, *Henry of Huntingdon* (Rolls Series, 1879), pp. xliv *sqq*.

[18] Rothwell, *op. cit.*, p. xxvi.

[19] cf. the introduction by A. O. and M. O. Anderson to the facsimile edn. of *The Chronicle of Melrose*, London, 1936, pp. xi-xii.

[20] He used other Durham histories as well, and had access to some ninth-century Northumbrian material not incorporated in HR.

[21] *MGH. SS.* XIX (1868), pp. 502 *sqq*. Strong doubts about the value of the earlier part of this compilation had already been expressed by L. Theopold, *Kritische Untersuchungen über die Quellen zur angelsächsischen Geschichte des achten Jahrhunderts*, Lemgo, 1872, pp. 71-2. For Levison's view, see his *England and the Continent in the Eighth Century*, Oxford, 1946, p. 114 and note. He did not live to publish the detailed examination of the *Annales* (ALD) there envisaged. They are found as marginal entries to a group of Easter tables at the beginning (fos. viii-xiii) of the Hunterian ms. T. 4. 2. in the University Library, Glasgow, which was formerly a Durham book; cf. R. A. B. Mynors, *Catalogue of the MSS. in the Cathedral of Durham*, Oxford, 1939, p. 55. The hands of the tables and of the marginal entries (as Mr R. O. Mackenna, University Librarian and Keeper of the Hunterian MSS., has been good enough to inform me) seem for the most part to belong to the second half of the twelfth century. For universal history these annals largely depend on the *Chronicon* of Marianus Scottus, which ends in 1082. A similar dependence on Marianus can be seen in the marginal entries to Easter tables in Durham Cathedral Library, Hunter ms. 100 (early twelfth century), fos. 27v-42. This ms. is closely related to the Glasgow ms. in other ways; cf. Mynors, *loc. cit.* After 1063 it has only 6 annalistic entries, 5 of which recur in ALD in almost the same words. ALD's entries for events in English history are mostly derived from known Durham sources of the early twelfth century, including HDE, HR and *De primo Saxonum adventu*. But even late compilers may have had access to early material now lost, and a few entries in ALD are perhaps worth further consideration: e.g. s.aa. 793, 797, 808, 820, 1018, 1046, 1047, 1059.

[22] BM. Cotton ms. Caligula A. VIII, fos. 36-43. The making of the abridgement may be dated by the mention on fo. 37v of Geoffrey as abbot of St Mary's, York *in presenti*. Abbot Richard died 31 December 1130, and Geoffrey 17 July 1132; H. H. E. Craster and M. E. Thornton, *The Chronicle of St Mary's, York* (Surtees Society, 1934), p.1. The style of the initials suggests to Professor Mynors, *Catalogue*, p. 8, a somewhat later date

for the writing of the ms. The passage referred to was printed, not quite completely or accurately, by J. Hodgson Hinde in his edn. of HR, p. 105. It seems worth repeating: [fo. 41, s.a. 1001] Eodem anno in estate xiii kal. Augusti applicuit Rodbertus comes Normannie cum nauali exercitu, ducens secum Rannulfum Dunelmensem episcopum aliosque proceres in loco qui Portesmuthe dicitur, ibique in riuaria de Walmesforde figi tentoria precepit. Rex autem eius aduentum apud Hastingas expectans, cum comitem uenisse audisset, cum exercitu suo maximo per Surreiam uenit ad Auwltune, ibique et ipse sua tentoria figi fecit. Ibique mediantibus utrorumque baronibus locuti sunt ad inuicem rex et comes, concordiaque inter eos prolocuta, uenerunt Guintoniam secundo die Augusti, et ibi sacramento et affidatione inter eos facta, reddite sunt unicuique baronum utrorumque terre, quas uel in Anglia uel in Normannia tempore dissensionis perdiderant, sicut prelocutum inter eos fuerat. Eodem anno circa festum omnium sanctorum rediit comes pacifice in Normanniam.

[23] The first form was printed by Hodgson Hinde, pp. 202-15, from Cotton ms. Caligula A. VIII, fos. 28-36, collated with Magdalen College ms. 53; and by Arnold, II, pp. 366-84, taking Cotton ms. Domitian VIII as his primary source. The revised version is to be found in Durham Cathedral ms. B. ii. 35, fos. 140-150, from which the short account of the archbishops of York was printed by James Raine the younger, *Historians of the Church of York* II (Rolls Series, 1886), pp. 513-30, and a fragment of the account of the bishops of Durham by Bedford, pp. 293-4 and Arnold, I, p. 169.

[24] B. ii. 35, fo. 148*: Qui tantam terrarum copiam eidem ecclesie contulit, ut monachi qui eatenus aquam tantummodo uel lac more Scottorum patrio unde uenere primum bibere consueuerant, exinde ceruisiam biberent.

[25] Hans Wolter S.J., *Ordericus Vitalis. Ein Beitrag zur kluniazensischen Geschichtsschreibung*, Wiesbaden, 1955, p. 90.

[26] cf. Barlow, *Durham Annals and Documents*, p. xxix.

[27] cf. A. G. Little, 'The Authorship of the Lanercost Chronicle', EHR xxxi (1916), 269-79, reprinted in *Franciscan Papers* [etc.], Manchester, 1943, pp. 42-54.

[28] The fourteenth-century annals at fos. 1-14, 15v of BM. Additional ms. 24059 (a Durham book) would perhaps repay investigation. Professor Rothwell hints at a possible surprise, *Walter of Guisborough*, p. xxxi.

[29] The domestic *Gesta episcoporum* give three lines to the battle. John of Tynemouth's account has been printed by Professor V. H. Galbraith, 'Extracts from the *Historia Aurea*', EHR xliii (1928), 214-15, from the Lambeth Palace ms. 12 which in 1395 formed part of the set in the Durham cloister library; cf. *Catt. vett.*, p. 56; M. R. James and Claude Jenkins, *Descriptive Catalogue of the MSS. in the Library of Lambeth Palace*, Cambridge, 1932, pp. 22-26. There is an account of Neville's Cross in the Latin Brut chronicle, now Durham Cathedral ms. B. ii. 35, fos. 1-35, but it does not appear from the catalogues that this work was in the library in 1395.

[30] The *Continuatio* of HDE printed by Bedford, pp. 249-92, and, under the title of *Continuatio prima*, by Arnold, I, pp. 135-160, seems in fact to be composed of two pieces. The first (a), covering Flambard's episcopate down to the phrase *sigillo confirmavit restituta* (Bedford, p. 260; Arnold, I, p. 141) would seem to have been written shortly after Flambard's death in September 1128. At this point the hand changes in the earliest ms., Cosin's V. ii. 6, fo. 102, and a further continuation (b) covers the episcopate of Geoffrey Rufus, Cumin's attempted usurpation, and the restoration of William of St Barbara in 1144 (Bedford, pp. 260-92; Arnold, I, pp. 141-60). This would appear to have been written before St Barbara's death in 1152. The *Continuatio altera* printed by Arnold, I, pp. 161-8 (and by Twysden, *Scriptores Decem*, coll. 63-8) occurs only in the Cambridge ms. Ff. i. 27 and its seventeenth-century copy, BM. Harley ms. 533. It begins after the death of Geoffrey Rufus, and for the years 1141-4 it seems a not very skilled compression and rewriting of (b). It completes St Barbara's episcopate, tells of du Puiset's election, and lists some of his building activities. These suggest a date after c. 1180.

[31] The title *Liber de statu Dunelmensis ecclesiae* occurs in the twelfth-century Durham library catalogue; *Catt. vett.*, p. 4. Holkham Hall ms. 468, fo. 3 has: Incipit liber Symonis

MEDIEVAL HISTORIANS OF DURHAM

(sic) monachi Dunelmensis de statu Lindisfarnensis et Dunelmensis ecclesie usque ad electionem Hugonis de Puteaco. York Cathedral ms. XVI. i. 12, fo. 99: Incipit [? libellus Symeonis monachi Dunelmensis *imperfectly erased*] de statu lindisfarnensis, id est dunelmensis ecclesie secundum uenerabilem Bedam presbiterum et postmodum de gestis episcoporum dunelmensium. BM. Cotton Titus A. II (fourteenth century), fo. 5 and Bodley, ms. Laud misc. 700 (late fourteenth century), fo. 14 show slight variations of the amended York *incipit*, making no mention of Symeon. Richard of Hexham refers to *Gesta episcoporum Dunelmensium* in his history of the church of Hexham, ii. 22. ed. J. Raine, *Priory of Hexham*, I (Surtees Society, 1864), p. 46. The title occurs in *Catt. vett.*, pp. 55-6 and in Bodley, ms. Fairfax 6, fo. viv.

³² The earliest ms. containing Geoffrey's continuation, the former Phillipps ms. 9374 (early thirteenth century), now in the Cathedral Library at Durham, ends at 1199. The next chapter (Raine, *SS. Tres*, p. 20) begins with a phrase which suggests a further continuation: Hiis adiicere libet que novorum tumultuum parturivit incursus. The Phillipps ms. has been described at length by J. Conway Davies, 'A recovered manuscript of Symeon of Durham', *Durham University Journal*, xliv (1951), 22-8. It may be added that a sixteenth-century transcript of it exists in Corpus Christi College, Cambridge, ms. 100 (1), pp. 7-122; by a slip Dr M. R. James in his catalogue of the Corpus mss. (I, Cambridge, 1912, pp. 189 and 319) suggested that this was a transcript of HR, not HDE. The Phillipps ms. was the source of the extracts from HDE etc. made by Laurence Nowell, now BM. Cotton ms. Vespasian A. V, fos. 93-127. He there describes it as 'De communi libraria monachorum Dunelmensium'; and there seems little doubt that it is to be identified with the 'Gesta Episcoporum incomplete . ii fo. prolatum est' of the Durham catalogue of books in the cloistral library in 1395: *Catt. vett.*, p. 56. Admittedly the second folio of the Phillipps ms. begins 'perlatum est', but the 'prolatum' of the catalogue is probably a slip, for the word does not seem to occur in the early parts of HDE or its related epitome. Possibly this ms. was at York in the late seventeenth century, and is the nr. 44 of Bernard's catalogue of 1697, one of the two copies of HDE seen at York by Thomas Rud (*Catt. vett.*, p. 149).

³³ Holkham Hall ms. 468, fo. 63; York XVI. I. 12, fo. 165v; Titus A. II, fo. 68.

³⁴ cf. e.g. *SS. Tres*, p. 41, where Graystanes imputes to Prior Thomas Melsanby, who resigned in 1244, a stay on Farne with the hermit Bartholomew and a death-bed vision, both of which really belong to Prior Thomas I a century earlier: *Vita Bartholomaei*, ed. Arnold, I, p. 307.

³⁵ *Anglia Sacra* I (1691), p. xlix.

³⁶ *SS. Tres*, pp. 35-6.

³⁷ Durham Cathedral Treasury, 2. 2. Pont. 1, 5 and 2 (duplicated).

³⁸ Raine's edn., though superior to Wharton's, leaves something to be desired. It omits, for instance, the whole of chapter 174 of the *Gesta episcoporum* concerning the dispute between Archbishop Melton and the convent about visitation rights in Howdenshire in 1328 and the following years. This chapter occurs as an addition in Bodley, mss. Fairfax 6, fo. 276v and Laud misc. 700, fo. 126; also in BM. Additional ms. 24059, fo. 51.

³⁹ Thus in the Phillipps ms. fo. 107 the attempt has been made to disguise the transition between the earlier continuators of HDE and Geoffrey of Coldingham. The division of HDE into books and chapters, as found in Bedford's and Arnold's edns., derives from the Cambridge University Library ms. Ff. i. 27, which stands outside the main textual tradition and did not find medieval imitators. Before the end of the thirteenth century a new continuous division of HDE, the anonymous continuators and Geoffrey into 122 chapters had been devised: the Phillipps ms., fos. ii-iiiv (in a later hand than the text) shows 122 chapters for the complete work; Holkham Hall ms. 468 fos. 1-3 shows 121, the discrepancy resulting from the accidental conflation of chapters 91 and 92. In the fourteenth century the whole history down to the end of Geoffrey continued to be treated as a single book, but it is now divided into 131 chapters, and in one group of mss. Symeon's text has been inflated by the addition of 5 miracles from the *De miraculis et translationibus Sancti Cuthberti*: York XVI. I. 12, Fairfax 6 and Laud misc. 700 show

insertions from *De miraculis* cc. 1, 4, 5, 8, 12 at chapters 31, 40, 67, 84 and 89. These insertions do not appear in the text of HDE in Titus A. II, nor in the incomplete Cotton ms. Vespasian A. VI. But all these mss. have the division into 131 chapters, Vespasian A. VI breaking off at c. 104. Graystane's chronicle originally existed as a separate work with its own chapter divisions: into 35 chapters in York XVI. I. 12, fos. 183-225v, the hand changing at fo. 195; into 38 chapters in Titus A. II, fos. 89-126v. Later in the fourteenth century it was thrown together with the 131 chapters of HDE etc. to form a single book: the *Gesta episcoporum* to 1334, in 184 chapters, as it appears in Fairfax 6. Before the end of the century the text was subjected to a final interpolation, when the treatise *De iniusta vexacione Willelmi episcopi primi* was inserted into the account of St Calais' episcopate. This form is represented by Laud misc. 700, into conformity with which the earliest ms. of HDE, Cosin's V. ii. 6, was altered in the sixteenth century. By 1400 the list of contents was provisionally complete; cf. Titus A. II, fos. 2-4v; Fairfax 6, fos. 213r-v; Laud misc. 700, fos. 14v-17r. By this time quite elaborate indices to the whole work were being drawn up: cf. Laud misc. 700, fos. 1-9, composed, it would seem, between 1374 and 1388; the *tabulatio* in Titus A. II, fos. 153-7v is shorter and less expert, and seems incomplete.

[40] Useful light on these continuations was thrown by Mr N. Denholm-Young's note on 'The Birth of a Chronicle', in *Bodleian Quarterly Record*, vol. vii, nr. 80, pp. 325-8. To the mss. he mentions should be added BM. Additional ms. 24059, which omits Bury's life but brings the substance of Prior Fossour's (fos. 61-2, as in *SS. Tres*, pp. 130-4) and gives an account of the death and benefactions of Bishop Hatfield (fos. 63-4) which is the same as the passage printed in *SS. Tres*, pp. cxlviii-cli. Cambridge, Corpus Christi College, ms. 138, in a insertion at fo. 97*, has a sixteenth-century version of the life of Bury, perhaps related to that in Titus A. II. Doubt may be felt whether the whole life of Bishop Hatfield as it appears in *SS. Tres*, pp. 137-142 belongs to the late fourteenth century. None of it occurs (as Mr Denholm-Young's argument suggests that it does) in Titus A. II or in York XVI. I. 12.

[41] *SS. Tres*, pp. 137-9; cf. Arnold, I, pp. 139-140; *SS. Tres*, pp. 1, 8, 12, 15, 91, 94, 96.

[42] 'The Red Book of Durham'; see note 6 above.

[43] Dr Robert Brentano, 'The *Jurisdictio Spiritualis*: an example of fifteenth-century English historiography', *Speculum* xxxii (1957), 326-32.

[44] The draft, Bodley, ms. Laud misc. 748, comes down to 1356; the most complete fair copy, BM. Cotton ms. Claudius D. IV, only to the death of Bishop du Puiset: see Craster, 'Red Book', pp. 509 sqq.

[45] *SS. Tres*, pp. 152-3.

[46] W. A. Pantin, 'English Monks before the Suppression of the Monasteries', *Dublin Review*, vol. 201 (1937), 257. Todd's volume of collections, now BM. Harley ms. 4843, provides the text of the twelfth- or early thirteenth-century *Miracles of St Cuthbert at Farne*, published by Sir Edmund Craster in *Analecta Bollandiana* lxx (1952), 5-19. It may be noted that there is a passage based verbally on the second and third of these miracles in the York Cathedral ms. XVI. I. 12, fos. 14v-15.

I

ADDENDA

p. 9 line 17 at 'Scottus:':
Presumably *via* the Worcester Chronicle; cf. R. R. Darlington & P. McGurk, 'The *'Chronicon ex Chronicis'* of 'Florence' of Worcester and its use of sources for English history before 1066', Anglo-Norman Studies: *Proceedings of the Battle Conference* 5 (1982), 185–96.

p. 11 line 9 at 'In 1131/2':
HSO suppressed the precise date In 1131/2, *substituting* Presumably in the last few years of Henry I's reign

p. 20 n. 8 line 2 at '(late twelfth century)':
D. N. Dumville, 'The Corpus Christi 'Nennius'', *Bulletin of the Board of Celtic Studies* xxv (1974), p. 371 thinks that CUL ms Ff.i.27 (together with Corpus Christi College Cambridge ms 66) was written in the early years of the thirteenth century.
[Subsequent work on CUL ms Ff.i.27, and Corpus Christi mss 66 and 139 was reported at the conference dedicated to Professor Offler's memory, see B. Meehan, 'Durham twelfth-century manuscripts in Cistercian houses', in *Anglo-Norman Durham 1093–1193*, ed. D. Rollason, M. Harvey & M. Prestwich, (Woodbridge, 1994), 439–49.]

p. 20 n. 8 lines 2–3 at 'Holkham Hall ms. 468':
Now Oxford, Bodleian Library, ms Holkham misc. 25.

p. 20 n. 9 line 2 at 'the edns.':
Cf. Derek Baker, 'Scissors and paste: Corpus Christi, Cambridge ms. 139 again', *Studies in Church History* xi (1975), 83–123.

p. 20 n. 9 line 4 at 'valuable part.':
Cf. J. M. Todd & H. S. Offler, 'A medieval chronicle from Scotland', *Scottish Historical Review* xlvii (1968), 151–9, reprinted as XI below.

p. 20 n. 9 line 6 at '89–100.':
Cf. P. Hunter Blair, 'Some observations on the *Historia Regum* attributed to Symeon of Durham', in *Celt and Saxon: Studies in the early British Border*, ed. N. K. Chadwick, (Cambridge, 1963), 63–118; H. S. Offler, 'Hexham and the *Historia Regum*', *Transactions of the Architectural and Archaeological Society of Durham and Northumberland*, n.s. ii (1971), 51–62, reprinted as X below; M. Lapidge, 'Byrhtferth of Ramsey and the early sections of the *Historia Regum* attributed to Symeon of Durham', *Anglo-Saxon England* x (1981), 97–122; D. W. Rollason, *The Mildrith Legend: A Study in Early Medieval Hagiography in England*, (Leicester, 1982), pp. 14–18.

p. 21 n. 13 line 3 at '559–63.':
Presumably these borrowings came *via* Florence of Worcester, whose

I

26 ADDENDA

borrowings are recognisable in the edition of William Howard, (1592), but not in that by B. Thorpe, (English Historical Society, 1848-9); cf. W. Levison, 'Die Annales Lindisfarnenses et Dunelmenses', *Deutsches Archiv für Erforschung des Mittelalters* xvii (1961), 447-506, at p. 449 n. 7. [See now *The Chronicle of John of Worcester* II, ed. R. R. Darlington and P. McGurk, (Oxford Medieval Texts; Oxford, 1995).]

p. 21 n. 17 after 'xliv sqq.':
Cf. D. Corner, 'The earliest surviving manuscripts of Roger of Howden's *Chronica*', *English Historical Review* xcviii (1983), 297-310; idem, 'The *Gesta Regis Henrici Secundi* and the *Chronica* of Roger, parson of Howden', *Bulletin of the Institute of Historical Research* lvi (1983), 126-44.

p. 21 n. 21 line 6 at 'envisaged.':
Published posthumously, see addition to n. 13 above.

p. 21 n. 21 line 17 at 'only 6':
7, according to Levison, 'Annales', p. 456.

p. 22 n. 22 line 2 at '*in presenti.*':
But in fact the date of Geoffrey's death is not certain (as Sir Charles Clay pointed out to me, and cf. M. D. Knowles, *Monastic Order in England*, (Cambridge, 1949), p. 231 n. 1), and he may have been abbot as early as 1123. The abridgement was certainly made while Henry I was alive, see fo. 32. It appears also in Liège, University Library, ms. 369C, fos. 95 -99v; cf. S. R. T. O. d'Ardenne, 'A medieval manuscript of British history', in *English Medieval Studies presented to J. R. R. Tolkien*, ed. N. Davis & C. L. Wrenn, (London, 1966), pp. 84-93. Dr d'Ardenne's contention that this ms. was the work of a Kirkstall scribe is not convincing; see her paper 'The Cistercian origin of MS Liège, University Library 369C' in *Studies in Language and Literature in honour of Margaret Schlauch*, ed. M. Brahmer et al., (Warsaw, 1966), p. 32. [On the Liège ms., cf. *The Gesta Normannorum Ducum* . . . , ed. E. M. C. van Houts, (Oxford, 1992), pp. ci–ii.]

p. 22 n. 22 final line:
The same annal in the Liege ms, fo. 98v reads *autunc* for *Auwltune* in line 5 and *Wintoniam* for *Guintoniam* in line 7 (*ex inform.* Dr Bernard Meehan). Much weight was laid on this passage by C. W. Hollister, 'The Anglo-Norman civil war: 1101', *English Historical Review* lxxxviii (1973), 316-7, 326-30, 334.

p. 22 n. 31 line 2 at 'Holkham Hall ms. 468':
Now Oxford, Bodleian Library, ms Holkham misc. 25.

p. 23 n. 32 line 2 at 'Durham':
As ms. A.IV.36.

p. 23 n. 33 at 'Holkham Hall ms. 468':
Now Oxford, Bodleian Library, ms Holkham misc. 25.

p. 23 n. 39 line 1 at 'Phillipps ms.':
Now Durham Cathedral Library, ms A.IV.36.

II

A NOTE ON THE LAST MEDIEVAL BISHOPS OF HEXHAM

The succession of the medieval bishops of Hexham ceased early in the ninth century in circumstances which are obscure. Our earliest source for the date would seem to be the chronicle of the church of Durham composed by a member of the pre-monastic congregation of St. Cuthbert between 1072 and 1083, and reconstructed by the late Sir Edmund Craster a generation ago. It tells us that the see of Hexham had come to an end 54 years before the Viking leader Halfdan devastated Northumbria in 875: that is, in or about 821.[1] Until the year 800 we are on firm ground concerning the succession at Hexham. According to the early Northumbrian annals which have survived embedded in the first part of the *Historia regum* attributed to Symeon of Durham, Bishop Heardred died in 800, this being the third year of his pontificate; then Eanberht was chosen and consecrated as his successor.[2] But what happened between 800 and 821? On this point there has been a difference of opinion among modern scholars. Stubbs, followed by Plummer and A. B. Hinds, has Eanberht dying in 806, and being succeeded by Tidferth, with whom the series of medieval bishops of

---

[1] H. H. E. Craster, "The Red Book of Durham", *EHR* 40 (1925), 524, lines 44-47.

[2] *Hist. regum*, ed. T. Arnold, in *Symeonis monachi Dunelmensis opera omnia* II (Rolls Series, 1885), p. 63. Eanberht's name is here given as *Eanbryth*. The place of Eanberht's consecration, *apud Cettingaham*, does not appear in related texts such as the *Historia post Bedam* and the Chronicle of Melrose. Possibly, as Arnold suggests, it is a later insertion in *Hist. reg.* from Hexham. Richard of Hexham, *De statu et episcopis ecclesiae Haugustaldensis*, ed. James Raine, *Priory of Hexham* I (Surtees Soc. Publns. 44, 1864), p. 41, reads *Ethingaham*.

By permission of The Society of Antiquaries of Newcastle upon Tyne.

164 THE LAST MEDIEVAL BISHOPS OF HEXHAM

Hexham came to a close in 821.[3] On the other hand James Raine the younger, who paid more attention to the antiquities of Hexham than any other nineteenth-century scholar, delayed the death of Eanberht and the accession of Tidferth until 814; and to this conclusion the *Handbook of British Chronology* approximates, giving the date 813 for the beginning of Tidferth's episcopate.[4]

The source of this discrepancy would seem to be Raine's reliance on Richard of Hexham, the first author to attempt a comprehensive account of the early bishopric. Richard, canon of Hexham, became prior of his house in 1141 and was confirmed in office during the next year; he witnesses as prior as late as 1163 x 1166.[5] His history of the church of Hexham has come down to us in a form completed after the great translation of the Hexham saints on 3 March 1155 [*De statu*, ii, 4, ed. Raine, *Priory of Hexham*, I, 49]. For the early part of his work Richard draws heavily on Bede's Ecclesiastical History and on Eddi's life of St. Wilfred; he also borrows from an earlier piece of his own, *De gestis regis Stephani*, which was probably composed between 1139 and 1141.[6] The first book of *De statu* brings the story down to 875, and in the last few chapters [i, 15-18] Richard's main authority is clearly the ancient Northumbrian annals, which he later refers to as *gesta veterum Northanhumbrorum* [ii, 13, p. 60]. For the most part he could have found these preserved in the first part of the Durham *Historia regum*, though it appears that Richard had a version of these annals before him which in one instance was more extensive than the surviving text of the Durham work. Under the year 788 Richard's entry has detailed information, corroborated in

---

[3] W. Stubbs, *Registrum sacrum Anglicanum* (2nd edn., 1897), pp. 17, 244; C. Plummer, *Two of the Saxon Chronicles Parallel* II (1900), p. 65; A. B. Hinds, in *Hist. of Northumberland* III: Hexhamshire. Pt. i (1896), pp. 115-16.

[4] James Raine, *Priory of Hexham* I, pp. xxxix-xl; *Handbook of British Chronology*, 1st edn. (1939), p. 184; 2nd edn. (1961), p. 232. Cf. C. E. Whiting, in AA4 24 (1946), p. 155.

[5] James Raine, *Historians of the Church of York* III (Rolls Series, 1894), pp. 79-81; cf. G. V. Scammell, *Hugh du Puiset* (1956), pp. 115, 126.

[6] *De statu*, i, 4, p. 17; cf. *De gestis*, ed. R. Howlett (Rolls Series 1886), p. 154.

part by the D and E versions of the OE chronicle, which is not to be found in *Historia regum* or in such derivatives from it as *Historia post Bedam* and the Chronicle of Melrose.[7]

The tale of Richard's borrowings can be lengthened. He knew the eleventh-century pre-monastic chronicle of Durham, already mentioned, and took over verbally from it the conclusion that the bishopric of Hexham came to an end in or about 821.[8] His account of the last two bishops is as follows: After the death of Heardred, *Eadbertus vel Osbertus* was chosen and ordained at the place called Ethingaham[9] and ruled over the church of Hexham for fourteen years [*De statu*, i, 18, p. 41]. Then, in the next chapter, *Eanbertus vel Osbertus* is listed as the eleventh bishop of Hexham, followed by the note *xiii*, indicating a thirteen-year pontificate. Twelfth and last appears Tydferdus,[10] with the note *sed tempus episcopatus hujus ignoratur*, although a few lines further on Richard repeats the sentence from the Durham chronicle which implies the end of the bishopric of Hexham in 821. To add to the confusion Richard computes (if we can rely on the surviving texts) that the bishopric existed for 144 years after its foundation in 674—*excepto ultimo episcopo cujus tempus ignoratur* [*De statu*, i, 19, p. 42]; for 674+144 would bring us to 818, not 814. In the first chapter of book ii of *De Statu* Richard tells us a little more about Tidferth: " as some relate, Tidferth the last bishop died on his way to Rome, and because of the violence of persecutions there was no one in that region to succeed him and take up his bishopric in his place ": and so

---

[7] *De statu*, i, 17, p. 38: Quo etiam anno tertio kalendas Octobris sinodus fuit in loco qui dicitur Aclech; cf. Chron. DE s.a. 789 [788], which mentions a synod at Aclea, but without a specific date. See Haddan and Stubbs, *Councils and Eccl. Docs.* III (1871), p. 464; cf. also K. Harrison, in *Yorks. Arch. Jnl.* 40 (1960), 246, note 1. There is evidence for a synod in south-east England at *Acleah* in September 787. Its relation (if any) to the synod mentioned in the northern sources is a dark question. *Handbook of Brit. Chron.*, 2nd edn., p. 548, plumps for a single synod, in southern England, and in 787.

[8] *De statu*, i, 19, p. 42 (cf. ii, 1, p. 43); *EHR* 40, 524, lines 18-20, 45-7.

[9] I can no more certainly identify this name than I can the alternative *Cettingaham* of *Hist. reg.*

[10] This reading of the York Cathedral ms. XVI. i, 12 seems preferable to the *Tilferdus* of Cambridge University Library ms. Ff. 1. 27, followed by the editors, Raine and Twysden.

the bishops of Lindisfarne took over [*De statu*, ii, 1, pp. 44-45].

Making the best they could, it would seem, of this confused construction, Raine and the *Handbook* have assumed that Tidferth succeeded Eanberht in 814 or 813. But there can be little doubt that Richard has gone astray. The earliest surviving collection of English episcopal lists, the Mercian fragment in Cotton ms. Vespasian B. VI, already notes Tidferth as the immediate successor of Eanberht;[11] and this fragment, in Dr. Sisam's view, " can be dated fairly closely about the year 812."[12] Because episcopal dates are themselves an important factor in dating the Mercian fragment, this piece of evidence alone is perhaps not quite conclusive that Tidferth was already bishop by 812. The decisive objection to Richard's construction comes from the OE chronicle, for versions D, E and F have Bishop Eanberht dying in 806. This is an annal of authority—the last of the entries from the early Northumbrian annals which are known to have been incorporated in the DE recension of the chronicle.[13] Chron. E correctly reports the lunar eclipse of 1 September 806.[14] The only doubt is, whether the other two items of the annal, the expulsion of King Eardwulf of Northumbria and the death of Bishop Eanberht, really belong to 806 rather than to 808, since the chronicle at this period sometimes falls a couple of years into arrears in its dating. Plummer's suggestions that the expulsion of Eardwulf " is probably to be referred to the end of 807 or beginning of 808 "[15] gains support from foreign sources,[16] and also from

[11] Printed by M. R. James, *Cat. of MSS. in Corpus Christi College, Cambridge* I (1912), pp. 434-5. The episcopal list for Hexham in the Corpus ms. 183, fo. 64b (James, *loc. cit.*), which comes from the early tenth century and was formerly a Durham book (cf. N. Ker, *Medieval Libraries*, p. 38), ends with Eanberht. Later lists, like those in Florence of Worcester, *Chron. ex chron.*, ed. B. Thorpe, i. 25, and in Durham Cathedral library ms. B. ii. 35, fo. 149v (middle of twelfth century), give the full succession Heardred—Eanberht —Tidferth.

[12] K. Sisam, *Proc. Brit. Acad.* 39 (1953), 289.

[13] Plummer, *Two Saxon Chronicles* II, p. 84.

[14] Plummer, II, p. 68. Chron. D. has a solar eclipse.

[15] *loc. cit.*

[16] Cf. Haddan and Stubbs, III, 561.

later English ones: the so-called *Annales Lindisfarnenses*, whose authority is discussed below, place the accession of King Aelfwald, which followed Eardwulf's expulsion, and also the death of Bishop Eanberht, s.a. 808; Roger of Wendover, writing indeed in the early thirteenth century, but with access to ancient Northumbrian material, also puts the succession of Aelfwald to Eardwulf s.a. 808, though he makes no mention of Eanberht's death.[17] On the other hand, if we accept the statement of Symeon's *Historia Dunelmensis Ecclesiae* that Eardwulf was driven out in the tenth year of his reign, this would suggest that he was expelled before 26 May 806.[18] And even if 808 is preferred to 806 for the ejection of Eardwulf, that does not necessarily carry the death of Bishop Eanberht to the later date also. But the margin of doubt is narrow: there is good evidence that Eanberht died either in 806 or 808, and Stubbs and those who followed him had justification for the date they chose. How long the vacancy at Hexham may have lasted until the accession of Tidferth, there seems no means of determining.

What led Richard of Hexham astray? The vicissitudes of the church of Hexham from the beginning of the ninth century onwards make it unlikely that there was much early local material available at Hexham for Richard in the middle of the twelfth century. He had to draw on more fortunate neighbours: and the obvious source was Durham. The version of the old Northumbrian annals used by the compiler of the first part of the Durham *Historia regum* did not extend beyond 802; nor apparently did the version known to Richard (whether or not that version was exactly the same as the one which lay behind the *Historia regum*). Thus he did not know the annal for 806 [? 808] which was the basis for the entry in the DE recension of the OE chronicle, and so he was

---

[17] Roger, *Flores Histor.* s.a. 808, in Matth. Paris., *Chron. maiora*, ed. Luard, I (Rolls Series, 1872), p. 370. See also Luard's introduction, p. xliii.

[18] Symeon, *Hist. Dunelm Eccles.*, ii, 5, ed. Arnold, in *Symeonis monachi Dunelmensis opera omnia* I (Rolls Series, 1882), p. 52; cf. *Hist. reg.* s.a. 796, p. 58.

denied the information from this source that the date of Eanberht's death was not 814, but 806/8.[19]

But how did Richard arrive at the date 814? An answer is suggested by his alternative name for Eanberht, the *Eadbertus vel Osbertus* of *De statu*, i, 18; the *Eanbertus vel Osbertus* of i, 19, when this is considered in the light of another Durham historical source. In 1862 the German scholar G. H. Pertz discovered in a former Durham manuscript, now Hunterian ms. T.4.2 in the University Library, Glasgow, a number of annalistic entries in the margins of a group of Easter tables. These annals Pertz esteemed very highly, taking them to represent entries made contemporaneously from the eighth century onwards; he published them in the folio series of *Scriptores* in the Monumenta Germaniae Historica under the title *Annales Lindisfarnenses et Dunelmenses*.[20] As the criticism of Theopold and Wilhelm Levison has shown, Pertz overestimated the value of these annals, particularly the early ones; they are not contemporary entries in the Easter tables, but the work of some compiler at Durham in the twelfth century.[21] Nevertheless, two of them are much to our present purpose. S.a. 808 we read: Aelfwald regnavit ii annis. Eanbert Hagulstadensis episcopus obiit; and s.a. 820: Osbertus ultimus episcopus Hagulstadensis obiit.[22] That Eanberht died in 808 is possible, as we have seen; 820 is not far out as the date of the death of the last bishop of Hexham. But Eanberht's successor was Tidferth, not Osberht: on that point the evidence of the fragment in Vespasian B. VI is definite. There seems in fact no room for an Osberht in the Hexham succession, and the *Annales Lindisfarnenses* would appear to be mistaken when they insert his name in place of Tidferth's.

---

[19] Though if he used (as is suggested below) the *Annales Lindisfarnenses* or a similar source, he would have found 808 given as the year of Eanberht's death.
[20] MGH *SS*. XIX (1866), pp. 502 *sqq.*
[21] L. Theopold, *Kritische Untersuchungen über die Quellen zur angelsächsischen Geschichte des achten Jahrhunderts* (Lemgo, 1872), pp. 71-2; W. Levison, *England and the Continent in the Eighth Century* (1946), p. 114 and note: H. S. Offler, *Medieval Historians of Durham* (1958), p. 21, note 21.
[22] MGH. *SS*. XIX, p. 506.

But it looks very much as if Richard of Hexham met this substitution in these annals or in some source akin to them, and allowed it to confuse him thoroughly. He knew that Tidferth, not Osberht, was the last bishop of Hexham; but instead of rejecting Osberht, he made room for him by equating him with Tidferth's predecessor, Eanberht. He may have reckoned that Osberht's pontificate, on the evidence of the *Annales Lindisfarnenses*, lasted twelve years; or thirteen, if the end of the succession of Hexham bishops came at what he thought was the correct date: 821. But then in Richard's mind Osberht became identified with Eanberht; and as the date of Eanberht's accession was firmly established as 800, Eanberht/Osberht had to be allowed to live on until 813 (according to *De statu*, i, 19, p. 42), or even until 814 (i, 18, p. 41). It seems possible to explain at least some of the confusion in Richard's account of the last two bishops of Hexham in this way: he led himself astray by conflating his genuine information, which did not go quite far enough, with an erroneous tradition based on the Lindisfarne annals or a cognate source. Thus the *De statu* is not good authority for the dates when Eanberht died and Tidferth succeeded. For the latter event, indeed, we cannot assign a date with certainty; for Eanberht's death the choice lies between 806 and 808.

III

THE EARLY ARCHDEACONS IN THE DIOCESE OF DURHAM*

The following abbreviations have been used in the notes:

AA   *Archæologia Aeliana* (the following number denotes the series).
EHR *English Historical Review.*
EYC W. Farrer, *Early Yorkshire Charters,* vol. 1-3 (1914-16).
FPD W. Greenwell, *Feodarium Prioratus Dunelmensis* (SS 58, 1872).
HED Symeon of Durham, *Historia Ecclesiae Dunelmensis,* ed. T. Arnold, in *Symeonis monachi opera omnia I* (RS, 1882).
HR   *Historia regum,* ed. Arnold, in *Symeonis . . . opera omnia II* (1885).
LV   *Liber Vitae Dunelmensis* = British Museum, Cotton MS. Domitian A. VII, cited from the facsimile edn. (SS. 136, 1923).
M   Durham Cathedral Library, MS. B.IV.24 (twelfth-century martyrology).
NCH *Northumberland County History.*
ND   J. Raine, *North Durham* (1852).
RS   Rolls Series.
SD   R. Surtees, *History and Antiquities of the County Palatine of Durham,* vol. 1-4 (1816-40).
SS   Publications of the Surtees Society.
ST   J. Raine, *Historiae Dunelmensis Scriptores Tres* (SS 9, 1839).
YAJ *Yorkshire Archæological Journal.*

WHEN in 1943 the late Professor Hamilton Thompson came to discuss the archdeaconries of the medieval church, it was natural that he should seek illustration for his argument among the Durham material which he knew so well. On his reading of the evidence, developments here began with the grant of the archdeaconry throughout the diocese by Bishop William of St. Calais to Prior Turgot in 1093; Turgot's promotion to the see of St. Andrews (1107 x 1109) provided Bishop Rannulf Flambard with a welcome opportunity to appoint a secular archdeacon for the first time. Before the death of Bishop Geoffrey Rufus in 1141 the

---

* Unless the contrary is stated, the documents cited are from the Treasury of Durham Cathedral, and now in the Prior's Kitchen.

office had become duplicated, and in this we are to see 'the beginning of the permanent division of the diocese into the two archdeaconries of Durham and Northumberland.'[1] Some years later Professor Barlow came to very much the same conclusions as the result of an independent approach to the problem. The first indisputable archdeacon of the diocese of Durham was Prior Turgot; he was succeeded by a single secular archdeacon, who had turned into two (and here Professor Barlow is rather more precise than Professor Thompson) even before the end of Flambard's episcopate in September 1128.[2]

Clearly, these views represent a considerable simplification, when we compare them with the lists of Durham archdeacons drawn up by earlier scholars: by William Hutchinson, for instance, in the eighteenth century, by Duffus Hardy in his revision of Le Neve, and by the Reverend D. S. Boutflower in the *Fasti Dunelmenses*. Perhaps they carry simplification too far. It may be profitable to look at the scanty and tangled evidence again, down to Bishop Hugh du Puiset's time when we reach more solid ground with the aid of Mr. Scammell's studies.[3]

Was Prior Turgot indeed the first Durham archdeacon whom we can name? Monks at Durham in the early twelfth century affected to believe that this was not so. Symeon of Durham was not among them. Writing his history of the church of Durham about 1104 x 1107, he tells how William of St. Calais appointed Turgot archdeacon in the summer of 1093, at the same time decreeing that all succeeding priors should also *ex officio* hold the archdeaconry.[4] There is no reason to doubt this account. But when somewhat later it came to be copied into the Durham *Liber Vitae* with other evidences of the convent's rights and

---

[1] A. Hamilton Thompson, 'Diocesan Organization in the Middle Ages' (Raleigh Lecture), *Proc. Brit. Acad.* 29 (1943), 164-5. Turgot was not consecrated until 1 August, 1109, but the choice of him as bishop seems to go back at least to 1108, and probably to 1107: Eadmer, *Hist. nov.*, ed. Rule (RS, 1884), p. 198; HR, p. 204.

[2] F. Barlow, *Durham Jurisdictional Peculiars* (1950), appendix: 'The earliest archdeacons of Durham', pp. 153-6.

[3] G. V. Scammell, 'A note on the chronology of the priors, archdeacons and sheriffs of Durham during the episcopate of Hugh du Puiset', AA4 xxxiii (1955), 63-4.

[4] HED iv, 8, p. 129.

THE EARLY ARCHDEACONS IN THE DIOCESE OF DURHAM

claims, Symeon's wording was deliberately elaborated to suggest that Turgot's predecessor as prior, Aldwine, had also been archdeacon: that in fact, as long as there had been a prior of Durham, he had been archdeacon too. A comparison of the texts reveals the fraudulent intention of the *Liber Vitae* entry, and there is no need to linger over it.[5] Prior Aldwine has no real claim to be numbered among the archdeacons.

But this line of our enquiry must be pursued further. There is no evidence for archdeacons in Durham before the Norman Conquest, though §§ 6 and 7 of the Northumbrian Priests' Law show that the office of archdeacon was known in the northern Danelaw in the first quarter of the eleventh century.[6] Possibly at Durham during this period, as Professor Barlow suggests, the dean or senior of the pre-monastic congregation of St. Cuthbert acted as the bishop's vice-gerent, when necessary.[7] However, by the end of the pontificate of the first of the Conqueror's appointees to Durham, the Lotharingian Bishop Walcher (1071 x 1080), there are indications of a different state of affairs. According to Symeon a large part in provoking the native resentment which led to the massacre of Walcher and his *familia* at Gateshead on 4 May 1080 was played by the misbehaviour of Walcher's followers, among whom an unnamed *archidiaconus* is twice mentioned.[8] Can he be identified? A longer and more informative account of the events which led up to the Gateshead massacre is given by the Latin chronicle of Worcester, here followed verbatim by the

[5] LV fo. 46ᵛ. The words italicized are not to be found in HED. ' Eo tempore memoratum priorem Turgotum ante totius episcopatus populos producens, *sicut et ante Alduinum priorem eius predecessorem fecerat*, uices suas *huic sicut et illi* etiam super illos ei iniunxit, ut scilicet per archidiaconatus officium *totius* christianitatis curam per totum ageret episcopatum, ita statuens ut quicunque illi successores fuerint in prioratu, similiter succedant et in archidiaconatu . . . Quapropter Willelmus antistes *eiusdem fundator ecclesie* ita in perpetuum constituisse dinoscitur, ut quicunque Sancti Cuthberti in ipsius ecclesia successores in prioratu fuerint *similiter* etiam in predicationis officium *et in summum archidiaconatus ministerium* curam agentes totius christianitatis *per episcopatum Dunelmensis ecclesie* eidem succederent.'

[6] F. Liebermann, *Gesetze d. Angelsachsen*, I (1898), 380; dated ' probably 1020-1023 ' by Professor D. Whitelock, *English Historical Documents*, I (1955), 434-5. Cf. R. R. Darlington, ' Ecclesiastical Reform in the late Old English Period ', EHR 51 (1936), 413 and n. 1.

[7] Barlow, p. 153.

[8] HED iii, 23, pp. 114-5.

Durham *Historia regum*.[9] These sources represent the killing of Walcher as a vengeance for the murder of the local notable Ligulf: a murder instigated by Walcher's chaplain *Leobwinus*, who had reached a position of eminent power in the diocese.[10] Is he our man? The Worcester chronicle and HR distinguish, as it seems to me, with care between this *Leobwinus* and another man who bore the same name, though in a less archaic form, *Leofwinus* the dean of Durham, who also perished at Gateshead.[11] Professor Barlow confuses Leobwine with the dean, and suggests that it was to 'Dean Leobwine' that the *archidiaconus* of Symeon was intended to refer.[12] It seems much more likely, however, that it is *Leobwinus capellanus* rather than Leofwine the dean who is the legitimate candidate for the title of archdeacon.

Leobwine's name at the head of the list should perhaps be followed by a question mark. The next claimant for inclusion needs no such qualification. Among the historical and pseudo-historical memoranda contained in the Durham *Liber Vitae* is the record of an agreement made between William of St. Calais and Abbot Vitalis of Westminster concerning prayers to be said at Westminster and Durham for dead brothers of the other house. It ends with the sentence: *Et huius conditionis sit particeps Turstinus dunelmensis archidiaconus*.[13] There is nothing to indi-

---

[9] Florence of Worcester, *Chron. ex chron.*, ed. B. Thorpe, II (1849), 13-16; HR, pp. 208-11.

[10] Florence, p. 14; HR, p. 209: 'suus capellanus Leobwinus, quem in tantum exaltaverat [episcopus], ut et in episcopatu et in comitatu fere nil sine illius arbitrio agitaretur.'

[11] Florence, p. 16; HR, p. 210. By an unfortunate slip Arnold has printed the dean's name as *Leobwinum*, HR, p. 210, line 28. But his source, Corpus Christi College, Cambridge, MS. 139, fo. 112va, quite unmistakably has *Leofwinum*, which is Florence's reading, and also Hodgson Hinde's in his edn. of HR (SS 51, 1868), p. 100. Medial and final *b* for *f* is not uncommon in Old English until the ninth century; its occurrence in 1080 is strange. Perhaps the explanation is that Leobwine the chaplain was not a native of this country, but a continental follower of Bishop Walcher, who came from Lorraine. I am grateful to Professor G. V. Smithers for his advice on this subject. No weight need be attached to the form *Signum Leobwini Decani Dunelmensis* found in the purported grant of the church of Tynemouth by Waltheof to Aldwin and the monks of Jarrow: Cart. I, fo. 83 =ST, appendix, p. xix. This is a spurious document.

[12] Barlow, p. 13 note 8, and p. 153.

[13] LV, fo. 48. Another version of this agreement, omitting all mention of William, Vitalis and Thurstin, survives in M. fo. 5, whence it was printed by Joseph Stevenson in his edn. of LV (SS 13. 1841), p. 134.

cate that this sentence was not copied into the *Liber Vitae* in the same hand and at the same time as the rest of the entry, or that it did not form part of the original agreement. The date of this can be determined within pretty narrow limits. There was no Durham monastery until William of St. Calais transferred the monks from Jarrow and Wearmouth at the end of May 1083; it would seem that Vitalis died on 19 June 1085.[14] Thus at some time between May 1083 and June 1085 there was a Durham archdeacon named Thurstin, who was not a member of the monastic community.

To establish this is not merely to restore substance to a figure who has sometimes been dismissed as a ghost.[15] It shows too that in the early years of the monastic chapter of Durham the diocese was aware of the tradition and was for some time under the sway of a secular archdeacon. The prior of the new monastery would take the lead in the chapter. What were to be his relations with an archdeacon—at this time the bishop's chief administrative assistant—who could not be a member of the cathedral chapter because he did not belong to the monastic community? Obviously there were here possibilities of controversy arising about matters of precedence and power. How long Thurstin survived in office is unknown. Our next notice of the archdeaconry comes when Bishop William, himself a monk, had found a solution wholly satisfactory to his monks. Clash between prior and archdeacon was to be ruled out by vesting both offices in a single man. At the beginning of the construction of the new cathedral in the summer of 1093, Symeon tells us, the bishop led out before the people of the whole bishopric Turgot, prior since 1087, and granted him the care of Christianity throughout the diocese, to be exercised by the office of archdeacon, which was to be held in the same way by all future priors.[16]

---

[14] J. A. Robinson, *Flete's History of Westminster Abbey* (1909), pp. 141-2. Flete, the fifteenth-century historian of Westminster, gives 19 June, 1082, as the date of Vitalis' death (*ibid.*, p. 84); but the present document provides an additional reason against accepting his date. E. H. Pearce, *The Monks of Westminster* (1916), p. 193, agrees with Dean Armitage Robinson.

[15] D. S. Boutflower, *Fasti Dunelmenses* (SS 139, 1926), p. 153, misplaces Thurstin under the date c. 1143; Hamilton Thompson, *loc. cit.*, makes no mention of him; Professor Barlow, p. 155, dismisses him: 'There appears to be no evidence for Thurstin's tenure beside the bare assertion of Le Neve and Hardy.'

[16] HED iv, 8, p. 129.

III

194 THE EARLY ARCHDEACONS IN THE DIOCESE OF DURHAM

Turgot remained prior of Durham until he was called to fill the see of St. Andrews, it would seem in 1107 or 1108. Can we assume that he was also archdeacon from 1093 to 1107/8? We know that his jurisdiction reached far and wide. A royal writ to be dated between 1092 and 1095 brought Carlisle within the spiritual sphere of the bishop of Durham and his archdeacon; between 1 January 1096 and 29 May 1099 another royal writ ordered the sheriff and king's barons of Carlisle to pay obedience to the archdeacon of Durham in spiritual matters as they had done in the time of bishop William.[17] A chance reference in a chronicle shows Turgot performing an act of archidiaconal jurisdiction in Teviotdale.[18] I do not know that any evidence has survived for his activity as archdeacon nearer Durham. But, favoured as he was by the long vacancy in the see after the death of St. Calais, and then by Flambard's early troubles with Henry I, Turgot, a masterful man, having influential connexions with the royal house of Scotland, must have become a very powerful figure in the diocese. *A priori* it seems unlikely that he would have surrendered any of his prerogatives as archdeacon before he left to undergo his unhappy experiences at St. Andrews.

But before we can accept this, a problem raised by a passage in Reginald of Durham's *Libellus de admirandis Beati Cuthberti virtutibus* must be considered.[19] For his chapter (written a couple of generations after the event) concerning the opening of St. Cuthbert's coffin on 24 August 1104 by Prior Turgot and the nine monks of Durham, Reginald relies very much on the older account preserved in the compilation *De miraculis et translationibus Sancti Cuthberti*.[20] But whereas this names only one of the monks, Reginald names them all, including *Henricus et Willielmus cognomento Havegrim utrique archidiaconi*. What are we to make

---

[17] Dugdale, *Monasticon*, I (1817), 241, nr. vi; cf. H. W. C. Davis, *Regesta Regum Anglo-Normannorum*, I (1913), nrs. 463, 478; H. H. E. Craster, ' A contemporary record of the pontificate of Ranulf Flambard ', AA4 vii (1930), 37-9.

[18] HR, pp. 197-8. Durham's jurisdiction in this area had been recognized before November 1100; cf. Craster, pp. 38-9.

[19] Ed. J. Raine (SS 1, 1835), p. 84.

[20] Printed by T. Arnold, in *Symeonis . . . opera omnia*, I, 247 sqq. Dated ' some twenty years or more after the translation ' by Dr. B. Colgrave, ' Post-Bedan Miracles and Translations of St. Cuthbert ', in *The Early Cultures of North-West Europe: H. M. Chadwick Memorial Studies* (1950), p. 331.

of these two monk archdeacons of 1104?[21] Reginald did not invent the names of his nine monks: they can all be found in the contemporary lists of Durham monks at the beginning of Cosin's manuscript of Symeon's history and on fo. 42 of the *Liber Vitae*.[22] In any case, invention would have been foolish; for it is reasonable to suppose that the names of those who took a chief part in the great events of August 1104 would long be remembered and honoured in the monastery. A more plausible case might be made for suggesting that Reginald made up the offices he assigned to the nine—were it not for this obit which is to be found in the twelfth-century Durham martyrology under the date *xiiii kal. oct.*: *Obier[unt] Columbanus anachorita et Heinricus archidiaconus*.[23] Attempts to identify William 'Havegrim' the archdeacon of 1104 with William the son of Thole, archdeacon of York or the West Riding, have been authoritatively rejected.[24] I do not think that we can argue *Henricus et Willielmus cognomento Havegrim utrique archidiaconi* out of the way: we have to take account of two Durham monk-archdeacons in 1104. Had Turgot by this date resigned his archdeaconry outright to a pair of his own monks? That surely would have prejudiced the system of prior-archdeacons on which the convent laid such stress. It seems more likely that Henry and William 'Havegrim' were Turgot's delegates, occupying a position rather like that of the

---

[21] Professor Barlow, p. 154 argues that 'Reginald's nine were the principal assistants at the second and impartial ceremony' [conducted by Ralf, abbot of Séez, some days later: cf. *De mirac.* pp. 258-9] and not the participants on 24 August. 'Hence the archdeacons were not necessarily Durham monks, nor in any way connected with the church of Durham.' I find this wholly unconvincing. Reginald's account when he names the nine is clearly based on the passage in *De mirac.* p. 253 which refers to the first opening of St. Cuthbert's coffin on 24 August. His additional reference to Algarus, as assisting Ralf of Séez, has indeed to do with the second ceremony. But it is by way of a note or gloss, identifying a brother whom the account in *De mirac.* p. 259 mentions but leaves unnamed.

[22] Alduinus appears 48th in the Cosin's list [HED, pp. 4-6], and 51st in LV. Leofwinus 4 in C, 7 in LV. Wikingus 17 in C, 20 in LV. Godwinus 18 in C, 21 in LV. Osbernus 24 in C, 27 in LV. Henricus 32 in C, 35 in LV. Algarus 49 in C, 52 in LV. Symeon 38 in C, 42 in LV. Willelmus may refer to any one of the three monks of that name: 3, 35 and 52 in C, 9, 39 and 55 in LV.

[23] M, fo. 32.

[24] C. T. Clay, 'Notes on the early archdeacons in the Church of York', YAJ 36 (1947), 284, 285 note 1. Nevertheless the suggestion has been repeated by R. L. G. Ritchie, *The Normans in Scotland* (1954), p. 411.

vice- or sub-archdeacons whom we find appearing in a number of English dioceses later in the twelfth century.[25]

William of Malmesbury has the story that Turgot carried matters so high that when he was promoted to St. Andrews Bishop Rannulf Flambard designed to leave the office of prior of Durham vacant.[26] This is likely enough. It is hard to conceive Flambard content with being anything less than full master of his diocese; it is hard to believe that he could have been this while Turgot was still active in Durham. Certainly the alacrity shown by Flambard in promoting the consecration of Turgot as bishop of St. Andrews struck St. Anselm as indecent.[27] As a member of the chapter of St. Paul's Flambard was acquainted with conditions in a secular cathedral, and he may well have thought them preferable to what he found at Durham.[28] To begin with, his relations with his monks were not happy, though a change for the better took place later;[29] from the terms of a confirmation of their privileges which they secured from Pope Calixtus II in 1123 it would seem that the monks still feared that their position in Durham was insecure.[30] It was to be expected, then, that once Turgot was out of the way Flambard would take steps to abolish the system whereby the prior was also archdeacon. He could not do without a prior for long, though quite when Algar was appointed as Turgot's successor is uncertain. It is clear, however, that Algar was not allowed to be archdeacon; Flambard returned to the older tradition of a secular clerk holding that position. The change he made was permanent. That does not mean that never after this shall we find a monk as archdeacon

---

[25] Cf. Clay, 'Notes', pp. 432-4; A. Morey, *Bartholomew of Exeter* (1937), p. 127.
[26] *Gesta pontific.*, ed. N. E. S. A. Hamilton (RS, 1884), pp. 273-4.
[27] Eadmer, *Hist. nov.*, pp. 198-9.
[28] C. N. L. Brooke, 'The Chapter of St. Paul's 1086-1163', *Cambridge Hist. Journ.* 10 (1951), 124, 129-31; *id.* in *A History of St. Paul's Cathedral*, ed. W. R. Matthews and W. M. Atkins (1957), pp. 21-2.
[29] The situation is summed up well in an anonymous short chronicle of Durham, probably written between 1164 and 1174: 'Iste in primordio suos monachos exosos habuit, sed postea illos plurimum dilexit.' Durham Cathedral Library, MS. B.11.35, fo. 149rb.
[30] W. Holtzmann, *Papsturkunden in England* II, ii (1936), nr. 5, pp. 138-40: 'prohibentes, ut nulli de cetero liceat eundem monasticum ordinem de eodem monasterio ausu quolibet amouere.'

III

THE EARLY ARCHDEACONS IN THE DIOCESE OF DURHAM 197

—we shall; but never again will the prior of Durham be archdeacon throughout the diocese *ex officio*. As the century wore on the monks themselves dropped further propaganda on behalf of St. Calais's constitution. Though controversy between priors and archdeacons continued endemic throughout the middle ages, its terms were no longer the claim of the prior to absorb the office of archdeacon. More limited, though still important issues came to the forefront: matters of precedence on ceremonial occasions, and the right of the prior to exercise archidiaconal jurisdiction in the convent's own churches.

The steps by which Flambard reversed St. Calais's policy are obscure. We must not say with Professor Knowles that 'almost immediately [after Turgot's departure] the secular clerks Rannulph and Robert are found as archdeacons.'[31] This would be to antedate developments by fifteen years or so. For the name of the next known archdeacon after Turgot was Michael. Beyond that, and the fact that he was not a monk of Durham, there is nothing to say about him. The evidence for his existence is only just sufficient. He heads the witness list in Flambard's purported grant of the hermitage of Finchale to the prior and convent.[32] I have no doubt that the text of this grant is spurious. But the witness list is not outrageous, and just possibly it may have been taken over from a genuine document. Besides Michael the archdeacon it comprises Master Rodbertus de Calfmonte, who may be identified with the Robert de Calzmonte of whose connexions with Flambard there is independent evidence;[33] William of Corbeil, the later archbishop, known to have been Flambard's clerk at one time;[34] Rodbertus the priest; Roger Conyers, a baron of the bishopric; and Osbernus, possibly the Durham monk of that name who was one of the sacristans in 1104, or possibly one of

---

[31] *The Monastic Order in England* (1949), p. 629.

[32] (a) 2.1.Pont.8; (b) Cart. III, fo. 274; (c) Bodley, MS. Laud misc. 748, fo. 38; (d) Lincoln's Inn, Hale MS. 114, fo. 89ᵛ. Printed from (a) and (b) by J. Raine, *Priory of Finchale* (SS 6, 1837), p. 20; by Dugdale, *Monasticon* IV (1823), 331-2, from (a)?

[33] C. Johnson and H. A. Cronne, *Regesta Regum Anglo-Normannorum*, II (1956), nr. 721.

[34] *De mirac.*, p. 258; HR, p. 269. For an interesting, if not wholly convincing argument that William acted as tutor to Flambard's sons at Laon, see T. A. Archer, 'Ranulf Flambard and his sons', EHR 2 (1887), 103-12.

Flambard's relatives.³⁵ If the witness list is acceptable, and if it was taken from some genuine document concerning Godric of Finchale, then its date would lie between c. 1110, when Godric first settled at Finchale, and 1116, by which date William of Corbeil had left the diocese.³⁶ But all this is in the highest degree conjectural. The only substantial evidence for Michael as archdeacon is a document issued by Bishop William of St. Barbara on 14 November 1147.³⁷ The bishop declared that Archdeacon Wazo had renounced his claims in his controversy with Prior Roger about precedence, after the wise old men of the bishopric had testified that in the past the priors had always occupied the

---

³⁵ For Osbernus the monk, see note 22 above. Brooke, 'Chapter', p. 130, note 18, mentions Osbern the royal chaplain, prebendary of Consumpta in St. Paul's, who may have been a brother of Flambard. Or the name may be a corruption of Osbertus, Flambard's nephew, who later became sheriff of Durham and witnessed a number of his uncle's *acta*.

³⁶ LV fo. 42ᵛ has Godric dying in 1170, with this note: 'hic aput finchale per ⟨ fere ⟩ lx annos uitam heremiticam ducens'; *fere* is added above the line. In 1116 William accompanied Archbishop Ralf d'Escures to the curia, according to Hugh the Chantor, *Hist. of the Church of York*, ed. C. Johnson (1961), p. 50. But William may well have left Flambard long before 1116. Hugh describes him as 'Dorovernensis canonicus', which I take to mean a canon of St. Gregory's, Canterbury. William's early career seems little known. But HR, p. 269, refers to him as 'venerandae memoriae archiepiscopo Anselmo saepissime ac familiariter conversatum'; and as Archer, *art. cit.*, p. 110 says, it would be difficult to assign this close familiarity with Anselm to a period other than that between Anselm's return to England late in 1106 and his death in 1109. Possibly it was at this time that William became a canon of St. Gregory's, remaining there until his appointment as prior of St. Osyth's, which occurred *c.* 1120, if we follow the account by Mr. J. C. Dickinson, *Origin of the Austin Canons* (1950), pp. 112-113. This would explain how William was 'familiarem' (HR, p. 269) to the monks of Christ Church at the Canterbury election in 1123; how he was available for the service of Archbishop Ralf in 1116; and indeed, if the canons of Laon came to England on their begging quest in 1113 rather than after 1123, how they could have found William at Canterbury, though the description of him as archbishop must have been an addition in the light of later events: cf. Hermann, *Lib. de miraculis s. Mariae Laudunens.* ii, 6, in Migne, *Patrol. Lat.* 156, 977; Archer, 'Ranulf Flambard', p. 105; R. L. Poole, *Exchequer in the Twelfth Century* (1912), p. 55; J. S. P. Tatlock, 'The English Journey of the Laon Canons', *Speculum* 8 (1933), 463-4. If William had left Flambard for Canterbury 1106 x 1109 he cannot, of course, have witnessed a document about Godric. Cf. n.91.

³⁷ 1.1.Archidiac. 1A and 1B (two verbally identical versions, written by different hands; both with the seals of William of St. Barbara and Robert abbot of Newminster, one of the bishop's assessors)=FPD, pp. lx-lxi. The date 'die prima kalendarum decembrium' is presumably to be rendered 14 November, not 1 December, as Professor Barlow suggests, p. 155.

THE EARLY ARCHDEACONS IN THE DIOCESE OF DURHAM 199

post of honour at the bishop's right hand, and that *Archidiaconos uero Michaelem et Rodbertum qui Wazonem precesserant nunquam ad hoc officium accessisse priore in quouis loco presente*.[38] Here we have the succession of what we may call the senior line of archdeacons of the Church of Durham: Michael—Robert—Wazo.

Robert had succeeded Michael before Flambard's death in September 1128, since he witnesses as archdeacon four or five of Flambard's surviving *acta*.[39] It is extremely difficult to date these documents precisely, but they all seem to come from the last few years of the episcopate.[40] If, as seems not unlikely, Robert is to be identified with the *Rodbertus clericus* who also witnesses under Flambard, he had not become archdeacon before 1121.[41] During the vacancy after Flambard's death Robert witnesses as archdeacon the grant by Prior Algar and the convent of Staindropshire to Dolfin son of Uchtred on 20 March 1131.[42] He is also found active during the episcopate of Geoffrey Rufus (1133 x 1141).[43] After Geoffrey's death he was won over to aid the attempt to gain the bishopric made by William Cumin, David of Scotland's chancellor.[44] He went south with Cumin's deputation to the Empress Matilda in the summer of 1141; we can assume that it was after Matilda's expulsion from London on 24 June that Robert made his way back to Durham to act as the mouthpiece of her

---

[38] The same clause occurs in 1.1.Archidiac.2 = FPD, p. lxii. But I feel no confidence in this document.

[39] 2.1.Pont.2 = SD I, i, appendix, p. cxxv, nr. v; 2.1.Pont.3 = EYC II, nr. 977; 2.1.Pont.5; 2.1.Pont.10 = EYC II, nr. 966 (from Cart. I, fo. 49). The *R. archidiaconus* who witnesses 2.1.Pont.3* (= EYC II, nr. 977 note) is almost certainly Robert.

[40] 2.1.Pont.2 can be dated early August 1128; 2.1 Pont.3, c. 1125-1128.

[41] *Robertus clericus* witnesses Flambard's grant of Ancroft to Papedy in fee, for the service of half a knight to be performed in the castle of Norham. The construction of Norham was begun in 1121: HR, p. 260. The grant was printed ND, p. 385, from an original in private possession which I have not seen. *Rodbertus clericus* also witnesses 2.1.Pont.6.

[42] Cart. II, fo. 186ᵛ = FPD, p. 56 note.

[43] 4.1.Pont.15 = SD III, 149 and FPD, p. 140 note; 4.1.Pont.17 = FPD, p. 205 note and EYC II, nr. 998. On 28 July 1137 x 1140 Robert publicly declared that he was present when Flambard made 'hanc donationem' to St. Cuthbert: 2.1.Pont.1* = FPD, p. 192 note. Whether this refers to Flambard's grants in 2.1.Pont.1, as Greenwell assumes, is uncertain.

[44] HED, *cont. prima*, p. 144.

order to the chapter to elect Cumin.⁴⁵ The order was not obeyed and Cumin was disappointed of his ambition, though he remained to make a pestilential nuisance of himself in the diocese for three years more. In view of his compromising connexion with Cumin we can hardly suppose that Robert was recognised as archdeacon by William of Saint Barbara (elected bishop on 14 March 1143), or can have survived in office after St. Barbara's effective occupation of the see in October 1144.⁴⁶ But though Robert had taken a line directly opposed to that of Prior Roger concerning Cumin's claim, he must before his end have made his peace with the convent and become a monk. His obit is entered in the martyrology between *ii id. octbr.* and *Idvs octbr.* as *Rodbertus archidiaconus et monachus.*⁴⁷ No note is added (as was normally the case when this was so) that this was just *ad succurrendum*.

Robert was succeeded as senior archdeacon by Wazo. But even before Flambard's death he had had a junior colleague: Rannulf, one of the bishop's many nephews. The grip exercised by Flambard and his relatives on the chapter of St. Paul's has been emphasised by Professor Brooke;⁴⁸ equally impressive was the spread of the clan in Flambard's bishopric. At the date of Flambard's grant of Hallowstell fishery to the monks of St. Cuthbert (after 1121) *Raulfus nepos meus* was ordered to give the monks seisin if Papedy sheriff of Norham failed to act.⁴⁹ Probably Raulfus is the *Rannulfus archidiaconus* who witnesses Flambard's charter of restitution to the monastery in August 1128, next after *Rodbertus archidiaconus.*⁵⁰ This document restored, among other things, Blakiston to the monks: a property which shortly before had been granted by Flambard to his nephew Richard, together with Ravensworth and *Hectona* [Eighton?]. The witness list

---

⁴⁵ *ib.*, p. 145; J. H. Round, *Geoffrey de Mandeville* (1892), pp. 85-6.

⁴⁶ HED, *cont. prima*, p. 160.

⁴⁷ M, fo. 34. Possibly Robert the archdeacon is the *Rodbertus* who comes 62nd in the list of monks in LV, fo. 42ᵛ, or the *Rodbertus iii* who comes 71st (59 and 68 in the list at the beginning of Cosin's MS. of Symeon: HED, p. 6).

⁴⁸ See note 28 above.

⁴⁹ 2.1.Pont.11 = SD I, i, appendix, p. cxxv, nr. iii and ND, appendix, p. 129, nr. dccxxviii.

⁵⁰ 2.1.Pont.2 = SD I, i, appendix, p. cxxv, nr. v. The copy in Cart. I, fo. 71ᵛ omits the *archidiaconus* after Rannulf, and so did Surtees, though it stands clearly in the original. Professor Barlow's conjecture, p. 155, that the second archdeaconry was in existence in Flambard's episcopate is thus justified.

of Flambard's grant to Richard is remarkable.[51] It is headed by Archdeacon Rannulf and includes at least four more members of the family: two other Flambard nephews, the brothers Osbert and Robert, and Archdeacon Rannulf's son, William Fitz Rannulf (to whom Flambard had previously granted Houghall, Harraton, the two Herringtons and Hawthorn),[52] as well as his nephew Paganus.[53] Prominent among the witnesses too figures *Papa monachus*. Papa is a strange name for a monk, though he is perfectly well authenticated as a member of the convent of Durham by the twelfth-century lists;[54] and the appearance of a single monk's name in this otherwise secular company provokes thought. It is likely that he too belonged to the clan: certainly not as Flambard's father,[55] but possibly as father of one or more of the nephews. The date of this document is uncertain, but probably it represents an attempt by the family to make the most they could for themselves out of the bishopric when Flambard was seen to be failing.[56] There seems no reason to suppose that Rannulf had been appointed archdeacon long before Flambard's death; during the vacancy which followed there is explicit mention of him as archdeacon on the Pipe Roll for 31 Henry I.[57]

In Geoffrey Rufus' time Rannulf on occasion witnesses as archdeacon alone; but also with, and then after, Robert.[58] The

---

[51] Society of Antiquaries of Newcastle upon Tyne, Ravensworth Deed 1; cf. H. E. Bell, 'Calendar of Deeds given to the Society by Lord Ravensworth', AA4 xvi (1939), 44-5, and plate iii, p. 70. Mr. Bell reads *Papamonus*, but the correct extension is *Papa mon(achus)*. The deed was printed from a late and bad copy in SD II, 210. The document was being talked about in Durham in the sixteenth century; cf. *Leland's Itinerary*, ed. L. Toulmin Smith, IV (1910), 128.

[52] 2.1.Pont.7, 6, and 7*. The first and third of these grants are printed SD I, ii, 181.

[53] For *Wibertus miles*, another nephew of Archdeacon Rannulf, see Reginald, *Libellus de vita et miraculis s. Godrici*, ed. J. Stevenson (SS 20, 1847), p. 106.

[54] 84th in LV fo. 42ᵛ; 81st in Cosin's MS., HED, p. 4.

[55] Papa's obit is *viii kal. iunii* : M, fo. 23ᵛ. Flambard's father's name was Thurstin and he died a monk of St. Augustine's, Canterbury. His obit is *kl. ian.*: M, fo. 13.

[56] HED, *cont. prima*, p. 140: 'Vivacis animi, et vegeti fuit corporis, in eodem incolumitatis statu usque biennium ante mortem perdurans. Abhinc enim et salus ei paulatim languescere, et acumen sensus coepit retundi.'

[57] *Pipe Roll, 31 Henry I*, ed. J. Hunter (Record Commission, 1833), p. 132. From a cancelled entry it appears that both Rannulf and Robert held a church, in each case valued at 40 shillings: *ibid.*, p. 128.

[58] E.g. 4.1.Pont.15 = SD III, 149 and FPD, p. 140 note.

parting of the ways for these colleagues came with Geoffrey's death in 1141. While Robert supported Cumin, Rannulf played a leading part with Prior Roger in defeating the Scottish bid for the bishopric. It was Rannulf who reported the matter to the legate, Henry of Winchester, and blocked the attempt of the Cumin faction to rush an election. When Cumin returned to Durham in September 1141 after his abortive visit to the empress he found Rannulf still obdurate, and drove him out, seizing and spoiling his possessions. Rannulf escaped with difficulty, first to York, then to King Stephen and the legate, from whom he obtained a sentence of excommunication against Cumin.[59] In co-operation with Prior Roger he sent envoys to the curia to state their case. These were successful, and on 6 December 1142 Pope Innocent II wrote to Roger and Rannulf ordering them to proceed to an election within forty days of receiving his letter. At the same time Henry of Winchester as legate was instructed to confirm the election when it had been made, and to see that full reparation for the injuries he had suffered was made to Rannulf.[60] Thus Rannulf, with Prior Roger, was the chief author of the election of William of St. Barbara, dean of York, as bishop of Durham on 14 March 1143. They met the newly elect at Wintringham on his way back to York from the council of London, and accompanied him to Winchester for his consecration by the legate on 20 June.[61] The record justifies John of Hexham's opinion that Rannulf was a good man in a tight corner.[62]

Rannulf witnesses half-a-dozen or so documents under William of St. Barbara as archdeacon without a partner;[63] but as soon as

[59] HED, *cont. prima*, p. 146.
[60] Holtzmann, *Papsturkunden*, II, ii, nrs. 29, 30, pp. 174-5.
[61] HED, *cont. prima*, pp. 148-50.
[62] John of Hexham, *Hist. XXV annorum*, ed. Arnold, in *Symeonis . . . opera omnia*, II, 312: 'vir praeclarae probitatis in ecclesiasticis necessitatibus.'
[63] (a) 1.2.Pont.4=SD I, ii, 97. (b) 3.8.Spec.9=SD I, ii, appendix, p. 280, note 1; FPD, p. 131 note; EYC II, nr. 649. (c) York Cathedral, Reg. Mag. Album, pt. iii, fo. 24=EYC III, nr. 1472. (d) Cartulary of St. Mary's, York, fo. 312ᵛ=EYC I, nr. 566. (e) Corporation of Newcastle upon Tyne, Liber Cartarum=A. M. Oliver, *Early Deeds relating to Newcastle upon Tyne* (SS 137, 1924), pp. 9-10. (f) 1.2.Pont.1=SD III, 385-6. (g) Public Record Office, Augmentation Office, Ancient Deed B 11535=J. Brand, *Hist. of Newcastle*, I (1789), 205 note. (h) **Cartuarium Vetus**, fo. 59ᵛ: chirograph dated 1148 of agreement between the prior and convent of Durham and Robert de s. Martino concerning the church of *bliburc* (Blyborough, Lincs.).

THE EARLY ARCHDEACONS IN THE DIOCESE OF DURHAM   203

he and Wazo appear as witnesses together, it is Wazo who is accorded first place, and thus held the senior of the two archdeaconries.[64] Presumably, therefore, Geoffrey of Coldingham is referring to Wazo when he relates that on the death of Bishop William (13 November 1152) both the prior [Lawrence] and the archdeacon were ambitious of the succession.[65] But it is clear that Rannulf played a prominent part in the controversy about the making of a new bishop. In 1141 x 1143 he had been aided by the Cistercian reformers, the great St. Bernard and William of Rievaulx, in maintaining at Durham the interests of the house of Blois against William Cumin, behind whom stood King David of Scotland, the uncle and the ally of the Empress Matilda. Ten years later he helped to bring Hugh du Puiset, a connexion and partisan of Blois, to the see of Durham, in defiance of the claim by the Cistercian archbishop of York, Henry Murdac, to have a decisive say in the matter. At the beginning of Lent 1153 Rannulf was one of the party of Durham ecclesiastics who came to York to seek absolution from the sentences Henry had fulminated against them for electing Hugh in January.[66] Neither popular agitation nor the intervention of King Stephen's son Eustace was sufficient to move Murdac. Only the efforts of Theobald of Canterbury as papal legate at last secured the absolution of du Puiset's electors. Over the question of consecrating Hugh, Murdac would not budge, and with Theobald's recommendation the Durham electors decided to go to Rome.[67]

John of Hexham does not name the members of the Durham delegation, other than Master Lawrence, later abbot of Westminster.[68] Coldingham reports that Prior Lawrence went, and also the archdeacon.[69] Probably Wazo is meant, for Rannulf

---

[64] Newcastle upon Tyne, Public Library, Greenwell Deed 3; cf. Joseph Walton, *Calendar of the Greenwell Deeds* (1927), p. 2 and pl. i.

[65] ST, p. 4.

[66] John of Hexham, p. 329.

[67] See A. Saltman, *Theobald Archbishop of Canterbury* (1956), pp. 120-2.

[68] John of Hexham, p. 330.

[69] ST, p. 5. The former Holkham Hall ms. 468 (now Bodleian Holkham misc. 25), fo. 64 reads *N archidiaconus* at this place in Geoffrey of Coldingham's chronicle. But this would seem to be no more than the conventional N. indicating the scribe's ignorance of the name.

was near his end. His obit in the martyrology is *xvii kal. ianr.*[70] By 1155 we know the name of his successor, John, and as there seems to be no evidence that he witnessed under Hugh du Puiset (consecrated at Rome on 20 December 1153) it is probable that Rannulf died about 16 December 1153. He had held his office through a stirring quarter of a century—together with his cousin Osbert the sheriff he had prolonged Flambard's influence in Durham far beyond the grave.

Whether his senior partner Wazo had been active in the diocese long before we hear of his controversy with Prior Roger being terminated in November 1147 is uncertain.[71] As Mr. Scammell has shown, Wazo's earlier connexions were with Henry of Winchester.[72] This may suggest that he was introduced to Durham as a result of Henry's co-operation with Prior Roger and Archdeacon Rannulf in opposition to William Cumin. Possibly he was brought in to take the place of the discredited Robert after William of St. Barbara had obtained real control of the bishopric late in 1144. He does not witness later than the end of Prior Absalon's regime (1158 or early 1159).[73] After him the system of two archdeacons set on foot under Flambard suffered an interruption for more than a dozen years, during which Rannulf's successor John acted as sole archdeacon in the diocese. John makes his appearance very early in du Puiset's episcopate,[74] and habitually his name comes after Wazo's when the two witness together.[75] But from c. 1158 until the arrival of Burchard du Puiset as archdeacon of Durham c. 1172 John had no fellow archdeacon; then for a couple of years he seems to fall back into the junior position,[76] in which he had been succeeded by Arch-

[70] M, fo. 38ᵛ.
[71] Above.
[72] G. V. Scammell, *Hugh du Puiset* (1956), p. 13 note 1.
[73] Scammell, 'A note', p. 63.
[74] Scammell, in YAJ 39 (1956), 88-9.
[75] The only exception I have noticed is 3.1.Pont.11 (=FPD, p. 100 note), where John tests before Wazo. I do not think any great significance need be attached to this single instance.
[76] He witnesses 3.1.Pont.12 (=FPD, p. 103 note) and 4.2.Spec.1 (=FPD, p. 100 note) after Burchard; but 4.1.Pont.8 (=FPD, p. 198 note) *before*. EYC II, nr. 985, where Burchard again precedes John, is dated by Farrer c. 1185-1195, amended by C. T. Clay, YAJ 35 (1943), 27 note 3, to *c.* 1185-1189. But if the dates suggested here for the two archdeacons are correct this document falls between c. 1172 and 1174.

deacon William by November 1174.[77] With Burchard and William a double series of archdeacons again becomes the normal situation, and so it remains.

We have, then, a more complicated story than has sometimes been supposed. Turgot was not the first of Durham's archdeacons, nor can we be sure that he held his office unaided. After him, no prior of Durham was archdeacon, except in the convent's own churches, but it would not be wise to stress too soon complete divorce between the monastic chapter on the one hand and the secular archdeacons on the other. For Archdeacon Robert died as a member of the monastic community; even more surprisingly, as I have pointed out elsewhere,[78] Archdeacon John, though in outward seeming a very secular character, turns out to have been a monk too. The system of two archdeacons begun in Flambard's last years did not enjoy unbroken continuity from that time on, as John's career shows. For much of the twelfth century there is an element of anachronism in neat tables showing parallel successions of 'archdeacons of Durham' and 'archdeacons of Northumberland'. Doubtless the succession Michael—Robert—Wazo represents the senior line of archdeacons of the Church of Durham: these men are what we may call the *archidiaconi majores*.[79] But not for a couple of full generations was a distinct territorial appellation applied to the junior archdeacons. After all, they too were archdeacons of the church or diocese of Durham. As Sir Charles Clay has pointed out, the phrase *archidiaconus Eboracensis* might be applied in the twelfth century either 'as the specific description of the Archdeacon of York' or to designate any of the archdeacons in the diocese.[80] The same was true in Durham. Ordinarily members of the junior line call themselves *archidiaconus*, and nothing more, as did their seniors. Exceptionally they may call themselves *archidiaconus Dunelmensis* or

---

[77] Scammell, 'A note', p. 64. The last known reference to John occurs in a document which can perhaps be assigned to the autumn of 1174: NCH VIII, 66 note. According to M, fo. 31ᵛ his obit is *v* or *iv idvs septembris* : *Johannes Archid(iaconus) mo(nachus) et prof(essus)*. Presumably he died in September 1174, or perhaps, though less probably, 1175.
[78] EHR 73 (1958), 96; see note 77 above.
[79] On this title see Hamilton Thompson, in *Proc. Brit. Acad.* 29 (1943), 159 sqq.
[80] C. T. Clay, 'Notes on the early archdeacons in the Church of York', YAJ 36 (1947), 270.

Dunelmi. Rannulf once appears with this title, when he was witnessing outside his diocese and there was need to identify him.[81] So too on occasion John is called archdeacon of Durham, and his seal bore that title.[82] Even John's successor William sometimes witnesses as archdeacon of Durham.[83] What Rannulf and John do not do, as far as I know, is use the title 'archdeacon of Northumberland'.[84] Nor can we say that there is anything like conclusive evidence of their activities being especially concerned with that part of the diocese which lay north of the Tyne.[85]

On the other hand, we do find William witnessing as *archidiaconus Northimbrie* on at least two occasions.[86] This is a significant change. It would seem to be during the later years of Bishop Hugh du Puiset that the distinction between the two archdeaconries was drawn firmly and consistently along territorial lines. After du Puiset's death the custodians of the vacant see rendered account of 20 marks *de hospiciis* of the archdeacon of Northumberland;[87] when the archdeacon of Northumberland is shown to have a revenue *qua* archdeacon, substantial existence can hardly be denied to his archdeaconry. Complaint was laid at the curia in 1202 against William's successor Theobald *de Pertico* for neglecting the duties of his archdeaconry of Northumberland, where he had not been seen since Bishop Philip had been

---

[81] EYC III, nr. 1472.

[82] 3.2.Spec.9 = NCH VIII, 145 note 1 (*Archidiaconus dunelmi*); Misc. Charter 1354 = ND, p. 111 (*archidiacono dunelmensi*). W. Greenwell and C. H. Hunter Blair, *Durham Seals* [= AA3 xv (1918)] no. 3252.

[83] EYC II nrs. 983, 987, dated by Farrer 1189-90 and 1189-95 respectively. Both these documents are witnessed by William's senior, Burchard. But he uses his new title of Treasurer of York; cf. C. T. Clay, 'The Early Treasurers of York', YAJ 35 (1943), 26-7.

[84] Mr. Scammell's statement, 'A note', pp. 63-4, that John is on one occasion 'specifically described as archdeacon of Northumberland' seems a slip. He refers to Cart. II, fo. 44ᵛ, which is an incomplete copy of 3.2.Spec.9, in which John's title is *Archidiaconus dunelmi*. The cartulary reads *archidiaconus dunelm̄*.

[85] Of the 17 documents witnessed by Rannulf as archdeacon which I have examined, only 3 relate to matters concerning the northern half of the diocese. These figures are not, of course, in themselves a conclusive argument; but they do give some indication of where the weight of Rannulf's interests lay.

[86] 3.7.Spec.21 = FPD, p. 125 note; 4.1.Pont.1 = Scammell, *Hugh du Puiset*, p. 261.

[87] *Chancellor's Roll, 8 Richard I*, ed. D. M. Stenton (Pipe Roll Society 45, 1930), p. 257.

consecrated in April 1197.[88] Early in the thirteenth century the distinction between the two archdeaconries is perfectly plain: Aimery appears in the public records as archdeacon of Durham, and Richard Marsh as archdeacon of Northumberland.[89] Soon we can find original documents witnessed by both archdeacons with their differing territorial titles.[90] The division of archidiaconal jurisdiction which lasted in the diocese of Durham till 1842 was now manifest. It had been foreshadowed, indeed, by the appointment of Rannulf as Robert's fellow archdeacon; but not till long after their day was it complete.[91]

[88] Cf. Pope Innocent III's letter dated 15 February 1203, in Migne, *Pat. Lat.* 214, 1170. The archdeacon is there described as *G. de Pertico*, but *Cal. Pap. Letters* I, 13 has *T. de Pertico*, which I take to be correct, and so identify him with the *Teobaldus de Pertico* of *Pipe Roll, 13 John*, ed. D. M. Stenton (Pipe Roll Society 66, 1953), p. 38.

[89] See *Rot. litt. pat.*, p. 93b; *Rot. Chart.*, p. 190.

[90] For example, 2.2.Pont.1 (=FPD, p. lxxxviii), dated 22 September 1219, and 2.2.Pont.5, of the same date: both witnessed by S(imone) *Dunelm. et A(lano) Northimbr. Archidiaconis*. Perhaps earlier instances than these could be found.

[91] In suggesting (note 36 above) that William of Corbeil became a canon of St. Gregory's I was influenced by the late Dr. Charles Johnson's rendering of 'Dorovernensis canonicus' as 'canon of Canterbury' (*Hugh the Chantor*, p. 50). Though he offered no reason for his choice, the authority of this vastly experienced scholar cannot be set aside lightly. But the more obvious translation would be 'canon of Dover', as Professor Barlow has pointed out in *History* 46 (1961), 238. As one of the unreformed canons of St. Martin's, Dover (where, incidentally, Rannulf Flambard had interest: cf. AA4 vii, 47) William would have been near enough to Canterbury to know Anselm and the monks of Christ Church and to meet the canons of Laon.

ADDENDA ET CORRIGENDA

p. 196 n. 25 at 'p. 127': C.R. Cheney, *English Bishops' Chanceries 1100–1250*, (Manchester, 1950), pp. 143–6.
p. 198 n. 36, l. 7 at 'Canterbury.': See further the final note to this study.
p. 199 n. 38 at '1.1.Archidiac.2': This should read '1.1.Archidiac.Dunelm.2'.
p. 199 n. 41, l. 4 at 'not seen.': It was given by the late Miss Alice Edleston to the Bowes Museum, Barnard Castle, and is deposited at the Durham County Record Office. [The reference is D/Bo/D/37; ed. H.S. Offler, *Durham Episcopal Charters 1071–1152*, Surtees Society 179 (1968), no. 19.]
p. 201 l. 14 at 'uncertain,': Probably before August 1127.
p. 201 n. 57, l. 2 at 'a church,': By gift of the king after Bishop Flambard's death.
p. 202 n. 63, l. 10 at 'Lincs.).': Original (4.3.Ebor.4) edited, with facing plate, p. 206 in K. Major 'Blyborough Charters', *A Medieval Miscellany for Doris Mary Stenton*, ed. P.M. Barnes & C.F. Slade, Pipe Roll Society new series xxxvi (1960), pp. 203–19.

IV

THE DATE OF DURHAM (*CARMEN DE SITU DUNELMI*)

The twenty-one lines of alliterative OE verse comprising *Carmen de situ Dunelmi* have evoked some interest as illustrating the long persistence of an old rhetorical form, the *encomium urbis*.[1] The text has been settled by Professor Dobbie; but doubt may be felt whether the piece can be dated within the precise and narrow limits that he suggests: i.e., between 1104 and 1109.[2] Clearly he is right in deciding that the posterior limit for dating the poem is determined by an unmistakable reference to it in Symeon's *Historia Dunelmensis Ecclesiae* (iii, 7; ed. Arnold, 1, 89).[3] Symeon completed his history between 1104 and 1107 (or, at the very latest, 1109). On the other hand, Dobbie's claim that the poem "cannot have been written before 1104, when the translation of St. Cuthbert to the new cathedral of Durham took place" is much less convincing. The textual tradition offers no help for the problem of dating;[4] and argument from the language of the poem does not seem to have been carried far.[5] (If it had, I would have no title to discuss the matter.) It may therefore be of value to emphasise, against Dobbie, that the contents of the poem seem perfectly compatible with a date before 1104.

The poem bases its praises of Durham partly on the city's site and natural surroundings (ll. 1–8); partly on the fact that here rest St. Cuthbert and the relics of other holy men. Mention is made of the head of the Northumbrian King, Oswald; and of relics of St. Aidan and three successive bishops of Lindisfarne between 688 and 740:

---

[1] See M. Schlauch, "An Old English *Encomium Urbis*," *JEGP*, XL (1941), 14–28.

[2] E. Van Kirk Dobbie, *The Anglo-Saxon Minor Poems* (London, 1942), p. 27 (text); pp. xliv–xlv (discussion of date).

[3] *Symeonis monachi Dunelmensis opera omnia*, ed. Thomas Arnold, Rolls Series, 2 vols. (London, 1882–85).

[4] The text depends on two twelfth-century MSS, of which Vitellius D. xx was destroyed in 1731 by the fire in the Cottonian Library; fortunately Hickes had already edited it. The other, Cambridge, University Library, Ff. 1. 27, comes from late in the century. See Neil R. Ker, *Catalogue of Manuscripts Containing Anglo-Saxon* (Oxford, 1957), nos. 14, 223.

[5] But see Schlauch, p. 16, who suggests that "the language of the poem points to a late date, probably early twelfth century"; Dobbie, p. xliv: "a typical English work of the transition period, with a number of spellings characteristic of that time."

© 1962 by the Board of Trustees of the University of Illinois. Used with permission of the University of Illinois Press.

Eadbert, Eadfrith, and Æthelwald (ll. 11–14), as well as of Bede and of Cuthbert's teacher, St. Boisil (ll. 15–17). Within St. Cuthbert's minster are also other uncounted relics (ll. 18–20). There is no reason why a Durham author should not have made these boasts long before the translation of August 1104. St. Cuthbert's body had been brought to Durham from Chester-le-Street in 995, and after finding two temporary resting places had been laid in Bishop Aldhun's new cathedral in 998 (Symeon, *HDE*, iii, 1–2, 4; Arnold, pp. 78–81, 82–83). At this date the saint's body was already accompanied by the relics of Oswald, Aidan, and the three bishops of Lindisfarne; indeed, as Symeon (*HDE*, ii, 6, p. 57) relates on written authority ("ut in veteribus libris invenitur"), these relics were in St. Cuthbert's coffin when it was removed from Lindisfarne in 875. Thus, by 995 all the relics named in the poem were at Durham, except those of Bede and Boisil. In the course of the eleventh century these, too, were acquired and placed with or near St. Cuthbert's body, by the efforts, Symeon tells us (*HDE*, iii, 7, pp. 88–89), of Alfredus (or Aluredus), son of Westou. This remarkable personage flourished as sacristan of Durham during the episcopates of Edmund, Æthelric, and Æthelwine, from about 1020, perhaps, until after 1056; the date of his death is not known.

Alfredus held the church of Hexham by gift of Bishop Edmund,[6] and was the great-grandfather of the Cistercian saint Ailred of Rievaulx. An active teacher—"Alured Larwa, id est doctorem," Ailred called him[7]—and familiar custodian of St. Cuthbert's body, he showed great energy in seeking out and elevating the relics of Northumbrian saints, many of which he brought to Durham. His elevation of the Hexham saints Acca and Alhmund took place certainly after 1031, and perhaps after 1056.[8] I do not know how we can date precisely his transference to Durham of the relics of Bede and St. Boisil.[9] We are told (*HDE*, iii, 7, p. 89) that Ælfred lived for many years after abstracting Bede's bones from Jarrow, which suggests a date before

---

[6] Brit. Mus., Add. MS 39943, fol. 149ᵛ, printed by James Raine, *Priory of Hexham*, Surtees Soc. Publns., 44, 46 (London, 1864–65), I, appendix, p. viii.

[7] Ailred, *De sanctis ecclesiae Hagustaldensis*, ch. 11, in Raine, I, 190.

[8] A Hexham interpolation in the Durham *Historia regum* (Arnold, II, 47) dates the elevation of Alhmund's relics "more than 250 years" after the saint's death in 781. Richard of Hexham, *De statu ecclesiae Hagustaldensis*, ii, 4 (Raine, I, 49), has Ælfred elevating Acca's relics and Alhmund's in the time of Bishop Æthelwine, i.e., between 1056 and 1070.

[9] The date commonly given is "about 1020"; see *Bede, His Life, Times and Writings*, ed. A. Hamilton Thompson (Oxford, 1935), p. 37. This seems no more than a guess based on *HDE*, iii, 7, p. 87.

rather than after 1050 for this pious theft.[10] At any rate, once he had brought these relics to Durham, there existed all the conditions which *Carmen de situ Dunelmi* describes. A much later author, Reginald of Durham, shows us Ælfred on one occasion in the midst of a circle of enthusiasts for the city: they begin "loci situm et murorum ambitum et altitudinem ecclesiae turrium, magnidici faustu eloquii vehementer extollere."[11] Reginald cannot have been writing long before 1167, but his anecdote derives some authority from the fact that it came to him as a piece of family tradition from Ailred of Rievaulx. The similarity between the state of feeling here recorded and that which produced *Carmen de situ Dunelmi* is striking, though it would be hopelessly rash to attempt to construct upon it any theory about the authorship of the poem. But undoubtedly Ælfred Westou had created the historical situation which made the poem's boasts plausible. Though he exhorted those in his confidence to secrecy about Bede's bones, there was an oral tradition at Durham concerning all the relics specified in *Carmen de situ Dunelmi*, even before the irregular congregation of St. Cuthbert was replaced by Benedictine monks in 1083. Probably there was a written tradition also;[12] and it may be that the author of the poem refers to this in line 20.[13]

In short, we can be sure that the poem had been written by 1109, at the very latest; but we cannot be sure that it had not been written before the translation of St. Cuthbert in August 1104—an event of which it makes no mention. As far as the contents of the poem are concerned, it could have been written fifty or sixty years before 1104:

---

[10] That Ælfred lived on into Æthelwine's episcopate is clear from Richard of Hexham, p. 49, and from HDE, iii, 7, p. 87.

[11] Reginald of Durham, *Libellus de admirandis virtutibus sancti Cuthberti*, ed. James Raine, Surtees Soc. Publns., 1 (London, 1835), ch. 16, p. 29. The identification of Reginald's "vir veteranus vitae honestae . . . qui singularem corporis beati Cuthberti custodiam optinebat" with Ælfred seems certain.

[12] On Symeon's use of the phrase "ut in veteribus libris invenitur," when telling of the presence of the relics of Oswald and the others in Cuthbert's coffin in 875, see above. A similar phrase in the account of the 1104 translation contained in the compilation *De miraculis et translationibus sancti Cuthberti* (Arnold, 1, 252) is probably derived from Symeon, for this account was presumably not written until twenty years or more after the translation; see Bertram Colgrave, "Post-Bedan Miracles and Translations of St. Cuthbert," in *The Early Cultures of North West Europe: H. M. Chadwick Memorial Studies* (Cambridge, 1950), p. 331. Latin lists of Durham relics have survived from the twelfth century and later; see *The Relics of St. Cuthbert*, ed. C. F. Battiscombe (Oxford, 1956), pp. 113-14. Possibly an earlier list of this kind was available to the author of the poem.

[13] "ðes ðe writ seggeð."

at any time, in fact, after Ælfred Westou had brought the relics of Bede and St. Boisil to Durham. The only possible grounds for assigning it, as Dobbie does, quite definitely to the first decade of the twelfth century would be linguistic.[14] And would not that be to ask of the argument from language more precise results than it can be expected to yield?

[14] Miss Schlauch's discussion of the date of the poem (pp. 15–16) suffers from her conviction that Symeon's *Historia Dunelmensis Ecclesiae* was not completed until 1129; she seems to have confused *HDE* with the *Historia regum* also ascribed to Symeon, which indeed ends in 1129. While she inclines to a late date, "probably early twelfth century," she admits the possibility that the poem refers to "an earlier verse account . . . now lost, dating from the eleventh century."

V

WILLIAM OF ST. CALAIS, FIRST NORMAN BISHOP OF DURHAM.[1]

ANY list of notable bishops of Durham would be incomplete without the name of William of St. Calais, to whom Durham owes the planning of its present cathedral and the foundation of the monastic house which for four and half centuries profoundly influenced religious and social life in these parts. About St. Calais little has been written, perhaps because there is not much to know.[1a] To what is already known it seems unlikely that substantial additions will be made. Probably there is something to subtract. For earlier accounts of St. Calais have relied much on the tractate "De iniusta vexacione Willelmi episcopi primi," commonly found in close connexion with the *Historia Dunelmensis Ecclesiæ*, which we ascribe to Symeon.[2] The claim of this tractate to be a contemporary account of St. Calais' controversy with William Rufus in 1088 has been accepted as authentic by all the very great historians who have had occasion to deal with it: by Stubbs, Freeman, Liebermann and Maitland. With every sort of diffidence I have come to disagree with them. In my

[1] I am grateful to Mr. B. Colgrave for a number of helpful suggestions about this paper.

[1a] An early attempt at a comprehensive account of St. Calais is in *Hist. litt. de la France*, VIII (1747), 433-7; the latest and best by Dom Léon Guilloreau, "Guillaume de St. Calais, Évêque de Durham," in *Revue historique et archéologique du Maine*, LXXIV (1913), and LXXV (1914); cf. also *Gallia Christiana*, XIV (1856), col. 457. Mandell Creighton's article in *DNB*, s.v. "Carilef," does not merit the charge of bias levelled at it by Professor Knowles, *The Monastic Order in England*, p. 169, n. 1.

[2] Most recently printed by T. Arnold in the Rolls Series *ed.* of *Symeon of Durham*, I, 170-95.

opinion the tractate is neither contemporary nor reliable; it is a tendencious piece of fiction, probably dating from the second quarter of the twelfth century. My reasons for so believing are, I hope, to appear elsewhere, and so they need not be rehearsed here. But if we reject the "De iniusta vexacione"—as I think we must—then we lose nearly all the evidence which has till now been used to reconstruct in detail what has undoubtedly appeared to be the most striking episode in the story of St. Calais.

The difficulties of evidence for that story are indeed extreme, for the atmosphere of calculated fraud is not wholly dissipated by the rejection of the "De iniusta vexacione." St. Calais was the founder of the monastery of Durham, and monastic foundations notoriously tended to surround their origins with a web of invention in order to cloak past usurpations, to protect present rights, or to prepare the way for future claims. The trouble is, that these monks who lied so hard for the good cause did not always—nor, indeed, commonly—invent completely. As long ago as 1872 William Greenwell[3] denounced as forgeries the foundation charters of Durham, including three of St. Calais, for which no less than seven different versions are extant as pretended originals.[4] In general, none can quarrel with his verdict. But there remains, after the initial recognition of their falsity, the more delicate task of deciding how much authentic information they nevertheless contain, by the aid of a more sophisticated criticism

---

[3] *Foedarium Prioratus Dunelmensis* (Surtees Soc., 58), pp. xxxi *et seq.*

[4] (1) " Ego Willelmus sedem episcopatus Sancti Cuthberti " : two pretended originals in Durham Dean and Chapter Archives, Ia Ie Pontificalium 2a and 2b (printed *Foedarium*, pp. xxxviii-xliii). (2) " In nomine Patris et Filii et Spiritus Sancti " : four pretended originals, Ia Ie Pontificalium 3a, 3b, 4a, 4b (3a and 4a printed *Foedarium*, pp. xlvii-li; 4b printed *Hist. Dunelm. Scriptores Tres* (Surtees Soc., 9), appendix, pp. xiv-xv). (3) " Venerabilibus patribus L. dei gracia Cantuariensi . . .": pretended original Ia Ie Pontificalium 1 (printed *Foedarium*, pp. lii-lvi).

than Greenwell could command.[5] The problem of the Durham foundation charters calls for a thorough re-examination in which all the resources of diplomatic shall be employed, and I have no wish to anticipate the findings of that enquiry. For my present purpose the foundation charters must be left on one side, and since the tractate "De iniusta vexacione" has already been discarded, the main source for St. Calais' career left to us is the fourth book of the *Historia Dunelmensis Ecclesiæ*, together with some scattered references in charters which we can be reasonably sure are genuine. We are, of course, lucky to have the author of the *Historia Dunelmensis Ecclesiæ* as a witness. For here was a monk of Durham—perhaps his name was Symeon—who wrote, in all probability, between 1104 and 1109: at the most, just over a dozen years after St. Calais' death. Almost certainly he had known St. Calais in person. But even in the use of this source caution is necessary. St. Calais was the benefactor and patron of the Durham monks; one of their number was unlikely to expose the reputation of their founder to the criticism of the outside world. But also, Symeon was a member of a monastic community whose interests, by the time at which he was writing, were becoming pretty distinct from, and sometimes even antagonistic to, those of the bishop who was its nominal abbot. By and large, Symeon is a candid witness, but it would be unwise to trust him too far either when he is obviously concerned to protect St. Calais' reputation, or when he imputes to him improbable grants of privilege in favour of the prior and convent.

Though not the first French speaking bishop of Durham, nor the first of the Conqueror's nominees, William of St. Calais was the first Norman to hold the see. Our information about his early life is scanty. As a young man, a secular clerk of the church of Bayeux, he followed his

---

[5] Illustrated, for example, by the work of Paul Kehr, Hans Hirsch and Albert Brackmann and their pupils on German monastic documents of this period; cf. V. H. Galbraith, "Monastic Foundation Charters of the Eleventh and Twelfth Centuries," *Cambridge Historical Journal*, IV (1934).

father, who had long before become a monk, into the monastery of St. Calais, which lay somewhat less than thirty miles south-east of Le Mans in the county of Maine.[6] Perhaps he was a native of the Bessin;[7] from the act of piety which caused him to have it inscribed in a Durham Martyrologium we know his mother's name: Ascelina.[8] The abbey of St. Calais was burnt down during the English occupation in the fifteenth century; among its few surviving records there seems to be no reference to William, though he prospered there, rising first to the office of "prior claustri" and then to that of prior.[9] To the house of his profession William gave solid tokens of continuing affection after he had become bishop of Durham: Durham lands in Lincolnshire, of an annual value of £4 according to the Domesday Book commissioners, continued in the possession of the monks of St. Calais until 1303;[10] among the agreements which the monastery of Durham made with other houses to pray, on reciprocal conditions, for their deceased members, is one with the abbey of St. Calais;[11]

[6] Arnold, *Symeon of Durham*, I (hereafter quoted as HDE), 119.

[7] As Guilloreau conjectures, *op. cit.* LXXIV, 210.

[8] In the Martyrologium in Durham Dean and Chapter Library, MS. B. iv. 24, fo. 12b, this entry stands between 1st and 3rd January: "Obiit Willemus Dunelmensis episcopus primus et Ascelina mater eius": printed by T. Rud, *Codicum Manuscriptorum Ecclesiae cathedralis Dunelmensis Catalogus Classicus*, p. 215, and by J. Stevenson, *Liber Vitae Ecclesiae Dunelmensis* (Surtees Soc. 13) p. 140; cf. *ib.*, p. 149, where Stevenson prints from a later Obituarium of Durham, now British Museum, Harleian MS., 1804, fo. 13, "Non. Januarii. Ob. Willelmus Dunelmensis episcopus primus et Anselma mater eius."

[9] HDE, 119; L. Froger, *Cartulaire de l'Abbaye de St. Calais*, p. xv.

[10] *D.B.*, 340b, 2; the priory of Covenham passed from St. Calais to Kirkstead in 1303 (Guilloreau, LXXV, 78).

[11] *Liber Vitae*, fo. 33b (Surtees Soc. facsimile, 1923): "Pro monachis de monasterio sancti carilefi tantum fiat quantum pro monachis de Westmonasterio," that is (cf. fo. 48) for each monk who dies seven full offices in the convent, a mass to be sung by each priest, a psalter by the other brethren, while the

a Durham missal now in the British Museum has a "Missa Sancti Karilefi abbatis" which was presumably introduced to Durham by William.[12] But further promotion awaited him elsewhere; by 1078 he had been elected abbot of St. Vincent's at Le Mans. There are a few indications of William's activity as the administrator of his new house; charters survive to show him receiving investiture of lands granted to the abbey and defending its rights to a mill site at St. Longis.[13] At some of his other activities we can only guess. Symeon tells us that the Conqueror made St. Calais bishop of Durham "quia eius industriam in rebus saepe difficillimis probatam habuit."[14] It may be conjectured that these most arduous matters were often political. Maine had only lately been seized by the Normans (1063) and was restive under their rule. From 1069 onwards Maine was in a state of revolt, fostered by the Normans' enemy, Fulk count of Anjou; though by his expedition to Le Mans in 1073 the Conqueror was able to re-establish his eldest son, the unsatisfactory Robert Curthose, in nominal possession of the county, neither native resistance nor the influence of Fulk had been finally broken. In this uneasy situation it was obviously profitable for the Conqueror to have a man whom he could trust at the head of the great abbey of St. Vincent's just outside Le Mans, especially during the years 1078-80 when Robert was badly at odds with the rest of his family.[15] It was

lay brethren who do not know the psalter are each to say 150 Pater Nosters. The same agreement recurs in Durham Dean and Chapter Library, MS. B. iv. 24, fo. 5.

[12] Harleian MS. 3289, fo. 334; cf. Guilloreau, LXXV, 79, n. 1.

[13] R. Charles and M. d'Elbenne, *Cartulaire de l'Abbaye de Saint Vincent du Mans*, nrs. 99, 100, 621. The original cartulary of St. Vincent's was lost in the disorders of the French Revolution, but a late seventeenth century copy survives in Paris, Bibliothèque nationale, fonds latin 5444. Its editors suppose that William succeeded Reginald as abbot in 1078.

[14] HDE, 119.

[15] Cf. W. J. Corbett, *Camb. Med. Hist.*, V, 517; C. W. David, *Robert Curthose, Duke of Normandy*, pp. 17-36; F. M. Stenton, *Anglo-Saxon England*, pp. 600-1.

wholly in accordance with the Conqueror's ideas of the proper relations between Church and State that a high ecclesiastic should be used to forward the political schemes of the secular ruler. Perhaps then we dare suppose that St. Calais while he held St. Vincent's acted as one of William's agents in Maine, and there disclosed—if indeed he had not already earned St. Vincent's by disclosing—the sort of capacity in practical affairs which was shortly to bring him to the see of Durham. At the same time he probably formed that connexion with Robert Curthose which afterwards involved his career in strange entanglements.

In May, 1080, Walcher the Lotharingian bishop of Durham was murdered at Gateshead. He had been appointed by the Conqueror in 1071; five years later the earldom of Northumbria was also committed to him, so that his secular sway extended from Tees to Tweed. This disordered area, where since the Conquest the Normans had exercised only an intermittent and precarious authority, was vitally important for the safety of the kingdom. The Scots were an ever-present menace, and the danger was felt more keenly when Malcolm of Scotland began to harbour Anglo-Saxon refugees; in 1070 he married the Etheling's sister Margaret. The Conqueror's invasion of Scotland in 1072 had compelled Malcolm's homage at Abernethy, but the northern frontier remained insecure. Sir Frank Stenton has reminded us that "the Norman government could do nothing to advance, and less than was needed to protect, the English frontier against Scotland"; in the east the line of the Tweed was as yet unfortified; in the west Scottish territory reached Stainmore, within two days' ride of York.[16] And in the exposed hinterland between Tweed and Tees Norman control was not patiently suffered. Few better illustrations of the character of this area can be found than the late eleventh century Durham tractate "De obsessione Dunelmi," with its account of a blood feud running through three and four generations.[17] It was an

[16] *Op. cit.*, p. 606.
[17] Printed by Arnold, *Symeon of Durham*, I, 215-20; cf. especially p. 219.

intensely conservative world, with deep loyalties to the house of the ancient earls of Bamborough which neither Danish invasion nor Norman conquest had been able to destroy. Even the Conqueror had found it prudent to attempt to rule through the native line of Bernicia. From it in 1066 he had appointed Cospatric as earl of Northumbria, and though two years later Cospatric forfeited for rebellion and treachery, he was restored in 1070 and ruled till further dealings with the Scots caused his deposition in 1072. Even then, his successor was a native: Waltheof, son of the great Danish earl Siward by a granddaughter of the Bernician earl Uhtred. In turn, Waltheof was implicated in conspiracy against the Conqueror, and after his removal the Northumbrian earldom was granted to bishop Walcher. There are indications that behind the massacre to which Walcher fell victim there was working the tradition of native loyalty to the Bernician line. But this was the second time that a Norman nominee in the north had been murdered, for in January, 1069, the Fleming Robert de Comines, appointed during Cospatric's first disgrace, had been burnt alive in the bishop's house in Durham. William the Bastard was not the man with whom to repeat such tricks, and after Walcher's death Odo of Bayeux was sent to ravage Northumbria. He did his work with Norman thoroughness, and in the autumn of 1080 Robert Curthose followed him by invading Scotland and building his new castle on the Tyne. A Norman, Aubrey de Coucy, was made earl of Northumbria, soon to be replaced by Robert of Mowbray, nephew of the great Norman ecclesiastic Geoffrey of Coutances. On 9th November, 1080, the successful abbot of St. Vincent's was chosen as bishop of Durham by the king: "ab ipso rege electus" says Symeon,[18] and that short phrase perhaps contains a good half of the Conqueror's philosophy about the right relations of Church and State. Though St. Calais' consecration at Gloucester on 3rd January, 1081, was performed by his metropolitan, Thomas of York, Lanfranc was busily con-

[18] HDE, 119.

cerned with the ceremony,[19] and perhaps this intervention may be taken as a guarantee that the Conqueror's choice, as usual, was sufficiently respectable. St. Calais had made himself a distinguished career in the reformed monasticism of the continent. But viewed in its context of northern danger and disorder it may be surmised that his appointment to Durham was not without political intention. The capacities which he had displayed in Maine were to be employed in another region of doubtful loyalty to the Conqueror.

We know St. Calais in the early years of his episcopate to have been much in the company of the great men of his time. "He had come," Symeon tells us, "by his energy and prudence to the notice and favour not only of the king of England and the king of France, but also to that of the pope."[20] For the rest of the Conqueror's reign William, bishop of Durham, frequently appears as a witness to royal charters. Rarely do we know the time or place at which they were issued, and so they cannot help us to construct even a skeleton itinerary for St. Calais, but they do show that he was assiduous at court and enjoyed the king's favour.[21] There is good reason to suppose that during the great Domesday enquiry of 1086 he was one of the commissioners for the south-western counties.[22] In September, 1082, he was with his king in Normandy,[23] and it was probably at the end of the same year that he went to the Curia. He was sent there with a double purpose: to talk

[19] The "Latin Acts of Lanfranc" (Earle and Plummer, *Two Saxon Chronicles Parallel*, I, 289) say that Thomas of York consecrated St. Calais at the Conqueror's order and with Lanfranc's consent. It was at Lanfranc's order that the bishops of Worcester, Exeter, Wells and Hereford assisted Thomas "eo quod a Scottorum episcopis qui sibi subjecti sunt habere adiutorium non potuit."

[20] HDE, 120.

[21] Cf. H. C. W. Davis, *Regesta Regum Anglo-Normannorum*, nrs. 220, 235, 236, 274, 275, 278, 282, 284.

[22] Cf. *D.B.*, 87b, 1; V. H. Galbraith, "The Making of Domesday Book," *English Historical Review*, LVII (1942), 174. The conjecture was first made by Eyton.

[23] Davis, *Regesta*, nr. 146a, 5 September, 1082.

with Pope Gregory VII on the king's behalf about some business which cannot now be specified, and to gain papal approval for a project touching his see: the creation of a monastic chapter for the cathedral of Durham.[24]

It is well known how monasticism, almost extinct in northern England as the result of the Viking invasions, began to be revived there from about 1074 by the efforts of Aldwin of Winchcombe and his companions. With the encouragement of bishop Walcher they reoccupied the monastery at Jarrow and attracted to themselves a body of monks, coming mainly from southern England. In a few years—the story has recently been well told by Professor Knowles[25]—the revival of monasticism spread to Melrose, Whitby, St. Mary's York and Wearmouth. The movement was protected and fostered by Walcher, who, according to Symeon, was frustrated only by his premature death in his intention of becoming a monk and of establishing a monastic foundation to care for the body of St. Cuthbert at Durham. He had already begun to build dwelling-places for the monks (on the site which they later occupied) when he was murdered.[26] Thus, at St. Calais' accession, there were monasteries close at hand, at Jarrow and Wearmouth, but in Durham the clergy living about the cathedral and having the custody of St. Cuthbert's body formed a community not easy to describe. For though it was a congregation, its members did not live under a monastic rule, nor were they regular canons.[27] Probably less than justice has been done to this congregation of St. Cuthbert, for it is from the monks who supplanted it that we have been

[24] HDE, 121: "Rex statim, ut ex omni parte tam utilis consilii roboraretur consensus, ad papam Gregorium tam de his eum consulturum quam de aliis quae mandaverat sibi locuturum eum misit." The likely date for St. Calais' journey to the pope seems the end of 1082: cf. H. Boehmer, *Kirche und Staat in England und in der Normandie*, p. 138, n. 3.

[25] *Monastic Order*, pp. 163-171.

[26] HDE, 113.

[27] HDE, 120. Walcher, it would appear, had imposed on the congregation the customs of secular canons: HDE, 106, and Knowles, *op. cit.*, p. 166.

content to learn about it. I suspect that in fact it was a society with a far greater care for tradition and the memory of its saint than the rather disparaging references to it by Symeon would lead us to believe; it may well be that a careful study of the sources of Symeon's own history would show that he owed a great deal to the labours of the predecessors whom he rather disdained.[28] But undoubtedly the congregation of St. Cuthbert represented something untidy, anomalous; there is a hint that it harboured connexions with those native Bernician conservatives who were not guiltless of the death of Walcher.[29] Here were reasons enough for its abolition by a Norman administrator. The tide of monasticism was flowing in the far north, and this admirably suited the ideas of the great Norman ecclesiastics, who had learned in their own country the value of reformed monasticism for the general purposes of the church. It may be—as the Durham historical tradition was later to assert[30]—that St. Calais convinced himself that the companions of St. Cuthbert and the early custodians of his body had been monks by reading the early life of the saint and Bede's history; certainly among the books which he afterwards gave to the convent

[28] For example, to the chronicle composed by a member of the congregation between 1072 and 1083 and inserted in the *Liber Magni Altaris.* This chronicle has been reconstructed by Sir Edmund Craster, " The Red Book of Durham," *English Historical Review*, XL (1925), 519-32.

[29] In what purports to be a bull of Gregory VII dated 6th January, 1083 (see note 36 below), there is a suggestion that political considerations may have had something to do with the dispersal of the congregation. After relating how the murderers of Walcher had been punished by the Conqueror, the " bull " goes on to say that the king has requested " etiam Dunelmensis ecclesie clericos maleactionales, *quosdam etiam eorum tam execrabili sacrilegorum prosapia oriundos*, propter vitam suam incorrigibilem auctoritate apostolica inde penitus eliminari." Even if the " bull " has to be wholly rejected as a forgery emanating from Durham, its evidence on this point retains some value.

[30] In the introductory section of the tractate " De iniusta vexacione ": Arnold, *Symeon of Durham*, I, 170.

was a copy of the *Ecclesiastical History of the English Nation*, which is still preserved in the Chapter Library.[31] But the decision to complete Walcher's plan of founding a monastery at Durham was so much in the Norman tradition as to leave its character as an individual resolution of St. Calais somewhat less than certain. The project for which he gained Gregory VII's assent at the beginning of 1083 had the support of the king and queen, and of Lanfranc.[32] It may be—though of this Symeon makes no mention—that the part of Lanfranc went beyond support. The organization of Canterbury as a monastic cathedral had been accepted and developed by Lanfranc, who also had introduced a monastic chapter at Rochester; both at Canterbury and at Rochester a two-fold division of the lands of the see was made between the prelate and the chapter.[33] In 1083 St. Calais is represented as doing precisely these things at Durham.[34] Can we suppose that something more than Lanfranc's example, that some positive act of promotion or suggestion on Lanfranc's part was here in play? Such a conjecture may seem over-bold, but it is noteworthy that the Benedictine customs under which the new convent at Durham was governed were those which Lanfranc had prescribed for Christ Church, and that the manuscript in which they were written—it is still in Durham—was written in a late eleventh-century Christ Church hand.[35] In any case, it seems proper to emphasize

[31] Durham Dean and Chapter Library, MS. B. ii. 35, fos. 38b-119.

[32] HDE, 121.

[33] Cf. Knowles, *op. cit.*, pp. 625-6; R. A. L. Smith, *Collected Papers*, p. 93. Whether Lanfranc was responsible for the division at Canterbury is perhaps doubtful: cf. B. W. Kissan, *English Historical Review*, LV (1939), 285-293.

[34] HDE, 123: "Denique terrarum possessiones illorum ita a suis possessionibus segregavit, ut suas omnino ab episcopi servitio, et ab omni consuetudine liberas et quietas ad suum victum et vestitum terras monachi possiderent." Symeon represents this as ancient custom in Durham, but this claim is refuted by Greenwell, *Foedarium*, pp. xiv-xxiv.

[35] Durham Dean and Chapter Library, MS. B. iv. 24, fos. 47-73 (on the hand cf. R.A.B. Mynors, *Durham Cathedral*

that when in May, 1083, St. Calais brought the twenty-three monks from Jarrow and Wearmouth to Durham and bound them to the service of St. Cuthbert and the cathedral his action must be viewed in a wider context, and perhaps as a less personal achievement, than the local tradition suggests.

The congregation of St. Cuthbert, except for its dean, who alone accepted St. Calais' invitation to become a monk, was dispersed; of the fate of its members we are ill informed, for at this point the earliest manuscript of the *Historia Dunelmensis Ecclesiæ* has suffered an erasure of some twenty lines.[36] Discussion of the organization and endowment of the new monastery by St. Calais must be pretermitted here. What lands he granted to the convent, what rights he allotted to the prior, how he regulated the relations of the prior with the archdeacon, are interesting matters which have been wilfully entangled in deceit since

Manuscripts, p. 44), has Lanfranc's monastic constitutions, in company, as usual, with a Martyrologium and the rule of St. Benedict: cf. J. Armitage Robinson, "Lanfranc's Monastic Constitutions," *Journal of Theological Studies*, X (1909), 381-2.

[36] Durham University Library, Bishop Cosin's MS., V, ii, 6, pp. 158-9. In the Chapter Archives and Library there are several documents purporting to be transcripts of a bull of Gregory VII dated 6th January, 1083, authorizing the foundation of the monastery of Durham (printed by W. Holtzmann, *Papsturkunden in England*, II, 2, p. 133; Holtzmann does not list the version, lacking the dating clause, in Dean and Chapter Library, MS. A. ii. 16, fo. 101v). This "bull" is a suspicious document, and is often rejected as a complete fabrication (cf. Knowles, *op. cit.*, p. 169, n. 2 and p. 629, n. 4). But I would hazard the opinion that it is heavily interpolated rather than completely false (Holtzmann, *loc. cit.*, leaves open the question whether a genuine mandate of Gregory VII, now lost, may have been used as a basis for it). Among the phrases which may well be genuine is a stipulation about the treatment of the members of the congregation of St. Cuthbert: " auctoritate et potestate nobis divinitus collata, eisdem clericis a Dunelmensi ecclesia irrefragibiliter recedere, et ubi fraternitas tua (i.e. St. Calais) eis victualia in vita sua sufficienter providerit pacifice conversari indicimus."

the early twelfth century; their unravelling must await a proper examination of the forged foundation charters. Symeon indeed suggests that in the endowment of the monastery the bishop's performance fell behind his promises,[37] and I confess to a general feeling that of late St. Calais' zeal for monasticism has been excessively praised. I do not wish to call in doubt the sincerity of his early profession; certainly he proved a good father to the monks whom he had called to Durham. But when we read the contemporary praises of him as a wise, firm, yet moderate disciplinarian,[38] we cannot forget that of necessity his control over his monastery must often have been somewhat remote. Significantly enough the piece of evidence most commonly adduced to illustrate his quality as a monastic superior is a letter addressed to the convent while he was absent from Durham—because he was hindered by the king's business, says Symeon, but more probably because he was in exile for treachery against his king.[39] The letter urges strict adherence to the rule, decent behaviour during the offices, frequent confession, full meetings of the chapter. These things are memorably expressed, but the sober eloquence of this letter must not cause us to forget that its author was one of the most slippery politicians of his age.

For the death of the Conqueror in September, 1087, did nothing to check St. Calais' activity in secular affairs. That under the new king, Rufus, he came into power so great "that all England went after his counsel, and so as

[37] HDE, 124 : "Episcopus quoque aliquantulum quidem terrae monachis largitus est; verumtamen ut sui indigentia et penuria Christo servirent, sufficientes ad victum illorum et vestitum terras eis unacum rege ipse providerat, et jam jamque daturus erat. Sed ne id ad effectum pervenerit, primo regis ac postea episcopi mors impedimento fuerat."

[38] HDE, 125.

[39] HDE, 125, says: "litterae, quas cum regiis impeditus negotiis venire non possit, ipse ad eos direxerat." But in the letter itself St. Calais refers to "tribulationes nostras" (HDE, 126), which would most naturally refer to the time of exile.

he would" rests on the doubtful interpretation of a single phrase in the OE Chronicle: the words may equally well be made to apply to Odo of Bayeux.[40] But we can be sure that St. Calais had a leading place in the counsels of Rufus during the early months of the reign.[41] This fact makes all the more discreditable his share in the rebellion of 1088, when the great Anglo-Norman feudatories, Odo of Bayeux, Robert of Mowbray, Roger of Montgomery, Geoffrey of Coutances, Hugh of Grantmesnil and others, made war on Rufus with the intention of replacing him on the throne by his elder brother Robert Curthose. On the extent of St. Calais' complicity with the unsuccessful rebels there is a severe conflict of evidence between the southern and the northern chroniclers.[42] The former depict St. Calais as a traitor, creating what disorder he could in the north, and then, when the rebellion had failed, being driven to surrender his castle at Durham to Rufus and to go into exile in Normandy. The northern chroniclers, on the other hand, say that the good relations between Rufus and St. Calais were disturbed by the machinations of their enemies, and then whisk St. Calais overseas without further comment. Only the tractate " De iniusta vexacione Willelmi episcopi primi " has something to add: it sets out to show St. Calais in the light of an injured martyr, who, having defended the rights and liberties of his order with great courage and resource in the presence of Rufus and the *Curia regis* at Salisbury in November, 1088, was forced by the unjust violences of his opponents to appeal to the pope and to leave England. But that plausible and attractive piece of evidence must be

[40] OE Chronicle, 1087: *ed*. Earle and Plummer, I, 222; cf. *ib*. II, 276-7, for an elaborate discussion of this point.

[41] Davis, *Regesta*, nrs. 304, 305, 306, show St. Calais as a witness to charters issued during the first few months of the reign.

[42] Examined at length by Freeman, *William Rufus*, II, 469-74. While he attempts to minimize the contradictions between the northern and southern accounts, Freeman concludes: " We can have little doubt in accepting the fact of the Bishop's treason."

rejected; it is an extraordinarily well-contrived piece of fiction, but fiction it is. And with it go the less determined attempts of the other northern sources to palliate St. Calais' conduct. In 1088 St. Calais the trusted counsellor became a defeated traitor, and as such went into exile. Freeman could not understand why St. Calais turned against Rufus.[43] What evidence we have suggests that his action was the political miscalculation of an ambitious man. In 1088 the cause of Robert Curthose looked promising; Rufus' qualities as a ruler were as yet untried, and many of the greatest Norman feudatories in England were Robert's supporters. St . Calais jumped too soon to what he wrongly thought would be the winning side.

The miscalculation did not cost him very dear. He did not go to the Curia, though he must have sent thither a specious account of his misfortunes, since in April-June, 1089, Pope Urban II addressed to Rufus a remonstrance for his ill-treatment of the bishop of Durham.[44] It was in Normandy that St. Calais chose to spend his exile, and there he found a welcome from Robert Curthose, who committed to him—so say the English sources—the care of the whole duchy.[45] That mark of confidence betokens his ability; it offers, too, a well-nigh conclusive answer to those who doubt his treason to Rufus in 1088. The charge must soon have proved onerous, for in 1090 Rufus went over to the attack on Robert's continental possessions. This

[43] *Loc. cit.* : " The great puzzle of the whole story, namely why Bishop William should have turned against the King at all, is not made any clearer on either side."

[44] S. Loewenfeld, *Epistolae Pontificum Romanorum ineditae*, p. 63.

[45] *Historia Regum*, ed. Arnold, *Symeon of Durham*, II, 216. Following Plummer, *Two Saxon Chronicles*, II, 278, and C. W. David, " A tract attributed to Simeon of Durham," *English Historical Review*, XXXII (1917), 385, I refer the phrase " Sed episcopus veniens Normanniam statim a Rodberto comite totius provinciae curam suscepit," to St. Calais, and not, as the text would appear to suggest, to Odo of Bayeux. St. Calais appears as a witness to Robert's charters in Normandy in 1089: Davis, *Regesta*, nrs. 308 (24th April) and 310.

WILLIAM OF ST. CALAIS 273

time St. Calais got the weights of men and chances right. As in 1088 he had deserted Rufus for Robert, so in 1090 he seems to have been willing to turn again. It may well have been he who acted as Rufus's agent in bribing Philip of France to abandon Robert;[46] Professor David has already conjectured that it was in part owing to his efforts that peace was made between Rufus and Robert in February, 1091.[47] One stipulation of the peace—that all Normans who had lost their lands in England because of their support of Robert should now recover them—would seem to have special relevance to St. Calais.[48]

Probably in accordance with that stipulation Rufus and Robert, now marching together in amity against Malcolm, king of Scots, brought St. Calais back to Durham on 11th September, 1091.[49] During the bishop's exile Rufus had behaved well to the monks of Durham, who had been able to build their refectory. But St. Calais, returning with continental treasures in ornaments and books, had

[46] HDE, 128 says that when the king's men were besieged in a castle in Normandy and were on the point of being captured, "eos episcopus a periculo liberavit, et consilio suo ut obsiaio solveretur effecit." Under 1090 the OE Chronicle has "Robert . . . sent to his lord Philip, king of the Franks, and he came to Normandy with a large army; and the king and the count, with an immense force, beset the castle about wherein were the men of the king of England. King William of England then sent to Philip king of the Franks, and he for his love, or for his great treasure, deserted his vassal, the count Robert, and his lands, and went again to France, and left them as they were" (Earle and Plummer, I, 225). If we combine HDE with the OE Chronicle it appears very probable that St. Calais won back Rufus's favour by acting as his agent in bribing Philip of France to desert Robert. Freeman, *op. cit.*, I, 228, suggests that the besieged castle was Eu.

[47] Cf. David, *Robert Curthose*, p. 59, n. 79.

[48] "Florence" of Worcester, *ed.* Thorpe, II, 27.

[49] *Historia Regum*, 218, says that this return occurred three years after St. Calais had had to leave Durham. On its joyful coincidence with the dispersal of the Scottish army which was blockading Durham, cf. the account in the collection "De Miraculis et Translationibus Sancti Cuthberti," in Arnold, *Symeon*, II, 340.

larger ideas about building than this. Soon he gave orders for Aldhun's church to be demolished, and on Friday, 29th July, 1093, he and prior Turgot began to dig the foundations of a greater structure; on Thursday, 11th August, they laid the first foundation stones of the present cathedral. This was to be erected at the bishop's expense; the conventual buildings were to be at the monks' charges.[50]

It is at this point—the culmination of the story in Durham eyes—that Symeon's account of St. Calais' active life comes in effect to a close. But there is in fact a fair amount more to be said, though it has to be gleaned from scanty and scattered sources. In the four years between his return from exile and his death St. Calais made himself again one of the most influential personages in Church and State in England, though he was hardly ostentatious of his power.[51] Twice he was in Normandy: in February, 1092, perhaps in an attempt to mediate between Rufus and Robert Curthose, who had recently fallen out again;[52] and again in February, 1093, for the funeral of Geoffrey of Coutances.[53] During 1092 he is witnessing charters of Rufus;[54] what part, if any, he took in the king's capital achievement of that year—the capture of Carlisle and the incorporation of Cumberland and Westmoreland into the English kingdom—we do not know, but we do know that it was to Durham that the spiritual jurisdiction over Carlisle was granted.[55] So high indeed did St. Calais rise in Rufus' favour that at the Christmas court at Gloucester in

[50] HDE, 128-9.

[51] Thus in the whole of that well-informed historian of the next generation, Ordericus Vitalis, there is only one mention of St. Calais, and that simply records his death (*ed.* Le Prevost, IV, 10).

[52] Davis, *Regesta*, nr. 327.

[53] 3rd February, 1093: *Gallia Christiana*, XI, *Instrumenta*, col. 224.

[54] Davis, *Regesta*, nrs. 330, 331, 332.

[55] H. H. E. Craster, "A Contemporary Record of the Pontificate of Ranulf Flambard," *Archæologia Aeliana*, 4th series, VII (1930), 37-9.

1093 he secured a charter allowing him henceforward to hold in free alms all those lands in England for which he had previously owed military service to the crown.[56]

However, there was one eminence which St. Calais could not attain. Lanfranc had died in 1089, and the archbishopric of Canterbury remained vacant until the nomination of Anselm in 1093. It would be interesting to know with what feelings St. Calais was present at the investiture of Anselm with the temporalities of Canterbury in September, 1093:[57] For a very different man from him had gained a promotion which he was suspected—though this is only reported as a rumour by a hostile witness[58]—of desiring for himself. St. Calais' later dealings with Anselm are beyond the power of apology to defend. It is likely that Rufus understood St. Calais, his capacities and his limitations, as thoroughly as he failed to understand Anselm; St. Calais, now perhaps the most eminent Norman ecclesiastic in England, became the natural auxiliary of the king in his transactions with a man whose character was outside the range of his experience. It was to St. Calais, together with Roger of Meulan, that Rufus referred at Rochester in the summer of 1093 the conditions on which Anselm made his acceptance of the archbishopric depend; it may well have been on St. Calais' advice that he gave his non-committal reply.[59] Nevertheless, Anselm became archbishop, and was soon involved in a violent

[56] *Op. cit.*, p. 36. Sir Edmund Craster says that this charter "probably dates from the king's Christmas court of 1093 "—at which we know St. Calais to have been present: Davis, *Regesta*, nr. 338.

[57] Davis, *Regesta*, nr. 336; cf. nr. 337.

[58] In his account of the Council of Rockingham in 1095 Eadmer, *Historia Novorum* (Rolls Series, ed. Rule), p. 60, says that St. Calais tried to contrive that Anselm should leave England: "ratus, ut dicebatur, ipso discedente, se archiepiscopatus solio sublimandum."

[59] *Historia Novorum*, pp. 39-40. Rule suggests July, 1093, for the date of this interview; Dean Church, *St. Anselm*, p. 227, puts it "in the course of the summer." In late July and early August St. Calais was busy at Durham with his new cathedral.

quarrel with Rufus because of his wish to go to Rome to receive the pallium from Pope Urban II, whom Rufus refused to recognize. The dispute was referred to the great meeting which opened at Rockingham on 25th February, 1095, and here St. Calais led the royal party. It is, of course, proper to remember that our witness for the council of Rockingham is Eadmer, monk of Christ Church Canterbury, and a devoted supporter of Anselm. The account which he gives of St. Calais' conduct may perhaps be over coloured, but it has not been suggested that it is substantially untrue. To Eadmer St. Calais appeared as the chief instigator of the quarrel between Anselm and Rufus, whom he had convinced that Anselm could be compelled either to renounce his obedience to Urban II or to resign his archbishopric (and then is hinted St. Calais' hope to be Anselm's successor). Eadmer depicts him at Rockingham using to Anselm the words and manner of a bully, and when these fail and he is beaten in the argument he advises the use of force; if Anselm will not bend to the royal will his staff and ring are to be taken away from him and he is to be driven from the kingdom.[60] The moral strength of Anselm, backed by the support of the lay feudatories, defeated St. Calais' efforts. The council of Rockingham came to an inconclusive end with Anselm still archbishop and still persistent in his obedience to Urban. St. Calais' failure can have done his credit with Rufus little good; his futile attempt to serve the king's pleasure—and perhaps his own interests—in this matter has rightly blasted his reputation with posterity.

With the fiasco of Rockingham our knowledge of St. Calais' public career is exhausted, for there is no need to accept Freeman's suggestion that he was guilty of a final disloyalty; the evidence for his complicity in Robert of Mowbray's plot to replace Rufus by Stephen of Aumâle is insufficient.[61]. Nevertheless, his relations with Rufus be-

[60] *Historia Novorum*, pp. 59-60.

[61] *William Rufus*, II, 38; 60-1: the evidence of Morel, quoted by Freeman from the OE Chronicle, 1095, does not specifically name St. Calais among Robert's accomplices.

came strained, and as a sick man he was forced to appear at the Christmas court at Windsor in 1095 to answer some charge of which we know nothing.[62] In his last illness he was comforted by the great men of the Anglo-Norman church: Anselm, Thomas of York, Walkelin of Winchester and John of Bath and Wells; he died at cockcrow on 2nd January, 1096. His body was brought back to Durham, and on 16th January he was buried in the monks' chapter house, for he had esteemed his corpse unworthy to enter the cathedral which sheltered the incorruptible body of St. Cuthbert.[63]

It is not easy to come to a short opinion about William of St. Calais. We cannot get close to him. James Raine tells us: "During the partial demolition of the Chapter House, in 1795, upon opening the grave of Bishop Carileph, there were found the bones of a tall man, portions of sandals, and fragments of a robe richly embroidered in gold, ornamented with griffins *passant* and other quaint devices."[64] For the rest, we have a single letter—written for publication;[65] a single conventional representation in the illumination of a contemporary manuscript;[66] the inventory of the robes and utensils of his portable chapel, on which the monks fastened together with the litter and horses which brought his corpse to Durham, and which by their limited magnificence remind us how primitive were the times in which he lived.[67] From these materials we cannot recreate a personality. Our estimate, then, has to be based on St. Calais' public

[62] William of Malmesbury, *Gesta Pontificum* (Rolls Series), p. 273.
[63] HDE, 133.
[64] J. Raine, *Auckland Castle*, p. 8, n. 1.
[65] See note 39 above.
[66] Durham Dean and Chapter Library, MS. B. ii. 13, fo. 102.
[67] J. Raine, ed., *Wills and Inventories Illustrative of the History, Manners, Language, Statistics etc. of the Northern Counties of England* (Surtees Soc. 2), pp. 1-2: five copes, three chasubles with a large stole and maniple, one white altar cloth, a small silver censer, a small silver vessel (*situla*), two bronze gilt candlesticks and one small silver candlestick.

actions. And consideration of these must tend to qualify some recent praises.[68] The portrait is two-faced. St. Calais was a good father to his monks, and he had the monastic virtues: he was sober, frugal and chaste. His intellectual abilities Symeon extols as eminent: he was of subtle genius in counsel (so that when he was on his deathbed men still came to him for advice), great eloquence, and marvellous powers of memory.[69] The books which he gave to the convent witness his care for things of the mind: some thirty-nine volumes, of which perhaps half are still to be found in the Chapter Library.[70] As manuscripts with a continuous history in a single place they are almost beyond price, but in content they form a rather conventional collection. A great Bible is accompanied by the standard theologians: Origen, Augustine, Jerome, Ambrose, Gregory, and Rabanus Maurus. There are homilies, but "of poetry, history and the ancient classics, there is almost nothing," except Bede.[71] It is likely that for his own reading St. Calais preferred a canon law book, his copy of Lanfranc's collections of decretals and canons which has now wandered to Peterhouse in Cambridge.[72]

[68] Those, for example, of Professor Knowles, *op. cit.*, p. 169, and Dr. A. J. Macdonald, *Lanfranc*, p. 267.

[69] HDE, 119, 133. Eadmer, *Historia Novorum*, p. 59, thinks less highly of his eloquence: "homo linguae volubilitate faecetus quam pura sapientia praeditus"; William of Malmesbury echoes Eadmer: "oris volubilitate promptus" (*Gesta Pontificum*, p. 272).

[70] A list of these books is in the second volume of the Bible which St. Calais gave to the convent, now Durham Dean and Chapter Library, MS. A. ii. 4. The most recent edition of it is by C. H. Turner, "The Earliest List of Durham MSS.," *Journal of Theological Studies*, XIX (1917), 124, who considers (p. 131) that sixteen of these MSS. certainly, and three not improbably, are still in the Dean and Chapter Library. Mynors, *Durham Cathedral Manuscripts*, p. 32, refers to a bequest of "nearly 50 volumes," and identifies 21 of them in the Dean and Chapter Library.

[71] Mynors, p. 33.

[72] Peterhouse MS. 74; cf. Z. N. Brooke, *The English Church and the Papacy*, p. 63 and 231.

For we must regard the other face. St. Calais was a very political prelate, and in politics his conduct was not pretty. There is a hint that even among his own monks his reputation in this respect was not beyond the shadow of a peradventure.[73] His desertion of Rufus in 1088, his ambiguous dealings with Robert Curthose in 1090-1 and his behaviour to Anselm all stamp him as an opportunist. In the inelegancies of his pursuit of power there was something of the new man on the make—which, of course, he was. But of his size there is no question. We who go about our daily avocations in the shadow of the cathedral which he planned have there a document of which the authenticity cannot be impugned. St. Calais' recoveries were as remarkable as his lapses; he was a proper representative to help to teach to a recalcitrant north the lessons of Norman organization and of Norman order.

[73] This may be inferred from the insertion into HDE of the strange " Visio Bosonis " in which a knight of Durham relates how in a vision during St. Calais' lifetime he saw his bishop in peculiar circumstances: " Inde in loco vastae ac tetrae solitudinis, magna altitudine domum totam ex ferro fabrefactam aspexi, cujus janua dum saepius aperiretur, saepiusque clauderetur, ecce subito episcopus Willelmus efferens caput, ubinam Gosfridus monachus esset, a me quaesivit. ' Hic enim,' inquit, ' hic ad placitum mecum adesse deberet.' " (HDE, 132.)

ADDENDA

p. 258 line 1 at the start:
    For a very different view of St Calais, especially of his part in the rebellion of 1088, see R. W. Southern, *Western Society and the Church in the Middle Ages*, Pelican History of the Church 2 (1970), pp. 184–5.

280   ADDENDA

p. 265 line 24 at 'counties.':
For evidence, almost exclusively palaeographical, that St Calais played a major rôle in the making of the Domesday enquiry, see P. Chaplais, 'William of Saint-Calais and the Domesday Survey', in *Domesday Studies*, ed. J. C. Holt, (London, 1987), 65–77 + iv pl. He argues (1) that the main scribe of Great Domesday, who wrote the list of contents, held a position of some importance in the Durham *scriptorium*, p. 74; (2) that 'it does look as if he [St Calais] was indeed 'the man behind the Survey'', p. 77; and (3) 'If he was, he could not have left England with the Conqueror in the latter part of 1086', p. 77. Thus, [if St Calais was not in the Conqueror's company during the last nine months of the king's life], the Pyrford writ (T. A. M. Bishop & P. Chaplais, *Facsimiles of English Royal Writs to AD. 1100*, (Oxford, 1957), no. 26) [witnessed by St Calais and dated by reference to the Domesday enquiry, 'post descriptionem totius Angliae',] must have been issued before the Conqueror departed for Normandy in 1086, [since 'it is usually, and doubtless correctly, assumed that William crossed the Channel (to Normandy) for the last time about the end of 1086', D. C. Douglas, *William the Conqueror*, (London, 1964), p. 357 n. 2. Cf. V. H. Galbraith, *The Making of Domesday Book*, (Oxford, 1961), pp. 206–7.]

p. 270 line 2 at 'foundation charters'
[For examination of the forged episcopal charters, see H. S. Offler ed., *Durham Episcopal Charters 1071–1152*, Surtees Society 179 (1968), nos 3–7.]

p. 273 line 12 at the start of the paragraph:
For St Calais' possible presence at the Council of Rouen in June 1091, see the witness-list of the charter of Archbishop William of Rouen in favour of Bec, possibly issued on that occasion, C. Johnson & H. A. Cronne, *Regesta Regum Anglo-Normannorum 1066–1154* ii, (Oxford, 1956), p. 400 no. 317b.

p. 275 line 3 at 'the crown.':
St Calais was present with Rufus at the consecration of the abbey church of Battle on 11 February 1094, which took place when the king's expedition against Robert Curthose was delayed at Hastings, E. Searle ed. & trans., *The Chronicle of Battle Abbey*, (Oxford Medieval Texts, 1980), pp. 96–7 and n. 3; *Regesta* ii, p. 401 no. 348a.

VI

The Tractate De Iniusta Vexacione Willelmi Episcopi Primi

I

FEW of the literary sources for the early years of the reign of William Rufus have been more thoroughly exploited than the Durham tractate *De iniusta vexacione Willelmi episcopi primi*. This short treatise, commonly found in close connexion with the *Historia Ecclesiae Dunelmensis* (HED) ascribed to Symeon of Durham, gives an account of the trial of the bishop of Durham, William of St. Calais, before the king's court at Salisbury in November 1088 for his part in the feudal revolt on behalf of Robert of Normandy earlier in the year. From it Freeman drew much of his narrative for 1088;[1] Liebermann, relying on Freeman, accepted it as undoubtedly authentic,[2] and with this weight of authority behind him, G. B. Adams did not hesitate to base on it an elaborate description of the procedure of the Anglo-Norman *Curia regis*.[3] Among the historians of English law, Maitland supposed the tractate to be a genuine source for the late eleventh century, and more recently Professor Goebel has used it to support his theories about the nature of the king's peace at that period.[4] Ecclesiastical historians and biographers have found in the *De iniusta vexacione* an exceptionally early example of the influence in post-Conquest England of pseudo-Isidorean principles and grounds for an appreciation of the character and abilities of an eminent Norman churchman.[5] All this extensive use of the

---

[1] *William Rufus*, i. 89–120.
[2] *Historische Aufsätze dem Andenken an Georg Waitz gewidmet*, p. 159, n. 10; *Gesetze d. Angelsachsen*, ii. 573.
[3] *Council and Courts in Anglo-Norman England*, pp. 43–69. Stubbs had already stressed the importance of the tract in this connexion : *Const. Hist.* (5th edn.), i. 476–7.
[4] *Hist. of English Law*, i. 117 ; J. Goebel, *Felony and Misdemeanor*, i. 284, n. 5, 430, n. 340, 432, n. 3.
[5] Z. N. Brooke, *English Church and the Papacy*, pp. 161–2 ; A. Fliche, *Querelle des Investitures*, p. 107 ; A. J. Macdonald, *Lanfranc*, pp. 235-43 ; L. Guilloreau, ' Guillaume de Saint-Calais, Evêque de Durham ', *Revue historique et archéologique du Maine*, lxxiv. 209–32 and lxxv. 65–79. Professor David Knowles, *Monastic Order in England*, p. 169, n. 1, supposes that the tract is probably 'entirely genuine ', and so ' must have been based on copious notes taken during the actual proceedings '. Elsewhere (p. 142, n. 2) he says that it was ' probably compiled by Symeon of Durham ', but gives no grounds for this ascription.

Durham tractate assumes that it is a truthful and contemporary account of the events of 1088 which it purports to describe : that it is the work of some one who was either present in person at the trial of William of St. Calais at Salisbury, or who had access to minutes written by an eyewitness of the trial. It is the purpose of this paper to subject that assumption to more rigorous examination than it has yet been given.

A preliminary problem may conveniently be treated here. Professor David has shown conclusively that in its present form the tractate is composite. To an original part, the *Libellus* proper, dealing with the events of 1088 and especially with the Salisbury trial, have been added an introduction summarizing St. Calais' career until 1088, and a conclusion which tells his story from his expulsion from England at the end of 1088 until his death in 1096.[1] Introduction and conclusion are by an author other and later than the author of the *Libellus*.[2] Professor David's further contention, that introduction and conclusion, while borrowing from HED, were known to and used by the compiler of the twelfth-century Durham secular history, the *Historia Regum* (HR), would imply that these two paragraphs had been written before *c*. 1150, which is perhaps as early a date as can now be assigned to HR.[3] But that contention seems unacceptable. The compiler of HR undoubtedly knew the *Libellus*, but there is no need to suppose that he knew or used the two paragraphs which were later attached to it. The echoes between these paragraphs and HR are more readily explained by supposing that the borrowing was the other way. Most of the introductory paragraph is taken from HED, bk. iv, cc. 1-3, but Professor David errs in maintaining that its author had no other source.[4] He could not have found in HED that the place of St. Calais' consecration was Gloucester, nor the date of Rufus' coronation. Both pieces of information were available in HR.[5] And while most of the concluding paragraph of the *De iniusta vexacione* is based on HED, bk. iv, cc. 8 and 10, it has two

---

[1] Reference will be made to the most accessible edition of *De iniusta vexacione*, that by T. Arnold, *Symeon of Durham* (Rolls Series), i. 170-95. The *Libellus* begins p. 171 : '*Rex Willelmus iunior dissaisivit*' ; it ends p. 194 : '*Rex permisit Episcopo transitum*'.

[2] C. W. David, 'A tract attributed to Simeon of Durham', *E.H.R.*, xxxii. 382-7, reprinted with slight revision in his *Robert Curthose, Duke of Normandy* (Harvard Historical Series, 25).

[3] The only surviving manuscript of HR dates from 1161-75 (J. Hodgson-Hinde, *Symeonis Dunelmensis Opera*, Surtees Soc. i. xxxi ; Arnold, *Symeon*, ii. 201 n.). The commonly accepted date of compilation, shortly after 1129, must be affected by Professor Darlington's contention (*Vita Wulfstani*, R. Hist. Soc., p. xvii) that the whole Worcester chronicle, which forms the main source of HR down to 1119, comes from one author, from its earliest stages down to its end in 1140.

[4] *E.H.R.*, xxxii. 383.

[5] Arnold, *Symeon*, ii. 211, 214, though here the date of St. Calais' consecration is given as 2 January 1081, while in the tractate it is 3 January.

VEXACIONE WILLELMI EPISCOPI PRIMI 323

important statements which HED omits but which do occur in HR :[1] (1) that Rufus and his brother on their expedition against Malcolm, king of Scots, restored St. Calais to his see on 11 September 1091, and (2) that Malcolm was present at the laying of the foundations of the new cathedral at Durham on 11 August 1093. Professor David assumes that for these details the author of the conclusion of the tractate was drawing on his own first hand knowledge, and that HR copies him. It seems more probable that the reverse is true, and that the introduction and conclusion added to the *Libellus* were composed by conflating information from HED and HR. If that is so, they may have been written by anyone to whom the Durham historical material was available, at any time between the compilation of HR and our first manuscript record of them, which is no earlier than the third quarter of the fourteenth century. Thus it is probable that they offer no help to the criticism of the main *Libellus* to which they were somewhat clumsily added,[2] and they need be discussed no further.

II

By the time that the surviving manuscript tradition of the *Libellus* begins, it had already acquired its introduction and conclusion. It has not been generally remarked how late this tradition is. Of the six manuscripts of the *Libellus* known to me, the earliest, Bodleian MS. Fairfax 6, fos. 207-12, (F) cannot be dated much before 1375.[3] The next in date, Bodleian MS. Laud misc. 700, fos. 66-74v, (B) may probably be referred to the episcopate of Bishop Fordham of Durham, 1382-8.[4] Shorn of its introduction and of all but a couple of lines of its conclusion, and slightly adapted at the beginning, the *Libellus* appears in two early fifteenth-century manuscripts of Prior Wessington's refashioned history of the church of Durham : Hale MS. 114, in Lincoln's Inn Library, fos. 63-75v, (L), and Cotton MS. Claudius D, IV, fos. 48-54, (C).[5] Lastly, two sixteenth-century

---

[1] Arnold, *Symeon*, ii. pp. 218, 220.

[2] Thus the concluding paragraph does not always agree with the body of the *Libellus*. It says that St. Calais was expelled from England in the eighth year of his episcopate, i.e. before 9 November 1088 ; the *Libellus* has St. Calais still at Southampton after 1 December 1088.

[3] *Summary Cat. of Western MSS. in the Bodleian Library*, vol. ii, pt. ii, nr. 3886, pp. 773-5. The statement on p. 773 that this version has a paragraph not to be found in D is incorrect.

[4] H. O. Coxe, *Cat. Cod. MSS. Laudianorum. Cod. Lat.*, cc. 501-2 ; Arnold, *Symeon*, i. xvii. This manuscript is commonly regarded as a transcript of F. But it is a composite volume, and in part (e.g. fos. 103-33) it may well be older than F.

[5] These manuscripts and their relation to each other are described by H. H. E. Craster, 'The Red Book of Durham ', *E.H.R.*, xl. 504 *et seqq*. Bodleian MS. Laud misc. 748, from which both derive, and which can be dated *c*. 1405-15 (*op. cit.* pp. 508-9) has only some fifty lines of the *Libellus*, on fo. 33 : ending *ad curiam suam cum abbate veniret*.

manuscripts have the *De iniusta vexacione* complete with introduction and conclusion, as in F and B : Harleian MS. 4843, fos. 224–31, (H),[1] and Durham, Bishop Cosin's Library MS. V. ii. 6, fos. 88–98, (D), where it exists as a late interpolation in a book of which the rest comes from the first half of the twelfth century.[2] Collation reveals that F is the best as well as the oldest of the manuscripts. B derives from it directly but inaccurately, and D seems a copy of B with some additional errors of its own. To this family, and probably deriving directly from F, H also belongs, though there are some indications that its scribe, William Tode, also consulted another version, akin to L and C. These two manuscripts belong to a different recension. C is later than L,[3] but not a direct copy of it ; both probably derive from a single exemplar known to the compiler of Bodleian MS. Laud misc. 748 but not transcribed in full by him. The relation of this exemplar to F is doubtful. Either it is a very free rehandling of F for the purpose of Wessington's history,[4] or—more probably— it is based on an independent version of the *De iniusta vexacione* now lost.[5]

In F the tractate still exists as a separate work, preceding the fourteenth-century version of the history of the church of Durham known as the *Gesta episcoporum*[6] which threw together into a single chronicle with continuous capitulation the original HED attributed to Symeon and the writings of his continuators : the anonymous author of the *Continuatio prima*, Geoffrey of Coldingham and Robert Greystanes. In H also, *De iniusta vexacione* stands alone. But in both B and D it has been inserted into the body of HED nearly at the end of Symeon's discussion of St. Calais, to form in B chapter 96 of the whole composite

---

[1] On this collection, transcribed by William Tode or Tod, who was first prebendary of the fifth stall in Durham in 1541, cf. B. Colgrave, *Two Lives of St. Cuthbert*, p. 29.

[2] Cf. R. A. B. Mynors, *Durham Cathedral Manuscripts to the end of the Twelfth Century*, pp. 60–1. Since the publication of this description the manuscript has been foliated.

[3] Craster, p. 514.

[4] Wessington knew and used F for the purposes out of which L and C grew : cf. Craster, p. 518, n. 1.

[5] In either case, both recensions ultimately derive from a version of the *De iniusta vexacione* into which an element of formalism had already entered. Both make St. Calais declare : *Talis enim dominus dedit michi terram quam habeo*, where in place of *Talis enim dominus* we would expect the name of William the Conqueror.

The first editor of the *De iniusta vexacione*, Thomas Bedford, who printed it as an appendix to his edition of Symeon's HED in 1732, based himself on F, noting variants in D, which he rightly regarded as a bad text. The version in the Caley, Ellis and Bandinel edition of Dugdale's *Monasticon* (1817), i. 244–50, is also from F. Arnold's edition for the Rolls Series in 1882, *Symeon*, i. 170–95, appears to have no independent authority, but to rely on Bedford, with occasional reference back to F and D. In 1855 Joseph Stevenson produced a translation from Bedford's edition, with a few notes : *Church Historians of England*, vol. iii, pt. ii. 731–50.

[6] Craster, *loc. cit.*

history.[1] Thus by 1382–8 *De iniusta vexacione* had been received into the official history of the church of Durham, and for the future its place was secure. When in the early years of the fifteenth century John Wessington decided on a restatement of that history, to be supported by documents, he incorporated the *Libellus* directly into his text, which we have as L and C. So much a part of the canon of HED did *De iniusta vexacione* become, that the oldest known manuscript of HED, D, suffered in the sixteenth century an erasure of the original hand at fo. 98 in order that the tract might be inserted. Yet it is noteworthy that this reception, though definitive, was late. By 1382–8, the date of B, *De iniusta vexacione* had become an established part of the text of HED. But a few years before this, when F was written, it was still 'extravagant'. It was not included in the original HED attributed to Symeon, though that is the piece of Durham historical writing nearest to the events of 1088.[2] Nor did it appear in the extension of the chronicle of the church of Durham to 1213 which was made up by adding to the original HED and its *Continuatio prima* the *Liber de statu ecclesie Dunelmensis* of Geoffrey of Coldingham.[3] Nor again, when in the fourteenth century the further continuation of the domestic history from 1213 to 1334 by Robert Greystanes was first placed alongside and then amalgamated with this extended chronicle,[4] is there any trace of *De iniusta vexacione*. Its absence from the successive expansions and revisions of the great chronicle of the bishops and the convent for nearly three centuries after the date when it is supposed to have been written can hardly be without significance.

Nevertheless, the *Libellus*—presumably without the introductory and concluding paragraphs—certainly existed and was known in Durham when the *Historia Regum* came to be compiled there about the middle of the twelfth century. For the period 848–1119 HR draws extensively on 'Florence' of Worcester. When it comes to the year 1088, however, HR for once deserts 'Florence', and bases itself on the O.E. Chronicle. But the Chronicle's comment on the conduct of St. Calais in this year is hostile, and it is clear that the compiler of HR has therefore edited his source in such a way as to suppress this unfavourable

---

[1] Shortly before the end of bk. iv, c. 10, after the phrase *in ecclesiam Sancti Michaelis deportaverunt*: Arnold, *Symeon*, i. 134; B, fo. 66; D, fo. 88.

[2] Represented by D in its unaltered state, and by Cotton MS. Faustina A, V, fos. 25–98.

[3] This extended chronicle, which only reaches 1199 in the former Phillipps MS. 9374, recently acquired by the Dean and Chapter Library in Durham, forms fos. 5–85 of Cotton MS. Titus A. II (the list of bishops of Durham on fo. 5v ends with Anthony Bek, who died in 1311), and fos. 95–182 of York Dean and Chapter Library MS. XVI. 1. 12 (where Bek again is the last name on the list of bishops, fo. 9v).

[4] I hope to discuss this process more fully elsewhere.

mention. By so doing, he has created confusion at the end of the annal for 1088. The story in the O.E. Chronicle is plain:

> 'Bishop Odo with the men who were within the castle (i.e. *Rochester*) went over sea; and so the bishop left the dignity which he had in this land. The king afterwards sent an army to Durham and caused the castle to be beset; and the bishop made peace and gave up the castle and left his bishopric and went to Normandy. Many Frenchmen also left their lands and went over sea.'[1]

Of this HR makes a pretty muddle. When Rochester had been captured:

> 'hi qui intus fuerunt se reddiderunt, et cum dedecore ejecti sunt de Anglia, et ita episcopus qui fere fuit secundus rex Angliae honorem amisit irrecupabiliter. Sed episcopus veniens Normanniam statim a Rodberto comite totius provinciae curam suscepit; cuius ordinem causae libellus in hoc descriptus aperte ostendit. Etiam Dunholmensis episcopus Willelmus, viii anno episcopatus, et multi alii, de Anglia exierunt.'[2]

Professor David's conclusion about this passage seems incontrovertible.[3] While the first *episcopus* is Odo of Bayeux, the second *episcopus* must refer to William of St. Calais, and the *libellus* describing the course of his case must be the Durham tractate under discussion. This reference to the *Libellus* recurs in another Durham compilation, the *Historia post Bedam*, which was drawn up between 1148 and 1161 from HR and was itself incorporated in Roger of Howden's chronicle, though now the apparent awkwardness of HR has been planed down and the confusion between Odo and St. Calais is complete:

> 'et ita episcopus qui fere fuit secundus rex Anglie honorem suum irrecupabiliter amisit. Sed veniens Normanniam statim a Rodberto comite totius provintie curam suscepit. Cuius ordinem cause libellus in hoc descriptus ostendit. Dunolmensis etiam episcopus Willelmus et multi alii de Anglia exierunt.'[4]

The compiler of HR about the middle of the twelfth century thus knew the *Libellus*. But that fact does not establish the *Libellus* as an authentic contemporary record of the events of 1088. Moreover, the first reference to it occurs in a context which is itself suspect. HR is concerned to protect the reputation

---

[1] C. Plummer and J. Earle, *Two of the Saxon Chronicles Parallel*, i. 225; B. Thorpe, *Anglo-Saxon Chronicle* (Rolls Series), ii. 193.

[2] Arnold, *Symeon*, ii. 216–7.

[3] *Op. cit.* p. 385. (Plummer, *op. cit.* ii. 278, had already come to the same conclusion.) Professor David has not, however, remarked that HR is here dependent on the O.E. Chronicle, and I cannot accept his proposition that HR is borrowing from the concluding paragraph of *De iniusta vexacione*, for I suppose that paragraph to have been written with the aid of HR; cf. *supra*, p. 323.

[4] British Museum, Royal MS. 13. A. VI, fo. 94v; cf. W. Stubbs, *Roger of Howden* (Rolls Series), i. xxvi *et seqq.*

of William of St. Calais. To that end it tampers with the annal for 1088 in the O.E. Chronicle, and for further information sends us to the *Libellus*. Had the *Libellus* not survived, it would have been reasonable to suppose that its tendency was the same as that of HR. It has survived, and gives an account of St. Calais' conduct in 1088 very much more favourable than that current in the other literary sources for this period. The O.E. Chronicle has some particularly damaging allegations against the bishop of Durham, whom it pillories as Rufus' trusted counsellor, who betrayed his master by joining the great feudal rebels, Odo of Bayeux, Geoffrey of Coutances, Robert Mowbray and Roger Montgomery in their scheme to make Robert of Normandy king in place of his brother. After taking an active part in the revolt, the Chronicle asserts, St. Calais was besieged in Durham Castle, and made peace with Rufus only at the cost of surrendering his stronghold, giving up his bishopric and leaving England for Normandy.[1] With this account Malmesbury substantially agrees, as does 'Florence' of Worcester, so far as he is interested in northern matters.[2] Trust, treachery, exile: that is the heavy indictment of the southern chronicle tradition against St. Calais, and once it had become established it must have raised an awkward problem for any monk writing history in Durham. To St. Calais, the convent was bound by very special obligations; he had been its founder, the builder of the great new cathedral, the energetic and kindly father of the monks, so that to preserve his memory untarnished was more than a matter of general *pietas*. Within twenty years of 1088 the original form of the *Historia Ecclesiae Dunelmensis* imputed to Symeon had been completed at Durham; the admiration of its author for St. Calais, whom we must assume him to have known, was great. But when he comes to the events of 1088 he treads with remarkable care. After telling of St. Calais' early friendship with Rufus he continues :

'Post non multum vero tempus, per aliorum machinamenta orta inter ipsos dissensione, episcopus ab episcopatu pulsus ultra mare secessit, quem comes Normannorum non ut exulem, sed ut patrem suscipiens, in magno honore per tres annos, quibus ibi moratus est, habuit.'[3]

That is all that is said of 1088, and the story is taken up again with St. Calais' return to England in 1091. That there is here an air of tactful pretermission of embarrassing detail can hardly

[1] *Sub anno* 1088.
[2] *Gesta Regum*, iv. 306 (Rolls Series, ii. 360-2); 'Florence' of Worcester, *English Hist. Soc.* ii. 21-2. Ordericus Vitalis has no mention of St. Calais in connexion with the events of 1088.
[3] Arnold, i. 128.

be denied.[1] Is it probable that had the author of HED, writing between 1104 and 1109, known and believed in the full and plausible version of St. Calais' conduct in 1088 which the *Libellus* presents, he would have been satisfied with this jejune statement ? Would he have neglected the opportunity, offered him by the *Libellus*, of depicting St. Calais as an injured defender of the privileges of the ecclesiastical order ? We may perhaps assume that the author of HED did not know the *Libellus* ; yet it was certainly known to the compiler of HR some forty years later. The inference that the *Libellus* was composed at some date between the writing of these two Durham histories, and therefore is not a contemporary account of the events of 1088, may seem to gain some support from the internal evidence of the tractate.

III

That is not apparent at a casual reading. The vigour and freshness of the *Libellus* have always provided the strongest argument for its authenticity. It brings St. Calais to Salisbury in November 1088 before the king's court, whose members discuss with freedom the issues at stake ; on occasion they are prepared to contradict the king. This, we feel, is how companions of the Conqueror might be expected to behave in the presence of his son. Individual characters at the trial are drawn with high verisimilitude. For long Rufus' patience with the debate is exemplary, but St. Calais' shifts to retain Durham Castle are more than he can bear, and at last he breaks out with his favourite oath : ' per vultum de Luca nunquam exibis de manibus meis donec castellum habeam '.[2] The study of the aged Lanfranc is

[1] That the author of HED knew that there were darker sides to St. Calais is suggested by the inclusion in his history of the strange *Visio Bosonis*. Boso, a knight of Durham, relates how, falling into a trance some time before the death of St. Calais, he had seen, among other things, his lord the bishop in an unenviable situation : 'Inde in loco vastae ac tetrae solitudinis, magna altitudine domum totam ex ferro fabrefactam aspexi, cujus janua dum saepius aperiretur, saepiusque clauderetur, ecce subito episcopus Willelmus efferens caput, ubinam Gosfridus monachus esset, a me quaesivit. " Hic enim ", inquit, " hic ad placitum mecum adesse deberet." Hunc namque episcopus procuratorem sui episcopatus constituerat ' (Arnold, i. 132). The trial at which Geoffrey the monk should have been may possibly have oblique reference to the Salisbury trial of 1088, but the context suggests rather that the ' placitum ' of the *Visio Bosonis* was not a terrestrial matter. Geoffrey the monk appears again in the *Libellus* (Arnold, i. 194). He can hardly have been a monk of Durham, for the first Geoffrey comes 194th on the list of members of the convent preserved at the beginning of D (fos. 7-8), and so falls well outside the episcopate of St. Calais. But it is noteworthy that in a similar but not identical list of the monks of Durham in the *Liber Vitae* of Durham (*Surtees Soc. facsimile ed.* fo. 42) the name ' Gosfridus ' appears as a later insertion after that of the second prior, Turgot. Perhaps we may identify this Gosfridus with the ' G. Dunelmensis ' of Durham Dean and Chapter Archives, Ia Ie Regalium, 8, who was perhaps custodian of the temporalities *sede vacante* after 1096 : cf. Davis, *Regesta*, nr. 412.

[2] The author of the *Libellus* could have learnt that this was Rufus' favourite oath from Eadmer : cf. *Hist. Nov.* (Rolls Series), pp. 30, 39, 101.

superb. He manages the assembly with all the skill of an experienced committeeman towards the ends which he desires: that St. Calais shall not escape judgement in the *Curia regis*, and that the king shall secure Durham Castle. Yet this determination is tempered by moderation and an overriding good sense, which, though cutting through St. Calais' legal subtleties, refuses to pursue him vindictively or beyond need. There is, we are made to feel, the essential Lanfranc in his answer to St. Calais' demand at the beginning of the trial that the ecclesiastics shall be robed: 'Bene possumus hoc modo vestiti de regalibus tuisque negociis disceptare. Vestes enim non impediunt veritatem.' But, above all, it is the minor characters who make the story so plausible. As Freeman says:

> 'We feel brought nearer to the real life of the eleventh century every time that we are admitted to see a Domesday name becoming something more than a name, to see Ralph Paganel, Hugh of Port, and Heppo the *Balistarius* playing their part in an actual story. The short sharp speeches put into the mouths of some of the smaller actors, as well as those which are put into the mouth of the King, both add to the liveliness of the story and increase our faith in its trustworthiness.'[1]

At this sort of instinctive acceptance Freeman's criticism of the *Libellus* stopped short, and his appreciation has hardly been questioned. There are, however, good grounds for suspecting that the air of naturalness and immediacy about the *Libellus* is delusive, the result, not necessarily of eyewitness contact with the events which it purports to describe, but of art. The *Libellus*, it will be suggested, has the air of a highly sophisticated document, composed some considerable time after 1088 with the intention of insinuating what its author knew not to be true: that William of St. Calais left England in 1088-9 as a wronged ecclesiastical appealing to the pope, rather than as an exile for manifest treachery against his king. The *Libellus* does not indeed suppress the accusation of treason, but it so contrives matters that the blame for refusing St. Calais' offers to clear himself of the charge by a procedure compatible with the privileges of his order is made fall upon Rufus and his advisers. The glimpse which Freeman caught of this tendency[2] did not lead him to scrutinize the credentials of the *Libellus* more closely. It may therefore be useful to examine the work again in detail.

A third of it is occupied by events preceding the actual trial at Salisbury in November 1088. The *Libellus* begins by telling

---

[1] *William Rufus*, i. 120.
[2] *Ibid.* p. 119: 'it made a fairer show in men's eyes to undergo forfeiture and banishment in the character of a persecuted confessor than to undergo the same amount of loss in the character of a convicted traitor'.

how Rufus disseized St. Calais of his lands on 12 March 1088 [1] and how St. Calais evaded attempts to take his person, and fled to Durham. The story of the next six months, as the *Libellus* tells it, is of Rufus' repeated attempts to get St. Calais away from the safety of Durham to stand his trial in the royal court on charges of disloyalty, and of the bishop's persistent thwarting of these efforts by recourse to the privileges of his order. St. Calais took his stand on the ground of the canonical maxim, ' Spoliatus ante omnia debet restitui ' ; he would accept the jurisdiction of no court until he had been restored to the full possession of his lands ; then he would be willing to stand trial, but only before an ecclesiastical tribunal. That is the purport, according to the *Libellus*, of his first letter to Rufus, which, if it be genuine, can hardly be dated much before the first week of April. Following another summons to the king's court brought to Durham by Wido abbot of St. Augustine's Canterbury, St. Calais, the *Libellus* tells us, sent a second letter to Rufus.[2] Again he claimed that he must have his lands restored to him before he would plead, and again he refused to accept the judgement of any but an ecclesiastical court. Alternatively, he was willing to clear himself by canonical purgation of any charge that he had failed in his feudal duty to the king. And though he proceeded, under safe-conduct, to Rufus' presence,[3] it was only to repeat the terms of his letter and to refuse the king's demand that, renouncing the guarantee of safe return to Durham under which he had travelled, he should plead as a layman (*laicaliter*).

The safe-conduct held, and once back in Durham, the *Libellus* reports, St. Calais addressed a third letter to Rufus.[4] This document is subtle to the point of disingenuousness. Once again St. Calais requests trial as an ecclesiastic. But if Rufus insists that he clear himself *laico more*, then on this question St. Calais is willing to submit to a preliminary judgement, though reserving the right to object to that judgement *secundum recta iudicia mei ordinis in eo loco ubi canonice iudicatum fuerit*. The gesture of concession was illusory, and St. Calais, it would seem, was already hinting darkly at an appeal to the pope. Again, as an alternative to trial, St. Calais offered canonical purgation. Rufus' answer to these propositions was to send an expedition against St. Calais.

[1] The southern chroniclers do not confirm the fact of dissension between Rufus and St. Calais before the middle of March. They have the great feudatories plotting in Lent, but put the overt acts of revolt after Easter (i.e. 16 April).

[2] Presumably, on the *Libellus*' own chronology, towards the end of May.

[3] There is no evidence of this meeting between Rufus and St. Calais except the *Libellus*. If it took place, this can hardly have been much before the end of June.

[4] To be dated about mid-July, if we accept the *Libellus*. The address of this letter is remarkable : Domino suo Willelmo Regi Anglorum, Willelmus Dunelmensis Episcopus salutem, et si placet fidele servitium. We may wonder if this is a likely impertinence to have been offered by a Norman bishop to a Norman king.

On 8 September the leaders of the royal force, earls Alan of Brittany, Odo of Champagne and Roger of Poitou, the *Libellus* relates, reached an agreement with the bishop. By the terms of this *convencio* the earls were to bring St. Calais safely to the king's court, and if Rufus would not grant him ecclesiastical trial [1] they were to see him safely back to Durham. They were to do likewise if a judgement was given to which St. Calais objected as unjust, and which Rufus and the judges failed to get confirmed *ubi contenciosa Pontificum iudicia iuste debent terminari*—which we can only understand as meaning at the papal court. But if the judgement could not be impugned, nor did king and judges fail to have it confirmed *ubi huiusmodi iudicia iuste debent confirmari vel destrui*, and St. Calais yet refused to accept it, then he was to have a royal safe-conduct overseas, and Durham Castle was to be surrendered to Rufus. No guarantees beyond the terms of the *convencio* were to be demanded of St. Calais; if Rufus infringed the agreement the earls were to withhold all service from him until St. Calais had released them from their engagements. For his part, the bishop accepted only two obligations. The fortifications of Durham Castle were not to be strengthened after the date of the *convencio*; once he had started his journey to the king's court St. Calais was to abstain from all hostilities towards Rufus until the hearing of his case at Michaelmas. This subtly phrased agreement is so extraordinarily favourable to St. Calais as to raise suspicion. To accept it as authentic it would seem necessary to assume either that Durham Castle was considered inexpugnable or that the earls were fools. By September 1088 Rufus was completely master of the feudal revolt, and according to the *Libellus* itself he had sent what must have been overwhelming military force against St. Calais. Nevertheless, the *Libellus* would persuade us, the bishop was able to make with the earls terms which guaranteed him from all drastic consequences even if his disloyalty to Rufus were proved. If he were denied ecclesiastical trial, or the right to appeal to the pope against the result of that trial, the earls were to restore him to Durham in that state which had been his before the attack upon him. And even if the court gave judgement against him, and the pope confirmed that unfavourable judgement, he was to be allowed to depart overseas unmolested.

In view of this careful formulation of principles of ecclesiastic privilege imputed to St. Calais in his letters to Rufus and the *convencio* with the earls, it is not surprising that there is a certain inevitability about the proceedings when St. Calais—according to the account in the *Libellus*—came before the king's court at

---

[1] secundum legem episcopi per tales iudices qui episcopum iuste iudicare deberent.

Salisbury on 2 November.[1] Every motion the bishop makes is informed with cautious legalism, and he will not go a step beyond the position which he had been developing between March and September. At the outset it is noted that St. Calais' metropolitan, Thomas of York, and his fellow bishops fail in their duty by neglecting to greet their brother with the kiss of peace, and their counsel is denied him by Rufus. Then St. Calais is made to raise the question of robes, with the intention of emphasizing that he had come as an ecclesiastic to be tried by an ecclesiastical court, and that it was only in so far as the Salisbury assembly was an ecclesiastical court that he would recognize its right to deal with him.[2] When Lanfranc had agreed that the bishops might be robed, in terms which suggested that he thought the question unimportant, St. Calais made his preliminary demand: before he pleaded, his bishopric must be restored to him, in accordance with the pseudo-Isidorean principle, ' Spoliatus ante omnia debet restitui ', which could be found so often repeated in that canonical collection which Lanfranc had introduced into England, and of which, the *Libellus* suggests, St. Calais had a copy in court.[3] Lanfranc's answer was to deny that St. Calais had been disseized of his bishopric, and to challenge him to say that he had ever seen a royal writ in which such disseisin was ordered. St. Calais' only reply was to rehearse the facts of the case: he had seen no royal writ, but he had seen his lands overrun and granted away to others, his men had been seduced from their allegiance to him, and he had been forced to leave his see. To Lanfranc's contention that he could expect the king to give him back his lands only after he had accepted the judgement of the king's court on the accusations which Rufus had to bring against him, St. Calais refused to agree, and when the lay members of the assembly noisily approved Lanfranc's opinion he sharply reminded them that he had no answer to make to them, for he wholly refused to be judged by laymen.

From this deadlock the trial, according to the *Libellus*, never broke free. Rufus, supported by Alan of Brittany and Roger of Poitou, repeated Lanfranc's argument that judgement must precede restitution: that the first step must be the hearing of

[1] Our only authority for this Salisbury meeting of the king's court seems to be the *Libellus*.

[2] Dixitque nichil se prorsus acturum ibi nisi canonice et secundum ordinem suum et sibi videbatur quod ecclesiastica consuetudo exigebat, ut ipse revestitus ante revestitos causam suam diceret.

[3] The *Libellus* makes St. Calais refer to ' Christianam legem quam hic scriptam habeo '. It is tempting to suppose that this was the Durham manuscript of Lanfranc's canonical collection, now Peterhouse MS. 74, on which cf. Brooke, *op. cit.* pp. 109, 162. On the extracts from Pseudo-Isidore touching the *Exceptio spolii* in Lanfranc's collection, cf. F. Joüon des Longrais, ' Les réformes d'Henry II en matière de saisine ', *Revue hist. de droit français et étranger*, 4ième série, 15, p. 548.

the charges against the bishop by the mixed assembly there present. St. Calais' only concession was neither new nor real. He declared himself ready to answer the charges even though still *dispoliatus*, provided that a preliminary judgement was given that he ought so to answer. But this judgement must be canonical; no layman was to have any part in it. When on Rufus' behalf Hugh de Beaumont appealed him of deserting his lord and king in his need, St. Calais refused to answer except on his conditions : either he must first be reinvested with his bishopric, or he must hear a canonical judgement to the effect that he should plead even though *dispoliatus*. And when the king's court—the mixed body of ecclesiastics and laymen—had at last declared that before the question of restitution was approached the bishop must answer the king's charges against him, St. Calais, the *Libellus* informs us, rejected this decision forthwith, in terms which were directly borrowed from the Pseudo-Isidore. He had not been properly cited, but had been forced to appear in court ; he had been compelled to state his case *dispoliatus*, outside his province, in the absence of his comprovincial bishops, in a lay assembly, before men who were his enemies, who had denied him their counsel and the kiss of peace, and neglecting what he had indeed said, had judged him for things he had not said. These men were at once his accusers and his judges.[1] Therefore he appealed to the pope—and here the quotation from Pseudo-Isidore becomes literal—*cuius dispositioni maiores causas ecclesiasticas et Episcoporum iudicia antiqua apostolorum eorumque successorum atque canonum auctoritas reservavit.*[2]

From this position St. Calais could not be moved by Lanfranc's assurance that the court was concerned with him not as bishop but as feudatory, in the same way as in the past it had judged Odo of Bayeux not as bishop but as earl of Kent. Despite St. Calais' recalcitrance, however, the *Curia regis* proceeded to a final sentence : since he would not plead to the charges of which he had been appealed, he must forfeit his fiefs. Again the bishop declined to recognize the competence of the king's court to judge him. He offered to clear himself of guilt in any place where justice and not violence reigned ; he would show at Rome that the judgement of the *Curia regis* was false. But Hugh de

---

[1] Cf. Hinschius, *Decretales Pseudo-Isidorianae*, p. 469 (Jul. ep. 2, c. xii) : ' Salva apostolicae aecclesiae auctoritate nullus episcopus extra suam provinciam ad iudicium devocetur, sed vocato eo canonice in loco omnibus congruo tempore synodali ab omnibus conprovintialibus episcopis audiatur, qui concordem super eum canonicamque proferre debent sententiam. . . . Nam si ipse metropolitanum aut iudices suspectos habuerit aut infensos senserit, apud primates dioceseos aut apud Romane sedis pontificem iudicetur.' *Ibid.* p. 504 (Damas. ep. 1, c. xvi) : ' Accusatores vero et iudices non idem sint, sed per se accusatores, per se iudices, per se testes, per se accusati . . .'.

[2] *Ibid.* p. 467 (Jul. ep. 2, c. xii).

Beaumont's offer to confirm that judgement he evaded, as the act of a tribunal of which he would not accept the jurisdiction. Then he sought in vain an interpretation of his *convencio* with the earls which would allow him to return to his castle at Durham; the decision of the court was that he must surrender his castle and leave England. At last St. Calais saw that further argument was futile, but before he withdrew he repeated his offer to show by canonical purgation that he had never failed in his feudal obligations. This Rufus would not accept, nor would St. Calais take Lanfranc's advice to throw himself on the king's mercy: ' Absit ' inquid ' ut iudicium contra canones immo ad destructionem canonum, suscipiam vel concedam '. On this note of defiance the trial in effect ended, though the *Libellus* reports that St. Calais was made to suffer many minor vexations before he was allowed to cross to Normandy.

IV

Several points in this story invite critical attention. The first is the very remarkable consistency in attitude imputed by the *Libellus* to St. Calais in regard to the charges arising from his quarrel with Rufus. He is willing to clear his reputation as a feudatory by canonical purgation, but he will not plead before any but an ecclesiastical tribunal, proceeding according to the rules of canon law, in the forefront of which he places the principle ' spoliatus ante omnia restituendus '; it is the right of the pope to decide *contenciosa pontificum iudicia*. Can we accept this account at its face value ? Can we suppose that in 1088 the new papal law was so strongly established in England as to provide a likely refuge for a high ecclesiastic involved in charges of treason ? Claims to clerical immunity had not availed Odo of Bayeux in 1082, and the *Libellus* itself shows the main author of the introduction of the new canonical jurisprudence into England, Lanfranc, not indeed formally denying papal supremacy, but denying in effect the right of appeal to Rome from the king's court.[1] Undoubtedly St. Calais was a man of great ability, possessed of notable powers of memory,[2] and very capable of conducting his own defence. But perhaps it is not captious to observe that it is precisely the apparently impeccable consistency imputed to St. Calais which leaves the impression that the *Libellus* is not so much a faithful contemporary report of what must have been a series of confused and disorderly personal encounters in 1088, as a *Tendenzschrift* composed at leisure with the reference books

---

[1] ' Non est ' inquid Lanfrancus ' iustum ut placitum vel iudicium Regis pro aliqua contradictione longius procedat, sed quociens in curia sua iudicium agitur, ibidem necesse est ut concedatur vel contradicatur.'

[2] HED remarks on St. Calais' extraordinary memory : Arnold, *Symeon*, i. 120.

available at a date when the new canon law was more freely current in England than was probable in 1088. The use of the Pseudo-Isidore in the *Libellus* is masterly, but it is used to suggest a falsehood : that St. Calais left England in 1088-9 so that he might go to the Roman court in order to pursue his appeal to the pope on a point of principle. In fact, he left England because he was exiled, as Odo of Bayeux and other rebellious feudatories were exiled, for traitorous conspiracy against Rufus on behalf of Robert Curthose. We do not know that he went to Rome in his exile ; we do know that he went to Normandy, and there served Robert until he was allowed to return to Durham in 1091, presumably as a result of the agreement between Rufus and Robert in February of that year that the former should restore their lands in England to all the Normans who had lost them because of their support of Robert.[1] St. Calais did in fact expose his griefs to Pope Urban II ; of that we are assured by a letter of remonstrance sent on his behalf by Urban to Rufus in April-June 1089.[2] But it seems proper to emphasize that in the conditions of 1088 such an appeal was not the simple and effective gesture which the *Libellus* pretends it to have been. The election of the imperialist anti-pope Clement III in 1080 faced Gregory VII and his successors with a formidable opponent. Between the two parties striving for the papacy William I and Lanfranc, we are told, ' remained neutral, awaiting the issue, and William II followed suit '.[3] This neutrality, according to Eadmer, lasted long after 1088. When in February 1095 Anselm approached Rufus at Gillingham with his wish to go to the pope to receive the pallium, Rufus immediately asked ' A quo papa illud requirere cupis ? ' And Eadmer comments :

' Erant quippe illo tempore duo, ut in Anglia ferebatur, qui dicebantur Romani pontifices a se invicem discordantes, et ecclesiam Dei inter se divisam post se tractantes ; Urbanus videlicet . . . et Clemens. . . . Quae res, ut de aliis mundi partibus sileam, per plures annos ecclesiam Angliae in tantum occupavit, ut ex quo venerandae memoriae Gregorius qui antea vocabatur Hildebrandus defunctus fuit, nulli loco papae usque ad hoc tempus subdi vel oboedire voluerit.'[4]

The difficulty would have been no less acute in 1088 than in 1095. Had St. Calais, as the *Libellus* suggests, based his defence in the last resort on appeal to the pope, the obvious rejoinder from the king's side would have been to ask to which pope he was appealing.[5] The *Libellus* gives no hint that that question was put, and

[1] ' Florence ' of Worcester, ii. 27.
[2] S. Loewenfeld, *Epistolae Pontificum Romanorum ineditae*, p. 63.
[3] Brooke, *op. cit.* p. 145. He points out (p. 162) that St. Calais' appeal ' must not be regarded too seriously. He was taking a very unusual step, but only to evade judgement, not as a matter of principle.'   [4] *Hist. Nov.* p. 52.
[5] At no time, in the *Libellus*' account, does St. Calais name the pope to whom he is appealing.

its silence on this point discredits its testimony that the need for the question arose. That St. Calais did appeal to Urban II is established, but that he made the appeal during the Salisbury assembly in the circumstances detailed by the *Libellus* seems extremely doubtful.

It may well be that we have here the sort of anachronism into which some one composing, say in the second quarter of the twelfth century, a supposedly contemporary account of events in 1088 could readily have fallen, for at the later date appeal to the pope would have been free of the complications of 1088. Much the same may be said of one of St. Calais' alleged objections to the preliminary judgement by the *Curia regis*. Among the grounds on which the *Libellus* makes him reject that judgement is the good pseudo-Isidorean principle that his comprovincial bishops were not present : *absentibus omnibus comprovincialibus meis*. It would be difficult to discover what comprovincial bishops Durham could claim in 1088. In 1072, in return for Thomas of York's acknowledgement of the primacy of Canterbury, Lanfranc had abandoned to York metropolitan jurisdiction over Durham and the bishops of Scotland, provided that Thomas could get his rights acknowledged by the bishops in question.[1] But it may well be doubted whether there existed in 1072 or 1088 any Scottish diocesan other than St. Andrews, and it is extremely unlikely that the last Celtic bishop of St. Andrews, Fothadh (1059-93), ever recognized the metropolitan rights of York. Until Alexander I and David had imposed a diocesan organization on the Scottish church, and the see of Carlisle had been founded in 1133, York had no suffragan but Durham. St. Calais' alleged complaint in 1088 that his comprovincials were not present was thus nonsensical from the point of view of the facts of 1088.[2] Even if we admit that it is the sort of legalist argument which a desperate ecclesiastic might have produced despite its unreality, can we believe that the *Curia regis* in 1088 would have left it unchallenged ? But the complaint need not have seemed nonsensical to some one inventing it in the changed conditions of the twelfth century.

To any attack on the credibility of the *Libellus* a real difficulty is presented by the long list it provides of characters participating in the events of 1088. Could any other than an eyewitness, or some one with access to the memoranda or the memory of an eyewitness, have produced in a plausible context, as does the

[1] Cf. R. Foreville, *L'Église et la Royauté en Angleterre sous Henri II*, p. 65. St. Calais had been consecrated in 1081 by Thomas of York with the assistance of suffragans of Canterbury, the bishops of Worcester, Exeter, Wells and Hereford : eo quod a Scottorum episcopis qui sibi subjecti sunt habere adiutorium non potuit (*Latin Acts of Lanfranc*, in Earle and Plummer, *op. cit.* i. 289).

[2] Freeman, *William Rufus*, i. 105, calls it ' grotesque '.

VEXACIONE WILLELMI EPISCOPI PRIMI 337

Libellus, a couple of dozen names of men of whose existence in 1088 we may be almost certain ? Some are figures whose activities in church and state are known from the chronicles : Lanfranc, Geoffrey of Coutances, Roger Bigod, Urse d'Abetot, Osmund bishop of Salisbury, Walchelin bishop of Winchester, earls Alan of Brittany, Odo of Champagne, and Roger of Poitou. Others appear as Domesday tenants and frequent witnesses to royal charters : Ralf Paynel, Walter d'Eyncourt, Ivo Taillebois, Erneis de Buron, Gilbert de Breteville, Hugh de Port, Ranulf Peverell, Robert de Lisle, Geoffrey de Trailli, even Heppo the royal *balistarius*. All are given likely enough parts in the Salisbury assembly and the events preceding and following it. Nevertheless, there are some suspicious circumstances about these varied dramatis personae. That charter corroboration seems to be lacking for two of the names, Robertus de Comtisvilla and Ricardus de Cultura, is, of course, not evidence that these men did not exist.[1] In view of the lateness of our first manuscript of the *Libellus* an otherwise unknown ' Reginaldus Paganellus ' can be explained away as a mistake for Radulfus Paganellus : some scribe may have extended ' R. Paganellus ' incorrectly.[2] Perhaps it is possible to explain similarly why the present text of the *Libellus* attributes to St. Calais the intention of crossing the Channel in November 1088 ' cum Rogero de Molbraio ', when we would expect to find the name of Robert Mowbray, earl of Northumberland 1080/1-95. But here an alternative explanation presents itself, which is damaging to the credibility of the *Libellus :* that ' Rogero ' is the true reading, and that the author has confused with Robert Mowbray, St. Calais' contemporary, Roger the son of Nele d'Aubigny and Gundred de Gournay, who was still a minor in 1129.[3] Even more remarkable is the part in the proceedings at Salisbury which the *Libellus* accords to a Hugh de Beaumont. Of all the laymen his voice is the most prominent. It is he who appeals St. Calais on behalf of the king ; he who is responsible for the defiant statement to the bishop : ' Si ego hodie te et tuum ordinem iudicare non potero, tu vel

---

[1] Freeman, *op. cit.* i. 115, n. 2, surmises that Robert de Conteville might be a ' kinsman of the husband of Herleva, the king's step-grandfather '. Richard de la Couture may possibly be a scribal error for Richard de Courcy (de Courceio) who is a frequent witness to charters in these years, including some dubious Durham charters : cf. Davis, *Regesta*, nrs. 205, 286.

[2] There is no reference to a Reginald Paynel in the Paynel pedigree in C. T. Clay, *Early Yorkshire Charters*, vol. vi. Elsewhere the *Libellus* refers to a ' Rogerus Paganellus ', likewise unknown.

[3] Cf. G. E. Cockayne, *Complete Peerage* (revised edn.), ix. 367-9. It is unlikely that the reference can be to Robert Mowbray's father Roger, for there seems no evidence for any activity of this Roger Mowbray in England, and probably he had died well before 1088. On him cf. Ordericus Vitalis, *Hist. Ecclesiastica* (*ed.* Le Prevost), ii. 121 and iii. 406 ; *Complete Peerage*, ix. 705-6.

tuus ordo nunquam me amplius iudicabitis'; he who announces to St. Calais the final judgement of the *Curia Regis*. But outside the *Libellus* there seems no trace of him. Henry of Beaumont, earl of Warwick, indeed appears often enough in the records of Rufus' reign, but for a Hugh de Beaumont we have to wait for Hugh, called le Poer, whom Stephen tried to make earl of Bedford : and this third son of Robert of Meulan was born after 1104.[1] Again, it is possible that the original exemplar of the *Libellus* read 'H.' or 'H. de Bellomonte', and that some later scribe is responsible for an erroneous extension into Hugh instead of Henry, which has passed into all the existing manuscripts. But it would be a singular coincidence if 'R. Paganellus', 'R. de Molbraio' and 'H. de Bellomonte' have all been distorted thus in the course of transmission ; the more probable alternative seems that the author of the *Libellus* wrote 'Reginaldus Paganellus', 'Rogerus de Molbraio', and 'Hugo de Bellomonte' in full, and so not only betrayed that his knowledge of the persons of 1088 was imperfect, but also gave a hint that he was writing at a time when at least the second and third of these names were in fact current.

One further doubt about a personage introduced by the *Libellus* may be added. On the sole evidence of that document Ralf Paynel is commonly described as sheriff of Yorkshire in 1088.[2] Yet during that year, when according to the *Libellus* he was much occupied with the affairs of St. Calais, an 'R. Paganellus' is to be found witnessing a charter in Normandy,[3] and there seems no Paynel except Ralf to fit this initial. Doubt has been expressed whether Ralf could have been in Normandy in 1088, because of the *Libellus*' report of his business in England in that year.[4] But if the *Libellus* be discredited, then the evidence of the charter may well stand.

Thus there are dubieties about the rich assembly of personages which is the most persuasive feature of the *Libellus*. These doubts, even when considered together with the weaknesses of the manuscript tradition and the tractate's lapses into what seems anachronism, do not amount to a complete demonstration that the *Libellus* was a calculated fraud. But they do raise a reasonably strong presumption against the claim of the *Libellus* to be accepted without question as a contemporary, or nearly

---

[1] *Complete Peerage*, vii. 526 n. c ; cf. *Gesta Stephani* in *Chronicles of the Reigns of Stephen, Henry II and Richard* (Rolls Series), iii. 30, 32 n. But Mr. G. H. White has recently doubted whether Hugh le Poer was ever known as Hugh de Beaumont : *Trans. R. Hist. Soc. 4th Series*, xiii. 77.

[2] W. Farrer, 'The Sheriffs of Lincolnshire and Yorkshire, 1066–1130', *E.H.R.*, xxx. 282–4, followed by C. T. Clay, *Early Yorkshire Charters*, vi. 2–4.

[3] Davis, *Regesta*, nr. 299 : R. Paganellus witnesses a charter of Robert, duke of Normandy to the abbey of Mont St. Michel.   [4] Clay, *op. cit.* p. 3, n. 10.

VEXACIONE WILLELMI EPISCOPI PRIMI

contemporary, account of the events of 1088. If it be objected that though there are a few uncertainties in the list of persons, the overwhelming majority of names mentioned by the author can be authenticated from the evidence of Domesday and the charters, that is no more than a tribute to the author's success in achieving what may be supposed to have been his intention. A twelfth-century monk of Durham could have purloined these names, so far as they were not in the chronicles, from charters and from Domesday Book itself. It is certain that the Domesday survey of Lincolnshire was known in Durham,[1] and perhaps it is not without significance that one in three of the names mentioned by the *Libellus* is that of a Domesday tenant-in-chief in Lincolnshire.

V

If we deny that the *Libellus* was written either in 1089 or soon afterwards, what indications are there why and when it was composed? The author of the first version of HED seems not to have known the *Libellus*; the compiler of HR did. The limits thus given (1104–9/1140–50) may be narrowed by conjecture. By 1112–3 the Canterbury monk Eadmer had put out the first issue of his *Historia Novorum*.[2] In its account of the council of Rockingham in 1095 this work made allegations about St. Calais' behaviour extremely damaging to his reputation. He is portrayed as the chief instigator of Rufus' persecution of Anselm, and as the leader of the opposition to the primate. His motive, Eadmer suggests, was ambition to supplant Anselm as archbishop, and to achieve that end he was willing to use disgraceful means; when Anselm had appealed to the pope, St. Calais advised Rufus to use violence against him.[3] How far Eadmer is a good witness need not here be discussed. Whether or not his story be true, by 1112–3 it had been published. Reply from Durham may well have seemed necessary, to clear the name of the founder of the convent from the charge of baseness towards a churchman universally regarded as great. What could better answer this demand than the *Libellus*, which showed St. Calais as the determined defender of the liberties of churchmen and of papal supremacy seven years before the council of Rockingham, and which at the same time, by suggesting that he was willing to defend these principles at the cost of exile, directed attention from the awkward fact that in 1088 St. Calais, to whom the monks of Durham owed so much, had been forced to leave

---

[1] Craster, *op. cit.* p. 529.
[2] *Hist. Nov.* introduction, p. xvi and n. 1; p. xxxvi.
[3] *Ibid.* p. 62: 'Verum mihi violentia videtur opprimendus, et si regiae voluntati non vult adquiescere, ablato baculo et anulo, de regno pellendus'.

England because he had been unable to clear himself of a charge of treason ? This is no more than conjecture, but it is a conjecture which does something to explain the undoubted correspondence in thought and sometimes in phrase between the *Libellus* and Eadmer's account of the council of Rockingham. When Anselm asks for delay in order to consider his reply to Rufus' demand that he should renounce his allegiance to Pope Urban II, St. Calais opposes the request in words which strike an echo. Addressing Anselm and referring to the king he says : ' Revesti eum primo, si placet, debita imperii sui dignitate, et tunc demum de induciis age '.[1] Inverted in its application it is the theme, central to the *Libellus*, of ' Spoliatus ante omnia restituendus '. There are other similarities between the two works which strengthen the supposition that the author of the *Libellus* was acquainted with the *Historia Novorum*.[2] The evidence is suggestive rather than conclusive. But if we suppose that the *Libellus* was written with Eadmer in mind, then we must conclude that it was written after 1112–3 ; its implicit claim to be a contemporary account of the events of 1088 fails, and the probability that some of it is fiction is increased. And if this be accepted, another date before which it can hardly have been written becomes likely. When St. Calais rejects the judgement of the *Curia regis* as an infringement of ecclesiastical liberty, the *Libellus* makes Lanfranc reply : ' Nos non de episcopio sed de tuo te feodo iudicamus, et hoc modo iudicavimus Baiocensem Episcopum ante patrem huius Regis de feodo suo, nec Rex vocabat eum Episcopum in placito illo sed fratrem et comitem '. If this story does not come from the immediate genuine knowledge of the author of the *Libellus* it is not easy to know whence he had it, if not from the *Gesta Regum* of William of Malmesbury, which was not finished before 1125.[3] If we cannot accept the

[1] *Hist. Nov.* p. 60.
[2] Anselm's appeal to papal judgement in Eadmer (*ibid.* p. 61) : ' Qui, propterea quod venerabilis sanctae Romanae ecclesiae summi pontificis oboedientiam abnegare nolo, vult probare me fidem et sacramentum violare quod terreno regi debeo, assit ; et in nomine Domini me paratum inveniet ei sicut debeo, et ubi debeo, respondere ' is made in the same sort of veiled terms which the *Libellus* has St. Calais use in his *convencio* with the earls on 8 September 1088 : ' Si vero tale iudicium Episcopo diceretur quod sibi videretur iniustum, et ipse contradiceret et in rege vel in iudicibus ad confirmandum iudicium illuc ire remaneret, ubi contenciosa Pontificum iudicia iuste debent terminari. . . . Again, St. Calais' stipulation in the *convencio* about a safe-conduct to the coast seems a mere elaboration of Anselm's demand : ' mandavit ei dare sibi conductum quo cum suis portum maris tuto petens regno decederet ' (*ibid.* p. 65). And the counsel of submission given to Anselm by the bishops at Rockingham is much like that which the *Libellus* has Lanfranc give to St. Calais in 1088 : Eadmer (*ibid.* p. 56), ' si pure ad voluntatem domini regis consilii tui summam transferre volueris, promptum et quod in nobis ipsis utile didicimus a nobis consilium certum habebis ' ; *Libellus*, ' Melius ageres, si in misericordia Regis totum te poneres, et ego ad pedes eius libenter tui causa venirem '.
[3] *Gesta Regum*, iii. 277 ; iv. 306 (Rolls Series edn., ii. 334, 361).

Libellus as an authentic contemporary account of the happenings of 1088, the probability is thus that it was a product of the period of brilliant literary activity at Durham in the second quarter of the twelfth century.

The grounds for these suggestions about the real date of the *De iniusta vexacione* are admittedly hypothetical. Even if they are found acceptable they cannot help to decide the question how much genuine information the author of the *Libellus* may have had at his disposal and faithfully transmitted. The proposition that he completely invented everything in his account could not possibly be sustained. Art he brought to its composition, but not art of that superlative order. Some of his material must have been authentic; his reproduction, for instance, of Rufus' safe-conduct for St. Calais to proceed overseas, seems unexceptionable in form and content.[1] Nevertheless there are good reasons for contending that circumstances in the tradition, the tendency and the details of the *Libellus* suggest that it is highly hazardous to treat it—as it has often been treated in the past—as a wholly trustworthy document contemporary with the events which it discusses.

[1] Arnold, *Symeon*, i. 192; this safe-conduct is accepted as genuine by Davis, *Regesta*, nr. 298.

ADDENDA

p. 322 at title:
[The edition of *De iniusta vexacione* prepared by Professor Offler will be published in the Royal Historical Society's Camden series.]

p. 332 n. 3 line 3 at '162.':
[For the close relationship between markings in the margins of Cambridge Peterhouse MS 74 and points in the *Libellus*, see pp. 131–2 in M. Philpott, 'The *De iniusta uexacione Willelmi episcopi primi* and canon law in Anglo-Norman Durham', *Anglo-Norman Durham 1093–1193*, ed. D. Rollason, M. Harvey & M. Prestwich, (Woodbridge, 1994), pp. 125–37.]

p. 337 line 6 at 'Roger of Poitou':
C. P. Lewis, "The King and Eye': a study in Anglo-Norman politics', *English Historical Review* civ (1989), 575 n. 5 remarks: 'The fact that the tract called Roger a Count, a title to which he was not entitled until 1091, argues that it was not composed before that year.'

VII

Rannulf Flambard as Bishop of Durham (1099-1128)*

WITHIN the experience of some here this evening the see of Durham will complete its first millenium. So far, it has known 68 bishops (counting Robert Graystanes, for I do not see why he should be left out). None of them, save Thomas Wolsey, has played anything like as prominent a part on the national stage as did Rannulf Flambard. After studies revised and expanded over many years, Dr. Southern has recently emphasized Rannulf's rôle as 'the chief legal and financial expert' of William Rufus. He calls Rannulf 'the first outstandingly successful administrator in English history', and reminds us that 'this son of an obscure priest in the diocese of Bayeux was the first man of ignoble birth in English history to climb from the bottom to the top of the social scale by the backstairs of the royal administration.'[1] That word 'backstairs' bothers me a little—for I take Rannulf to be of the kind that never hesitates to hammer on the front door. But otherwise Dr. Southern's appreciation of what Rannulf did in the service of his king carries conviction. There is no need to undertake the task again. My intention is to concentrate on a much narrower theme: on Rannulf as manager of the diocese of Durham and of St. Cuthbert's patrimony. For, unlike Wolsey, whose interest in Durham was for the most part limited to the financial profit which he could expect to extract from the see, Rannulf was extremely active in these parts for more than twenty years. He was bishop at a time when the flow of western church history was more than usually disturbed, as the impetuous freshets of reform swirled round the deeply anchored snags of traditional lay influence in church affairs. Rannulf stood at the opposite pole to the doctrinaire reformers, who were vehement for the Church's freedom from undue secular control and its concomitant evils, and tireless— since they included many of the best speculative intelligences of the age—in refining on what was to be understood by 'freedom' and 'undue'. But he cannot have been unaware (for sometimes he was present at it) of the work of the synods and councils, where in less spectacular and perhaps more useful fashion legislation of reforming tendency was being hammered out. It is some sort of token of Rannulf's efficiency that the sources for his episcopate are tolerably abundant, measured by the standards of the early twelfth century. We have a better opportunity with him than with many of his contemporaries of measuring both the innovatory and the obsolescent in his career as bishop.[2]

Let us not flatter ourselves: in a sense much of Rannulf's activity in Durham was involuntary. Rufus had made him bishop at Whitsun 1099 in circumstances which, though they were not unusual at this period, St. Anselm was later to deplore as

---

* The Cathedral Lecture for 1971, given in the Monks' Dormitory at Durham on 4th March 1971. The pagination for this lecture is shown in square brackets.

[1] R. W. Southern, 'Ranulf Flambard', in *Medieval Humanism and other studies* (Oxford, 1970), pp. 184, 186, 188. This amplifies his earlier essay, 'Ranulf Flambard and early Anglo-Norman administration', written in 1930-1 and published in *Trans. Royal Hist. Soc.*, 4th series, xvi (1933).

[2] An account of Rannulf written in Durham not long after his death was added to Symeon's *Historia Dunelmensis Ecclesiae*; it is cited here as HED *cont. prima* from Thomas Arnold's edn. of Symeon, vol. i (Rolls Series, 1882). In the fifteenth century Prior Wessington incorporated in his history of the Church of Durham an important series of documents for Rannulf's episcopate, which presumably he found in the episcopal archives; they have since disappeared. Wessington's copies were brought to light and published by H. H. E. Craster, 'A contemporary record of the pontificate of Ranulf Flambard', in *Archaeologia Aeliana*, 4th series, vii (1930), 33-56 [cited here as CR]. Rannulf's charters are edited in *Durham Episcopal Charters 1071-1152*, Surtees Soc., vol. 179, 1968 [cited as DEC]. Material from the royal chancery concerning Durham at this time will be found registered in *Regesta Regum Anglo-Normannorum*, vol. i, ed. by H. W. C. Davis (Oxford, 1913), and vol. ii, ed. by C. Johnson and H. A. Cronne (Oxford, 1956) [cited as RAN i and ii].

simoniacal and uncanonical.³ At this time Rannulf can have had no grounds for suspecting that his promotion in the Church was likely to interrupt his services to the king: after all, the promotion of another Norman priest, Roger, to the see of Salisbury in 1102 did not prevent him remaining the leading minister of the crown for thirty seven years. What brought Rannulf's career as the king's chief agent to a catastrophic close was the mysterious death of his patron Rufus in the New Forest on 2nd August 1100. Henry I, so conveniently poised to take up his brother's inheritance, found in the Bishop of Durham a badly-needed scapegoat for the unpopularity of the previous régime. Within a fortnight he had committed Rannulf to the Tower of London on a charge of malversation. It looked to be all up with Rannulf—and the applause was general.

The story of his escape from the Tower on 3rd February 1101 is pure Gilbert and Sullivan. It was superbly told by their slightly older contemporary, Edward Augustus Freeman, whom I quote:

'At last the means of escape were given to him; a rope was brought in hidden in a vessel of water or wine. The Bishop made a feast for his keepers and plied them well with the wine. When they were snoring in their drunken sleep, Flambard tied his rope to the small column which divided one of the double windows usual in the architecture of his day. Even at such a moment, he did not forget that he was now a bishop; he took his pastoral staff with him and began to let himself down the rope. But he had forgotten another, and at that moment a more useful part of the episcopal dress. He left his gloves behind; so his hands suffered sadly in his descent. Moreover, the Bishop was a bulky man and his rope was too short; so he fell with a heavy fall, and lay groaning and half-dead. But his friends and followers were at the foot of the Tower ready to help him.'⁴

And so they did, over the Channel to Normandy, to join Henry's elder brother and rival, Duke Robert Courthose. Bruised and groaning though he may have been at the foot of the Tower, the Bishop's human affections did not fail. He took with him his old mother, whom his opponents derided as a witch.

During the next five years this resilient man conducted himself so deviously as to defeat historians' attempts to elucidate the complications of the double game he played between Henry and Robert. From the start Rannulf seems to have been able to manipulate Robert to his own advantage. There is no doubt that he was behind that rather feckless magnate's armed expedition to England in the summer of 1101; indeed, we are told that by counselling the corruption of Henry's sailors, he made Robert's passage of the Channel possible. It did not come to battle between Robert and Henry in 1101; instead, they made a peace at Alton in Hampshire which might have been designed to suit Rannulf's purposes. Robert's supporters were to be restored to their lands in England from which Henry had dispossessed them, and Rannulf appears to have benefited from this amnesty clause.⁵ In August, Henry ordered that the lands and men of the bishopric of Durham were to be restored to Rannulf, and by September the latter was back in England, seemingly on a friendly footing with Henry, even if not fully restored to favour.⁶

I do not share the confidence of some scholars⁷ that by this time Rannulf was already wholly committed to acting as Henry's agent for the conquest of Normandy from his brother. Long before Henry's conclusive victory at Tinchebrai in 1106 Rannulf will have read the omens. But until Robert had been defeated and captured Rannulf enjoyed some freedom to play one brother off against the other; in my opinion he found the nerve—it needed a great deal—to use that freedom. He can be shown to have visited

---

³ Anselm. Cantuar., *Ep.* 214 (to Pope Paschal II, early 1101), in *Opera omnia*, ed. F. S. Schmitt, iv., 112-3.

⁴ E. A. Freeman, *William Rufus*, ii (Oxford, 1882), 397-8.

⁵ Florence of Worcester, *Chron. ex chron.*, ed. B. Thorpe, ii, 48; *cf.* C. W. David, *Robert Curthose* (Harvard, 1920), pp. 130, 134-6.

⁶ CR nos. x-xii; RAN ii nos. 539-41.

⁷ e.g. F. Barlow, *The Feudal Kingdom of England* (1955), p. 176.

VII

[5] 16

England in 1102, 1104 and 1105, but most of the time he spent in Normandy.⁸ In June 1102 he jobbed his brother, Fulcher, into the vacant Norman bishopric of Lisieux; on Fulcher's death a few months later Duke Robert was persuaded to invest two of Rannulf's sons, scarce twelve years old, with the bishopric, on the understanding that if the elder, Thomas, died, the younger brother should succeed. The administration of Lisieux Rannulf took over himself, and despite the scandal which this whole transaction provoked among the Norman reforming churchmen and their attempts to secure a canonical election at Lisieux, he continued to retain the see—possibly with an interruption in 1104—until 1106 or 1107. In all this he needed, of course, the connivance of Duke Robert, but he also obtained at a critical moment—perhaps in 1105—the support of Henry I. From that time on, there can be no real doubt, he came down on Henry's side in Normandy.⁹

With Henry's triumph over Robert in 1106 and the accession of John of Seéz as bishop of Lisieux in 1107, Rannulf was free to concentrate his attention on Durham, the see he had held since 1099. The bitter fact was, he had not much else to do. Though on the surface his reconciliation with Henry I was complete, he did not gain the king's full confidence. Never under Henry was he allowed to play the part he had invented for himself under Rufus: the supreme, permanent administrator of royal business, through whose hands ran all important matters of justice and finance. Henry had found another man for such tasks in Roger of Salisbury, the contrast between whom and Rannulf Dr. Southern has painted vividly.¹⁰ Rannulf's position was now that of a great prelate and territorial magnate in England; but he was only one among a number of such. It was not in him, of course, to desert the seats of power completely. 'Either first or up with the leaders' remained his motto: which afterwards became attached to Bishop Thomas Hatfield only as the result of intellectual bankruptcy on the part of a late medieval chronicler.¹¹ For the rest of his lifetime there can have been few really great occasions of church and state in England from which he was absent. He appears quite often in the king's company and was with him in Normandy at least thrice.¹² The suggestion that he cherished serious hopes of succeeding Anselm at Canterbury is almost certainly based on a misapprehension.¹³ But Ralph d'Escures who did obtain Canterbury in 1114 was an old acquaintance, and Ralph's successor, William of Corbeil, had once been Rannulf's clerk. It would be wrong to suppose that during the last twenty years of his life Rannulf had no influence at all in high affairs. But for the most part his time and tremendous energy and intelligence were now available for Durham.

There, much needed to be done. The heavy losses suffered by the see during the first few years of Henry's reign provide an argument of some weight against the view that the disgrace and imprisonment of Rannulf were no more than gestures in a sham fight. Whatever may have been the true nature of the bishop's misadventures, in the thrusting, colonial society of the time there were greedy neighbours eager to turn them

---

⁸ RAN ii, nos. 595-6; *De miraculis et translationibus s. Cuthberti*, vii, in *Symeonis monachi opp. omn.*, ed. T. Arnold, i (Rolls Series, 1882), 254, 258, 260; RAN ii nos. 683, 699, 701, 703, 706.

⁹ Ivo Carnotensis, *Epp.* 157, 153, 154, in Migne, PL clxii, 162, 157-8 (David, *op. cit.*, pp. 152-3 is surely right in dating *Ep.* 154 later than *Ep.* 157; and *Ep.* 154 takes *Ep.* 153 with it). Ordericus Vitalis, *Hist. eccles.* x, 16, in Migne, PL clxxxviii, 763.

¹⁰ HED *cont. prima*, pp. 138-9; Southern, *Medieval Humanism*, p. 231.

¹¹ HED *cont. prima*, p. 139: 'ut in conventu procerum vel primus vel cum primis contenderet esse'; *cf.* the so-called chronicle of Willielmus de Chambre, in *Hist. Dunelmensis Scriptores Tres*, ed. J. Raine, Surtees Soc., vol. 9, 1839, p. 137.

¹² In 1115, 1116 and 1118-9; *cf.* Hugh the Chantor, *Chronicle of the Church of York*, ed. C. Johnson (1961), pp. 37, 48, 74; RAN ii nos. 1204-5, 1210, 1215.

¹³ The cryptic passage in Gerard of York's letter to Anselm (in Anselm. Cantuar., *Ep.* 373, *Opp. omn.* ed. Schmitt, v, 317), referred to Rannulf by the editor in his note, seems more probably to have had Roger of Salisbury in mind; *cf.* F. Liebermann, *Quadripartitus* (Halle, 1892), p. 158, note 5.

to their own advantage. In the fifteenth century Prior Wessington brought the loss of Durham's spiritual jurisdiction over Hexham into connexion with Rannulf's imprisonment. Though that foreshortens unduly what was in fact a much longer story, this is the time when Durham's jurisdiction over Carlisle and Teviotdale was finally lost.[14] From August 1101 onwards numerous royal writs ordered that Rannulf was to be reseised with his lands and men and their services. But it is clear that some of these royal orders were put into effect only very slowly, and others not at all.[15] The three extensive Yorkshire manors of Northallerton, Welton and Howden, the proceeds from which amounted to perhaps a third of the revenues of the bishopric, seem to have remained in the king's hands until 1116.[16] It may well be that it was during Rannulf's disgrace that Harold's great manor of Waltham in Essex, granted by William the Conqueror to Bishop Walcher, slipped permanently from Durham's control.[17] Despite Henry's order, the lands at Marske by Sea and in its neighbourhood which Copsi, Earl Tostig's deputy, had granted to St. Cuthbert even before the Norman Conquest were never recovered.[18]

Rannulf indeed found it easier to recover his ecclesiastical status than his temporal possession. To Anselm—whose enthronement at Canterbury in 1093 he had interrupted in an unmannerly fashion, breaking in like a bum-bailiff at a wedding breakfast—Rannulf was almost everything detestable: 'by profession a priest, but in fact not only a tax collector, but the most infamous prince of tax collectors, known as Flambard on account of his cruelty, which was like a devouring flame.'[19] Gerard of York was more accommodating; in the early autumn of 1101 he wrote to the prior and convent at Durham to tell them that he had received Rannulf in order to restore him to his see, by the king's grace and with the assent of his fellow bishops.[20] Though Pope Paschal II had urged this course,[21] no more than Anselm did he regard the case against Rannulf as thereby closed. Writing to the bishop in April 1102 Paschal did not mince his words: if what has been reported at the Curia about Rannulf's offences before he became bishop and at the time of his promotion is true, Rannulf should not only have forfeited his bishopric but also have been unfrocked.[22] He must present himself to Anselm and clear himself of the charges by an oath of canonical purgation supported by six other bishops; should he fail to do this, he must be sent to the Curia; if he then refuses to be examined by the pope, the penalty will be expulsion from his see.[23] Rannulf must have found six bishops to support him and have survived the test, and so avoided having to appear before the pope. For though the medieval and the modern biographers of Anselm have little or nothing to say about this unedifying

---

[14] Lincoln's Inn, Hale ms. 104 (114), fo. 83v (cf. DEC pp. 22-23); CR nos. iii-vi, pp. 38-9; RAN i no. 478; HED cont. prima, p. 139.

[15] CR nos. xi-xvii, xx-xxi, xxiii, xxvi; RAN ii nos. 540-1, 545-6, 560-2, 575, 589-90, 642.

[16] Pipe Roll, 31 Henry I, ed. J. Hunter (1833), pp. 132-3; CR no. xxx; RAN ii no. 1124.

[17] Cf. DEC p. 23.

[18] HED iii, 14, ed. Arnold, p. 97; CR no. xxi; RAN ii no. 590. These lands do not appear to have been held by Durham in 1086.

[19] Eadmer, Hist. nov., ed. M. Rule (Rolls Series, 1884), p. 41; Anselm. Cantuar., Ep. 214 (to Pope Paschal II), in Opp. omn. iv, 112. According to Ordericus, Rannulf's nickname was given him by Robert, the royal dispenser: Hist. eccles. viii, 8, in Migne, PL clxxxviii, 580. Presumably this was Robert FitzTurstin, who appears as dispenser under William I and Rufus: RAN i p. xxvii.

[20] CR no. xix. Rannulf had been present at the royal council at Windsor in early September 1101: RAN ii nos. 544-6, 548. Gerard set off to Rome for his pallium in the autumn of 1101.

[21] Cf. Paschal, in Anselm. Cantuar., Ep. 223, Opp. omn. iv, 128. Possibly Paschal, like Anselm, was concerned that the canonical principle, 'spoliatus ante omnia restituendus', should be preserved.

[22] CR no. ix, p. 41; Paschal, in Anselm. Cantuar., Ep. 225, ed. cit. iv, 130. I accept the date suggested by W. Holtzmann, Papsturkunden in England ii (Berlin, 1935), no. 4, pp. 137-8.

[23] Paschal, in Anselm. Cantuar., Ep. 223, ed. cit. iv, 128-9.

business, the formula according to which Anselm absolved Rannulf—perhaps in the autumn of 1102—has survived.[24] However dark the circumstances, whatever Anselm's doubts, Rannulf was now respectable according to the law of the Church. How thick a vein of impudence ran in him he showed in the last year of the archbishop's life, when he exposed himself to rebuff by urging Anselm to allow him to cut a canonical corner.[25]

At his consecration Rannulf had been careful to avoid making any profession of obedience to his metropolitan.[26] Nevertheless, his relations with the archbishops of York were easy and loyal; he did not conceal his sympathy with the vigorous concern of Thomas II and Thurstan to foil Canterbury's claims to superiority. When Thomas was in the midst of his struggle for equality with Canterbury we hear of Rannulf making a characteristic offer. If the king will allow the issue to be settled in York's favour by a canonical judgement, he is prepared to give Henry 1000 marks of silver, with the usual 10 per cent commission for the queen. 'But', says the York chronicler (not, of course, a wholly unprejudiced witness), 'the king would not listen, well knowing which side could bid the higher.'[27] Though Archbishop Thurstan was to earn a reputation for piety which Rannulf never achieved, up to a point there was much in common between the two. Both came from the same part of Normandy; both had been members of that extraordinary club of ambitious Norman clerics in London, the chapter of St. Paul's; it was Rannulf, so it seems, who ordained Thurstan priest in 1115; for years in diocesan business they shared the same auxiliary, Ralph Nowell, titular bishop of Orkney. There is something attractive about Rannulf's friendship for Thurstan, though at times it needed to be cautious.[28]

Within his own diocese the crucial question for Rannulf was how he would be able to get on with his cathedral chapter, the monks of the convent established in Durham by his predecessor, the imposing monk-bishop, William of St. Calais. 'At the beginning of his episcopate he hated his monks exceedingly, but later on greatly cherished them' —that sentence, written in Durham some forty years after Rannulf's death, over-simplifies a line of development.[29] I doubt whether Rannulf ever really hated his monks. But to begin with there were certainly tensions. Rannulf's was not a naturally Benedictine soul. All his earlier experience had accustomed him to the outlook and practices of the secular rather than the monastic clergy. He and his brothers and sons were embedded in the chapter of St. Paul's, in which he had held the prebend of Tottenham and maybe also the deanery with which that prebend often went.[30] At one time or another we hear of him in connexion with the colleges of secular canons at Christchurch in Hampshire and at St. Martin's, Dover; he held prebends (perhaps from policy, for he himself contributed to their endowment) in the cathedrals of Salisbury and Lincoln.[31] A prejudice on his part in favour of the system of cathedral organization which he knew best would be natural. Expert in administration as he was, he could hardly be

---

[24] CR no. xviii, p. 48. Rannulf, it seems, was in England in late September 1102: RAN ii nos. 595-6. Anselm may have left England in the spring of 1103. Rannulf does not appear among the bishops recorded as attending the English council at Westminster in the autumn of 1102: Eadmer, *Hist. nov.*, pp. 141-2; and the Durham *Historia regum*, ed. T. Arnold (Rolls Series, 1885), p. 235, states categorically that he was not there. But his absolution must date from about this time.

[25] Anselm. Cantuar., *Ep.* 442, ed. cit., v, 389.

[26] HED *cont. prima*, p. 138.

[27] Hugh the Chantor, *History of the Church of York*, ed. and trs. C. Johnson, p. 29.

[28] Hugh the Chantor, pp. 37 and note, 74; *cf.* D. Nicholl, *Thurstan, Archbishop of York, 1114-1140* (York, 1964), p. 51.

[29] Durham, Dean and Chapter Library, ms. B. ii. 35, fo. 149b: Iste in primordio suos monachos exosos habuit, sed postea illos plurimum dilexit.

[30] C. N. L. Brooke, 'The Chapter of St. Paul's, 1086-1163', *Cambridge Hist. Jnl.*, x (1951), 124, 129-31.

[31] RAN i no. 361; CR no. xvi; RAN ii nos. 562, 753, 1104.

blind to the practical difficulties of running a diocese in conjunction with a monastic chapter, which could offer him few or no opportunities for supporting and rewarding his familiar clerks in the usual fashion. His political sense would be alert to the danger of a corporate monastic opposition to his régime emerging. For a time the monks may have feared that Rannulf envisaged overturning the cathedral constitution established so much in their favour by William of St. Calais.

It is likely, too, that there was a clash of personalities between the prior of Durham, Turgot, and the new bishop. Turgot was a masterful man, and powerfully connected, above all with the royal house of Scotland. During the long vacancy after St. Calais's death and during Rannulf's early troubles and absences—say roughly from 1096 to 1106—he had been the dominant figure in the diocese. According to the terms of St. Calais's constitution, as prior he was also archdeacon: and that made him in effect the bishop's right-hand man in diocesan affairs. Durham was not big enough to hold comfortably two such sizable characters. When Turgot was chosen to be bishop of St. Andrews in 1108 Rannulf showed an eagerness to get him consecrated and safely out of the way which Anselm clearly felt to be indecent.[32] But Turgot's departure for Scotland gave the bishop his opportunity to break with the practice of monk-archdeacons. From about this time dates the appearance of a secular cleric as archdeacon in Durham, and before the end of Rannulf's episcopate he had been given a fellow, so that the ground was being prepared for the division of the diocese into the two archdeaconries of Durham and Northumberland which was to last until 1842. We ought not to underrate the significance of what may appear to be no more than an opportunist shuffle of persons. Without engaging in a noisy battle of principle, Rannulf had very considerably reduced the monastery's capacity to influence the administration of the diocese.[33]

Certainly he did not always defer to his monks' susceptibilities. When his active career in Durham began, only the choir of the new cathedral had been completed. To hasten matters along and get the walls of the nave up, he diverted into the cathedral fabric fund the altar dues and burial fees which the monks thought should have been used for the domestic buildings of the monastery. It is hard to believe that there was anything abusive about this, or indeed that there are substantial grounds for accusing Rannulf of treating his monks harshly. The documents of restitution which he issued at the end of his life do little to support such a charge, and the balance of the evidence points the other way.[34] Rannulf knew quite a lot about monks: his father died a monk of St. Augustine's, Canterbury; it is likely that at least one close relative of his became a monk at Durham; his friend, Abbot Richard of St. Albans, thought well enough of him to invite him to dedicate the chapel of St. Alexis in the priory church there; he was in confraternity with Hyde Abbey and perhaps also with Thorney.[35] He was not to be gulled by the chapter of Durham nor persuaded into uselessly combative attitudes on its behalf.[36] In time the monks settled down on appreciative terms with their nominal abbot. The account of Rannulf written not long after his death by a Durham monk and added to Symeon's *History of the Church of Durham,*

---

[32] Anselm. Cantuar., *Ep.* 442, ed. cit., v, 389.

[33] H. S. Offler, 'The early archdeacons in the diocese of Durham', *Trans. Archit. & Archaeological Soc. of Durham & Northumberland,* xi (1962), 193-202.

[34] DEC nos. 24-5 and pp. 110-11; *cf.* Southern, *op. cit.,* p. 202. More than half of Rannulf's surviving *acta* record grants made by him to the monastery: DEC nos. 14-18, 20-21, as well as the restitution charters.

[35] Offler, 'Early archdeacons', p. 201; *Gesta abbatum mon. s. Albani,* ed. H. T. Riley, i (Rolls Series, 1867), 148; Southern, *op.* 192 and note. It seems likely that the *Randulfus episcopus* entered among the confraternity in the Thorney cartulary is indeed our Rannulf, though the *passeflambardus* has been added afterwards: British Museum, Add. ms. 40,000, fo. 10, col. 2.

[36] Thus he seems to have kept quite clear of the monks' efforts to gain possession of the church at Tynemouth, granted long before by Earl Robert Mowbray to St. Albans; *cf.* DEC pp. 43-5.

though it does not deal in flattery, is by no means unfriendly. A dozen years later another monk, Lawrence, who afterwards became prior, writing amid the disorders after the death of Bishop Geoffrey Rufus, looked back longingly to Rannulf's episcopate as a golden age of peace and plenty for the monastery. Both authors agree on this: Rannulf was a man of great heart and spirit.[37]

It would be pointless to challenge that judgement. Great-hearted men can, of course, also be foolish—as that other magnanimous bishop of Durham, Antony Bek, was at times foolish. But, despite the deficiencies of the evidence, study of Rannulf's management of the temporal affairs of the bishopric leaves the impression of a dominant and designing intelligence. It is not just that, for all the early losses, material prosperity increased, though this is undoubted: during the vacancy after Rannulf's death the crown received twice as much a year from its regalian rights as during the vacancy after William of St. Calais.[38] More important, we can glimpse Rannulf in his capacity as a great territorial magnate diagnosing the political problem of the north and defining an attitude towards it.

For much of the twelfth century the cult of the Northumbrian Saint Cuthbert was as popular in Scotland as in England; local notabilities like Prior Turgot and Ailred of Rievaulx turned quite naturally at certain points in their careers to the court of the king of Scots. The question where the frontier between the English and Scottish kingdoms was to be fixed—whether along Tweed or Tyne or Tees—remained open down to the reign of Henry II. Less than ten years after Rannulf's death King David I of Scotland disclosed his ambition to create what has been called a Scoto-Northumbrian state governed from Carlisle, and his efforts in that direction came near success.[39] It is true that between 1097 and David's accession in 1124 the kings of Scotland were at peace with their neighbours, 'because they accepted the lordship of William II and Henry I.'[40] There are strong indications that Rannulf realized how precarious this situation was. Had he been taught a lesson as early in his episcopate as 1100, by being deprived of Durham lands in Berwickshire granted only shortly before by Edgar king of Scots? Professor Duncan's argument that Edgar did indeed take some such action has not wholly convinced me.[41] But the bridge which Rannulf built from the peninsula of Durham across the Wear to the world outside—Framwellgate Bridge—opened easier access to the north. His fortification of Norham on Tweed in 1121 and the organization at about this time of the Durham lands in Norhamshire and Islandshire into a separate sheriffdom for the episcopal vassal Papedy need to be seen in a wider context of Anglo-Norman unease about Scotland. It is hard to dismiss as mere coincidence the fact that 1121-2, the years of Rannulf's patent concern with Norham, when he built in Durham, running from the chancel of the cathedral to the Castle keep, that defensive wall of which a portion has recently been exposed in Bailey Court, saw too the establishment of Eustace Fitzjohn near Bamburgh and perhaps of Walter Espec at Wark on Tweed, as well as Henry I's visit to Carlisle to

---

[37] HED *cont. prima* (ed. Arnold, pp. 135-141) has been added to the earliest ms. of Symeon's history of the Church of Durham: Durham University Library, Cosin's ms. V. ii. 6. Originally it ended at *confirmavit restituta* (Arnold, p. 141), where the hand changes (fo. 102). Lawrence of Durham, *Dial.* ii, 235-6, ed. James Raine the younger, Surtees Soc., vol. 70, 1880, p. 22, wrote: Nomen ei Rannulphus erat; quo praesule nobis / Aurea felici saecla fuere statu.

[38] Between 1096 and 1099, we are told, Rufus was able to exact £300 a year from Durham for the royal treasury: HED *cont. prima*, p. 135. In the two years between Rannulf's death and Michaelmas 1130 the Exchequer received £1238. 1. 5d. from the bishopric: Margaret Howell, *Regalian Right in Medieval England* (1962), pp. 25-9, on the basis of *Pipe Roll, 31 Henry I*, pp. 128-133. There may be an element of special royal impost in this total, as Dr. Howell suggests, but it will not have amounted to as much as £120.

[39] G. W. Barrow, *Feudal Britain* (1956), p. 145.

[40] A. A. M. Duncan, 'The earliest Scottish charters', *Scottish Hist. Rev.* xvii (1958), 135.

[41] Duncan, p. 111.

get work going on the walls and castle there.[42] How prescient such measures had been was shown at the end of 1135, when among the strong points which David had to seize on his sweep southwards were Norham, Carlisle and Wark, while he tried and failed at Bamburgh.[43] And that even at the height of his power in 1141 David was unable to bring off the coup which would have projected his influence down to the Tees and beyond, by intruding his chancellor William Cumin as bishop of Durham, was in large part due to the strength of Rannulf's system, maintained for more than two decades after his death by his nephews, Osbert the sheriff and Rannulf the archdeacon of Durham.

Rannulf's government of the patrimony of St. Cuthbert owed nothing to what are sometimes called his palatine rights there; that anachronistic language had best be avoided at this date. The essence of the great ecclesiastical immunity which Rannulf ruled in Durham, Northumberland and Yorkshire was financial; normally it was supposed to be exempt from payment of the king's geld.[44] Possibly Rannulf was not able to maintain the claim wholly intact, to the understandable annoyance of his subjects.[45] Beneficiaries of episcopal grants still thought it prudent to obtain recognition that the grants had been made by royal permission as well as with capitular assent; at times they sought direct confirmation by the king.[46] It was the king who gave the bishop leave to hold a market every Sunday in his vill of Norton.[47] Clearly, it would be wrong to imagine that Rannulf exercised anything like full regal power within the patrimony. Yet he did enjoy considerable freedom, at times in fashions which opened wider perspectives for the future. His hunting rights were protected by sanctions as weighty as those protecting the king's in the New Forest.[48] On occasion a charter of Rannulf's will echo the peremptory language of the royal chancery which he knew so well, and we know that he had able clerks in his household.[49] We ought not, of course, to exaggerate the extent to which the machinery of administration in the bishopric had developed. Only one household officer, William the chamberlain, occurs among the charter witnesses; until late in the episcopate the interests of the steward, Hugh son of Pinceon, were largely in Lincolnshire, and he attests none of the bishop's surviving *acta*. Quietly, however, at least one important development did take place. As in Norhamshire and Islandshire with Papedy, so in Durham Rannulf proved capable of appointing a sheriff depending on himself, not on the king. His nephew Osbert is called sheriff in a couple of Rannulf's charters. It is not certain that Osbert acted in that capacity under Bishop Geoffrey Rufus, but he was recognized as sheriff again in 1141 and was still in office as late as 1148.[50] This was an important precedent.[51] The king had no regular financial rights in the heart of the patrimony, and therefore no incentive to establish there any permanent officer of his own lower than the bishop. Possibly this practice of the bishop appointing the sheriff, which Henry I seems to

---

[42] Symeon, *Historia regum*, pp. 260, 267; HED *cont. prima*, p. 140; RAN ii no. 1279. From the addresses in RAN ii nos. 1264 and 1279 it may perhaps be inferred that Walter Espec had achieved his footing in Northumberland by mid-1121.

[43] Richard of Hexham, *De gestis regis Stephani*, ed. R. Howlett (Rolls Series, 1886), p. 145.

[44] *Cf.* the interesting though obscure story of the misfortunes of a would-be royal tax-gatherer in Durham in William I's time, as told by Symeon, HED iii, 20, p. 107. His name was Rannulf.

[45] CR nos. xxiv, xxix; HED *cont. prima*, pp. 138-9.

[46] DEC nos. 11-12 (but *cf.* no. 13), 23(*a*), 32(*c*).

[47] RAN ii no. 925.

[48] CR no. xxv; RAN ii no. 709.

[49] DEC no. 20.

[50] DEC nos. 17 and 20, and pp. 85-6.

[51] I do not know of any evidence to support the supposition that the Bishops of Durham had had their own sheriffs from the time of the Norman Conquest, as is claimed by G. T. Lapsley. *The County Palatine of Durham* (1900), pp. 81, 160.

have accepted so casually, was not viewed as a casual matter at all by Rannulf. Its significance for the future progress towards quasi-autonomy of the bishop's secular administration was considerable.

In Rannulf's time that administration still depended less on official or bureaucratic machinery than on the faithfulness of a handful of vassals. A major fascination of Rannulf's episcopate is the opportunity it provides of observing the emergence into at least the half-light of the class of episcopal tenants-in-chief, the barons of the bishopric. For the most part the members of the honorial baronage of Durham were not very big men, for they held little except from Durham. It may have been precisely this lack of external distractions which made them so active locally: the story how their heirs and successors during the thirteenth century created the feudal community of the bishopric remains one of the more interesting unwritten chapters of Durham's history; in some ways, I suspect, it parallels on a miniature scale the growth of the communities of the realm in England and Scotland. Not all nor perhaps even most of these families owed their status as Durham vassals to Bishop Rannulf. Conyers, Amundeville, Humez and Bonnville, for instance, may first have done fealty to Bishop William of St. Calais. The greatest land-owning family in the county, sprung from the Anglo-Scandinavian thegn Meldred, whose estates in west Durham stretched from Staindrop to Winlaton, most of the way between Tees and Tyne, had probably been tenants of St. Cuthbert since well before the Norman Conquest. These ancestors of the Nevilles cannot be shown to have been in direct feudal relationship to the bishop in Rannulf's time or for long afterwards.[52] But others, like the Escollands at Seaham and Ralph of Winchester in Bedlingtonshire, probably owed their first footing in the north to Rannulf, while earlier-established families certainly had their fiefs augmented and their services more precisely defined.[53] Much must probably remain obscure about the details of the feudal map of Durham in the first quarter of the twelfth century. But it was then that the main lines were settled. In the generation after Rannulf tenancies from the bishop changed hands as the result of death or marriage or forfeiture, but few new ones needed to be created.[54]

These barons, bearing names from Normandy or Brittany or Anjou, formed the bishop's court and witnessed his charters; with their knights and dependents they provided the bishopric with elements of defence, of coercive force and of public opinion. Intermingled with them, scarcely by chance, were Rannulf's own relatives. Those four of his sons of whom we have certain notice—Ralph, Elias, Thomas and his unnamed brother—were all destined for careers in and at the expense of the Church. None of them left any mark on Durham's history except Ralph, patron of St. Godric, parson of Middleham and member of the Canterbury family of Archbishop Theobald. It was on his nephews and their descendants that Rannulf lavished grants of land Osbert the sheriff and Rannulf the archdeacon have been mentioned already Osbert was settled on the great episcopal fee of Bishop Middleham. William FitzRannulf. son of the archdeacon (so I continue to regard him, though Dr. Southern argues that he was son of the bishop), was granted a fief comprising Houghall, Harraton in Chester-le-Street, the two Herringtons in Houghton-le-Spring and Hawthorn in Easington.[55] Osbert's brother, Robert, though he met his violent end in the bishopric. seems to have held his lands from the Durham fee in Lincolnshire.[56] But yet another nephew, Richard, received fiefs at Horden, Silksworth, Eighton, Ravensworth and Blakiston in Norton, assessed for service at the extremely low figure of $1\frac{1}{4}$ knights

[52] DEC pp. 76–7.

[53] DEC nos. 19, 22, 26(a).

[54] On this the evidence of the returns of 1166 seems conclusive: *Red Book of the Exchequer*, ed. Hubert Hall, i (Rolls Series, 1896), 415–8.

[55] Southern, *op. cit.*, p. 201 and note; DEC nos. 11–13.

[56] DEC pp. 88–9.

RANNULF FLAMBARD AS BISHOP OF DURHAM (1099-1128)

in all.[57] Leave Durham for Newcastle or Wearmouth or Hartlepool or Yarm, and within an hour or so you would be riding by the lands of one or other of Rannulf's kinsmen. It was a situation in which the strands of hard-headed policy can no longer be unravelled from those of family affection and duty, about which the social anthropologist may still find a word to say.

However successfully, even beneficially, Rannulf's exploitation of the bishopric in the interests of his kindred may have worked, it makes a very secular story. Maybe it is a scandalous one. Rannulf's was the kind of reputation round which shadows gathered. The shadows have seemed to grow darker as the result of the publication by Dr. C. H. Talbot a dozen years ago of a twelfth-century *Life* of Christina, the notable recluse and later prioress of Markyate, near St. Albans. According to the *Life*, before he became bishop Rannulf had had children by Christina's maternal aunt. Afterwards he married the aunt off to a townsman in Huntingdon, and was wont to lodge at their home in that town on his journeys between the north and London. On one such occasion—the date would be about 1114, when Christina was perhaps sixteen years old—he had the girl brought to his curtained chamber while, most regrettably, her parents were getting drunk in the hall below. Rannulf and Christina being alone, 'the shameless bishop' (I quote Dr. Talbot's translation) 'took hold of Christina by one of the sleeves of her tunic . . . and solicited her to commit a wicked deed.' The quick-witted girl asked, would it not be better to bolt the door first? The bishop agreed, and so she did, but with herself safe on one side of it and Rannulf on the other. Well, there is some amusement to be had from the picture of Rannulf biting his nails in baffled rage like bad Sir Jasper foiled in a Victorian melodrama. But if this story is true, it is really infinitely discreditable to him: after all, he was a bishop.

Is it true? It was not written down until forty or fifty years after the event which it purports to describe. If not invented by the biographer, its only source can have been Christina herself, and her evidence is not corroborated. Moreover, it serves almost too neatly to explain what Christina's biographer may well have felt embarrassment about explaining: why Christina, having taken a vow of chastity when very young, afterwards did get married (though, it is maintained, without breaking her vow). For the *Life* goes on to relate how Rannulf, in order to avenge himself, coerced Christina into marriage with a young nobleman. One suspects that Rannulf, long after his death, may be being made use of in no very scrupulous fashion. The *Life* is a work of edification. Its heroine had to be perfect, and to the ascetic ideals of the twelfth century marriage seemed to derogate from perfection. So Christina's putative marriage needed to be shown to be involuntary, and Rannulf's reputation was such that the worst could be expected of him. Evidence of the sort provided by the *Life* would hardly have convicted him in any court of law. Should historians be less exigent than lawyers in their demands for proof?[58]

This is not the only example of the way in which posterity was to make free with Rannulf's character. About the middle of the twelfth century Henry of Huntingdon put out an unlikely story concerning a papal legate in the past, John of Crema. Having legislated in his legatine council at Westminster in September 1125 against the English clergy's wives and women, Henry tells us, John was discovered that very same evening with a whore, and consequently left the country in haste and confusion. Fifty years later we find a monk at Winchester, possibly Richard of Devizes, improving this fiction by writing into it prominent and indecorous (though entertaining) parts for Bishop Rannulf and a niece of his.[59] Clearly, it was invention. But mud sticks—and

---

[57] DEC no. 23.

[58] *The Life of Christina of Markyate*, ed. C. H. Talbot (Oxford, 1959), pp. 40-44.

[59] Henry of Huntingdon, *Hist. Angl.*, ed. T. Arnold (Rolls Series, 1879), p. 246; *Ann. Wintoniae*, in *Ann. Monastici*, ed. H. R. Luard, ii (Rolls Series, 1865), 47-8; cf. J. T. Appleby, 'Richard of Devizes and the Annals of Winchester', *Bull. Inst. Historical Research* xxxvi (1963), 70-7.

VII

the learned German lady who demonstrated both the dependence of the Winchester account on Henry of Huntingdon and the worthlessness here of Henry, yet felt obliged to refer to Rannulf as 'the profligate [*sittenlos*] bishop of Durham'.[60]

We need not follow her in this. But when the more lurid tales are discounted, the problem of assessment remains. Was Rannulf just a vastly talented, jovial, full-blooded ruffian? To say that he was no worse than many of his kind, and outdid nearly all of them in courage, energy and intelligence, though probably true, does not close the question. Had he, who did so well out of the Church for himself and his in material terms, any sense of his responsibilities as distinct from his privileges as a churchman? A flat negative would be unjust. One would look in vain for any evidence of refined spirituality in Rannulf, or any hint of active sympathy with the ideals of the church reformers of his time. In no sense was he an intellectual: if Hildebert of Lavardin can be reckoned among his correspondents, it is only on the strength of a single, very short letter.[61] But he was judge of quality. He picked a clerk, William of Corbeil, who in twenty years had become archbishop of Canterbury; the hermit whom he chose to support was Godric of Finchale. The great translation of St. Cuthbert's body to the new cathedral on 29th August 1104 gives us glimpses of Rannulf's sense of occasion. There he was, outside the east end of the unfinished building, this sturdy, well-favoured and short-headed man, with his sloping forehead and bulging occiput, pomping a little, perhaps in his cope decorated with the myriad small pearls (his green cope embroidered with the large griffons had been lent to cover the body of the saint). Aloft for all to see he held that already venerable copy of St. John's Gospel, which maybe still survives at Stonyhurst. Was his crosier that English piece of work, of which the crook and ferule were found in 1874: 'made in a smithy where the traditions of Viking craftsmanship were still in active operation', and of a pattern perhaps especially congenial to Rannulf 'because he was at heart a Viking too'? Was his ring that massive gold circlet set with a single unengraved sapphire which was found at the same date as the crosier? For monkish tastes, Rannulf's sermon on that day was largely irrelevant and far too long; the sudden rain storm which brought it to a close seemed providential. But the point surely is, that he was capable of preaching and did preach.[62]

It might be argued, I suppose, that it was just his ambition and feeling for magnificence which led him to drive work on the cathedral triumphantly forward. But it was he who gave the land for Godric's hermitage and founded and endowed St. Giles's church in Durham and its hospital for the poor—and the record of that transaction (though we cannot assume that Rannulf drafted it himself) is very far from suggesting that he was an impious man.[63] Sometimes when prompted, sometimes spontaneously, so one of his monks tells us, he was indeed a genuinely charitable being.[64] It must be of some weight that the opinion of the convent turned in his favour. Above all, he was not insensitive to currents of opinion which he did not share. On 28th December 1115 King Henry attended the consecration of the new abbey church at St. Albans,

---

[60] Helene Tillmann, *Die päpstlichen Legaten in England bis zur Beendigung der Legation Gualas, 1218* (Bonn, 1926), p. 29, note 95.

[61] Ordericus calls him 'pene illiteratus', but this is hostile comment: *Hist. eccles.* x, 15, in Migne, PL clxxxviii, 758. Hildebert, *Epp.* iii, 1, in Migne, PL clxxi, 283.

[62] 'Corpore pulcher', says Ordericus, viii, 8, *ed. cit.,* col. 580; we can get an impression of Rannulf's physique from the description of his skeleton in J. T. Fowler, 'An account of the excavations made on the site of the Chapter-house of Durham Cathedral in 1874', *Archaeologia* xlv (1880), 387–9. *De miraculis et translationibus s. Cuthberti,* vii and xxi, *ed. cit.,* i, 260, ii, 361; *Wills and Inventories* i, ed. J. Raine, Surtees Soc., vol. 2, 1835, p. 2; T. D. Kendrick, 'Flambard's Crosier', *Antiquaries Jnl.* xviii (1938), 236–42, from whom I quote.

[63] DEC no. 9.

[64] HED *cont. prima,* p. 140. Even Ordericus has to admit it, x, 15, col. 758: 'licet crudelis et iracundus, largus tamen et plerumque jucundus et ob hoc plerisque gratus et amandus.'

performed by Bishop Robert Bloet of Lincoln supported by, among others, Roger bishop of Salisbury and Rannulf of Durham—as eminent a trio of high Caesarean prelates as even that reign could show.[65] Probably a few days before or after this, a significant transaction occurred. The king was persuaded to grant to Lincoln cathedral the churches of King's Norton in Northamptonshire and the land in Horley, Oxfordshire, which Rannulf bishop of Durham held from him. Churches and land were to go to increase the endowment of the prebend which Rannulf and his son Elias possessed in the church of Lincoln. Elias was to hold the prebend thus augmented for his lifetime; if he died before his father, the prebend was to remain with Rannulf. But after both were dead, it was to fall free and quit to God, St. Mary and the church of Lincoln and its bishop.[66] As usual, Rannulf had not neglected his family interests. But the charter suggests also that he had become aware of the emergence of a new sentiment and a new set of conventions. Elias was not expected to have an heir; the permanent alienation of church endowments for the profit of a clerical dynasty was no longer being felt tolerable. Ground was being yielded, however slowly, to the pressure of the church reformers; tribute was being paid, however grudgingly, to the success of their ideas. If, measured by their standards, Rannulf was often a bad churchman, at least he became better.

When all is said, perhaps he is able to withstand our scrutiny more successfully than we could his. He cleared Palace Green of its encumbrances—in the words of his biographer: 'He made as clear and level as a field the space between the cathedral and the castle, which had been invaded by numerous dwelling-places, lest the Church be soiled by their filth or emperilled by their fires.'[67] What would he make of us who, combining myopia with greed, now allow the skirts of one of the nobler buildings of the West to be defiled by a noisy congestion of smelly tin boxes?

[65] RAN ii no. 1102.
[66] *Registrum Antiquissimum* i, ed. C. W. Foster, Lincoln Record Soc., vol. 27, 1931, no. 33, pp. 26–7.
[67] HED *cont. prima*, p. 140.

VII

ADDENDA

p. 3/14 n. 1 line 4 at '(1933).':
The discussion of Rannulf in W. Fröhlich, 'Die bischöflichen Kollegen Anselms, ii', *Analecta Anselmiana*, ed. F. S. Schmitt, II (1970), 135–41, adds, I think, nothing significantly new.

p. 4/15 n. 7 at '176.':
Fröhlich, pp. 139–40. Cf. C. W. Hollister, 'The Anglo-Norman civil war: 1101', *English Historical Review* lxxxviii (1973), 333.

p. 7/18 lines 7–8 at 'At his ... metropolitan':
This statement (and cf. *Durham University Journal* lxvii (1974), p. 108) probably needs to be revised in the light of the authenticated transumpts of Scottish bishops' professions to York, made by John Pakenham, official of the Court of York and Mag. William Layton, notary public, on 13 November 1464, and surviving in British Library MS Harley 433. Among the 11 *scedule* of profession transumpted is one (fo. 260^v): 'Ego R[anulfus] sancte Lindisfarnensis ecclesie pontifex electus promitto sancte Ebor[acensis] ecclesie et domino Archiepiscopo Th[ome] eiusque successoribus canonicam obedienciam.' My attention was drawn to this by Mr M. G. Snape and Dr D. M. Smith. [Fuller treatment of this, together with Professor Offler's other additions and corrections to his *Durham Episcopal Charters 1071–1152*, Surtees Soc. clxxix (1968), will appear in M. G. Snape, *English Episcopal Acta: Durham 1153–1237*.]

p. 8/19 lines 37–8 at 'the chapel of St Alexis in the priory church':
[The word 'priory' appears to be a slip: although the entry referring to the dedication of the chapel of St Alexis does not specify its whereabouts, as similar entries at this point do, there seems no reason to think that it was not at St Albans abbey. See *Gesta abbatum monasterii S. Albani* (Rolls series 28) IV, 147–8; discussed O. Pächt, C. R. Dodwell and F. Wormald, *The St. Albans Psalter*, (London, 1960), p. 135.]

VIII

A NORTHUMBERLAND CHARTER OF KING HENRY I

While working on the Alnwick Castle muniments in 1965 Miss S. D. Thomson discovered a torn and crumpled scrap of parchment which she identified as a charter of King Henry I. With one possible exception,[1] this is the earliest royal charter known still to survive in Northumberland. This fact by itself would be sufficient justification for publishing it; but the document is interesting also for the light it throws on an obscure corner of Northumbrian feudal history. All the credit for the discovery is due to Miss Thomson, but my efforts to persuade her to publish it herself have been unavailing. I am most grateful to her for her generous assistance with the charter, and to its owner, the Duke of Northumberland, for his permission to print it.

The charter is now numbered Alnwick Castle ms. X. II. 1(2), and measures 7·25" × 3·25", excluding the seal tongue. It has suffered much hard treatment over the centuries: the seal has disappeared; most of the seal tongue has been torn away; and parts of the nine lines of text have been lost as the result of rubbing and tears. The scribe used unruled parchment. The hand appears very like that of a scribe known to have been active in the royal chancery late in Henry I's reign and into Stephen's. He is designated as Scribe XIII by Mr. Bishop, who gives 1127-1139 as the narrowest limits of his chancery career.[2] The charter is not endorsed. It has now been expertly repaired.

---

[1] That is, the Society's Ravensworth Deed no. 2, deposited at the Northumberland County Record Office. This too is a Henry I charter though it is concerned with lands in Co. Durham. Its date is probably August 1127; cf. P. Chaplais, EHR 75 (1960), 275.

[2] T. A. M. Bishop, *Scriptores Regis* (Oxford, 1961), pls. V(c) and XVII(a).

By permission of The Society of Antiquaries of Newcastle upon Tyne.

VIII

182

In the text which follows contractions in the original have been expanded without comment when there is no doubt what was intended; expansions about which any doubt can be felt have been put within parentheses and italicized. Conjectures to complete the mutilated text stand within square brackets.

H. rex Anglorum episcopo Dunelmensi et justic' et vic' et baronibus et omnibus m[inistris] et fidelibus suis de Norhu-(*m*)berlant francis et anglis, salutem. Sciatis me concessisse Radulfo de Chalgio in feodo et hereditate sibi et heredibus eius post eum terram Ellingeh(*am*) et Dochesf(*ord*) et Osburwic, quas Nic(*olaus*) de Grainuilla ei dedit cum nepte sua, sicut ipse eas ei dedit et [conce]ssit. Et volo et precipio quod bene et in pace et quiete teneat in bosco [et] plano, in pratis et p[ascuis,] in ecclesiis et molendinis, et cum omnibus earum [appe]nditiis, cum omnibus quie[tationibus] et libertatibus illis pertinentibus sicut [Nic(*olaus*) unquam] melius et quietius et hon[orificentius eas tenuit.] T(*estibus*) W(*illelmo*) de Alb-(*ineio*) et E[. . . . . .] et R(*oberto*) de Brus. Apud Wint(*oniam*).

Translation:
Henry king of the English to the bishop of Durham and his justiciar(s) and sheriff(s) and barons and all his officials and faithful men of Northumberland, both French and English, greeting. Know that I have granted to Ralph de Gaugy in fee and inheritance to him and his heirs after him the land Ellingham and Doxford and *Osburwic*, which Nicholas de Grenville gave him with his niece, just as Nicholas gave and [granted] them to him. And it is my will and command that he (Ralph) holds (them) well and in peace and without disturbance, in woodland and open field, in meadows and [pastures], in churches and mills and with all their [appurtenances], with all the immunities and franchises belonging to them, just as [Nicholas ever held them] best and most peaceably and [honourably]. Witnessed by William de Albini and E[. . . . . .] and Robert de Brus. At Winchester.

A NORTHUMBERLAND CHARTER OF KING HENRY I

No precise date can be suggested for this charter. William de Albini attests very frequently under Henry I, and Robert Brus not rarely; they witnessed at least one other royal charter together at Winchester, probably in the spring of 1121.[3] Just possibly the fact that the Bishop of Durham is given neither name nor initial indicates a date when the see was vacant, between the death of Bishop Rannulf in September 1128 and the appointment of Bishop Geoffrey Rufus in May 1133. But there are no really substantial grounds for narrowing the dating limits between *c.* 1120 and August 1133, when the king crossed over to Normandy for the last time. Nicholas's niece was Mabel, the elder daughter of his brother Walter. *Osburwic*, as Edward Bateson argued,[4] has probably been absorbed into what today is Newstead.

This discovery adds something to our knowledge of the tangled early history of the barony of Ellingham or Jesmond. As its alternative names suggest, this was a scattered fee, of which the northern members (Ellingham, Doxford and *Osburwic*/Newstead) lay far apart from the southern lands in Cramlington, Jesmond, Heaton and Hartley. One result of this has been that the barony has been discussed in at least three volumes of the *Northumberland County History*: by Edward Bateson in 1895, by H. H. E. Craster in 1909 and by Miss Hope Dodds in 1930.[5] It is common ground to them all that at the death of Henry I in 1135 the original grantee, Nicholas de Grenville, held the barony from the crown by service of three knights; they have good authority for this, as it seems, in the returns made by Nicholas's heirs to Henry II's enquiries in 1166.[6]

Miss Thomson's discovery shows, however, that by 1135

---

[3] *Regesta Regum Anglo-Normannorum* II, ed. C. Johnson and H. A. Cronne (Oxford, 1956), no. 1279.

[4] *NCH* II, 225.

[5] *NCH* II, 225 ff.; IX, 97 ff., XIII, 309 ff. There is a compact survey of the barony in I. J. Sanders, *English Baronies* (Oxford, 1960), p. 41.

[6] *Red Book of the Exchequer*, ed. Hubert Hall (Rolls Series, 1896), I, 438 (*carta* of Hugh de Ellington), 443 (*carta* of Ralph II de Gaugy). The editor's confusion about the text of Ralph's *carta* is not cleared up in his note. Ralph was claiming "esnecy" as son of the first-born sister.

Nicholas's immediate control was limited to the southern parts of his barony. Without knowing this evidence, Sir Edmund Craster inferred that Ellingham and its northern adjuncts must have been subinfeudated to Ralph I de Gaugy before 1161, though he supposed that this had happened in the time of Nicholas's nephew and heir William de Grenville.[7] Henry I's charter demonstrates that this enfeoffment had been carried out by 1133, as part of a marriage arrangement between Ralph and Nicholas's niece Mabilia. Ralph's title as a mesne tenant to Ellingham, Doxford and *Osburwic* was, then, clearly established by 1133; certainly the Gaugy claim to these lands was not just the result of the inheritance of the barony by Mabilia de Gaugy and her sister Alice on the death of their childless brother William de Grenville c. 1161-2.[8]

At this point a complication must be faced. On succeeding his father Eustace Fitz John as lord of Alnwick in 1157, William de Vesci secured from Henry II confirmation of the lands and fiefs which he claimed Eustace had held. Among them was "the whole fief of Ralph de Gaugy, that is to say Ellingham and Doxford and Osberwick and Heaton with their appurtenances".[9] What lay behind this claim that Ralph held his lands (including Heaton, part of the southern complex of the barony) not under Grenville, but under Alnwick? Craster's solution was to suggest that Ralph I de Gaugy must have died shortly before 1157, leaving an heir, Ralph II, under age, the wardship of whom came "by grant from Grenville or otherwise" to Eustace Fitz John.[10] Though this suggestion disposes very neatly of a difficulty, doubts may be felt about it. The crucial problem is the year

---

[7] *NCH* IX, 97.

[8] On the date of this succession, see Sir A. M. Oliver, *Early Newcastle Deeds* (Surtees Society vol. 137, 1924), p. 36, note. William accounted at the Exchequer at Michaelmas 1161: *PR* 7 Henry II, p. 23. The representatives of Mabilia and Alice, Ralph (either I or II) de Gaugy and Hugh de Ellington, accounted for relief at Michaelmas 1162: *PR* 8 Henry II, p. 11.

[9] *The Percy Chartulary*, ed. M. T. Martin (Surtees Society vol. 117, 1911), no. dcclix, p. 292.

[10] *NCH* IX, 97.

of Ralph I's death. He was certainly alive in 1154, which is the earliest possible date for his grant of Ellingham church to the convent of Durham;[11] he was dead by 1166, when it was his son, Ralph II, who made the return for the fee.[12] But the mentions of Ralph de Gaugy on the Pipe Rolls for 1162 and 1165 might apply to either father or son; the suggestion that Ralph I died in 1161 or 1162 is no more than reasonable conjecture.[13] Sir Edmund's theory demands not only that Ralph died five or six years before this, but also that his heir was under age at the time of his death. On the evidence of Henry I's charter, Ralph's marriage to Mabel de Grenville may have taken place in the 1120's; there would thus have been plenty of time for an heir to have reached full age before 1156/7. These considerations make the suggestion of Vesci wardship over Gaugy seem less attractive. But even if this suggestion is rejected, the evidence that Gaugy held under Alnwick is not confined to the royal confirmation of William de Vesci's claims in 1157.

The Grenvilles were benefactors of St. Cuthbert's monastery at Durham. At an early date Nicholas granted to the monks the church of Ellingham together with land in Cramlington and a fishery in the Tyne.[14] The grant of Ellingham church did not take effect; it was not included in Pope Eugenius III's confirmation of the monks' possessions in 1146, though the other items in Nicholas's grant were.[15] Henry I's charter suggests the reason: Ralph de Gaugy had become established at Ellingham and kept the church under his own control. Nicholas de Grenville must have survived

---

[11] Durham, Treasury of the Dean and Chapter, 4.2. Spec. 2: printed in *Feodarium Prioratus Dunelmensis*, ed. William Greenwell (Surtees Society vol. 58, 1872), p. 100, note; *NCH* II, 228, note 5. The dating limits are given by the attestation of Prior Absalon and the inclusion of Ellingham church among the monks' possessions confirmed by Pope Hadrian IV on 3 February 1157: W. Holtzmann, *Papsturkunden in England* II (Berlin, 1935), no. 94, p. 276.
[12] *Red Book* I, 443.
[13] *PR* 8 Henry II, p. 11; 11 Henry II, p. 28; Oliver, p. 37.
[14] Durham, 4.2. Spec. 7: printed in *Feodarium*, p. 99, note; *NCH* II, 226, note 3.
[15] Holtzmann, *Papsturkunden* II, no. 51, pp. 205-7.

for some years into Stephen's reign, for he secured from Henry, son of King David of Scotland, confirmation of his grant to Durham of the Tyne fishery and the land in Cramlington, and it seems safe to assume that this was after Henry had become Earl of Northumbria in April 1139.[16] Again there was no mention of Ellingham church: presumably because by this time Ralph was its lord, not Nicholas. But the monks persisted in their aim of acquiring St. Maurice's church at Ellingham. Between 1154 and 1156 they succeeded in persuading Ralph I de Gaugy to give it to them, though the grant was hedged round with various safeguards for the rights of the existing incumbent and the reversion of the living was secured to whichever of Ralph's sons should be most suitable for it.[17] Most significantly, this grant was confirmed "so far as pertains to me" by William de Vesci, presumably in or soon after 1157, in a charter which implies his position as feudal superior over Ralph I rather than as guardian of Ralph II during the latter's nonage. Immediately after printing this document nearly a hundred years ago William Greenwell wrote: "Ellingham, when it was possessed by Gaugy, was held under Vesci."[18]

For the 1150's, at any rate, Greenwell seems right. On the other hand, Miss Thomson's discovery shows that by 1133 Ralph de Gaugy had been enfeoffed with Ellingham, Doxford and *Osburwic* to hold from Nicholas de Grenville. How had this change in his tenure taken place? Probably we shall never know in detail. In general there come to mind the exposed situation of the small Gaugy fief, so close to the strong Alnwick field of influence, and also the disordered conditions in the north-east during much of Stephen's reign. Small tenants like Grenville and Gaugy were liable to intense pressures from a local magnate of the standing of Eustace

---

[16] Durham, 4.2 Spec. 46: printed in *Feodarium*, p. 103, note.

[17] See note 11 above. The conditions were set out by Bishop Hugh du Puiset in a separate document, Durham, 3.1. Pont. 11: printed in *Feodarium*, p. 100, note; *NCH* II. 268, note 1.

[18] Durham, 4.2. Spec. 3: printed in *Feodarium*, p. 101, note. It seems clear that this document refers to Ralph I's grant in c. 1154-6, rather than to that by Ralph II c. 1172-4, on which see note 24 below.

Fitz John; they had little to hope from the king after 1139, and much to fear from the illwill of Eustace, especially after he had quarrelled with Stephen.[19] Though the fashion escapes us, there is no doubt about the fact: by some means or other Eustace acquired the service of Gaugy, and in 1157 William de Vesci was prepared to claim, and apparently was able to gain, recognition of this superiority as a matter of right. Nicholas de Grenville's barony seemed hopelessly split, and Gaugy fated to dependence on Alnwick.

In the event, matters took a different turn: the barony of Ellingham was reunited in the hands of Ralph de Gaugy's descendants. As we have seen, Nicholas's heir, William de Grenville, who can never have enjoyed more than the southern part of his uncle's barony, died childless in 1161-2. The inheritance which his sisters, Mabel (either already or soon to become the widow of Ralph I de Gaugy) and Alice (wife of Hugh de Ellington),[20] divided between them was the whole original Grenville fee, including the northern members once subinfeudated to Ralph. Mabel and her son, Ralph II de Gaugy, left the southern estates to the Ellingtons, and took Ellingham, Doxford and *Osburwic* for themselves.[21] In the capacity, it seems probable, of his mother's representative rather than of his father's heir, Ralph II contrived to step out of dependence on Vesci and into the position of tenant-in-chief occupied by his Grenville uncle and great-

---

[19] Cf. R. H. C. Davis, "What happened in Stephen's reign", *History* 49 (1964), 4.

[20] On Alice, see Oliver, pp. 36, 67.

[21] There was a complication caused by Nicholas de Grenville's enfeoffment of a knight called Galo or Golo with a third (or perhaps a quarter) of a fee: *Red Book* I, 443, 438. Robert the son of Gualo witnesses a charter by William de Grenville: *Feodarium*, p. 104. note. As Craster argues (*NCH* IX, 98), it is likely that Galo's fee was Hartley in Earsdon chapelry, and that this was the purpresture or concealed escheat for which William de Vesci accounted as sheriff in 1166, when it was called "terra Radulfi de Calgi" and was held by William himself: *PR* 12 Henry II, p. 76, cf. *PR* 13 Henry II, p. 73; these entries, it seems, misled Dr. Sanders into thinking that Ralph II de Gaugy was a minor until c. 1168 (*English Baronies*, p. 41). Hartley remained in the hands of the crown until 1176-7, when it was returned to Ralph II de Gaugy and Hugh de Ellington in exchange for their claims in Newburn: *PR* 23 Henry II, p. 82.

uncle. This phase of the story ends about 1180. By Michaelmas of that year Hugh de Ellington was dead; his wife Alice had predeceased him; his two daughters, the wives of Ralph Baard and Robert Bulmer, were, it is surmised, the children of another marriage, and did not inherit from Alice.[22] By paying a fine of 5 marks for 1½ fees Mabel and Ralph II de Gaugy gained possession of the southern members and so reconstructed the barony as it had once been held by Nicholas de Grenville.[23]

There is a small final puzzle. When Ralph II granted (or rather confirmed) Ellingham church to the monks of Durham c. 1172-4, he did so " with the consent and will of my heir Ralph ".[24] Ralph II had died by Michaelmas 1184, and his heir Ralph III, because he was under age, did not acquire the fief until 1194.[25] This makes it almost impossible to identify him with Ralph the heir in c. 1172-4. The latter may have been a collateral rather than a son of Ralph II; if he was a son, he may have died early, so that his name became available for a younger son, perhaps by a later marriage, who inherited as Ralph III in 1194.

[22] *NCH* XIII, 311.
[23] *PR* 26 Henry II, p. 142; cf. 27 Henry II, p. 49; 28 Henry II, p. 48.
[24] Durham, 4.2. Spec. 1: printed in *Feodarium*, p. 100. note; *NCH* II, 228, note 2. The limits of date are given by the attestations of Archdeacons John and Burchard; cf. *AA*[4] 33 (1955), 63-4.
[25] *PR* 31 Henry II, p. 10; 34 Henry II, pp. 5, 100; 2 Richard I, pp. 20-1; 6 Richard I, p. 124

IX

A note on the early history of the Priory of Carlisle

THE evidence for the early history of the priory in Carlisle has been thoroughly sifted by local scholars. It is so scanty that even a scrap of additional material may be worth noting. This consists of a short entry in an unpublished chronicle, a "Liber de gestis Anglorum" composed substantially of extracts from the Durham *Historia Regum* and the *Historia XXV Annorum* of John of Hexham in some Scottish monastery during the last quarter of the 12th century. Since 1899 the manuscript has been in the Bibliothèque nationale in Paris, and is numbered nouv. acq. lat. 692. On fo. 39 we read *Anno .M.c.ii. fundata est domus Karleoli*: "In the year 1102 a house [of religion] was founded at Carlisle." The main text of the chronicle at this point jumps from 1100 to 1105; the words quoted have been neatly added to complete a line at the end of the entry for 1100. They are not in the text hand, but do not appear much later than the text, and can be assigned with fair confidence to the end of the 12th century.

This seems by nearly a century the earliest chronicle notice of a post-Conquest religious foundation at Carlisle. In two manuscripts coming from the second half of the 14th century — British Museum, Cotton Claudius D.VII (the *Lanercost Chronicle*), and the Ingilby manuscript of the *Anonimalle Chronicle* of St Mary's, York, edited by Professor Galbraith — are to be found entries almost identical with each other concerning the early history of Carlisle Priory.[1] Since it is highly probable that the entries

[1] The passage is found in Claudius D. VII as an addition at the foot of fo. 58; printed by Canon J. Wilson in his introduction to Sir Herbert Maxwell's translation of the *Chronicle of Lanercost* (1913) pp. xiv-xv. Ingilby MS. fo. 2, printed by V. H. Galbraith, *The Anonimalle Chronicle* (Manchester, 1927), pp. xlvi-vii.

in these two manuscripts were drawn from a single source, the early lost part of the chronicle of Richard of Durham, who was at work between c. 1280 and 1297,[2] the tradition they represent can be carried back at least to the late 13th century. There seems little doubt that a similar though more concise statement in the 15th-century *Scotichronicon* was taken by Abbot Bower from the same line of tradition.[3]

Here we have a much more circumstantial account of the priory's foundation than the Paris manuscript affords. It goes thus: In 1101 or 1102 King Henry I, as the result of the activity and counsel of his queen, Matilda, set up a body of regular canons in the church of Carlisle. A certain priest named Walter who had come to England at the conquest with William the Bastard received from King William as his reward for arduous services the church of Carlisle, many other churches and a number of neighbouring vills. He founded the church of St Mary of Carlisle, and died not long afterwards. King Henry gave his lands and possessions to the canons regular, and made Adelwald, prior of Nostell, their first prior.[4]

Some, but by no means all, of this 13th-century tradition finds support in the record sources. A return of 1212, preserved in the Book of Fees, stated that Henry I gave to Walter his chaplain Linstock and Carleton for an annual cornage of 37s. 4d., and that later Walter, at the desire and with the permission of the king, took the religious habit in the priory of St Mary of Carlisle and gave all this land to the priory.[5] A royal charter for which the editors of the *Regesta Regum Anglo-Normannorum* suggest a date between May and August

---

[2] Galbraith, pp. xlvi-vii; cf. A. G. Little, "The authorship of the Lanercost Chronicle", *Franciscan Papers, Lists and Documents* (Manchester, 1943), 48.
[3] v 39, ed. Goodall (1759), i 289.
[4] Claudius gives the date 1102; Ingilby, 1101. The latter does not give Walter's name, nor call Adelwald the *first* prior of the canons of Carlisle. Canon Wilson's reading, *Henricus [episcopatum]*, from Claudius should presumably be amended to *Hic ecclesiam*, as in Ingilby.
[5] *Book of Fees* i 199.

1127 does indeed grant in alms and quit of cornage to God, St Mary and the canons of Carlisle all the churches and land which Walter the priest had possessed (*que fuit Walteri presbiteri*)[6]; on the Pipe Roll for 31 Henry I the canons appear relieved of 37s. 4d. for cornage, which it is safe to identify as Walter's annual render for Linstock and Carleton. But this evidence, while it points to Walter the priest or chaplain as a benefactor of the regular canons of Carlisle, suggests that he became so pretty late in Henry I's reign rather than at the beginning of the century, and Henry's other known grant to the canons also belongs to the 1120's.[7]

Such considerations, together with inferences drawn from the history in general of the establishment of the Austin canons in England and of Henry's I's dealings with them, have caused scholars in modern times to conclude that the Augustinian priory which was afterwards to form the cathedral chapter of Carlisle was founded not in 1101/2, as the 13th-century tradition would have it, but as a consequence of Henry I's visit to Carlisle in 1122.[8]

The evidence of the Paris manuscript does not invalidate this conclusion, which I do not wish to contest. But it does strengthen the case for treating seriously the suggestion that before the Austin canons were established at Carlisle there was an older foundation, dating back to 1101 or 1102, for a religious community of some unspecified kind — a possibility not absolutely neglected nor denied by modern scholars, but to which some have been reluctant to attach much weight.[9]

[6] *Regesta Regum Anglo-Normannorum* ii, ed. C. Johnson and H. A. Cronne (1956), no. 1491.
[7] *Ibid.*, no. 1431, for which the editors suggest the date October 1125.
[8] J. E. Prescott's discussion in *The Register of Wetheral*, appendix B, 478 ff. is still fundamental. Cf. J. Wilson in *VCH Cumberland* ii 7 ff and 131; J. C. Dickinson, "The origins of the cathedral of Carlisle", CW2 xlv 134 ff.; id., *The Origins of the Austin Canons* (1950) 245 ff.
[9] Cf. Dickinson, "Origins", 136, n. *. Dr D. Nicholl, *Thurstan, archbishop of York* (York, 1964) 147 and n. 143, allows the possibility of an earlier religious community at Carlisle, though by a slip he puts the beginning of this community, on the evidence of the Ingilby MS., in 1100 instead of 1101.

IX

179 EARLY HISTORY OF THE PRIORY OF CARLISLE

When a Carlisle jury in 1278-9 alleged that a house of religion had been founded there about 180 years before, it was wrong if it meant the Augustinian priory, but perhaps not far off the mark if it was referring to an earlier house.[10] The Paris manuscript does not name the founder of this house, but in the light of Henry I's charter of 1127 and the entry in the Book of Fees it would be difficult to reject the Lanercost tradition that he was Walter the priest or chaplain: a tradition repeated (rather than confirmed) by such later witnesses as a note in the lost register of Bishop Strickland (1400-1419) and John Leland in the 16th century.[11]

If we accept a foundation by Walter of some sort of conventual religious establishment at Carlisle in 1101/2, had Henry I anything to do with it, as the jurors of 1278-9 asserted and the 13th-century chronicle tradition seems in a rather muddled fashion to suggest? This has been rejected as improbable, on the grounds, *inter alia,* that at this time Henry was "far too much occupied in the southern part of his kingdom to trouble himself about the ecclesiastical affairs of a northern border town, which ten years before had been for two centuries an uninhabited heap of ruins."[12] It seems worth remarking that Richard of Durham, as reflected in the Lanercost and Ingilby manuscripts, and, presumably following him, Bower in the *Scotichronicon* have the king acting at the instigation of Queen Matilda. Since she died in 1118 this can hardly refer to the Augustinian priory founded in or after 1122. Possibly, of course, her name was dragged in by this line of tradition quite gratuitously: in the hope, for example, of gaining the benevolence of the Scots, to whose ruling-house she belonged. But we do not know at what date Henry granted Linstock and Carleton to Walter; it may have been quite early in the reign — as early, e.g. as he granted to his chaplain Richard d'Orval four of

---

[10] Cumberland Assize Roll 132, m. 32, quoted *VCH Cumberland* ii 9.
[11] *Ibid.,* ii 8, n. 1; John Leland, *Collectanea* i (ed. alt., 1774) 120-121.
[12] Prescott, 482; cf. Dickinson, *Austin Canons,* 246; "Origins" 136.

the six Northumbrian churches which later went to increase the endowments of the Austin canons at Carlisle.[13] If so, Henry's grant to Walter may have represented a benefaction to the latter's foundation. However this may be, *a priori* argument against any early action on Henry's part based on his alleged lack of interest in the north at this time is unconvincing. There are, on the contrary, indications that his accession in 1100 precipitated an important change in the ecclesiastical administration of the far north-west. For a few years after William Rufus's seizure of Carlisle and its district in 1092 it seems to have been intended that this new acquisition should be subjected to the ecclesiastical authority of St Cuthbert's see, which had connexions with this area going back to the 7th century.[14] Between 1092 and 1095 a royal writ ordered W. son of Thierry and all the king's lieges of Carlisle and all who abode beyond the Lowther to accept the spiritual jurisdiction of the Bishop of Durham and his archdeacon; Archbishop Thomas I of York reinforced this order with his metropolitical authority.[15]

During the vacancy of the see of Durham between 1096 and 1099 another royal writ ordered the sheriff and barons of Carlisle to obey the archdeacon of Durham in all spiritual matters as in the time of Bishop William (of St Calais).[16] We shall never know what part, if any, in formulating these orders was played by Rufus's right-hand man, Ranulf Flambard, who himself became Bishop of Durham in June 1099. But we do know that one of Henry I's first actions after his accession in August 1100 was to disgrace and imprison Flambard, and that during Flambard's subsequent exile Durham's claims to

---

[13] *Regesta Regum Anglo-Normannorum* ii, no. 572, with 1102 as a possible date.

[14] Cf. Sir Edmund Craster, "The patrimony of St Cuthbert", *Eng. Hist. Rev.* lxx (1954) 181.

[15] Dugdale, *Monasticon* (1817), i 241, no. vi; Craster, "A contemporary record of the pontificate of Ranulf Flambard", *Archaeologia Aeliana*, 4th series, vii (1930) 38.

[16] *Monasticon* i 241, no. vii.

jurisdiction over Carlisle were lost for good and all.[17] Into the sphere thus left vacant stepped York, with the Bishop of Glasgow attempting to intervene from the north, until the setting up of the see of Carlisle in 1133. It seems clear that at the beginning of his reign, round about the year 1101/2, Henry I had indeed good reasons to interest himself in ecclesiastical arrangements in the Carlisle area. There might be calculable profits for him in supporting the foundation in Carlisle of a house of religion by a locally influential royal chaplain. But this can be no more than conjecture, based on a tradition a century younger than the laconic but quite definite entry in the Paris manuscript.

---

[17] Symeon of Durham, *Historia Dunelmensis Ecclesiae, cont. prima*, ed. T. Arnold (Rolls Series, 1882), 139.

X

HEXHAM AND THE *HISTORIA REGUM*

The *Historia Regum* attributed to Symeon of Durham is a tricky source to handle. The more welcome, then, was Mr. P. Hunter Blair's scrutiny of it in 1963, carrying a good deal further the survey he had published in 1939.[1] His argument that the only surviving manuscript of the whole work—Corpus Christi College, Cambridge, ms. 139—comes from the Cistercian monastery of Sawley in the West Riding has been most happily clinched now that Professors Vaughan and Cheney have been able to make out the Sawley *ex libris* mark on the first page.[2] The date, *c*. 1170, which he suggests for the compilation of this manuscript [C] as a whole, seems an acceptable approximation.[3] Especially valuable is Mr. Blair's careful separation of the various layers which make up this highly composite history. He distinguishes no less than nine of these and groups them into three main divisions. To the first he allots the material from the beginning of the compilation down to 887, which has been worked over by a single idiosyncratic editor; this part comprises the legends of the Kentish saints, the list of Northumbrian kings from Ida to Ceoluulf, material derived from Bede, a series of annals from 732 to 802, and another series from 849 to 887, derived mainly from Asser. The second main division contains a chronicle from 888 to 957; the third, a chronicle from 848 to 1129. This scheme refines on the division of HR into two overlapping chronicles, 732 to 957 and 848 to 1129, made by the nineteenth-century editors and generally accepted since.[4] There are good reasons for the change Mr. Blair proposes. It seems that in future we shall need to speak not just of SD[1] and SD[2], as W. H. Stevenson did,[5] but of SD[1] (to 887), SD[2] (888 to 957) and SD[3] (848 to 1129). And if on stylistic grounds it is difficult, as Mr. Blair hints,[6] to avoid the conclusion that SD[1], which relies extensively on Asser, was worked over by a single editor in the tenth century, here is an obstacle to be surmounted by those who think it a plausible hypothesis that Asser's *Life* was not written until the first half of the eleventh.[7]

Mr. Blair's essay has notably helped our understanding of HR, and in particular of its earlier and intrinsically more important sections. One aspect of his discussion, however, seems to call for further consideration. It is that concerned with the fortunes of HR between the completion of its latest section, SD[3], which we assume to have occurred at Durham soon after 1129,[8] and the only complete surviving version of it finding a place *c*. 1170 in the miscellaneous collection of Northumbrian historical material which now makes up Corpus Christi ms. 139.

Obviously, any debate must begin from this manuscript, C. That C, like the companion collection of historical treatises now divided between the two Cambridge mss., University Library Ff. 1. 27 and Corpus Christi 66,[9] once belonged to Sawley is now beyond doubt. It is true, as Mr. Blair points out, that the contents of C as a whole show much interest in Yorkshire material and some special knowledge of Yorkshire geography;[10] whether C's concern with Cistercian affairs is more pronounced that it is natural to expect in a Northumbrian monastic compilation at this period is perhaps less certain. But Mr. Blair's inference that, since C comes from the same scriptorium as the Sawley elements in the other two Cambridge manuscripts just mentioned, it 'therefore must itself be a Sawley book'[11] need, I think, be true only in the sense that Sawley once owned these manuscripts. No proof is

X

offered that they were written there, and Mr. Blair hardly seems justified in going on to refer to C as a book 'written at Sawley'.[12] It may have been written there, but it is not certain that it was. Together with its companion volume it may have come to Sawley as the result of gift or purchase.

    This point has some significance. It has long been accepted that C offers a version of HR which to some extent departs from the lost Durham original (let us call this O); commonly it has been assumed that this rehandling of O took place at Hexham. His conviction that C was written at Sawley, however, has encouraged Mr. Blair to deny this supposed Hexham influence.[13] Though he allows that S.aa. 740 and 781 SD[1] has been interpolated by a propagandist writing in the interests of Hexham, he is reluctant to admit that this was done at Hexham itself. His supposition throughout seems to be that such alterations as C may show from the original form of HR were made either when C was being written at Sawley or in the course of, as it were, a Cistercian circuit via Fountains and Newminster on the way to Sawley.[14] It is true that earlier scholars made somewhat facile use of the hypothesis of Hexham influence on the evolution of C. For the Rolls Series editor of HR, Thomas Arnold, the Hexham explanation served as a kind of master key for every sort of difficulty; M. R. James called C itself the work of a Hexham scribe, though this claim does not seem susceptible of proof.[15] Mr. Blair's reaction is thus natural, and to some extent it is justified. But I feel that he has carried it too far. That no direct Hexham influence was felt anywhere along the line of tradition between O and C, as he infers,[16] seems questionable for a number of reasons.

    In the first place this conclusion pays too little attention to the evidence of the version of part of HR to be found in the late twelfth-century Paris manuscript, 'Bibliothèque nationale, nouv. acq. lat. 692'.[17] This manuscript [P] contains a 'Liber de gestis Anglorum' composed of extracts from HR (a few from SD[1], but mostly from SD[3]) and (*pace* Mr. Blair)[18] almost the whole of John of Hexham's *Historia XXV Annorum*, which continued HR from 1130 to 1153 and is found immediately following HR in C. Both for its extracts from HR and for John of Hexham's chronicle the text of P is very close to, and at times rather better than, that of C.[19] Neither can derive directly from the other. It seems necessary to postulate a common (and probably not very distant) ancestor to both. This ancestor (let us call it X) already had John's *Historia* following HR as its continuation. There seems no doubt that John's chronicle was planned as a continuation of HR; it is reasonable to suppose that before John could form his plan a copy of HR was available to him. Already at the stage of X John's work had been written and combined with HR. And surely the obvious place for this combination to have occurred at was the home of the author of the continuation, i.e. Hexham? The existence of X, which the nature of P's text makes it necessary to assume, rules out any theory that HR and John's continuation were first brought together in C, whether it was at Sawley or elsewhere that C was written. If it was in X that the two works were first combined, then probability points to Hexham as the place whence X originated.[20]

    Again, if we accept that the long interpolations concerning the Hexham bishops Acca and Alchmund which appear in HR 740 and 781 were, as Mr. Blair says,[21] 'the work of a skilful Hexham propagandist', it is natural to assume, as Arnold assumed, that propaganda for Hexham was made at Hexham. Mr. Blair's objection that this is not a necessary assumption is doubtless formally correct.[22] But he is hardly entitled to give no weight at all to inherent probability and to go on to say later that there is no reason for supposing that the interpolations were written at Hexham,[23] especially as there seem good grounds for disqualifying his alternative candidate for authorship, Ailred of Rievaulx. Ailred indeed had strong sympathies with Hexham, where his forbears had flourished for generations. His account of the Hexham saints, *De sanctis Ecclesiae Haugustaldensis,* written in connexion with the great translation of 1155, shows some similarities, even verbal ones, to the Acca and Alchmund interpolations in HR. But this does not demonstrate that Ailred was the interpolator. Other explanations for the similarities can be offered. Ailred may have used a version of HR already containing the interpolations; or both Ailred and an interpolator may have used a common source now lost;[24] or, as seems most likely to me, the interpolator may have borrowed from Ailred. What can hardly be explained, if Ailred is to be made responsible for the interpolations as well as for *De sanctis,* is the fact that the interpolator, by inference, refers to Acca a miracle of protection against Malcolm Canmore for which *De sanctis* gives the credit to St. Wilfrid and St. Cuthbert.[25] Another line of argument, admittedly more subjective, drawn from stylistic considerations, also makes it difficult to accept Ailred as the author of the interpolations. The Acca miracles in *De sanctis* Chapters 8, 9 and 11 are presented with artistry; their equivalents in the HR interpolations do not exceed the level of ordinary craftsmanship. The account of the wonder at Alfred Westou's translation of Alchmund found in *De sanctis* Chapter 12 is probably the basis for the paraphrase in the HR interpolation at 781.[26] If we conclude that the 740 and 781 interpolations, though not to be ascribed to Ailred, derived from *De sanctis,* they cannot have been made before 1155.[27] The likelihood that they were composed at Hexham remains strong.

There are other indications that HR was known at Hexham by the middle of the twelfth century. In his treatise *De statu Hagustaldensis ecclesiae* Richard of Hexham used a version of the early Northumbrian annals 732-802 very similar to, if not exactly the same as that preserved in the part of the C version of HR we designate SD^1.[28] No source other than HR is known from which he could have taken them. Moreover, comparison of Richard's *De statu* i, 14-15 with the first part of the HR interpolation for 740 shows that here either Richard was copying the interpolator, or vice-versa.[29] Whichever way the influence flowed, Hexham is the most likely place for it to have occurred.

Thus there is still a reasonable case for supposing that between its original form *O* and its surviving form in C the text of HR experienced a Hexham interlude. Against it Mr. Blair brings no more than two arguments, neither of which seems conclusive.[30] To the first, that 'nowhere in the whole book is there any hint of an awareness of the Hexham translations of 1155', it seems a fair answer that C offered no opportunity to discuss the translations at the appropriate date, 1155, since HR ended in 1129 and its continuation, *Historia XXV Annorum,* in 1153. That the interpolator did not mention s.a. 740 or 781, the translations of 1155, does not prove that he did not know of them: as has been pointed out, there are indications that he may have used Ailred's *De sanctis,* which was written for that occasion. Mr. Blair's second objection, that the disjunct and interrupted presentation of John of Hexham's *History* in C cannot have been the work of a Hexham scribe, would be convincing only if the case for Hexham influence on C assumed a Hexham scribe for the manuscript. But it need make no such assumption. Moreover, P, deriving from the same ancestor, *X,* as C, presents John of Hexham in a continuous and orderly fashion. Why the scribe of C indulged in a muddle about the order of John of Hexham is a mystery; but the muddle cannot be used to argue away a Hexham influence on C's ancestry. It is now fully established that C

x

was once owned by Sawley; where it was written is still uncertain, though clearly we must be chary of attributing it to a Hexham scribe. Nevertheless there are still good grounds for believing that the text of HR was considerably rehandled and interpolated at Hexham, and that its presence there supplied the impulse for John of Hexham to compose his continuation of it.

By excising the obvious interpolations in C s.aa. 740 and 781 we can get somewhat nearer to the original form of HR. Can means be found to arrive at a more detailed assessment of the discrepancies between C and O? Two facts may help us to make at least some progress in this direction. First, until half way through his entry for 1118 Symeon, the author-compiler of the third part of HR, SD^3, extracts copiously and on the whole literally from the Latin chronicle of Worcester attributed to Florence [LCW], which forms the stock on to which Symeon grafts the rest of his material; to complete 1118 and for 1119 he borrows in the same fashion from Eadmer.[31] Second, other chronicles survive which had used HR as a main source before it had been rehandled in the fashion C displays. When the text of these chronicles agrees with HR's habitual sources, while C departs from them, there are grounds for suspecting that what C offers did not stand in O.

Among the chronicles which used HR thus are the Durham *Historia post Bedam* and the first part (732 to 1171) of the *Chronicle of Melrose*.[32] For purposes of comparison with C and LCW it is the *Historia post Bedam* [HPB] which offers by far the widest basis. This work, completed shortly after 1148,[33] was in turn taken over by Roger of Howden to form the first part of his chronicle. Two good manuscripts of HPB survive, one of which—now St. John's College, Oxford, ms. 97—was listed among the books in the monastic library at Durham in 1395 and has an index dated 1532 compiled by the Durham monk Thomas Swalwell; the readings of both manuscripts are to be found in the apparatus of the Rolls Series edition of Howden.[34] From them it is possible to trace HPB's dependence on HR. From time to time excising rhetoric and abbreviating its source, HPB follows SD^1 pretty faithfully from 732 to 802. Then Henry of Huntingdon becomes its source for a history of the West Saxon kings from 752 down to the accession of Æthelberht in 860. At this point HPB starts to transcribe SD^3 (from its beginning in 848), and continues to do so (though occasionally giving preference to SD^1 or SD^2)[35] down to the close of 1121, after which it relies again on Henry of Huntingdon until it ends in 1148.

Comparison between the text of HR offered by C, HPB and the ultimate source of both, LCW or Eadmer, is especially illuminating in passages found in HR s.aa. 1070, 1107, 1108 and 1119 (see Appendix, where they are set out in full). In all five examples (the year 1107 provides two) the text of HPB is quite clearly closer to the sources of HR—LCW and Eadmer —than is that given by C. Since HPB is based on a version of HR current by 1148 (either O or a cognate manuscript), its discrepancies from C can be explained in one of two ways. Either C does here follow O, while the compiler of HPB has taken the trouble in these instances to refer to O's sources and has decided to adhere to them more closely than O had done. This seems no more than a theoretic possibility. Or—much the more likely alternative—HPB is in fact following O as usual. If that be so, then the differences between C and HPB indicate differences between C and O. On this hypothesis C at times departs considerably from the original form of HR.

This process, it would seem, was already reflected to some extent in X, the common ancestor of C and the Paris manuscript we have called P. In the only one of the examples cited in the Appendix (no. 1) reproduced by P, the readings of C and P coincide; they will thus have stood in *X*. C's reading s.aa. 1003, 1047, 1048 and 1069 of *Danubia* for the *Denemercia* or *Danemarcia* of LCW and HPB is substantiated by P 1069, the only one of these entries which it contains; C's *Brittones* for the *Waloni* of LCW and HPB s.aa. 1063, 1064, 1065, 1102 and 1116 appears in P 1063 and 1064 (P does not give the other entries). So in all probability *Danubia* and *Brittones* appeared in *X*. Even if C was written at Sawley—which is by no means certain—the fact that these alterations had already occurred in C's exemplar would mean that they were not made at Sawley. As has been indicated above, it is likely that the interpolations shown by C s.aa. 740 and 781 were introduced at Hexham. There seem better reasons for affirming than denying that other alterations also were made there.

Let us revert to the examples in the Appendix. Numbers 1-3 and 5 all disclose a single tendency on the part of C: to soften statements in the southern sources, LCW and Eadmer, which were hostile or injurious to York and its archbishop. In No. 1 C tones down the Worcester chronicler's outspoken condemnation of what he alleges had been Thomas I of York's attempts to depress and subject the church of Worcester. C's departures from its habitual source in numbers 2 and 3 seem concerned to blunt any claim to supremacy of Canterbury over York which might be built on LCW's account of Gerard of York's promise to Anselm in 1107. To present a better showing of the York case against Canterbury also seems to be the motive for C's deviating from Eadmer in number 5, the account of Thurstan's consecration by Pope Calixtus II at the Council of Rheims in 1119.[36] All this marked tendency of C in favour of York, it deserves to be stressed, is an argument for rather than against a Hexham phase in the evolution of C. Writing to Bishop Tunstall of Durham in 1532 Archbishop Edward Lee could say: 'I have a litle lordeshippe adioninge too youre Diocese nyar as I am enfourmed too Duresme than too Yorke, called Hexham.'[37] The harsh facts of border history in the late middle ages had made Hexham remote from York. Conditions were very different in the twelfth century. The house of regular canons at Hexham had been established by Archbishop Thomas II as a kind of York colony north of Tees, and it owned property and rights in Yorkshire; the prebend of Salton in the church of York was attached to the prior's office at Hexham;[38] during the century when both the known Hexham historians, Richard and John, held that office, we are entitled to suppose that Hexham's connexions with York were intimate. Its concern for the privileges of the church of York was not likely to be less than that of a Yorkshire Cistercian house like Sawley, whose filiation was extra-diocesan. Possibly the explanation why C in example number 4 shows the preamble to the statutes of the council of 1108 formulated in a slightly different fashion from LCW and HPB is that regular canons (as the canons of Hexham were) wished to emphasise that the statutes were not aimed directly at them. These departures of C at one and the same time from its sources and from HPB can thus serve to reinforce the case for supposing that substantial alterations in the original form of HR were made at Hexham.

Though it is a stronger case than Mr. Blair allows, it would not be safe to claim that all the alterations were made there. We must allow the possibility that after *O* had been rehandled at Hexham and *X* had been produced, it was subjected to further changes in Yorkshire as well as being joined there to the other Yorkshire material which bulks large in the contents of the Corpus Christi ms. 139 as a whole. In two passages which P otherwise gives in full, C shows slight additions deriving from specifically Yorkshire interest or Yorkshire knowledge; these additions are absent from LCW, HR's source, as well as from P.[38a] But even if one

X

assumes a Yorkshire as well as a Hexham phase in the emergence of the text of C from that of *O*, the Yorkshire phase need not, in any very significant fashion, be connected with Sawley.

Mr. Blair has indeed indicated four ways in which *O* may have been revised to produce C and he canvasses the possibility that some or all of this revision may have taken place at Sawley.[39] He mentions first the possibility that the compiler of *O* began SD[3] at 450, with the beginning of LCW, not at 848, as it stands in C. Second, that the Sawley scribe when dealing with the entry in SD[3] s.a. 1074 brought up to date the names in the lists of the abbots of York and Whitby. Third, that the account of the Northumbrian earls which appears s.a. 1072 in C had been moved there from an original position earlier in the chronicle (it stands s.a. 953 in HPB and s.a. 950 in *Chron. Melrose*). Fourth, that after HR had left Symeon's hands, in the SD[3] entries for 848 to 887 passages from Asser taken from the annals for the same period in SD[1] were combined with the main source, LCW.

The first point does not seem of much substance. If Symeon when compiling SD[3] had available—and there seems no reason to suppose that he had not—the material of SD[1] and SD[2], and his purpose was, as the initial rubric declares, to compose a history of the English kings from the death of Bede,[40] why should he have begun SD[3] at 450? As to Mr. Blair's second point, it seems doubtful whether the bringing up to date of the abbots' names s.a. 1074 can 'confidently be attributed to Sawley'. P omits the whole passage, but the additions may already have appeared in *X*. On the other hand we can feel confident that wherever the alterations touched on in Mr. Blair's third and fourth points were made, it was not at Sawley. For in both these cases the alterations appear in P as well as in C, and so derive from *X*.[41] If there is a specific Sawley contribution to C, it is probably to be sought in the various marginal additions and alterations made to the manuscript by hands later than that of the text, and also in the element of confusion caused by mistaken tampering with dates which were originally written correctly.[42] Such instances are not without interest. But in weight they cannot match the occasions when there are strong grounds for supposing that C preserves traces of a determined Hexham intervention to reshape the text of HR: for example, in SD[1] s.aa. 740 and 781; in SD[3] s.aa. 1070, 1107, 1108, 1116, 1119 and perhaps also 1112 and 1113.[43]

When HR is cited as a witness, then, it must be with discrimination. In SD[1] and SD[2] it preserves early materials of great importance, and Mr. Blair's study enables us to recognise the nature of their authority more readily than before. It is in its third section, SD[3], that HR shows most signs of having been altered between its original form, put together at Durham in or shortly after 1129, and the form in which it survives in C, the only basis for the printed versions. At times the right way to deal with a difficulty in HR may be to challenge the reliability of the printed text. We read for instance in HR s.a. 1018 of a mighty battle fought at Carham between the Scots and English, with Uhtred Waltheof's son, earl of the Northumbrians, opposed to Malcolm II, King of Scots, aided by Owen the Bald, King of Strathclyde. The battle at Carham is of capital importance in the history of Anglo-Scottish relations, if we can regard it as sealing the acquisition of Lothian by the King of Scots. But how could Earl Uhtred have taken part in this battle in 1018? For as HR (here following LCW) had already reported two years earlier, he was killed in 1016 by the order or with the connivance of King Cnut. It is hardly satisfactory to suppose that Uhtred is mentioned by HR in 1018 simply in error for his brother and successor Eadulf Cudel,[44] particularly as there is reason to doubt whether Owen the Bald was alive as late as 1018.[45] On the grounds that names are better remembered than dates, Sir Frank Stenton suggested that the battle of Carham should be set in some earlier year than 1018.[46] Before accepting this solution it seems worth remarking that HPB and *Chron. Melrose* s.a. 1018, both following a version of HR which is not C, mention the battle without naming the leaders. Very significantly, so too does P, fo. 30, which is here verbally identical with HPB. Possibly, then, the names of the leaders formed no part of HR's entry for 1018 about the battle of Carham in *O* or in *X*, and their appearance in C is the result of a late and presumably muddled addition from an unknown source. If the authority of C is reduced in this way there is little difficulty in accepting 1018 as the correct date of the battle of Carham. And this fits admirably with the account of the date, the antecedents and the nature of the battle which Mrs. Anderson has based on other Durham sources such as Symeon's *Historia Dunelmensis Ecclesiae* and the *De obsessione Dunelmi*.[47]

If C does depart here from its exemplar, there is no reason at all to suppose that this happened at Hexham. Nevertheless, it may be suggested, the character of HR as a Durham historical work was to some extent overlaid in the forty years or so between 1129 and the writing of C by what may broadly be called Hexham-York influences. Durham's standard national history after Bede became the *Historia post Bedam*, not the *Historia Regum*. The appropriation of HR by the Hexham-York historical tradition had for the most part already occurred before C was written. Despite Mr. Blair's objections, Hexham is the most likely place for this to have happened, though possibly Hexham was not solely responsible. The most likely time seems in the decade following 1155.[48] Possibly the text of HR was re-handled when John of Hexham's *History*, which was not finished until after May 1162, was added to it. If these suggestions are justified, the *Historia Regum* as we have it in print belongs not to the first third, but to the second half of the twelfth century.

APPENDIX

Italics denote coincidence of C and HPB with LCW or (in example 5) with Eadmer; omissions from their source texts are indicated by dots.

(1) LCW 1070 (ed. B. Thorpe, ii, 8): His gestis, reverendi Wlstani, Wigornensis episcopi, mota est iterum querela, episcopo jam consecrato Thoma, qui pro Eboracensi loqueretur ecclesia; et in consilio, in loco qui vocatur Pedreda celebrato, coram rege ac Doruberniae archiepiscopo Landfranco, et episcopis, abbatibus, comitibus, et primatibus totius Angliae, Dei gratia adminiculante, est terminata. Cunctis siquidem machinamentis non veritate stipatis, quibus Thomas ejusque fautores Wigornensem ecclesiam deprimere, et Eboracensi ecclesiae subjicere, ancillamque facere modis omnibus satagebant, justo Dei judicio ac scriptis evidentissimis detritis, et penitus annihilatis, non solum vir Dei Wlstanus proclamatas et expetitas possessiones recepit, sed et suam ecclesiam, Deo donante ac rege concedente, ea libertate liberam suscepit, qua primi fundatores ejus, sanctus rex Aethelredus, Osherus Hwicciorum subregulus, caeterique Merciorum reges, Kenredus, Aethelbaldus, Offa, Kenulfus, eorumque successores, Eadwardus Senior, Aethelstanus, Eadmundus, Edredus, Eadgarus ipsam liberaverant.

X

C: *His gestis, reverendi Wlstani Wigornensis episcopi mota est iterum querela, episcopo jam consecrato Thoma, qui pro Eboracensi loqueretur ecclesia; et in concilio in loco qui vocatur Pedreda celebrato, coram rege ac Doroberniae archiepiscopo Lanfranco, et episcopis, abbatibus, comitibus, et primatibus totius Angliae . . . terminata est . . . Siquidem . . . non solum vir Dei Wlstanus proclamatas et expetitas possessiones recepit, sed et suam ecclesiam, Deo donante ac rege concedente, ea libertate liberam suscepit, qua primi fundatores ejus . . . eorumque successores . . . ipsam liberaverant.*

HPB: *His gestis, reverendi Wlstani Wigornensis episcopi mota est iterum querela, episcopo jam consecrato Thoma, qui pro Eboracensi loqueretur ecclesia; et in concilio, in loco qui vocatur Pedreda celebrato, coram rege ac Doroberniae archiepiscopo Lanfranco, et episcopis, abbatibus, comitibus, et primatibus totius Angliae, Dei gratia adminiculante, est terminata. Cunctis siquidem machinamentis* nequaquam *veritate* suffultis, *quibus* Thomas *Eboracensis archiepiscopus ejusque fautores Wigornensem ecclesiam deprimere, et Eboracensi ecclesiae subjicere, ancillamque facere modis omnibus satage*bat, *justo Dei judicio, ac scriptis evidentissimis, detritis et penitus annihilatis, non solum vir Dei Wlstanus proclamatas et expetitas possessiones recepit, sed et suam ecclesiam, Deo donante* et *rege concedente, ea libertate liberam suscepit, qua primi fundatores ejus, sanctus . . . Athelredus* et *Osherus Hwicciorum subregulus,* sanctus videlicet, *Cenredus, Athelbaldus, Offa,* sanctus *Kenulfus* pater Kenelmi martyris, *eorumque successores* ac postea totius Angliae monarchiam obtinentes, scilicet *Eadwardus senior, Athelstanus, Eadmundus, Edredus, Eadgarus* pater Eadwardi regis et martyris illorumque successores *liberaverant.*

(2) LCW 1107 (Thorpe, ii, 56): Gerardus Eboracensis archiepiscopus sua manu imposita manui Anselmi, ut ipse volebat, interposita fide sua, pollicitus est, se eandem subjectionem et obedientiam ipsi et successoribus ejus in archiepiscopatu exhibiturum, quam Herefordensi ecclesiae ab eo sacrandus episcopus illi promiserat.

C: *Gerardus Eboracensis archiepiscopus sua manu imposita manui Anselmi . . . pollicitus est se* illam *subjectionem et obedientiam ipsi . . . in archiepiscopatu exhibiturum, quam Herefordensi ecclesiae ab eo sacrandus episcopus . . . promiserat.*

HPB: *Gerardus Eboracensis archiepiscopus sua manu imposita manui Anselmi, ut ipse volebat, interposita fide sua, pollicitus est, se eandem subjectionem et obedientiam ipsi et successoribus ejus in archiepiscopatu exhibiturum, quam illi promiserat* cum ad *Herefordens*em *ecclesi*am *ab eo sacrandus* esset.

(3) LCW 1107 (Thorpe, ii, 56): Willelmus Wintoniensi, Rogerus Searesbyriensi, Reignelmus Herefordensi, Willelmus Excestrensi, et Urbanus Glamorgatensi ecclesiae, quae in Walonia est, electi episcopi, simul Cantwariam venerunt, et in die Dominica, quae fuit iii idus Augusti, pariter ab Anselmo consecrati sunt, ministrantibus sibi in hoc officio suffraganeis ipsius sedis, Gerardo, scilicet, archiepiscopo Eboracensi, Rotberto Lincoliensi, Johanne Bathoniensi, Hereberto Northwicensi, Rotberto Cestrensi, Radulfo Cicestrensi, Rannulpho Dunholmensi.

C: *Willelmus Wintoniensi, Herefordensi Reinelmus, Searesberiensi Rogerus, Willelmus Execestrensi, et Urbanus Glamorgacensi ecclesiae, quae in Walonia est, electi episcopi simul Cantuariam venerunt, et in die Dominica, quae fuit iii idus Augusti, pariter ab Anselmo consecrati sunt, ministrantibus sibi in hoc officio suffraganeis ipsius sedis.* Gerardus etiam Eboracensis archiepiscopus eorum consecrationi, rogatu Anselmi, interfuit.

HPB: *Willelmus* Giffard *Wintoniensi, Rogerus Searesberiensi, Reinelmus Herefordensi* ecclesiae, *Willelmus Excestrensi, et Urbanus Glamorgacensi ecclesiae, quae in Walonia est, electi episcopi simul Cantuariam venerunt et . . . iii idus Augusti, Dominica, pariter ab Anselmo consecrati sunt, ministrantibus sibi in hoc officio* suo *suffraganeis* suae *sedis, Gerardo scilicet archiepiscopo Eboracensi, Roberto Lincolniensi, Johanne Bathoniensi, Hereberto Nortwicensi, Roberto Cestrensi, Radulfo Cicestrensi, Rannulfo Dunelmensi.*

(4) LCW 1108 (Thorpe, ii, 57): Haec sunt statuta de archidiaconibus, presbyteris, diaconibus, subdiaconibus et canonicis in quocunque gradu constitutis.

C: *Haec sunt statuta de archidiaconibus, presbyteris, diaconibus, subdiaconibus et canonicis* saecularibus.

HPB: *Haec sunt statuta de archidiaconibus, presbyteris, diaconibus, subdiaconibus, et canonicis in quocunque gradu constitutis.*

(5) Eadmer, *Hist. nov.* 1119 (ed. Rule, p. 256): Ne putet rex me de negotio quo de (*sic*) agit quavis ratione secus acturum quam ipse velit. Nec enim me unquam ad hoc mea voluntas tulit, ut Cantuariensis ecclesiae dignitatem, cui tot praeclari patres, ut pene toti mundo notissimum est, praesederunt, quoquo modo humiliem.

C: *Ne putet,* inquit, *rex me de negotio de quo agit . . . secus acturum quam* ratio exigit. *Nec enim me . . . ad hoc mea* fert *voluntas, ut Cantuariensis ecclesiae* justam *dignitatem . . . humiliem.*

HPB: *Ne putet,* inquit, *rex, me de negotio de quo agit, quavis ratione secus acturum quam ipse velit: nec enim me unquam ad hoc mea tulit voluntas, ut* antiquam *Cantuariensis dignitatem . . . humiliem.*

NOTES

1. 'Some observations on the *Historia Regum* attributed to Symeon of Durham', in *Celt and Saxon. Studies in the early British Border,* Cambridge, 1963, pp. 63-118; 'Symeon's History of the Kings', *A.A.*[4], XVI, (1939), 89-100.
2. 'Obs.' 118.
3. 'Obs.' 70; but cf. pp. 78 and 112, where Mr. Blair comes down more definitely for 1164 as the date when HR was copied at Sawley: a less tenable suggestion, to my mind.
4. J. Hodgson Hinde, *Symeonis Dunelmensis opera et collectanea* (Surtees Soc., li. 1868), pp. xiv-xxxi; Thomas Arnold, *Symeonis monachi opera omnia* II (Rolls Series, 1885), p. xi. Mr. Blair distinguishes two components of the 848-1129 section: a chronicle from 848 to 1118 and another from 1119 to 1129. He inclines to the view that Symeon was responsible for both: 'Obs.' 107-12. Stubbs in the introduction to his edn. of Roger of Howden's *Chronica* I (Rolls Series, 1868), p. xxx, argued that the break occurred in 1121, so that 1122-9 represents a later continuation. But this interesting question has no great relevance to the present discussion, and the section 848-1129 will be treated as a unity; cf. Arnold, p. xxi.
5. *Asser's Life of King Alfred,* Oxford, 1904, pp. lviii-ix; cf. J. Armitage Robinson, *The Times of St. Dunstan,* Oxford, 1923, p. 51, n. 1. Stevenson's suggestion that for its extracts from Asser HR probably used B. M. Cotton Otho A. xii is shown to be untenable by Professor Dorothy Whitelock, *The Genuine Asser* (Stenton Lecture for 1967, Reading, 1968), p. 19.
6. 'Obs.' 117-18.
7. Cf. V. H. Galbraith, 'Who wrote Asser's "Life of Alfred"?', in *An Introduction to the Study of History,* London, 1964, p. 98. In her Stenton Lecture, *The Genuine Asser,* Reading, 1968, Professor Dorothy Whitelock uses the dependence of HR on Asser in defence of the traditional date of the latter (pp. 17-20).

X

8. It would seem that the section 848-1118 of SD³ was completed before the death of Henry I in 1135, and after the accession of David as King of Scots in 1124: HR 1072, 1070, ed. Arnold, pp. 199, 192.
9. 'Obs.' 73.
10. 'Obs.' 66, 72-3.
11. 'Obs.' 74.
12. 'Obs.' 76, 78; cf. p. 112: 'the scribe at Sawley'. Sir Roger Mynors discerned in Ff. 1. 27 a type of ornamental lettering characteristic of Durham: *Durham Cathedral Manuscripts*, Oxford, 1939, p. 8.
13. 'Obs.' 70-2.
14. 'Obs.' 90, 115 ('There is no reason for supposing that they [the interpolations] were written at Hexham'), and, rather more cautiously, 117; cf. 'Obs.' 113.
15. *Catalogue of the Manuscripts of Corpus Christi College* I, Cambridge, 1912, 323.
16. 'Obs.' 111 n. 3: 'I do not believe that Arnold's Hexham writer ever existed.'
17. See J. M. Todd and H. S. Offler, 'A medieval chronicle from Scotland', *Scottish Historical Review* XLVII, (1968), 151-9.
18. 'Obs.' 66.
19. See, for example, HR 848, where C, ed. Arnold, p. 98, reads *plaga,* and P fo. 3 (probably correctly), *paga;* moreover P has the smoother *Aelfredus rex erat filius Athelwlfi regis occidentalium Saxonum* for C's awkward *Elfredus rex erat regis occidentalium Saxonum filius Athelvulfi.* Later in the same year, P fo. 3v *aut exules aufugerant* seems preferable to C's *aut exules aut fugerant.* HR 866 C's *Elfredus id est clito Atheling iugi* etc. (p. 104) looks like a misplaced gloss, when compared with P fo. 5: *Aelfredus clito iugi* etc. Cf. Todd and Offler, 'A medieval chronicle', p. 153, note 4.
20. Possibly the rubrics to HR from which Mr. Blair has extracted the date 1164 ('Obs.' 77-8; cf. Arnold, p. xi) were copied by C from its ancestor *X*, which would thus have been written in that year. John, described as prior of Hexham on the same fo. 129 v of C which has the colophon of HR, can have become so only about this time, for his predecessor Richard appears as late as 1163 X 1166: cf. J. Raine, *Historians of the Church of York* III (Rolls Series, 1894), 79-81; G. V. Scammell, *Hugh du Puiset,* Cambridge, 1956, pp. 115, 126.
21. 'Obs.' 89.
22. 'Obs.' 90.
23. 'Obs.' 115.
24. As is suggested by J. Raine, *Priory of Hexham* I, (Surtees Soc., xliv, 1864), p. 173, n. *o.*
25. HR 740, p. 37; Ailred, *De sanctis,* ch. 2, ed. Raine, *Priory of Hexham* I, 177-81.
26. *De sanctis,* ch. 12, pp. 195-8; HR 781, pp. 47-50.
27. This involves rejecting Mr. Blair's suggestion, 'Obs.' 89-90, that the date of the interpolations lay between 1113 and 1155.
28. Cf. *A.A.*⁴, XL, (1962), 164-5.
29. Richard, *De statu,* ed. Raine, *Priory of Hexham* I, 32-5; HR 740, pp. 32-3. Though the conclusion is perhaps not quite as obvious as Raine, p. 36, n. *q,* suggests, I agree that Richard was probably copying the interpolator. The latter finishes his extract about Acca from Bede, *Hist. ecclest.* v. 20 with the words *et suis subjectis tradidit,* which are not in Bede's text. Richard, it may seem, copied the interpolator without verifying the reference, for after *tradidit* he adds: *Hucusque verba Venerabilis Bedae presbyteri.*
30. 'Obs.' 71.
31. The case for treating Symeon as the author-compiler of SD³ is judiciously stated by Mr. Blair, 'Obs.' 112.
32. In their introduction to the facsimile edition of the *Chronicle of Melrose,* London, 1936, p. xi, A. O. and M. O. Anderson point out that the Melrose chronicle does not borrow directly from that version of HR which we have called C.

33. HPB ends in that year. S.a. 1074 Benedict is named as the present abbot of Whitby, an office he held from *c*. 1138 to 1148; cf. J. C. Atkinson, *Chartulary of Whitby* (Surtees Soc., lxix, 1879), p. 210. The reference in the same place to Severinus as abbot of St. Mary's, York, *qui et in praesenti*, is less helpful, for the date when he succeeded Geoffrey is doubtful, and he lived until 1161.
34. *Chronica Magistri Rogeri de Houedene*, ed. W. Stubbs, I, (Rolls Series, 1868), pp. xxxi-xl.
35. For instance, s.aa. 869, 870, 874 (in part), 914 (in part), 916, 925 (*rectius* 934), 937, 941.
36. Cf. D. Nicholl, *Thurstan, Archbishop of York*, York, 1964, p. 66, n. 68. For a discrepancy of similar tendency between LCW and C s.a. 1116, see *ib*. p. 54. Here again HPB is closer to LCW than to C.
37. *Register of Cuthbert Tunstall*, ed. Gladys Hinde (Surtees Soc., clxi, 1952), p. 19.
38. Cf. Raine, *Priory of Hexham* I, 50, n. *i*, 58 n. *n*, 140 n. *1*.
38a. Cf. HR s.a. 1014, ed. Arnold, p. 146: et apud Eboracum sepultus fuit—only in C. HR s.a. 1066, p. 180: et Eboracum gravi pugna obtinuerunt—only in C. apud Fulford—only in C.
39. 'Obs.' 112.
40. Of course Symeon himself was not responsible for the rubrics.
41. The account of the earls of Northumbria appears in P fos. 32-3v, s.a. 1072, as in C; similarly in the *Annales* of Alfred of Beverley, ed. T. Hearne, 1716, pp. 132-3. Books vii-ix of Alfred's compilation are extracted verbatim from HR, and show that he used a text in many ways similar to C. This is interesting, in view of the fact that Alfred would seem to have begun putting his book together just before 1150. The Asser passages HR 848, 851 and 866 (cf. 'Obs.' 108-9) are there in P fos. 3, 5. I see no reason to suppose that the absorption by SD3 of the Asser passages from SD^1 took place elsewhere than at Durham.
42. These additions have not been treated very systematically by the editors. Thus Arnold, p. 230, does not mention that the first four lines he prints for HR 1100 are a later addition in the lower margin of C. At the beginning of 1128 (*rectius* 1127) he incorporates without comment in his text a passage concerning the transfer of the monks of Selkirk to Kelso, which stands in C in the lower margin as an addition in a later hand. His note on p. 247 about the additions concerning the monks of Tiron at the beginning of HR 1113 is misleading. Neither Arnold nor Hodgson Hinde points out that the year of John of Crema's legatine synod has been clumsily and wrongly altered in C from MCXXV to MCXXVI, and that this mistake has been continued in the annal heading for the next two years, turning 1126 into 1127 and 1127 into 1128.
43. For the likelihood of interference with HR 1116, see note 36 above. The account of the founding of the priory of Hexham in HR 1112, though it occurs in P, is absent from LCW, HPB, *Chron. Melrose* and Alfred of Beverley. There seem to be echoes in it of Richard of Hexham, *De statu*, ii, 5 and 8, and of Ailred, *De sanctis*, ch. 11, p. 192. The lines in praise of Archbishop Thomas II of York in HR 1113 are not found in LCW or HPB; but cf. Richard, *De statu*, ii, 6.
44. As does Dr. D. P. Kirby, 'Strathclyde and Cumbria', *CW* LXII, (1962), 91, n.79.
45. *Ann. Cambriae* (ed. J. W. ab Ithel, Rolls Series, 1860), p. 22, assign the death of Owen son of Dunawal to 1015, the year before Cnut took over kingship in England.
46. *Anglo-Saxon England*, p. 412, n. Professor Whitelock, 'Dealings of the Kings of England with Northumbria', in *The Anglo-Saxons. Studies . . . presented to Bruce Dickins*, ed. P. Clemoes (1959), p. 86, seems to support this position. Miss Janet Cooper, 'The dates of the bishops of Durham in the eleventh century', *Durham University Journal*, n.s. XXIX, (1968), 132-3, argues for 1016 as the date of Bishop Aldhun's death and the battle of Carham. Though her argument deserves serious consideration, I do not find it wholly convincing. In particular, her claim that the phrase *Cnut regnum Anglorum disponente*, in *Hist. Dunelm. Eccles*. 'is much more appropriate to 1016 than to 1018' seems doubtful. After all, 1018 was the year of the great Oxford assembly, the oaths taken at which, as Sir Frank Stenton wrote (*ASE*, 405), 'were the real foundation of the Anglo-Danish state'.
47. M. O. Anderson, 'Lothian and the early Scottish kings', *Scottish Hist. Rev.* XXXIX, (1960), 111-12. Possibly Mrs. Anderson goes too far when she conjectures that Eadulf Cudel was 'actually on the side

X

of the invading army' at Carham. The *De obsessione Dunelmi* calls him *ignavus* and *timidus*—epithets which suggest slothful cowardice rather than active treachery.

48. If we accept, as is suggested above, that the interpolator at HR 740 and 781 made use of Ailred's *De sanctis*. But there is no need to suppose that all the alterations were made at a single time. For the possibility that the date of *X*, C's exemplar, was 1164, see above, note 20.

XI

A medieval chronicle from Scotland

J. M. TODD AND H. S. OFFLER

At the end of the last century the Bibliothèque nationale in Paris purchased a parchment manuscript, formerly no. CXII of the Asburnham Appendix, and earlier the property of T. Martin of Palgrave; it is now numbered Nouv.acq.lat. 692 [henceforward P].[1] Originally the early gatherings of this manuscript (each of eight folios) were occupied by a chronicle 'Liber de gestis Anglorum', extending from 793 to 1153 and written in a square, rather squat hand of the late twelfth century. This came to an end on the seventh line of the verso of the fourth folio of the eighth gathering; it was followed immediately on the same folio by the beginning of the 'De excidio Trojae' of Dares Phrygius. At this stage the foliation must have been: fos. 1-60v, 'Liber de gestis Anglorum'; fos. 60v ff., 'De excidio'. Later the wish was felt to extend the chronicle beyond 1153. Room was made by inserting at least one new gathering of eight folios (the parchment is of noticeably different quality) after fo. 56v. On the first three folios and at the top of the recto of the fourth of this new gathering was copied that part of the 'Liber' which had formerly occupied fos. 57-60v: the rest of the insertion was thus blank and available for further entries. The old fos. 57-59 were removed; but the former fo. 60 (now 65) had to be preserved, since the 'De excidio' began on its verso. The present foliation is thus as follows: fos. 1-60, 'Liber de gestis Anglorum', 793-1153; fos. 60-64v, continuations to the 'Liber', extending from 1153 to 1164; fo. 65, the last folio of the first form of the 'Liber', in the original hand; fo. 65v, first seven lines erased; then the beginning of the 'De excidio'.[2] The additional chronicle material for 1153-1164 breaks off in the middle of a speech at the foot of fo. 64v, which is the end of the inserted gathering. Possibly further additions once existed; there is sufficient distortion in the binding between fos. 64v and 65 to support the view that a second inserted gathering once filled the gap.

1   H. Omont, *Bibliothèque nationale: Inventaire sommaire des nouvelles acquisitions du Département des manuscrits pendant les années 1898-1899* (Paris, 1900), 13.
2   'De excidio' ends on fo. 80v; fos. 81-107v have part of Fulcher of Chartres, 'Gesta Francorum Jherusalem peregrinantium'; fos. 108-110 anonymous verses in a fifteenth-century hand concerning the destruction of Jerusalem by the Romans.

J. M. TODD works with a firm of solicitors in West Cumberland and H. S. OFFLER is professor of medieval history in the university of Durham. Some time ago they discovered that from quite independent beginnings they had reached conclusions about this chronicle which were in part similar and in part complementary. They have thought it sensible to join forces in this paper, and wish to thank Mrs M. O. Anderson and Professor G. W. S. Barrow for much help, not least in making them known to each other.

By permission of the Trustees of the Scottish Historical Review Trust.

152

As Léopold Delisle pointed out in 1899,[1] the 'Liber de gestis Anglorum' from 793 to 1153 contains almost nothing which is unknown. Save for a preface (printed by Delisle) and a genealogy of the kings of Wessex from Cerdic to Beorhtric taken from Florence of Worcester, the 'Liber' depends wholly and literally on the Historia regum attributed to Symeon of Durham and on John of Hexham's Historia xxv Annorum, though neither of these authors is named.[2] The compiler has taken the annals for 793, 794 and 802 from the earliest and most important of the overlapping chronicles known as Historia regum [henceforward HR]; all his other borrowings from this source are from its last two sections, which run from 848 to 1129.[3] His choice of what to reproduce and what to omit seems wholly haphazard: at one juncture he will follow his source for a dozen consecutive years; at another he summarises the entries for fourteen years in a single line[4]; at times he gives no more than the torso of the annal in HR. Neither principle nor art is to be discerned in his erratic method.[5] On the other hand, when his source changes on fo. 42v, with the beginning of John of Hexham's history in 1130, the compiler ceases to select. He does indeed quite deliberately omit the long and eulogistic obituary notice of Archbishop Thurstan from the entry for 1140.[6] This is natural enough if, as seems likely, the 'Liber' was put together in Scotland, as the continuations to it certainly were. A Scottish chronicler would see no reason to expatiate on the merits of an archbishop of York whose claims to ecclesiastical authority in Scotland had been pressed hard and firmly resisted.

1   L. Delisle, 'Vente de manuscrits du comte d'Ashburnham', *Journal des Savants*, June 1899, 330–2.
2   For a slightly later insertion on fo. 39, of some interest for the early history of Carlisle, see *Trans. Cumberland & Westmorland Antiq. & Archaeol. Soc.*, n.s. lxv (1965), 176.
3   On these components of HR, see P. Hunter Blair, 'Some observations on the "Historia Regum" attributed to Symeon of Durham', *Celt and Saxon. Studies in the Early British Border* (Cambridge, 1963), 76 ff. The first three entries come from the chronicle which Mr Blair numbers (4); the rest from his (8) and (9).
4   The only entry between 979 and 994 is: *Iterum uenerunt danici pirate in angliam regnante rege Æthelredo* (fo. 13v).
5   The annals from HR which P reproduces (most often more or less truncated) are: 793–4; 802; 848; 851; 855; 860; 863–4; 866; 870–1; 875–7; 883–4; 888; 899 (dated 901 in P); 906 (dated 817 in P); 924 (dated 828 in P); 925–6; 940–3; 946; 955–960; 963–4; 967–79; 994–5; 1011–19; 1031–2; 1035–7; 1040; 1042–3; 1053–5; 1057; 1062–4; 1066; 1069–73; 1075 (dated 1074 in P); 1080; 1087; 1093; 1096; 1098–1100; 1106 (dated 1105 in P); 1107; 1112; 1120–5; 1126 (misdated 1127 in Arnold's edn. of HR, for which see n. 9 below); 1127 (misdated 1128 in Arnold); 1128–9.
6   There is little doubt that the eulogy was in P's exemplar, as it was in that of the other MS of John's chronicle, C (for which see below). C begins the entry for 1140 (fo. 139rb) thus: *Anno mcxl sancte memorie Turstinus*.... Then, the obituary completed, it turns to other events of the year (fo. 140ra): *Eodem anno Henricus comes*.... P (fo. 49v) begins the entry for the year: *Anno mcxl. Eodem anno Henricus comes*.... The use of the scissors is apparent.

A MEDIEVAL CHRONICLE FROM SCOTLAND   153

Apart from this single omission, however, the 'Liber' offers the complete text of John of Hexham's chronicle.

In itself, then, the 'Liber de gestis Anglorum' is a feeble and completely unoriginal piece of work. Its value lies in the light it can throw on the textual history of its sources. The text of HR and of John of Hexham's Historia is known only from a single manuscript, Corpus Christi College, Cambridge, MS 139 [henceforward C], the basis for all the editions.[1] This manuscript has been dated c. 1170 by Mr Hunter Blair; it cannot be much earlier, for John of Hexham did not complete his chronicle until after May 1162.[2] There are serious doubts how faithfully C represents the text of HR as it was when its various elements were first put together, presumably before the death of Henry I, or the text of John's Historia as it came from his pen. Both internally and externally C shows signs of later additions and alterations (not always adequately indicated by the editors); at times extraneous material has been introduced, resulting in disorder in the arrangement of the text and in chronology.[3] It does not seem rash to assume that the compiler of the 'Liber' used a manuscript in which, as in C, HR was followed by John of Hexham. Collation of P with C shows that the former did not depend on the latter, for despite the deficiencies of its scribe P at times preserves manifestly superior readings.[4] It seems necessary to conclude that both manuscripts derive at no great distance from a common ancestor, one or two idiosyncrasies of which both preserve,[5] and whose readings P has on occasion saved when the original readings of C have been

---

1   HR in R. Twysden, *Historiae Anglicanae Scriptores Decem* (1652); J. Hodgson Hinde, *Symeonis Dunelmensis Opera et Collectanea*, i (Surtees Soc., 1868); Thomas Arnold, *Symeonis monachi Dunelmensis opera omnia*, ii (Rolls Series, 1885). John of Hexham in Twysden, Arnold and James Raine, *Priory of Hexham*, i (Surtees Soc., 1864).
2   'Some observations', 70. It is now established that C was once owned by Sawley abbey (ibid., 118). John (ed. Arnold, p. 324) records the end of Richard de Belmeis II bishop of London, who died on 4 May 1162.
3   For example, at C, fos. 132rb–138ra, discussed by Mr Hunter Blair, 'Some observations', 66–68. We are grateful to the master and fellows of Corpus Christi for permission to examine their MS. and acquire photographs of it.
4   Both at the beginning and end of the entry for 848 and at the beginning of 851 (Arnold, pp. 98, 100) P (fos. 3, 3v) is nearer HR's source, Florence of Worcester, than C. So too in the entries for 969, 973, 1013 and 1066 (Arnold, pp. 130, 131, 144, 182), where P (fos. 11v, 12, 15, 27) gives *monachizauit, Juchil, archipresulatum, Heortfordensem*. For John, cf. Arnold, p. 285, l.27: *iiii nonas* in P, rightly, against *iii nonas* in C. Page 286, l. 6: *que* P; *quod* C. Page 291, ll. 22–23: *abduxit* P; *adduxit* C. Page 293, l. 15: *in eo* P; *in eos* C. Page 293, l. 25: *quantam* P; *quam* C (later corrected to *quantam*). Page 301, l. 34: *promulgatis* P; *prouulgatis* C. Page 306, l. 26: *de Soilli* P; *de Coilli* C (as a later addition). Page 314, l. 20: *merore* P; *memore* C. Page 318, l. 24: *Selebi* P; *Salesbia* C.
5   See Arnold, p. 287, l. 23: both P and C aspirate *eundem* into *heundem*. Page 299, l. 12: P and C both read *Albano*, *sancto* being added later in C. Page 299, l. 27: Arnold reads *ex ea*, with a later hand in C, as the sense demands, but P and C read *ea*.

lost by later rehandling.[1] By taking P in conjunction with C, which Arnold has sometimes misread,[2] it would be possible to better the Rolls Series text of the Historia xxv Annorum in a couple of dozen places, and incidentally to deprive of most of its point the charge of chronological confusion so often laid against John of Hexham. P's usefulness for the text of HR is less, because of its numerous arbitrary omissions. But even here its help, when available, is not to be despised, as an example may suggest. C's statement [pp. 155-6 in Arnold's edition of HR] about the leaders at the battle of Carham in 1018 raises difficulties, possibly only to be met by supposing that the battle took place in some earlier year.[3] It is worth noting that P's entry for 1018 (fo. 30), while it records the battle, does not name the leaders, resembling in this Roger of Howden and the Melrose chronicle, both of which depend for this part of their text on HR. It is difficult to avoid the suspicion that what C offers here is an elaboration unknown to the common ancestor of C and P: whatever its authority, it is not that of HR.

The continuation of the 'Liber de gestis Anglorum' commencing on fo. 60, which we have edited in part as an appendix to this article, is a disappointing jumble of material from various sources. Its compiler seems to have had the best intentions of bringing the 'Liber' nearer to his own time, but to have been at a loss for material with which to do this. The continuation begins with an additional entry for 1153 and an annal for 1154 down to Stephen's death in October. This material is very close in substance and in language to entries for 1153 and 1154 in the Chronicle of Holyrood [henceforward H].[4] Two entries in the corresponding sections of H are not in P: the death of the traitor Arthur is dated *iiii kal. Marcii* in P and a day later in H; whilst H contains no mention of Ness of Calatria.[5] These discrepancies rule out the possibility of direct dependence of H on P or P on H, and we must postulate a common source, particularly concerned with the affairs of Scotland and Northumbria. Possibly this source ended in 1154 as the continuation makes no further use of it,

---

1 Arnold, p. 291, l. 18: *in Crafna circa Cliterhou* P; *circa Clitherou*, preceded by an erasure, C. Page 328, l. 30: *die sancte Agnetis* P; *die sancti Vincentii* C.
2 For example, Arnold, p. 294, l. 15: *unus*; P and C: *in ius*. Page 331. l. 4: *apud Scottiam*; P and C: *apud Sconam*. The second instance is noticed by G. W. S. Barrow, *Regesta Regum Scottorum*, i, *Acts of Malcolm IV* (Edinburgh, 1960), 7, n. 3.
3 Sir Frank Stenton, *Anglo-Saxon England* (Oxford, 1947), 412. But the date 1018 finds support from Mrs M. O. Anderson, 'Lothian and the early Scottish kings', *ante*, xxxix (1960), 112.
4 *Chron. Holyrood*, 124-6. There is no such similarity to *Chron. Melrose*, 35 at this point.
5 For the identification of *Nesius de Kaletirio*, see Barrow in *Regesta Regum Scottorum*, i, 8. The way in which this reference to Ness is tacked on to the end of the sentence suggests that in the manuscript from which the entry was copied it was an interlinear or marginal addition.

A MEDIEVAL CHRONICLE FROM SCOTLAND

unless the next element (*princeps quidem* onwards) also comes from there.

This eulogy of King Henry II reads like a prospectus for a history of his reign which has perhaps already been written (*ut in sequentibus clarebit*). The substance of this passage would seem to imply that it was written after the Irish campaign of 1171-2 and the capture of William the Lion in 1174: indeed its recapitulatory tone suggests that it was written after the end of Henry's reign. We have not succeeded in locating any similar passage elsewhere.

The remainder of fo. 60 is blank, save for what could be the remains of four year-numbers in the right hand margin. These may mark spaces for material for the years 1155-8 which never came to hand, or may be later marginalia.

At the top of fo. 60v is an entry about the fortification of Wark, undated but belonging to the year 1158. This must have been taken from a source akin to the Melrose Chronicle [henceforward M],[1] since it is not in H. After the papal letter, on which we comment below, come several more entries on fos. 62v-63 for the years 1158 (an error for 1159), 1159 and 1162. These seem closer to M than to H, although they occur in both.[2] They are only a selection of the material in M for these years, and it is possible only to guess the reason—a hasty copy, a defective source, or deliberate choice on grounds unknown. Spaces have been left between these annals, as if for more material to be added later.

In the bull *Eterna et incommutabilis* Alexander III proclaimed to the world the validity of his election in September 1159. Several copies of the letter are known, with broadly similar texts and different addresses.[3] We have therefore printed only the opening and closing sentences of the text in P, which bears the date 29 October (1159). The main point of interest is that the letter was sent to Scotland at all. At the time it was being sent out, however, William bishop of Moray and Nicholas the king's chamberlain were in Rome, the former at the time of Alexander's election, and the latter probably shortly after, on business concerning the succession to the see of St Andrews. There can be little doubt that they brought this letter home with them.[4] The pope addressed the letter to the Scottish

1   *Chron. Melrose*, 35.
2   *Chron. Holyrood*, 132-4, 140-1; *Chron. Melrose*, 36. For example, both the continuation and *Chron. Melrose* say simply that Malcolm 'was made a knight' by Henry II: *Chron. Holyrood* with a flourish says 'gladio militie accinctus est'.
3   P. Jaffé, *Regesta Pontificum Romanorum*, 2nd edn. (Leipzig, 1885-8), nos. 10584, 10587-92, 10601-2, dating from 26 Sept. to 13 Dec. 1159. The most accessible full text is that addressed to the bishops of England: D. Wilkins, *Concilia*, (London, 1737), i, 432 (Jaffé no. 10602). But textually the Scottish letter is closest to one addressed to the clergy of northern Italy, dated 13 Dec. 1159 (Jaffé no. 10601).
4   *Chron. Melrose*, 36; *Chron. Holyrood*, 134-5; *Vita Sancti Waldeni*, in *Acta Sanctorum*, August, i, 270.

bishops, thereby implicitly recognising the autonomy of the church in Scotland. This was the first sign that Alexander, unlike his predecessors, was prepared to consider the Scottish church as something more than a part of the province of York. It seems that the Scottish mission was prompt to recognise Alexander as the rightful pope and so made a good impression at the outset. This shrewd move was the turning-point in the tide which took the church in Scotland on to its position of *filia specialis* thirty-three years later.[1]

The list of schismatic popes which follows the letter on fo. 62v is an extract from a list of schisms in Ralph de Diceto's Opuscula.[2] It was another of Ralph's works which provided the compiler of the continuation—or perhaps his successor, for there may be a change of hand at this point—with ample pabulum from 1162 onwards. The remainder as it survives (fos. 63–64v) is copied from the beginning of an account of the 'Becket affair', which Ralph abridged from his own Ymagines Historiarum.[3] The source of both sections was a manuscript which Diceto presented in 1195 to William Longchamps bishop of Ely, and which passed to Robert, William's brother, who became abbot of St Mary's, York in 1197.[4]

The continuation is thus not a very successful or resourceful piece of chronicle-making, adding but two facts to our knowledge of the period: that one Ness of Calatria was a fellow-traitor with Arthur in 1154,[5] and that a copy of Pope Alexander's letter justifying his election was addressed to the Scottish bishops. The diversity of its sources, however, is an interesting indication of the breadth of the literary contacts of a Scottish monastic house at this time.

The case for a Scottish origin of P rests largely on the address of the papal letter, but also on the parallel passages with the two Scottish chronicles and on the reference to the king without adding *Scotie* or *Scottorum*. We have found nothing which clearly links the manuscript with a particular monastic house. In view of their known chronicles, it is perhaps unlikely that the manuscript came from Melrose or Coupar Angus. Possibly as much might be said of

1   For comments on these developments see Barrow in *Regesta Regum Scottorum*, i, 14.
2   *Historical Works of Master Ralph de Diceto*, ed. W. Stubbs (Rolls Series, 1876), ii, 195.   3   Ibid., ii, 279–85.
4   Ibid., i, pp. xcvii–xcviii. The manuscript is now in the British Museum, Add. MS 40007. The list of popes is on fo. 8v and the Becket narrative is on fos. 12–15. This is the only manuscript of Ralph's Opuscula which contains both the list and the Becket narrative. Moreover where the readings of the three known manuscripts of the narrative differ, P invariably follows the York MS.
5   For an interpretation of this 'Calatrian' rising, see *Regesta Regum Scottorum*, i, 8. It seems (to one of us at least) possible that 'Arthur' may be identified with Arthur 'Finboga' who occurs in the (admittedly suspect) witness-list to a charter of Robert bishop of St Andrews (Lawrie, *Charters*, no. 230). Gilbert 'Fimboga' joined Dufoter of Calatria in witnessing a charter of David I (ibid., no. 109). These scraps of evidence point to Arthur's being of Calatria.

Kelso, where the Historia Danorum as it existed in the middle of the thirteenth century seems to have been a version of the Historia post Bedam; certainly it was not the 'Liber de gestis Anglorum' as contained in P.[1] We mention one possible pointer for what it is worth. John of Hexham states that in 1147 John bishop of Glasgow was buried in the church of Jedburgh 'in qua conventum regularium clericorum ipse disposuit'. This is the reading in C, and the original reading in P (fo. 56) also. But a later hand has altered the phrase to 'in qua conventum canonicorum regularium instructu ipsius episcopi idem rex David disposuit', an alteration which comes nearer to the truth.[2] Had at some time a reader with special concern for the history of Jedburgh access to P? It would be rash to build much on so slight an indication. If the names on the final sheet (which appear to be those of late medieval owners) could be identified, we might be clearer on this score.[3]

As for the date of the manuscript, the handwriting of the continuation appears to be of the late twelfth or early thirteenth century. The earliest date for the section based on the Diceto manuscript is 1195, or more probably 1197, while the remainder would scarcely be written much if at all earlier.

---

1   This we base upon the extract concerning the death of Malcolm III Canmore sent from the Historia Danorum of his house by R. *dictus de Dunelmo* monk of Kelso to Ralph prior of Tynemouth, and preserved in British Museum, Cotton MS Vitellius A. xx, fo. 75v (printed by Raine, *Priory of Hexham*, i, app. xi, pp. xiv–xvi). The text of this extract is close to that of the Historia post Bedam; it is not the text of the account of Malcolm's end in P, fos. 36v–37.
2   See G. W. S. Barrow, 'Scottish rulers and the religious orders', *Trans. Royal Hist. Soc.*, 5th ser., iii, 92–93; Easson, *Religious Houses*, 77.
3   On fo. 110 the name *Willelmus Pateryk* appears. By the aid of ultra-violet light Dr A. I. Doyle has made out the following erased entries on fo. 110v and has been so good as to communicate them to us: *Remembrans rest reuyth Radcliff: Cuthbert Radcliff Radclifeus* (early sixteenth century); *Henricus Northumbrie* (hand of the sixteenth/seventeenth century); *Comes Wissingamus* [?] (late sixteenth century). The inscription *Remembrans . . . radclyff* appears also in Trinity College, Cambridge, MS O.3.55, fo. 59, formerly belonging to Durham priory (cf. M. R. James, *Western Manuscripts in the Library of Trinity College, Cambridge*, iii [Cambridge, 1902], 243; we owe this reference also to the kindness of Dr Doyle). The Cuthbert Radcliff whose name is written in P is more probably Sir Cuthbert Radcliffe of Cartington and Dilston in Northumberland, who died in 1545, than either of his great-grandsons of that name, Cuthbert (d. 1644) son of Sir Francis Radcliffe, or Cuthbert son of Anthony Radclyffe of Blanchland (see *Northumberland County History*, x, ed. H. H. E. Craster (1910), 280 for the pedigree of Radcliffe of Dilston and Derwentwater). As warden of the Middle Marches (1540–3) and captain of Berwick (1544) he could have found plenty of opportunity to profit from the plunder of a lowland monastery.

XI

APPENDIX

Extracts from 'Liber de gestis Anglorum' covering the years 1153–1162. Paris, Bibliothèque nationale, MS Nouv. acq. lat. 692, fos. 60–63.[1]

fo. 60 ... Die Sancti Leonardi[2] Sumerled et nepotes eius insurgunt in malcolmum regem puerum.

*A*nno.m.cliiij.[3] Willelmus ille pie recordationis Archiepiscopus Eboracensis permittente pio papa Anastasio ad cathedram suam summo cum honore reuersus est. Et infra.vii^am. septimanam obiit.

Hugo puteacensis Rome consecratus dunelm*ensem* episcopatum su*s*cepit.

Fames maxima et alienarum[4] pestilencia aput scottos.

Arturus regem mal*colmum* proditurus duello; periit iiij. k*alendas* marcii.[5] et nesius de kaletirio

Rog*erus* de ponte Episcopi in Archiepiscopatum ebor*acensem* Rome consecratur.

Obiit Stephanus Rex Anglie .viij. k*alendas* nouembris.[6] et Henricus dux supradictus regni diademate insignitur. princeps quidem in ex*se*quendis iudiciis indagatur discretissimus multis predecessorum suorum dignitate potencia pariter ac gloria superior nam ut in sequ*en*tibus clarebit fines regni sui dilatauit reges et principes ab eo prelio uincti captique sunt quamplurimi eorumque terras et castella partim iussit dirui partim eorum manibus potenter extorsit· ac per hoc totam Angliam simulque finitimas regiones in sui potestatem reredegit.[7] Genuit hic ex uxore sua videlicet regina Helienor q[   ][8] filios[   ][9]

fo. 60v Iterum firmatum est Werc.[10]

Magna his temporibus habita est rome contencio et dissensio de summo pontifice eligendo et ut hoc clarius legentibus innotescat exemplar literarum domini pape A*lexandri* .iij. huic pagine inserere iudicauimus

1   Letters in italics have been supplied by the editors.
2   6 Nov. 1153.
3   The initial letter of *Anno* and of other words commencing lines in the text have been omitted, presumably for rubrics to be inserted later.
4   So P: the correct reading *animalium* is in *Chron. Holyrood*, 125.
5   26 Feb. 1154: *Chron. Holyrood*, 126 has 27 Feb.
6   25 Oct. 1154. Another hand adds in the margin: *anno domini m°cliiii° mense Octobr' et anno regni sui xix°*. A later hand also adds *obiit Stephanus* above and after *m°cliiii°*.
7   So P: *re* is at the end of one line and *redegit* at the beginning of the next—a copyist's error.
8   Most of the word has been erased in P: it was probably *quattuor*.
9   After *filios*, which is the first word on line 16 of fo. 60, four and a half lines have been erased. In the left-hand margin opposite *filios* is written *Willelmum*, as if Henry's eldest, short-lived son had come to mind. The lower part of the page, about 13 lines, is left blank, but in the right-hand margin are four year-numbers on alternate lines, all of which, following the trimming of the page, appear as *mc*, but could have marked spaces for the years 1155, 1156, 1157 and 1158.
10   The entry is undated but belongs to 1158: *Chron. Melrose*, 35.

A MEDIEVAL CHRONICLE FROM SCOTLAND 159

Alexander episcopus seruus seruorum dei Uenerabilibus fratribus episcopis et dilectis filiis abbatibus prioribus et uniuersis ecclesiarum prelatis per scociam constitutis. Salutem et apostolicam benedictionem. Eterna et incommutabilis prouidencia . . . .[1]

fo. 62v   Datum terracin' .iiij. kalendas nouembris

octauianus itaque intrusus in scismate moritur et Gwido Cremensis item intrusus simili fine decessit Johannes autem licet intrusus reconcciliatur

Anno .m.clviii.[2] Henricus ii^{dus} Rex Anglie Tholosam cum exercitu adiit et melcolmus Rex[3] miles factus est Thuronis a predicto rege.[4]

ADrianus[5] papa obiit cui successit Alexander[6] sicut superius expressum est.[7]

Anno .m.clxii.[8] Obiit Ærnaldus Episcopus Sancti Andree.
fo. 63   Cui succes/sit Ricardus capellanus Regis.[9]

1   The text of the letter follows, copied without a break, taking up the remainder of fo. 60v, fos. 61–62, and the first twelve lines of fo. 62v.
2   More correctly mclviiii: Chron. Melrose, 36.
3   After Rex, scocie has been added above the line in a later hand.
4   After rege, four lines are blank. In the left-hand margin, in another hand, is the year-number mclviii, followed, with gaps of four lines between each number, by mclix, mclx, mclxi and mclxii, the missing digits being due to page-trimming.
5   This annal appears, correctly, opposite the year-number mclix in the left-hand margin.
6   iii is inserted above Alexander.
7   The next ten lines are blank, except for the marginal numbers.
8   The marginal number mclxii also comes opposite this entry.
9   The remainder of the text down to 1164, which follows without a break, is derived from Ralph de Diceto.

XII

Re-reading Boldon Book*

Whether by accident or design – more probably the latter – Durham together with the rest of England north of Tees escaped the great survey of 1086 of which the results were set out in Domesday Book. Its bishop, William of St. Calais, was certainly one of the Domesday commissioners, and recently Dr Chaplais has argued not only that his role was predominant in the whole enterprise – 'it does look as if he was indeed "the man behind the Survey"' – but also that the main scribe of the Great Domesday was connected with the Durham scriptorium. Then too it is almost unbelievable that William's successor at Durham, Rannulf Flambard, already by 1086

---

* It is a pleasure to acknowledge how much this essay has benefited from comments and suggestions by Martin Snape, Paul Harvey, Richard Britnell and Alan Piper. Responsibility for its deficiencies remains wholly mine.

Documents cited with the prefix DC Mun. are at Durham among the muniments of the Dean and Chapter.

Printed works of series frequently cited are denoted by the following abbreviations:

AA	*Archaeologia Aeliana* [a suprascript number for the series]
Additamenta	*Libri censualis vocati Domesday-Book Additamenta ex codic. antiquiss.*, ed. Henry Ellis, Record Commission, London, 1816.
Austin	*Boldon Book. Northumberland and Durham*, ed. David Austin, Chichester, 1982 (no. 35, Supplementary Volume to *Domesday Book*, ed. John Morris).
BF	*Book of Fees, pt.i, 1198-1242*, London, 1920
'Boldon Book'	G.T. Lapsley, art. 'Boldon Book' in *Victoria County History*: Durham, vol.i, London, 1905.
DEC	*Durham Episcopal Charters 1071-1152*, ed. H.S. Offler, SS clxxix (1968)
FPD	*Feodarium Prioratus Dunelmensis*, ed. W. Greenwell, SS lviii (1872)
Greenwell	*Boldon Buke*, ed. W. Greenwell, SS xxv (1852)
Hatfield Survey	*Bishop Hatfield's Survey*, ed. W. Greenwell, SS xxxii (1857)
HD	R. Surtees, *The History and Antiquities of the County Palatine of Durham*, 4 vols., 1816-40
PR	Pipe Roll
PR Soc.	Publications of the Pipe Roll Society
RS	Rolls Series
SS	Publications of the Surtees Society

in or on the outskirts of royal service, was not somehow or other involved in that mighty business.[1] Yet no Domesday account of Durham survives, and those concerned with its history have lacked this firm basis for their studies of the decades before and after the Norman Conquest. Naturally enough, when Bishop Hugh du Puiset's survey of 1183/4 was first printed in 1816 among the *additamenta* to the Record Commission's edition of Domesday Book, there was some tendency to treat Boldon Book as a sort of belated surrogate for the record which had not been made a century earlier. It has long been recognised that this approach will not do. Neither in purpose nor range did Boldon Book represent a substitute for Domesday Book in part of the neglected north. In essence Boldon Book did not differ from similar surveys made in the late twelfth century for other large ecclesiastical estates.[2] Its aim was to give an account of the rents and customary services due from the bishop of Durham's demesne, that is to say, from the lands more or less under his direct economic control.[3] Not even all these were included, for the survey was restricted to the area of *Haliwerfolc* between Tyne and Tees, together with ancient episcopal estates in Northumberland: in Bedlingtonshire, lying between the river Blythe and the Wansbeck, and in Norhamshire immediately south of the Tweed. It makes only one reference to Islandshire, the complex of the bishop's lands adjoining Norhamshire to the east, and none at all to his considerable estates in Yorkshire and elsewhere. Within the areas which were surveyed, intermingled with the bishop's possessions, were, of course, considerable holdings in demesne by other landowners: most notably, the Prior and Convent of Durham and laymen holding fees from the bishop. All such lands fell outside the purview of the bishop's survey; if mentioned at all, it was only incidentally. Thus what we can expect to find in the Boldon Book is much more limited than the information resulting from the comprehensive remit to the Domesday commissioners a century earlier.

Equally obvious is another contrast. It has become commonplace of modern scholarship that understanding of Domesday Book can be much deepened by investigating in detail how it was made. The student of Boldon

---

1 Pierre Chaplais, 'William of Saint Calais and the Domesday Survey', *Domesday Studies*, ed. J.C. Holt, London, 1987, pp.74, 77. For Rannulf, see R.W. Southern, *Medieval Humanism and Other Studies*, Oxford, 1970, pp.187, 190; V.H. Galbraith, *Domesday Book: its place in administrative history*, Oxford, 1974, pp.104-5.

2 As P.D.A. Harvey remarks, *Manorial Records*, British Records Association, *Archives and the User* no. 5, 1984, p.19.

3 G.T. Lapsley's description of Boldon Book as 'in reality no more than a polyptichum designed to meet the administrative needs of a great estate' is true enough, even if unhelpful to those not quite sure what polyptichum means: 'Boldon Book', p.259.

Re-reading Boldon Book

Book has no such opportunity, since genuinely external evidence about the making of this survey is lacking. He is driven back to the short historical preamble to the text: an introduction not necessarily contemporary with the bulk of the document. It says that in the year of our Lord's incarnation 1183 at the feast of St. Cuthbert in Lent Hugh, bishop of Durham, present in person and accompanied by his feudatories, caused to be set down in writing (*fecit describi*) all the rents of assise of his bishopric and its customary renders and services, both as they were then and had been previously.[4] This statement is less easy to interpret than may appear at first sight. It would be unsafe to be too definite even about the date. St. Cuthbert's feast in Lent causes no trouble: it was 20 March, one of the four major rent days in the bishopric annually. If the year of incarnation was reckoned as beginning at Christmas, the date can be settled in our terms as 20 March 1183. On the other hand, if the beginning of the year was reckoned from Lady Day after Christmas, following the practice of the *calculus florentinus* – as was not unusual in England from the late twelfth century – then the date when Bishop Hugh met his feudatories according to the preamble was 20 March 1184. What happened at the meeting? Various renderings of *fecit describi* are possible.[5] The bishop caused the fixed rents and customary renders and services due to him to be transcribed or described in writing, or defined, or properly ordered. But was this the occasion when the results of enquiries already completed were formally promulgated? Or was it when, in circumstances of some pomp, the process of enquiry was set on foot? No evidence appears on which to base an assured answer.

Indeed, any account of the making of Boldon Book must be largely a matter of conjecture. If it be supposed that the enquiries were complete by 20 March 1183 or 1184, the task of carrying them out, which involved the investigation of about 150 separate settlements, must have begun some considerable time before. It cannot be believed, of course, that the estates of the bishops of Durham had earlier been administered without any recourse to written record. Besides the holdings it describes as being by charter, Boldon Book itself tells of stock and seed leases at Little and Great Haughton-le-Skerne, Ketton and Wolsingham with Rogerley where the

---

4 The better textual reading seems: omnes redditus tocius Episcopatus sui assise et consuetudines sicut tunc erant et ante fuerant; thus the technical term 'redditus assise' is rather awkwardly split. In fact Boldon Book was very little of a 'now and then' survey, and the preamble sounds suspiciously like a later addition.

5 The phrase calls to mind Robert Losinga's *facta est descriptio*, on the making of Domesday Book: cited in W. Stubbs, *Select Charters*, 9th edn., Oxford, 1929, p.95.

conditions had been specified in indentures: *sicut in cirografo continetur.* Nevertheless, arduous work must have gone into compiling Boldon Book. Information would have to be collected and authenticated locally; then consolidated and edited at one centre or more. About all this we are in the dark. No evidence survives that local juries were used to ascertain the facts, as they certainly were at about this time in producing the surveys of other great ecclesiastical estates.[6] Possibly they were; we do not know. For the Bedlingtonshire and Norhamshire entries the ancient territorial unit, the Northumbrian small shire, could have served as the agency for collecting information about individual settlements. But between Tyne and Tees, in *Haliwerfolc* proper, though we hear in Boldon Book of Quarringtonshire, Heighingtonshire and Aucklandshire, it seems doubtful whether survivals of this ancient system were strong or comprehensive enough to serve the purposes of the whole survey. The smaller judicial and administrative groupings of the English communities south of Tees had not evolved in episcopal Durham; in 1183/4 the wapentake of Sadberg was still in royal hands. There is no conclusive evidence that by this date Durham was divided for administrative purposes into the four wards of Chester, Easington, Stockton and Darlington, which later undertook some of the functions falling elsewhere to hundred or wapentake; probably, indeed, the wards in Durham failed to develop courts.[7] We are reduced to assuming that the local enquiries were conducted by the bishop's bailiffs from convenient centres within the various groups of episcopal vills which Lapsley claimed were already well established by this time.[8] It would be easy to guess at about a dozen likely places: Durham, Chester-le-Street, Houghton-le-Spring, Easington,

---

[6] For example, by Glastonbury, Shaftesbury, St. Paul's cathedral and the Templars in Essex; see R.V. Lennard, 'Early manorial juries', *EHR* lxxvii (1962), 511-8.

[7] The surviving fragment of an enquiry into free tenures in the bishopric made *sede vacante* 1208-10 adumbrates the existence, at least in embryo, of what will later be called the Stockton ward: *BF* i.28-31. K. Emsley and C.M. Fraser, *The Courts of the County Palatine of Durham*, Durham, 1984, p.14 deny that the Durham wards had courts. Lapsley, *The County Palatine of Durham*, New York, 1900, p.194 had taken a different view, but his evidence, so far as courts are concerned, is late and inconclusive.

[8] 'Boldon Book', pp. 260-6. The survey does not name any bailiff directly, though the West Auckland entry refers to *ballia Radulphi callidi*. By the late fourteenth century this had become *Warda de Auckland: Hatfield Survey*, p.30.

Re-reading Boldon Book

Sedgefield, Stockton, Darlington, Heighington, Bishop Auckland, Wolsingham, Lanchester, Consett, Whickham. But we cannot be sure.[9]

What is quite clear, however, is that the information collected locally was edited at some centre or centres. By the fourteenth century the survey had come to be called the Boldon Book. The reason for this was that Boldon was the first township listed where the customary villein services were set out in detail; later in the survey, with other townships where the same conditions prevailed, the obvious economy was practised of simply noting that the villeins held and served as did *illi* (or *villani*) *de Boldona*. The entries for 19 townships display that formula.[10] We can hardly believe that informants about somewhere pretty remote from Boldon, say Preston-on-Tees, when asked what services the villeins of their township owed, had come out with the crisp answer: *sicut illi de Boldona*. It must be assumed that they had given the appropriate details, and that subsequent editorial effort had reduced the bulk of repetitive information. Perhaps not all the editing was done at one centre. The Boldon Book entries running from New Ricknall to Frosterley, comprising the townships which later fell within Darlington ward, never refer to the Boldon pattern of services; all cross-references are to other entries in the New Ricknall-Frosterley section.[11] Of course, that may simply be because the Boldon pattern did not match the facts existing in the west of the county. But it is significant that this section shows in one recension of the survey (called *x* below) a consistent variation from the common form used elsewhere. Throughout the survey records seasonal variations in liability for weekwork by cottars (sometimes by villeins too); they may, for instance, owe work for two days weekly in autumn and one for the rest of the year. Normally the survey reports this in the terms: so many days a week *a festo Sancti Petri ad Vincula* [1 August] *usque ad festum Sancti Martini* [11 November], and so many *a festo Sancti Martini usque ad festum Sancti Petri ad Vincula*. The *x* recension of the New Ricknall-Frosterley section, however, habitually

9 The guess derives some support, as Richard Britnell informs me, from the evidence about the grouping of the Durham episcopal vills for Halmote court purposes in the middle of the fourteenth century: PRO Durham 3/12 (1349-62). The court centres were then Chester-le-Street, Houghton-le-Spring, Easington, Middleham, Stockton, Darlington, Bishop's Auckland, Wolsingham and Lanchester (together with Sadberge and Bedlington). Durham and Whickham owed suit at Chester, Sedgefield at Middleham, Heighington at Bishop's Auckland, and Consett at Lanchester.
10 Cleadon, Whitburn, Wearmouth, Tunstall, Ryhope, Burdon, Easington, Thorpe, Shotton, North Sherburn, Shadforth, Cassop, Sedgefield, Middleham, Cornforth, Norton, Stockton, Hartburn and Preston.
11 Greenwell, pp.15-30.

replaces the correlative 'from St. Martin's feast to the feast of St. Peter in chains' by the shorter phrase *e contra*.[12] It is not certain that this peculiarity reflects the primitive text of Boldon Book. If it does, it would suggest that the initial editing of the raw materials took place at two centres rather than one, or at any rate was the work of more than one team of clerks. At the least, this example serves to emphasise that interpretation of Boldon Book needs to pay close attention to the textual problems which its tradition presents.

The problems are not easy. Whereas the manuscript evidence for Domesday Book is more or less contemporary with the enquiry itself, the text of Boldon Book has been transmitted only by four witnesses written long after the survey was made. The oldest manuscript (henceforward A) may perhaps be dated *c.* 1320-1340; B, written shortly before 1400, is perhaps a little older than C; D, the youngest, comes from the late fifteenth century or even the early sixteenth.[13] An original version of the text (*o*) must have been produced *c.* 1183/4; given the tendency of bureaucrats to duplicate documents, it would probably be unwise to suppose that *o* existed in no more than a single copy. Any attempt to recover *o* from the evidence of the surviving manuscripts must thus involve an exercise in textual criticism. But here analogy with the business of establishing a literary text from late witnesses is not wholly apt. An editor of the literary work can assume that its author expressed his thought, made his final corrections, and laid down his pen for the last time, thus leaving a 'definitive' text to be reconstructed (ready, maybe, for literary critics to 'de-construct' at will). Boldon Book, however, was no literary text, but a document produced for administrative purposes. Its usefulness, it might reasonably be thought, could be increased by conscious efforts to keep it up to date amid changing circumstances. It is likely that our available witnesses, which are all so late, will preserve traces of efforts of this kind. And so the modern editor of Boldon Book faces a double demand: to recover *o*, the text as it was in 1183/4, so far as this is possible; and to identify deliberate later alterations to the original text. He will realise that

---

12   At New Ricknall, Heighington, Redworth, North Auckland and Little Coundon: Austin, pp. 38, 58, 64, 68.

13   A = London, BL Stowe ms.930, ff.36r-51r. B = London, PRO SC/12/21/28, no ancient foliation; now pp.197-219. C = Durham, DC Mun. Priory Register I, pt.ii, ff.51r-62r. D = Oxford, Bodleian Library, Laud misc. ms. 542, ff.1r-9r. In order to avoid compounding existing confusion, the sigla assigned by Lapsley (1905) and retained by Austin (1982) have been used here. Care remains necessary, for Greenwell (1852) designated the Laud ms. (here D) as B, using no siglum for the ms. here called B. Moreover Lapsley in the notes to his translation (as distinct from his discussion of the mss.) denoted B's readings by the siglum A. The date of A is discussed below.

Re-reading Boldon Book

sometimes success in achieving the second aim will frustrate his pursuits of o. Finally he has the problem of presenting his results in such a way that his degrees of success with each task can be readily distinguished.

These exacting requirements are not fully met by any of the existing editions. Boldon Book was first printed in 1816 by Henry Ellis in his volume of *Additamenta* to Domesday Book. Though he knew of C and had available a transcript of B, his edition, printed in Record Type and noting variants from B, was unwisely based on the youngest manuscript, D, of which his opinion was far too favourable.[14] A much more serious attempt to elucidate Boldon Book appeared in 1852, when the Surtees Society published the Reverend William Greenwell's edition of the Latin text, accompanied by a translation, appendices and a valuable glossary.[15] He based his text on B, printing variants from C and D (for the latter he confusingly used the siglum B). Though he was aware that A existed, he was denied permission to see this manuscript by its then owner, the fourth earl Ashburnham.[16] Only after the purchase of the Stowe manuscripts by the British Museum in 1883 did A become easily available to scholars. The first to use it was G.T. Lapsley, to whom had been entrusted the account of Boldon Book for the first volume of the Victoria County History for Durham. Though Lapsley did not print a Latin text, he produced there in 1905 a complete translation of Boldon Book based in essentials on A, with some translated variants from B. His elaborate general discussion of Boldon Book was accompanied by a detailed examination of the textual tradition, the first to take account of all four manuscripts.[17] In 1982 Dr David Austin produced for the Phillimore Press Domesday series a text of Boldon Book based on A, with variants from B, C and D, a translation *en face* and a gazetteer of place-names.[18]

---

14 *Libri censualis vocati Domesday-Book Additamenta ex codic. antiquiss.*, ed. Henry Ellis for the Record Commission, London, 1816: text of Boldon Book, pp.565-87; indices, pp.631-5; introduction, pp.xvi-xvii. At p.xvii Ellis wrote of D: 'While such a transcript remains, it is a subject of comparatively little regret that the autograph is lost; as many reasons might be adduced to render it very probable that this is a faithful copy of the original Boldon Book.' This confident nonsense was echoed half a century later by Thomas Duffus Hardy, *Descriptive Catalogue of Materials relating to the History of Great Britain and Ireland* ii, RS, 1865, pp.443-5.

15 *Boldon Buke*, ed. William Greenwell, SS xxv (1952): Latin text, pp.1-41; translation, pp.43-75; documentary appendices, pp.i-xlix; glossary, pp.l-lxxii.

16 For Greenwell's two main applications, c. 1849 and in 1880, for access to A, see A. Hamilton Thompson, *The Surtees Society 1834-1934*, SS cl (1935), pp.124,177.

17 Art. 'Boldon Book' in VCH *Durham* i, London, 1905, pp.259-341: general discussion, pp.259-317; examination of the textual tradition, pp.321-6; translation, pp.327-41.

18 *Domesday Book*, ed. John Morris. No. 35: Supplementary Volume. *Boldon Book: Northumberland and Durham*, ed. David Austin, Chichester, 1982.

These efforts have made the varying readings of all four manuscripts readily accessible. Comparison rapidly reveals two markedly different recensions of Boldon Book's text. One, represented by A, C and D, derived, in Lapsley's view, from a lost ancestor x, common to these three manuscripts. B, the representative of the other recension, can be traced back, he claimed, to another lost exemplar, z. From his detailed scrutiny of the text Lapsley concluded that x was the superior line of tradition, with A as its earliest and best surviving example; x and A, he thought, thus offered the best route in any attempt to recover o. This conclusion, accepted without question by Dr Austin, has determined the basis of his recent edition.[19] It would be foolish to underrate Lapsley's authority. He was a formidably clever man: 'glittering like a diamond, polished, hard as nails', 'eager, epigrammatic, smart, sociable' – so A.C. Benson found this New Yorker on his translation to Cambridge, England in 1904.[20] A pupil of Charles Gross at Harvard, he had made his name as a scholar before the age of thirty by his book *The County Palatine of Durham*, a pioneering study of a great English franchise.[21] This work, almost precociously mature, even now after nearly nine decades, though inevitably overtaken in part, is far from being superseded as a whole. In my own memory from the early 1930s he was still one of the most impressive medievalists teaching in Cambridge – certainly not the most learned, but a superb oral expositor of English constitutional history during the middle ages.[22] Much is pertinent and valuable in Lapsley's discussion of the textual tradition of Boldon Book. Nevertheless, his argument and conclusions ought not to be allowed to harden into accepted orthodoxy without challenge.

As the first scholar to use A, Lapsley not unnaturally made much of its virtues. Indeed, he exaggerated them. His claim that A 'was copied in the thirteenth century' and was 'written in a hand which cannot be later than 1300' ran counter to the view of the experienced cataloguers of the

---

19   Lapsley, 'Boldon Book', pp.321-6; Austin, p.8.
20   Quoted by David Newsome, *On the Edge of Paradise*, London, 1980, p.175.
21   Published as vol.viii of the Harvard Historical Series at New York in 1900.
22   Hindered, it may be, by indifferent health and the claims of a busy social life, this sub-Jamesian figure published no book after *The County Palatine* (though well-acquainted with Henry James, he was far closer to Edith Wharton). Nine of his shorter contributions to constitutional history were collected after his death in *Crown, Community and Parliament in the Later Middle Ages*, Oxford, 1951. The editors, Helen Cam and Geoffrey Barraclough, prefixed an interesting and generous account of Lapsley's career.

Re-reading Boldon Book

Stowe manuscripts, who dated the hand 'about 1320'.[23] Some modern opinion, including my own, would not reject a dating two or even three decades later than that. Even though A still offers the oldest surviving version of Boldon Book, its seniority to B and C is much less than Lapsley supposed, reduced in effect from a century to perhaps no more than fifty years. Moreover, his suggestion that A, C and D were probably copied independently from a common original fails to convince. His account of the discrepancies by which he justifies his view does not stand up to an examination of the manuscripts;[24] the six instances he adduces all in fact point in another direction.[25] It would, I think, be difficult to prove that D is not a somewhat inaccurate copy of C. A and C present very similar texts. C may be a copy of A, though its direct derivation from an exemplar common to both cannot be ruled out.[26]

Though these objections may cast some doubt on the soundness of Lapsley's arguments, it still remains necessary to postulate an exemplar for A, and *x* may continue to stand for that exemplar, from which C and D, directly or indirectly, also derived. Much more vulnerable is his contention that *x* is a superior line of tradition to *z*, the assumed ancestor of B, so that consequently ACD offer a 'better' version of Boldon Book than B. For that contention does not explain (nor even adequately stress) the preposterous ordering of the entries as they appeared in *x*. In *z* the entries are given for the most part in a rational and comprehensible geographical sequence. Pride of place goes to the only city, Durham; then, starting from Gateshead, the entries proceed southwards in a more or less consistently clockwise direction down the eastern half of *Haliwerfolc* to the Tees, then northwards through the western half to end on the Tyne. A short, geographically miscellaneous series of thirteen entries follows; the significance of this important section will be discussed below. After this the survey is rounded off by the entries for Bedlingtonshire and Norhamshire. In stark contrast, *x* as reflected in ACD presented a

---

23 'Boldon Book', pp.322-3; cf. *Catalogue of the Stowe Manuscripts in the British Museum* i, London, 1895, p.615.
24 'Boldon Book', pp.322.
25 (i) ACD in fact agree about the cottars at Wearmouth against B. (ii) In the Middridge entry the reversal (compared with B) of the last two clauses in the sentence *Wekemann ..... Episcopi* is common to ACD. (iii) At Stanhope the first half of the sentence *Punderus ..... ova* is indeed omitted by A, but also by CD. (iv) In the Langley entry *Domino* is lacking before *Henrico* only in B. (v) At Bedlington B correctly shows *tassum*; *cassum* appears in ACD. (vi) for B's *Tilmouth* AC offer *Eillemuthe* (C correcting to *Tilmouth* in a much later hand), and D *Ellemouth*.
26 Austin's note, p.77, to the Frosterley entry, B *Rogerus*, is mistaken: It should be AB *Radulfus*; CD *Rogerus*. This is a significant variant.

disorderly and incoherent picture. Starting off in the same way as z, after Norton it goes on to entries for Butterwick, Brafferton, Binchester and Urpeth, all in different areas of the county; then to Bedlingtonshire and Norhamshire; then to West Auckland, whence the order of entries is the same as in z until Winlaton; then to another group of nine dispersed settlements until with Stockton it begins another sequence in common with z, concluding the whole at Newton Cap. On the inescapable assumption that the survey was intended for practical use, so that administrators could turn up any of its 150 or so entries rapidly by reference to some ordered scheme, this is a nonsensical jumble. All the same, this is the sequence shown by ACD, and therefore, Lapsley concluded, of x, which he esteemed to display here the original state of the Boldon Book. So this is the order he maintained in his translation; as a corollary he attempted – and thus really did sin against the light – to explain away B's manifest superiority in this respect by arguing that the sequence in B does not result from adhering to a correct exemplar, z, but rather from a deliberate recasting of the disposition of the materials, made after Hatfield's Survey had been compiled towards the end of the fourteenth century.[27] Basing his edition on A, Austin has perceived the difficulty and offered advice on how to obviate it.[28] Nevertheless he has preserved x's sequence, which he knows to be wrong, and so presents us Boldon Book in a form inconvenient for use in any century.

Little ingenuity is needed to suggest what went wrong with x. Early copies of the survey will have been composed of unbound sheets and gatherings. We may conceive of an antecessor of x consisting of four gatherings (maybe three quires each of four leaves plus a bifolium): conforming to the sequence in z, the first gathering (a) contained the entries running from Durham to Norton; the second (b) those from Stockton to Newton Cap; the third (c) those from West Auckland to Sheraton; the fourth (d) those from Butterwick to the end of the final entry for Horncliffe in Norhamshire. In all this it will have matched the logic and doubtless original order of the survey, preserved in z and B. By mischance the gatherings of x's antecedents became confused: perhaps someone dropped them. They were reassembled in the wrong order: (a) was now succeeded by (d), while the displaced (b) was tacked on at the end of (c). When x came to be written as a continuous text,[29]

27   'Boldon Book', p.326.
28   Austin, pp.8-9; appendix i, p.73.
29   If it ever was. It is possible that A was copied directly from the disordered gatherings.

Re-reading Boldon Book

it followed the disarray caused by this shuffle; its progeny, direct or indirect, ACD, inherited the error.[30]

The dislocation in x, retained by Lapsley in his translation and condoned by Austin's edition, impairs quite unnecessarily the credibility of Boldon Book as a useable administrative document. Equally important is the fact that it masks the considerable significance of an apparently miscellaneous section in the survey, which according to z, and doubtless according to o, immediately followed the main entries for *Haliwerfolc* and preceded those for the estates north of Tyne.[31] This section comprises entries for thirteen places widely scattered in or on the margin of *Haliwerfolc*. It falls into two parts; the components of each are related by theme rather than just by geography.

The first part has entries for Sunderland, Winston, Newsham and Barford. These four places had clearly been felt to fall somewhat outside the routine organisation of the bishop's demesne; in one way or another they were all debatable lands. Sunderland – the *sonder land or* separated area – is not to be identified as the port at the mouth of the Wear.[32] It is the Sunderland from which Sunderland Bridge by Croxdale takes its name, as is indicated by the entry's reference to Roger of Audre, lord of Croxdale, Butterby and Coxhoe. What factors contributed to Sunderland's distinctive status in 1183/4 are not wholly clear; some may have been very ancient.[33] The survey treats it as a possession in some way out of the ordinary, as it

---

30 Three other instances where the order of the entries varies between x and z are so slight as perhaps to call for no explanation beyond scribal inadvertence or idiosyncrasy: (i) the account of Penshaw in x follows Little Burdon, not Newbottle, as in z; (ii) the entry for Preston follows Stockton in x, Hartburn in z; (iii) [Newbiggin] by Thickley follows Thickley in x, but Redworth in z. In these cases it must remain uncertain what was the order displayed in the original survey.

31 Greenwell, pp.35-8. In Austin the entries are split between pp.26-9 and pp.50-4, and the two blocks are in the wrong order.

32 As the map-reference given by Austin, p.92, would suggest. The port does not appear in Boldon Book under the name Sunderland; it lurks at the end of the Wearmouth entry as the *burgus* or *burgum* rendering 20/-. Its charter, granted *burgensibus de Weremue*, can have been only two or three years older than the survey: Greenwell, app.iv, p.xli; cf. M.W. Beresford and H.P.R. Finberg, *English Medieval Boroughs: a hand list*, Newton Abbot, 1973, p.107. The name Sunderland for the port (*villata de Sunderland*) has not been noticed before 1196, when its liability for tallage was set at 58/-: *Chancellor's Roll 8 Richard I*, ed. D.M. Stenton, PR Soc. n.s. vii, 1930, p.255.

33 This Sunderland was almost the navel of St. Cuthbert's lands between Tees and Tyne. When ward demarcations became clear, its relation to them was striking and perhaps significant. It lay immediately south of the boundary between Chester and Easington wards along the river Wear, and close to the point in Tursdale where the Darlington, Stockton and Easington wards met: see Surtees, *HD* I.ii, p.iv.

does Winston, Newsham and Barford in the Tees valley at the westernmost limits of Boldon Book's demesne record.[34] This trio of estates lay in an area where the extensive rights centred on Gainford, granted to St. Cuthbert and his church by Bishop Ecgred (850-45), had been prejudiced before the Norman Conquest by land-loans and leases made by Bishops Cutheard (900-15) and Aldhun (990-1013) to Northumbrian earls; after 1066 Gainford and its appurtenances formed the barony granted to the Balliols by the Conqueror.[35] Winston and Newsham were among the settlements returned, so it was claimed, by Robert Mowbray, earl of Northumbria, to St. Cuthbert and his bishop in 1094. But the evidence for this comes from the late twelfth century, and must be regarded with some suspicion.[36] Barford was one of the properties loaned out by Bishop Aldhun; no record of how the bishops of Durham recovered it has been found.[37] It is clear that by c. 1200 the effective mesne lordship of these three Teeside estates lay with the descendants of Meldred son of Dolphin, the lords of Staindrop and Raby.[38] A tantalisingly imperfect document appears to show that c. 1163 X 1176 Bishop Hugh had granted to Meldred in fee and inheritance Winston and Newsham together with Winlaton and Sunderland, for an annual rent of £20 and other unspecified free services.[39] In 1183/4 Meldred's eldest son and heir, Robert, was still a minor; presumably the bishop claimed prerogative wardship over him. The survey's sequence of entries Sunderland-Winston-Newsham-Barford emphasises that, unlike Staindrop, which the family held from the prior and convent

---

34 Confusion has been caused here by one of Greenwell's few slips in transcription; he printed *Winestona* as *Wivestoua*. Combined with the *Wynestowe* in ACD this led to Lapsley's mistaken identification as Weston and Austin's, pp.51,92, as Westoe.
35 See H.H.E. Craster, 'The Patrimony of St Cuthbert', *EHR* lxx (1954), 187-95.
36 DC Mun. 1.1.Reg.17 = *FPD*, p.lxxxii; cf. *DEC*, p.11.
37 See *Historia de Sancto Cuthberto*, in *Symeonis Monachi Opera Omnia* i, ed. Thomas Arnold, RS, 1882, p.213. Barford, lying west of Little Newsham and south of Cleatlam, is not the Barforth in Yorks NR, as G.V. Scammell, *Hugh du Puiset*, Cambridge, 1956, pp.232, 330, supposed.
38 Robert Fitzmeldred granted lands and rights in free alms to the monks of Durham at Winston and Newsham; similarly his brother Gilbert at Barford: *FPD* 51n-55n, 153n-155n. Robert refers to *molendinum meum de Winestona*.
39 London, BL Landsdowne ms.902, f.67v. This is a transcript, made perhaps by Ralph Gowland early in the eighteenth century, of what purports to be the confirmation by the Prior and Convent of Durham of the bishop's grant to Meldred, which has not survived. If the transcript was made from a genuine document and the prior named, *Jerrardus*, is a mistake for Germanus, the date of the confirmation cannot be before 1163. Meldred died after 1172 and before 1178. Martin Snape will deal with this very corrupt text in his collection of Hugh du Puiset's *acts*.

Re-reading Boldon Book

of Durham, this part of his inheritance was episcopal demesne, and so liable to be exploited in the bishop's interests. It should be read in connection with the entry immediately preceding Sunderland in the survey: that for Winlaton, where the tenancy of Robert Fitzmeldred's family can be assumed.[40] This first part of the miscellaneous section is thus wholly concerned with the holdings of a single family, which by the accident of a minor's succession happened to be at the bishop's mercy. It was a passing phase; so far as is known none of the four settlements in the series Sunderland-Barford occurs in later accounts of the bishop's demesne.

The second part of this section has a different interest. It presents the entries, running from Great Usworth to Urpeth, for eight (or more precisely seven and two-thirds) townships in *Haliwerfolc*, if Hulam is reckoned as a single unit with Hutton Henry.[41] The grouping is not geographical but thematic. With one exception these entries show a common characteristic: while in only two instances, at Herrington and Sheraton (both divided estates), is a tenant specified by name, all the entries refer to a dreng, unnamed, who renders no money but is liable for certain services, clearly antique in origin. He must feed a dog and a horse (for the service of his lord, the bishop); attend the bishop's great hunt with two greyhounds and five ropes;[42] pay suit at the bishop's court and go on the bishop's errands. At Herrington, Hutton Henry and Urpeth he must also cart wine for the bishop, and a millstone too at Hutton Henry and Urpeth: *corvées* the survey records elsewhere as communal rather than personal liabilities. The exceptional case is Brafferton, where no dreng but an unnamed thegn is involved; he must attend the great hunt and owes suit of court, but his freedom from the duties of feeding dog and horse is specifically noted.[43]

---

40 In 1183/4 Winlaton is recorded as at farm for £15 p.a.; the farmer is not named; Greenwell, p.35. But cf. *DEC*, p.76. While the farm for the four estates Winlaton-Sunderland-Winston-Newsham had been set at £20 in Bishop Hugh's grant to Meldred, in the survey the total for them amounts to more than £38.

41 Greenwell, pp.35-8. Hulam, for which the entry is extremely brief, may be counted as a single unit with Hutton Henry, with which it was closely associated; cf. *Hatfield Survey.*, p.153.

42 The 15 ropes stipulated at Urpeth, according to all the mss., is possibly an example of a very early scribal aberration.

43 Greenwell, p.37 mistranscribed *Theinus* in B as *Themus*; ACD read *Henricus*. Lapsley rather desperately amended B's reading to *Thomas*.

The problem of drengage in northern England, with its ministerial colouring and perplexing combination of military socage and almost unfree tenure, has attracted much attention since Maitland indicated its importance in 1890.[44] Mentions of drengage abound in Boldon Book, emphasising the persistence on the bishop's estates of that 'underlayer' of ancient Northumbrian shire custom, on which the heavier organisation of the manor had as yet been superimposed only incompletely.[45] Normally, however, such entries in Boldon Book show a named tenant and a stipulated rent; at least fifteen examples of this can be observed before the beginning of the miscellaneous section.[46] Obviously the seven entries concerning unnamed drengs and the entry about the unnamed thegn at Brafferton have been removed from their natural geographical contexts and brought together for some special purpose, after the information on which they were based had been acquired in the ordinary course of the survey.[47] They amount in effect to a homogeneous block of estreats.

No doubt their purpose was to promote in some way the more efficient and profitable administration of the bishop's estates. But it is not easy to suggest exactly why these estreats were made. It cannot have been just a matter of replacing hoary, obsolescent and uncertain services from anonymous drengs and thegns by money renders from clearly identified free tenants. As Paul Harvey has pointed out to me, the identity of the unnamed drengs can hardly have remained unknown to those responsible for the survey. It seems likely enough that named tenants at Herrington and Sheraton, Hugh *de Herinas* and Thomas, were responsible for the personal liabilities of the unnamed drengs at those places, while by 1184 an episcopal charter had confirmed a grant from William, patently the dreng at Butterwick who remains unnamed in the

---

44 Early milestones in the discussion are F.W. Maitland, 'Northumbrian Tenures', *EHR* (1890), 625-33; G.T. Lapsley, 'Cornage and Drengage', *American Hist. Rev.* ix (1904), 670-95; *id.*, 'Boldon Book', pp.284-91; J.E.A. Joliffe, 'Northumbrian Institutions', *EHR* xli (1928), 1-42. For more recent treatments, see G.W.S. Barrow, 'Northern English Society in the early middle ages', *Northern History* iv (1969), 1-28; William E. Kapelle, *The Norman Conquest of the North*, London, 1979, pp.50-85.
45 Kapelle, pp.181-90. But positive evidence for Kapelle's contention that the 'manorialisation' of many Durham townships was the direct result of the Conqueror's ravages in 1069 seems scanty indeed.
46 See in particular the very detailed entries for Oxenhall and Whessoe: Greenwell, pp.18-20.
47 For Great Usworth perhaps in conjunction with Gateshead; for Herrington with Newbottle; for Hutton Henry, Hulam and perhaps also Sheraton with Shotton; for Butterwick with Sedgefield; for Brafferton with Darlington; for Binchester with Coundon; and for Urpeth with Chester-le-Street.

Re-reading Boldon Book 15

Boldon Book entry.[48] To postulate from these estreats some comprehensive anti-drengage programme set on foot by Bishop Hugh's administrators would neglect the fact that in practice the supersession of drengage tenure in Durham proved a very slow business. Two centuries after Boldon Book the Hatfield Survey provides evidence in plenty for its persistence as a form of landholding carefully distinguished from free tenure: thus late in the fourteenth century the lordly Nevilles were still liable for typical drengage services – at least nominally – at Oxenhall and Little Burdon, just as their direct forbear Robert Fitzmeldred had been at Whessoe in 1183/4.[49]

Nevertheless, Boldon Book can show change already on foot in this area, as well, perhaps, as preparation for further changes. William of Hertburn's holding at Washington looks much like a former drengage recently converted to fee-farm.[50] At Heworth near Aycliffe Gilbert is now holding for an annual rent of three marks, and is quit of the ancient works and services 'which he used to do as form a thegnage'.[51] An alteration to the text of Boldon Book when combined with charter evidence makes clear that by 1200 Thomas of Aycliffe had come to hold Whitworth by knight's service; it had still been a drengage in 1183/4.[52] And among the estreated entries themselves, that for Sheraton invites speculation. As the Boldon Book text now stands, a moiety of the vill is held by John for the rent of three marks, quit of the works and services which were wont to be rendered from half the drengage, in return for Crawcrook which he has quitclaimed. Thomas holds the other moiety of Sheraton in drengage, and the personal liabilities of the unnamed dreng are explicitly reckoned as half the normal.[53] Boldon Book records Crawcrook as at farm, without naming the farmer; by 1189 the bishop had granted it in fee-farm to his chamberlain Lawrence.[54] It may well be that the original form of Boldon Book had

---

48 Bishop Hugh's confirmation, printed *Early Yorkshire Charters* ii.308-9, survives in only a late copy, incomplete and probably corrupt; cf. Bishop Philip of Poitou's charter for the heir of the original grantee: Oxford, Bodleian Library, ms. Dodsworth 7, f.353r-v. I owe these references to Martin Snape. A William *de butrewic* witnesses a charter of Bishop Hugh, DC Mun. 4.1.Pont.3, printed by Scammell, AA[4] 34 (1956), 84-5 and dated by him '*c.* 1190'.
49 *Hatfield Survey*, pp.9,145; Greenwell, p.20.
50 Greenwell, p.3.
51 Greenwell, p.16: *que inde sicut de theinagio facere solebat.*
52 Greenwell, p.27 and app.vi, p.xliii.
53 Greenwell, pp.36-7. AD says that John *quietam clamat* Crawcrook; BC offer the preferable *quietam clamauit.*
54 Greenwell, p.35; London, BL Landsdowne ms.902, f.78r. The royal confirmation of Bishop Hugh's charter is dated 30 November 1189, *ib.* f.78v.

displayed Sheraton still as an undivided drengage, so that the situation now shown by the manuscripts had resulted from the transformation of half of it after 1183/4 into a free tenure to recompense John for giving up Crawcrook.

At Butterwick the process of change can be followed in some detail. By 1208-10 the Butterwick dreng, unnamed in Boldon Book (though doubtless known in 1183/4 to the bishop's officials), is now identified as William, holding *hereditarie in drengagio de antiquo tenemento*.[55] By 1248 Roger, William's son and successor, had sold out his drengage rights to Bishop Nicholas Farnham for 50 marks, whereupon the bishop granted the whole vill of Butterwick, its demesnes, services, villeins and all other possible profits to William, son of William of Sadberge. William is to hold in fee and inheritance for an annual render of 10 marks, in order to compensate the bishop for the services due to him while Butterwick was held in drengage; he is liable for the amount of forinsec service appropriate to a sixth of a knight's fee, and owes suit at the three major meetings of the bishop's court at Durham; his heirs will pay a relief of 10 marks.[56] For an outlay of 50 marks the episcopal administration had tidied up the tenurial situation at Butterwick, with the prospect of a steady annual rent which would soon defray the cost of the operation; moreover, though this was not made explicit in the charter, henceforward the tenants of Butterwick would presumably be liable for the free tenants' tax, the *commune auxilium*, which drengs may have claimed to escape.[57] Binchester and Urpeth had gone the same way as Butterwick by the time of the Hatfield Survey, which shows them now being held at fee-farm for considerable money rents and forinsec service.[58]

It can be accepted, then, that there was movement on the bishop's estates away from drengage. But difficulties remain about attempting to explain the estreated entries simply as part of some conscious plan in 1183/4 to reform this ancient tenurial system. If such a plan existed, its execution was neither quick nor effective. According to the Hatfield Survey some drengage characteristics persisted in five of the estreated townships late in

---

55 *BF* i.31.
56 See Appendix I.
57 It may be significant that none of the estreated entries makes reference to *utware* among the dreng's personal liabilities, though elsewhere in the survey, at Oxenhall and Whessoe, this is recorded: Greenwell, pp.18,20.
58 *Hatfield Survey*, pp.34,82. But drengage burdens had persisted at Urpeth as late as 1365: Surtees, *HD* ii, pp.191-2. Even the *Hatfield Survey* shows the tenant liable to cart wine.

Re-reading Boldon Book

the fourteenth century. While John de Ask holds half of Sheraton by rent and forinsec service alone, the other half, in Neville hands, is paying 6/- a year *pro redditu dringagii* and commutation for the metrith cow; it is still liable for the same cornage as the half-drengage of 1183/4, and for renders of grain and meal; its tenant owes forinsec service.[59] Great Usworth now has knightly tenants, holding for rent and forinsec service, but they also pay cornage, commutation for the castleman and metrith cow of 1183/4, and must still cart a tun of wine, though the dreng's services set out in Boldon Book have disappeared.[60] If the Hatfield Survey shows the ville and most of the land at Hutton Henry being held by Henry of Esh as a free tenant by rent and forinsec service, Henry is also named among the drengage tenants who owe payments in commutation for some of the services listed in Boldon Book.[61] The tenants of East Herrington are still described as holding *in dringagio*. The major tenant is a knight, holding by forinsec service; he is liable for finding a castleman, commutation payments for cornage and the metrith cow, and for renders of oats and meal and malt. But the dreng's classic personal services (attendance at the bishop's hunt, keeping dog and horse, going on the bishop's errands etc.) are recorded as resting on a smaller tenant holding by rent and forinsec service.[62] And at Brafferton remarkably little seems to have changed in two centuries, except for the disappearance of the thegn and the commutation into money renders of the metrith cow and the castleman.[63]

Such evidence counsels caution before supposing that the estreats in the second part of the miscellaneous section of the Boldon Book foreshadowed a radical attack on drengage tenures on the bishop's estates. But it seems quite certain that they must have had some programmatic significance, even if their real concern was less with forms of tenure as such than with the status and personal liabilities of drengs. Only z, represented by B, it must be emphasised, allows us to perceive that Boldon Book here presents an important problem. The mistaken sequence of entries in the x tradition destroys the unity of this miscellaneous section; by

---

59 *Hatfield Survey*, p.152. The cartage of wine and a millstone, specified as burdens on the drengage half of Sheraton in Boldon Book, is now said to rest on the whole vill.
60 *Hatfield Survey*, p.102.
61 *Hatfield Survey*, p.153. Commutation is due for cornage, metrith cow and castleman. There is no mention of the Boldon Book dreng's liabilities for dog and horse, cartage of wine and millstone, attendance at the bishop's hunt, suit of court and messenger services.
62 *Hatfield Survey*, pp.157-8.
63 *Hatfield Survey*, p.27.

following A Lapsley and Austin were led to print it disjointed into two widely separated parts, neither of which, taken by itself, reveals the sense of the whole.[64] On the other hand, apart from this major dislocation, Lapsley's claim that in general x preserves a more primitive form of Boldon Book than does z can be accepted. What must be stressed above all, however, is that neither line of tradition presents the survey exactly as it was written down in 1183/4; sometimes o can be recovered only by conjecture, and at other times not at all. Boldon Book is in fact a labile document; the original text was not regarded as sacrosanct and almost at once alterations and additions began to be made to it. In differing degrees and by varying routes these found their way into both lines of tradition. Undoubtedly this process of incorporation came to an end in x before it did in z; x, so to speak, was the earlier to fossilise. That fact, it may be said in anticipation, does not necessarily recommend x as the 'better' basis for a modern edition.

Some of the post-1183/4 additions are common to x and z. The most obvious is a long insertion to the Bedlingtonshire entries in both recensions, which cannot have been made before the episcopate of Walter Kirkham (1249-60). It is a memorandum about the terms on which Bishop Walter had released the free men and their tenants in Netherton, West and East Sleekburn, Cambois and Choppington from the ancient carting and building duties which they had been recorded in 1183/4 as owing in aid of Bedlington. These services are now superseded in return for annual cash payments totalling £12 13s 8d. In addition there are notes about the farming of the fishery at Cambois to Adam and his heirs and the manumission by Bishop Walter of a Bedlingtonshire serf.[65] Neither recension offers a completely reliable text here. In x the memorandum is spatchcocked into the middle of the original short entry for Netherton, instead of ending the Bedlingtonshire account, as it does, no doubt correctly, in z.[66] Moreover, x makes William rather than Walter (as in z) the bishop of Durham

---

64 'Boldon Book', pp.331, 336-7; Austin, pp.26-28, 50-54.
65 Greenwell, pp.39-40. Stephen, son of Adam of Cambois, forfeited his holding in West Sleekburn for complicity in Gilbert Middleton's attack on Louis Beaumont and the two cardinals at Rushyford in September 1317: James Raine, *The History and Antiquities of North Durham*, London, 1852, p.372.
66 Possibly this memorandum originally existed on a single detached sheet, with a more or less adequate note about where it was to be inserted, i.e. at the end of the original entries for Bedlingtonshire, where it stands in B. It may be that in the course of x's evolution a scribe, using an exemplar in which the original entry for Netherton extended from one folio to the next, picked up the additional sheet and heedlessly inserted it where the first folio ended, completing Netherton at the end of the insertion.

Re-reading Boldon Book

responsible for the commutation of the ancient customary services at Netherton, West Sleekburn and Cambois.[67] It is beyond belief that the survey would have recorded in 1183/4 – as it did – customary services at these townships if they had already been commuted by Bishop William of St Calais (1081-96) or Bishop William of Ste Barbe (1143-52). The correct reading must be Walter. But there is also inaccuracy in the other line. Perhaps in z, though more probably in the copying of its sole representative, B, confusion is caused by what seems an easily explicable scribal slip. B imputes the release from ancient services of two free tenants in Choppington to Bishop Antony Bek (1283-1311), rather than to Walter Kirkham. The reference is intended to be to the bishop already named, i.e. Walter. ACD give the correct reading: *Dominus autem Episcopus*. In B, however, something like *aut' Episcopus* was expanded in error as *Antonius*. A charter of Bishop Robert Stichill in May 1262 shows that release from the *antique operaciones* was already effective in Choppington as well as the other Bedlingtonshire townships two decades before Bek's accession.[68] This scribal blunder in B has no necessary bearing on the date of z.

At least one more addition from Bishop Walter's time found its way into z, sandwiched with two other entries between the survey's accounts of North Biddick and Chester-le-Street; this little block of added matter is absent from x.[69] But in their account of Whickham both x and z offer clear indications of a later rehandling of o, made in order to reflect changed circumstances there.[70] As it stands in the editions this entry shows unusual features; above all, it combines information from two distinct dates. This

---

67   ACD give *Willelmus*; B *Walterus*. The editors are unhelpful. Greenwell mistakenly shows C reading *Walterus*. Austin in his text and apparatus does not record B's reading at all, though he refers to it on p.81 in a note to p.30 line 12 which is wholly unconvincing.

68   DC Mun. Priory Reg. I, pt.ii, ff.23r,42v: a copy of an inspeximus and confirmation of Stichill's charter by Prior Hugh and the chapter of Durham, 30 October 1263.

69   These entries comprise: (i) a record of the acquittal *per patriam* from an allegation of serfdom of two brothers in West Auckland (what Austin, p.74, means by reading *per palam* for *per patriam* defeats me); (ii) a grant by an unnamed bishop of land on the moor at Newbottle for rent, made to Gilbert son of Humphrey of Durham; (iii) an undated grant by Bishop Walter of 48 acres at Helmington (west of Willington) to Roger Bernard. This grant was confirmed by the prior and convent on 8 September 1259: DC Mun. Priory Reg. I, pt.ii, f.11r. The date of (i) is uncertain. Possibly the Gilbert fitz Humphrey of (ii) is the deponent in 1221 X 1223, whose memory went back to 1195-6: *FPD* 282-3. A man named thus sealed shortly after 1219, DC Mun.2.4. Pont. 8 = *FPD* 218-9, and witnessed *FPD* 173-4nn. Presumably all three entries were originally made in the margin of z and later incorporated in the text.

70   As Lapsley suspected, 'Boldon Book', pp.325-6. Text: Greenwell, pp.33-4; Austin, p.48.

resort to a *then* and *now* form, though advertised in the preamble to Boldon Book (of uncertain date), is not in fact characteristic of the survey as a whole. This difficulty can be resolved by accepting that when the enquiries were first made the demesne at Whickham was in hand, being directly exploited by the bishop through his reeve; consequently the villein holdings, works and services were enumerated in detail, doubtless in the present (and, where appropriate, the future) tense, as was normal throughout the survey. At some later date the manor of Whickham was put out to farm, making much of this information irrelevant. But instead of them being scrapped, the original entry was rehandled by the expedient of changing its verbs into the past tense, and the conditions of the farm were specified (in the present tense) in a new clause beginning *Nunc autem*. This process of reworking is so clear that it seems possible to reconstruct with fair confidence the original form of the Whickham entry.[71] Unfortunately, it is not known when Whickham was put out to farm, so the date of this alteration remains uncertain. It may even have been made during the course of the survey: we do not know.

No other additional material common to x and z, except the Bedlingtonshire insertion, needs be dated much later than the episcopate of Philip of Poitou (1197-1208). The few instances seem tolerably easy to identify. Whitworth, said to be held by Thomas of Aycliffe by service of a quarter of a knight's fee, had not been transformed from a drengage tenure until about 1200, as the bishop's charter of enfeoffment shows.[72] The vills of Cornsay and Hedley Hill had been granted by Bishop Hugh to his chamberlain Simon before 1183/4; Simon duly appears in Boldon Book as holding them. Later he contrived to pass the vills over to his nephews, Robert fitz Roger and Walter fitz Hugh of Caen: Bishop Hugh's charter of ratification is to be dated 1190 X 1195.[73] The note added to the Cornsay entry about the exemption of Robert and Walter from suit of court at Durham and Sadberge respectively cannot have been introduced into x and z before c.1190, even supposing that Bishop Hugh's acquisition of the wapentake of Sadberge in September 1189 was followed almost immediately by the setting up of an episcopal court there. In the entry for Marley the reference to an exemption from services granted by Philip of Poitou must have been added to x and z later than 1196. The note in the

---

71 This is attempted in Appendix II.
72 See note 50 above.
73 Now at Ushaw College. Printed by Greenwell, app.vii, p.xliv, and better by G.V. Scammell, *AA*[4] xxxiv (1956),87.

Re-reading Boldon Book 21

Heighington entry about Simon Dorward's holding (more explicit in *x* than in *z*) must be later than Bishop Hugh's grant to Simon, which was made after August 1190 and probably near the end of the episcopate.[74]

These examples of later additions to *o* seem quite certain. A few more can be surmised. The tenant at *Smalleia* (near Birtley) is now known as Robert of Cogesall' (Rogershall in *x*), who was active in Durham under Bishop Richard Marsh (1217-26) and later;[75] it seems unlikely that he could have appeared in *o*. At Byermoor the tenant is a Philip *de Gildeford*, who is not met with as a witness to local charters much before the second decade of the thirteenth century.[76] If the unnamed son of William the moneyer shown as holding at Stella is William fitz William fitz Erkembald, he too may have found his way into Boldon Book after 1183/4, for his father lived on until 1190 at least, and the earliest other evidence for William fitz William comes from 1196.[77] In these three cases there are reasonable grounds for conjecturing that both *x* and *z* bear witness to later amendment of *o*, though the evidence falls short of proof.

For some time, then, the two lines of tradition must have run together. Yet, as will later be illustrated further, *z* shows modifications of *o* not to be found in *x*. To the problem how and when the two lines diverged perhaps no wholly satisfactory answer can be found. But a useful starting point for this enquiry is the differing codicological histories of the two recensions. There must have been at least one 'office' version of the original survey, kept for use by the bishop's administration and liable to alteration as circumstances changed on the estates. Everything points to B, continuously in the custody of the episcopal administrators for five centuries, until nineteenth-century legislation decreed its removal to London,[78] as being the official descendant of the original 'office' version, *o*. Naturally, though regrettably, when B was written at the end of the

---

74 Hugh's charter and Bishop Philip's confirmation survive in a fifteenth-century inspeximus: DC Mun., Misc.Ch.7243 mm.203. I owe this reference to Martin Snape.
75 See Northumberland Record Office, Gosforth, Ravensworth Deed no. 20, dated 1223. In 1221 X 1223 Robert's memory went back to local events in 1208: *FPD* 243. But he was still witnessing as late as 1237 X 1241: DC Mun. 2.14. Spec.23 = *FPD* 202n.
76 See DC Mun. 2.6. Spec. 3 & 4; 3.3. Sacr.7 (Robert of Coggleshall too witnesses the second and third of these documents); *Early Deeds relating to Newcastle upon Tyne*, ed. A.M. Oliver, SS cxxxvii (1924), no. 175, p.113.
77 DC Mun. 3.6 Spec.4; cf. *Early Deeds relating to Newcastle*, pp.198-9.
78 According to Lapsley, 'Boldon Book', p.321 and n.4, B was still in the Halmote Court offices at Durham in 1905. But by 1908 it had been listed at the PRO in London: *List of Rentals and Surveys ..... preserved in the Public Record Office*, Lists and Indexes xxv (1908), p.79.

fourteenth century, it was thought to supersede the materials from which it was transcribed. They were allowed to disappear, perhaps the more readily because a comprehensive new survey of the episcopal estates (the Hatfield Survey) had become available. Thus today B is the only surviving witness of the z recension. Because the survey of 1183/4 was intended for use, attempts were certain to be made, at least sporadically, to keep it up to date. This, it may be supposed, was done by making marginal and interlinear corrections to the 'office' copy of o; only the memorandum about Bishop Walter Kirkham's dealings with Bedlingtonshire was too long to be handled in this fashion and was kept on a separate sheet. Possibly, at some date after c.1260, this 'office' copy, as amended and including the Kirkham memorandum, was transcribed as a continuous clean version incorporating all the post-1183/4 material. If that happened, the result would have been z, the hypothetical ancestor or exemplar of B. Alternatively, B may have been based directly on the amended 'office' version of o; it would thus have been the first clean copy of the survey and its amendments available to the bishop's officials since shortly after 1183/4. In either case, what had happened to o had occurred within the bishop's exchequer.

In contrast, the contexts in which the witnesses for x appear to indicate an un- or extraofficial history for that recension. A and C are found in books which belonged to the Prior and Convent of Durham; though D was once owned by Bishop Cuthbert Tunstall, it is not certain that it was specially written for him, and the textual evidence suggests that it may have been no more than a copy of C. Motives of capitular responsibility and neighbourly inquisitiveness will have urged Prior and Convent to acquire a copy of Bishop Hugh's great survey. It seems that they were not successful immediately. But later they came into possession of a version already showing official amendments made down to a decade or so after 1200.[79] Even later, probably, they secured the Kirkham memorandum about Bedlingtonshire, and incorporated it maladroitly in their text. It is likely that the x tradition, represented by ACD, originated in some such way. In so far as its modifications of o (except for the Kirkham memorandum) come to an end by c. 1220, it does indeed offer a less extensively rehandled text of the survey than does z.

---

[79] This can hardly have been the main amended 'office' version, which presumably was kept closely safe by the bishop's administrators. But, as has been pointed out, more than one copy of o may have been produced.

Re-reading Boldon Book 23

That fact does not force us to accept Lapsley's claim that *x* is 'in the main a much better version' than *z* and consequently is the basis for a modern edition of the survey.[80] Admittedly, it stopped growing before *z* did; but more primitive does not necessarily mean better.[81] It would be unwise to follow Lapsley in exaggerating *x*'s merits. Somewhere in the course of its evolution to its earliest surviving representative A this line of tradition had fallen into careless or ignorant hands. Its renderings of placenames betrays the work of a scribe who knew or cared little about the geography of the bishop's demesnes: *Suyfela* for Twizel by Easington;[82] *Eillemuthe* for Tillmouth; *Audeham* for Duddo; *Ungeleia* for Migley; *Birdeia* for Birtley; *Reyhermore* for Byermoor; *Wynestowe* for Winston; *Horton*' for Hutton (Henry); *Bolum* for Hulam. Personal names have suffered too: Richard *de Yrseley*, holding in Stanhope, was really *de Hyfpherlea*, as Bishop Hugh's charter for him shows.[83] The *Ormus filius Coket Vttingus* holding a carucate at Preston disguises joint tenants, Orm son of Toki and Utting.[84] The unnamed thegn at Brafferton is garbled into a man called *Henricus*; Lawrence son of Odard at East Sleekburn has become the son of Edward;[85] a convincing Nigel at Edderacres is transformed into an implausible Seal.[86] Manifest errors crop up elsewhere in the text. The three 'coroners' at Wolsingham with their annual render of wooden trenchers have long since recovered their proper identity as turners.[87] No sense can be made of *x*'s *lallia Radulfi Callidi* in Aucklandshire; it is *z*

---

80 'Boldon Book', p.325.
81 Thus, when discussing the editorial problem raised by the existence of two or more manuscripts of a document, R.F. Hunnisett, *Editing Records for Publication*, British Records Association, *Archives and the User* no. 4, 1977, p.19, though maintaining that 'if no original version survives, that which is nearest to the original must, if possible, be used', feels bound to allow that 'if one document was treated by contemporaries as having greater administrative authority than its fellows, or as being "of record", it is that the document which should be transcribed.'
82 *Tuisela* in B; cf. the grants made by Bishops Richard Poore and Nicholas Farnham of services from land at *Suthe- twysle* and *Northtwisill* to support a chaplain in the chantry of the Blessed Virgin in Easington church: DC Mun. Misc.Chs. 5155,6157; cf. Priory Reg.I, pt.ii, ff.4r, 9v. This is not the Twizel north of Craghead, as the grid-reference in Austin, p.92, suggests.
83 Printed from DC Mun. 3.1.Pont.17 by Scammell, *AA*[4] xxxiv (1956), who dates it *c*. 1160 X 1170. Scammell prints *de Hyspherlea*, but the preferable reading seems to be *de Hyfpherlea*.
84 As is obvious from the later situation described in B: *Ormus filius Toki et Willelmus filius Uttingi j. carucatam*, Greenwell, pp.14-15.
85 Greenwell, p.40, makes him the son of Edmund, having misread B's *Edardi*; for the true name of Lawrence's father see *Monasticon* VI.ii, 1830, p.734, no.18.
86 ACD *sigillo*; B *Nigillo*.
87 ACD *coronatores*; B *tornatores*.

24

which gives us 'the bailiwick of Ralph the Crafty'.[88] It was the prior of Brinkburn who held two bovates and a fishery at Whickham as alms from the bishop, as *z* states and charter evidence confirms, not the prior of Guisborough, as *x* records.[89] Only reference to *z* allows repair to quite considerable omissions by *x* towards the end of the entries for Bishop Middleham, Stanhope, Blackwell and Thornton. Other readings in *x* are on the face of it so inferior as hardly to call for comment.[90]

In comparison *z*, as represented by B, comes out by no means badly. B's text is not immaculate. It starts unhappily, with a redundant first *sicut tunc erant* in the preamble, where it reads *assisas* wrongly for *assise*. It goes on to make about a couple of dozen omissions. These are mostly very small, amounting to no more than a single word or numeral, though at Heighington a later insertion has perhaps led to the loss of a note about the reeve, and at Witton (Gilbert) a clause has fallen out *per homeoteleuton*. In the text of the Kirkham memorandum about Bedlingtonshire the reference to carriage services from Darlington seems erroneous; as can be seen from *x*, what was intended was cartage from Bedlington to Gateshead. A few lines later B's *nichil* (corrected by a later hand) is a mistake for *vel*, while the false reading *Dominus Antonius Episcopus* for *Dominus autem Episcopus* has been discussed already. A few more aberrations could be adduced.[91] Overall, however, Lapsley's contention that B presents an

---

88 B *Baillia Radulphi callidi*: Greenwell, p.26. It is likely that this Ralph was the *Radulfus cautus* noted in Boldon Book at Stanhope and Frosterley; possibly the *Radulphus canutus* at Bushblades was a different man. *Radulfus queinte* witnesses DC Mun. 4.1.Pont.3 = Scammell, *AA*[4] xxxiv (1956), 85, dating from *c*.1190. Ralph le Cu<i>nte was among Hugh du Puiset's servants who made fine after the bishop's death; in 1196 he was liable for £40, of which he had paid £26 13s. 4d.: *Chancellor's Roll 8 Richard I*, p.259. Together with *Robertus Cautus* he witnesses DC Mun. 3.7.Spec.7 = *FPD* 136n.

89 Hugh du Puiset's charter for Brinkburn (before 1174) is printed in *The Chartulary of Brinkburn Priory*, ed. William Page, SS xc (1892), p.180; cf. pp.186,197.

90 For example: at Farnacres, A *pro dimidia parte*, CD *et dimidia parte* (correctly: pro decima parte); at Whickham, ACD *solebant inpiscari in Tyna* (B *solebant facere iii. piscaries in Tina*); in the Bedlingtonshire insertion, ACD *singuli in communi* (B *singulis annis in communi*) and just above this ACD also omit *pro relaxacione*; at Winlaton, AC *suis instaur'* for *sine instauramento* (D has corrected this).

91 B's figure of 20 chalders of corn as the render of the farm of the ten ploughteams on the demesnes at Stockton and Hartburn seems absurdly low; the 200 chalders shown by *x* is clearly preferable. It makes smoother sense to read *scillicet* with *x* rather than B's *sunt* as the third word in the entry for Quarringtonshire. In the account of the villeins' services at Boldon it would seem that when they make the lodges and do their carting of wood, *then* they are quit of other works: reading *tunc* with *x*, rather than *ducunt* with B.

Re-reading Boldon Book

inferior text to x is contradicted by the facts. In its sequence of the entries and general accuracy in geographical matters B is clearly more comprehensible than ACD. Rather grudgingly Lapsley pointed to a dozen or so passages where it seemed to him that B had 'preserved a purer reading' than x.[92] That number could be multiplied at least sixfold. Though A is an earlier manuscript than B, it does not undermine the latter's authority.

Confrontation of x and z, though interesting in itself, has, of course, only limited value for recovering the survey as it was committed to writing in 1183/4. To seek a completely unadulterated o from the surviving manuscripts is to pursue an *ignis fatuus*. For many of the instances in which x and z or one of the two departed from o were not the consequences of mere scribal inefficiency; they were later alterations deliberately made. It has been suggested that x ceased to undergo substantial change $c.1220$.[93] With z alteration continued longer and was more extensive. The changes it shows in the run of entries from Durham city to Mainsforth are not particularly striking, comprising little more than minor adjustments to the acreage of holdings or to renders of hens and eggs due from pinders.[94] In the run between Norton and Hunwick, however, they were far more numerous.[95] Many take account of a change in tenants, as one generation replaced another. At Norton Gilbert of Hardwick's holding is now in the hands of his son Alan, who has 60 acres where his father had held 36. At Preston the holding which according to x (as corrected above) belonged to Orm son of Toki and Utting is now in the hands of Orm and William son of Utting. At Great Haughton (-le-Skerne) the widow of Alfred the dreng, holding three acres by the bishop's alms in x, must have died or married again, for z does not mention her. At Heighington the wife of Hugh Brown, mentioned in x, has disappeared from the record in z, which shows that Hugh's two bovates had been granted to Thomas *de Pemme* for an increased render. In the entries for Stockton, Darlington and North Auckland x and z diverge markedly, with z clearly being the later state of the text.[96] But

---

92 'Boldon Book', pp.324-5.
93 Except for the somewhat botched insertion after $c.1260$ of the memorandum about commuted services in Bedlingtonshire.
94 Greenwell, pp.1-12. On the whole the tendency seems upwards: the 40 hens due according to x from Boldon, Newbottle and Sedgefield have in z become 80, 60 and 80 respectively. On the other hand z shows diminished annual receipts from the mills of Durham and Quarringtonshire: 36 marks as compared with 60 in x.
95 Greenwell, pp.12-27.
96 At Darlington, for example, z shows changes among the tenants, further definition of the cottars' services, and an increase in the expected receipts from the borough, the dyers and the town ovens.

from Wolsingham onwards there is less evidence of rehandling in z. Thence to the end of the survey difference in substance becomes infrequent, though at Lanchester z records 20 villeins against 10 in x, while in Norhamshire z produces an entirely new entry (for Cornhill) and significantly varies the villein renders at Horncliffe.[97]

Probably not many of the alterations exhibited by z were made long after c. 1220, although its reduction to *nil* of the thousand eggs which x shows the villeins at Heighington, Killerby, Middridge and Thickley owing annually may have occurred at a much later stage. What detailed examination of the changes undergone by o reveals unmistakably is that they were haphazard, not the result of any comprehensive review made on the basis of consistent principle. Both x and z show Whitworth held in fee by Thomas of Aycliffe, who is known to have been enfeoffed with this former drengage by Bishop Philip of Poitou c. 1200.[98] But they give no indication that before that date Richard I had restored to Durham the right of coinage which they record Henry II as having taken away.[99] Nor do they show that before his death in 1195 Bishop Hugh had granted Little Haughton in fee to William son of William of Harlsey and Witton (Gilbert) in fee-farm to Gilbert de la Ley.[100] A detail in the entry for Bishop Auckland can be used to reinforce this contention. According to x the survey revealed that a small tenement of $1^1/_2$ acres being held there by William Scott, Elstan and William Boie, rendering annually a dozen iron bars.[101] According to z, however, the holding is in the hands of the bishop's sergeant, Monk Cook, together with $19^1/_2$ acres of cultivable land within and outwith the bishop's park, and another 10 acres of non-cultivable land; Monk Cook holds all 31 acres for his service and at the bishop's will.[102] This change must have been made, and recorded in z, quite soon after 1183/4, because well before the end of Bishop Hugh's episcopate Monk Cook had secured a charter granting him these 31 acres in fee and inheritance, in return for the yearly payment of a pound of cumin:[103] a

97 Two *oras* of farm from each villein in z, as against two chalders of wheat in x.
98 See note 50 above.
99 See Lapsley, 'Boldon Book', pp.304-5.
100 Little Haughton: DC Mun. 3.1.Pont.21 = Surtees, *HD* iii, p.339. Bishop Hugh's charter for Gilbert de la Ley is printed from DC Mun. Cart.Elemos., p.223 by Scammell, *AA*[4] xxxiv (1956), 86.
101 Lapsley was defeated by the phrase (though Greenwell could have helped him), translating the render as '12 *esperducta* of wheat'. CD certainly show something which looks very much like *esperductas frumenti*. But Austin has made A yield *esperductas ferri*, and so arrived at the preferable reading and translation.
102 Greenwell, p.24.

Re-reading Boldon Book 27

development not noticed in *z*. The inescapable conclusion from examples of this kind is that no systematic effort was made to keep *o* up to date, though sporadically piecemeal alterations were made to it. From time to time the bishop's exchequer received report of local changes since 1183/4; sometimes they were entered up, sometimes, it seems likely, disregarded. Beneficiaries of altered circumstances will at times have pressed to have their new claims inserted in the record; how often and with what degree of success is for the most part unknown. But it must be accepted that our texts of Boldon Book reflect, however spasmodically and irregularly, considerable effects of intervention later than 1183/4.

The results sometimes puzzled Durham bureaucrats later on in the middle ages. At Killerby, *x* tells us, Simon Dorward holds the demesne for a rent of 4 marks (possibly in the light of later evidence, this was a mistake for 3 marks); in itself this looks like an amendment to the original 1183/4 entry. Clearly reflecting a later situation, *z* shows Simon holding one carucate at Killerby by the service of 1/12th of a knight's fee. That this change in the terms of Simon's tenure at Killerby had been confirmed by Bishop Hugh in a charter can be safely inferred from later evidence.[104] But somehow the 'official' record must have been altered imperfectly (though B shows no sign of this); perhaps an earlier entry, more or less as it appears in *x*, was cancelled inadequately. At any rate, confusion about whether Simon's holding at Killerby was solely by knight's service or by rent of 20/- a year and forinsec service has left traces in the Hatfield Survey and was still calling for resolution between 1423 and 1437.[105]

How in practice were the alterations made? It may be helpful to approach that question by trying to form some idea of how *o* appeared to the eyes of those who used and amended it. It seems reasonable to suppose that *o*, an administrative document, was (like Domesday Book) written with many abbreviations, since the inevitable repetition of set phrases would encourage truncation of verbal, nominal and adjectival endings. For the routine purposes of a twelfth-century administrator a note in some form as *Gatesheued cum burg' molend' piscar' et furn' et cum iii. part' terr' arab'*

---

103 DC. Mun. 4.1. Pont.7 = *FPD* 177n and *AA*[4] xxxiv (1956), 84, where Scammell's proposed dating, *c.* 1185, is perhaps too early; Robert Fitzmeldred would have been a very young witness at that date. By 1197 X 1208, when Bishop Philip of Poitou issued a charter for Monk Cook, the latter had exchanged that part of his holding which lay within the park for 13 acres of the bishop's moor at Auckland: *FPD* 177-8n.

104 Charter of Bishop Philip, surviving in a fifteenth-century inspeximus: DC Mun. Misc.Ch. 7243 m.3.

105 *Hatfield Survey*, p.23. I depend here on information from Martin Snape.

de ead' uill' redd' lx. marc' would tell him what he needed. To surmise abbreviation of this kind in *o* is not gratuitous, for it is amply illustrated in the surviving witnesses of *x*. It is less obvious in B, perhaps because that manuscript was written when the primarily administrative function of Boldon Book at the bishop's exchequer was being superseded by the new Hatfield survey of episcopal lands; as Boldon Book was becoming history the scribe took room to spell out some of the earlier contractions. That can be useful nowadays, when we try to resolve the ambiguities inherent in truncated words. Was there just a single borough, mill, fishery and oven at Gateshead in 1183/4 or, so far as some items were concerned, more than one? B gives a definite answer, as the *x* manuscripts do not. Of course a Durham scribe in the late fourteenth century was not perfectly placed to describe a situation two centuries earlier; but he was better placed than a modern scholar faced by the same abbreviations. The point will bear emphasis at a quite elementary level. In a survey recording payments various forms of *reddere* were certain to abound. But the abbreviation *redd'*, so frequent in the manuscripts, can be extremely troublesome.[106] It may be intended for *reddit* or *reddunt* or *reddet* or *reddent* or, at a pinch, *reddebat* or *reddebant*; in any particular case choice has to be made by resort to context, which can itself be ambiguous. It is B's special merit to offer on the whole more and better guidance in such dilemmas than do the representatives of *x*.[107] B's willingness to expand contracted forms can elucidate the real meaning of the text, as the following example shows. *Hercia* or *hercea* = a harrow; *hercharius* or *hercarius* = a beast used for harrowing; *carruca* = either a plough or a plough team. That the carpenters at Wearmouth and Sedgefield hold their dozen acres apiece *pro caruc' et herc' faciend' et reparand'* is straightforward enough: 'for making and repairing the ploughs and harrows'. But the demesne at Boldon is at farm *cum instauramento iiii. caruc' et iiii. herc'*. Only B, by spelling out *herc'* as *hercariorum*, makes it clear that the bishop stocks his demesne at Boldon – and, no doubt, elsewhere – not with such ploughs and harrows as the

---

106 As Dr Edward Miller pointed out when reviewing Austin's edition, *Northern History* xx (1984), 241-2.
107 Even so, that guidance must sometimes be rejected. At Thickley B's *reddit* would impose on individuals liabilities for quite impossibly heavy corn renders; in a similar situation at Heighington B rightly shows *reddunt*: Greenwell, pp.20-22. At Stanhope Lambert the marble mason *will* pay 4/- p.a. for his holding when he leaves the bishop's service, but B gives *reddit* instead of *reddet*: Greenwell, p.30. At Grindon in Norhamshire B's *quadrigant et faciunt* should probably be *quadrigabunt et facient*: Greenwell, p.41; cf. Austin, p.34.

Re-reading Boldon Book 29

carpenters make and repair, but with ploughteams and beasts for harrowing.[108]

Such general considerations may offer help in clearing *o* of some of the accretions it has collected in the course of the textual tradition. Something has already been said about the Whickham entry.[109] A few more examples seem worth discussion in detail. The Whitworth entry, already noticed, now shows the situation created perhaps fifteen or twenty years after 1183/4 by Philip of Poitou's charter of enfeoffment. B states baldly: Thomas of Aycliffe holds Whitworth by the free service of a quarter of a knight's fee. But *x* prefaces the same statement with an unfinished sentence: *In Wyteworth' sunt xvi. villani quorum unusquisque tenet i. bouatam de xx. acris et reddit et operatur omnibus* ... Obviously this sentence originally continued with some such words as *modis sicut villani de Westaukland'* (or some other township where villein services had been enumerated previously).[110] This surely is a fragment of *o*'s entry for Whitworth, made when it was still held in drengage and the burdens of its villeins still needed to be described. When revising the entry, after Whitworth had been turned into a fief and so passed outside the direct episcopal demesne, *x* failed to cancel *o* adequately; *z* made no such mistake.

A second example concerns Elstan, a dreng at West Auckland. According to all the manuscripts he was dead and his four bovates were in the bishop's hands until his heir should have grown up. The bishop has granted 12 acres to Elstan's widow to support her children in the meantime; the rest of the land is paying 13/- rent and doing the services Elstan used to perform. Superficially the entry seems quite clear and unexceptionable. Only when it is probed in detail do reasons appear for doubting whether it had this form in *o*. In B the conditions of Elstan's tenure are all expressed in past tenses, with one revealing exception: *et facit iii.* [iiii. in ACD] *precaciones*. In *x* there is a rare muddle, the verbs changing from perfect tense to present, from present to future and from future to imperfect.[111] These difficulties can be obviated by supposing that when the survey was made Elstan was still alive, so that *o*'s original entry about him read thus:

---

108 The point is missed in all translations. One harrowing beast (often doubling as a cart horse) to each ploughteam would seem a pretty normal ratio. I am indebted to Richard Britnell for advice about this.
109 See pp.19-20 above and Appendix II.
110 Austin, p.39, has gone sadly astray in his attempt to translate this fragment.
111 Greenwell, p.26; Austin, p.36.

Elstanus drengus ten(et) iiii. bouatas et redd(it) x. solidos et fac(it) iii. [*rectius* iiii.?] precaciones in autumpno cum omnibus hominibus suis excepts propria domo sua et [om.B] ar(at) et herci(at) ii. acras et ib(it) in legacionibus Episcopi inter Tinam et Teisam cum suo custamento et inuen(iet) iiii. boues ad vinum ducendum.

In order to adapt this text to the changed situation after Elstan's death, all *z* needed to do was to manipulate verb endings, probably already contracted in *o*, thus producing B's readings *tenuit, reddidit, facit* (the slip which gives the game away), *arauit, herciauit, ibat* and *inueniebat*. Much less adriot was *x*, which gives as the verbs *tenuit, reddit, facit, arat, herceat, ibit* and *inueniebat*, thus departing first and last from consistent cohesion to *o*. In their different ways both *x* and *z* brought the record up to date here. But it is a reasonable conjecture that they did so only at the cost of falsifying the historical situation in 1183/4, when Elstan was probably still living.

A final example, taken from the closely related entries for Norton, Stockton and Preston, is a good deal more complicated. For Stockton *x* gives the earliest surviving form: Adam son of Walter holds one carucate and one bovate, rendering one mark. Robert of *Cumba* holds four bovates for half a mark, and another bovate on loan from the bishop (*de accomodatione Episcopi*). While he is in the bishop's service he is free from obligatory works; but if he quits that service he shall be liable for as many works as are due from Walter's half carucate. In addition Robert has the old toft of the hall next to his house, paying 16d. for it.[112] In *z* the entry was altered at some date after Robert's death; B gives William of *Cumba* as tenant of the five bovates instead of Robert.[113] But *z*'s alteration to the entry was incomplete. B still shows *idem Robertus*, whom it has not previously mentioned, holding the old toft, in error for William, who by this time will have succeeded his father. That seems mere carelessness. What remains puzzling is the statement that Robert's (later William's) five bovates are contingently liable for as much obligatory work as is due from a half carucate of Walter's. For Walter's services are nowhere specified in the surviving texts, though in the Preston entry (immediately following Stockton) the terms of the tenure of a Walter of Stockton, together with those of Alan of Normanton in Norton (immediately preceding Stockton), are cited as the norm for what is due from four drengage tenures in

112 Austin, p.54. A reads *Robertus de Coumbus*; CD *Robertus de Cambous*. B renders his son's name as *Willelmus de Tumba*. This is partly corroborated by the Book of Fees; see next note.
113 Greenwell, pp.13-14. According to the Book of Fees in 1208 X 1210 William of *Cumba* and his mother held 5 bovates in Stockton for half a mark yearly: *BF* i.29.

Preston.[114] The first tenant named at Stockton by both *x* and *z* is Adam son of Walter, who undoubtedly was the son and successor of Walter of Stockton.[115] But whereas Walter's tenancy at Stockton in 1183/4, as its equation with Alan of Normanton's at Norton indicates, amounted to one carucate held for 10/- a year together with stipulated field works, Adam, on the evidence of *x* and *z*, had managed to enlarge this holding by a bovate and shed all liabilities for works (none being mentioned) in return for an increase in rent to one mark.[116]

Both in *x* and *z*, then, alterations made to *o* in order to adapt it to later circumstances have caused incoherencies in the Stockton entry. Probably its original form can be conjectured. Instead of the opening sentence in the surviving texts about Adam son of Walter, *o* will have shown something like: *Walterus de Stokton' tenet i. carucatam et reddit et operatur omnibus modis sicut Alanus de Normanton'* (specified in the previous entry for Norton). Robert of *Cumba* holds his four bovates (i.e. half a carucate) and in addition one bovate on loan from the bishop for a rent of half a mark, free of works for as long as he remains in the bishop's service. If he leaves that service, he will be liable for field work amounting to half that due from Walter's carucate (the loss of his bovate on loan is assumed).[117] Robert also holds the old toft by a separate payment of rent.

In the light of this result it is possible to clarify the original terms of the four drengage tenures at Preston, which Boldon Book defines by reference to the holdings of Alan of Normanton (i.e. at Norton) and Walter of Stockton (i.e. at Stockton). In *x* the names of the Preston tenants appear as Walter (not, I think, Walter of Stockton) and *Waldewini*, each holding a carucate, the corrupt composite *Orm fil' Coket Vtting* holding a carucate

---

114 Greenwell, pp.14-15; *et reddunt et operantur modis omnibus sicut Alanus de Normanton et Walterus de Stockton*; Austin, p.54, wrongly gives *redditt et operatur*. The Norton entry reports Alan of Normanton's rent (10/-) and predial obligations in full.

115 He is described thus in a charter of Bishop Hugh to be dated *c*. 1190 X 1195: DC Mun. Priory Reg. I, pt.ii, f.6r. So also is an amendment of Boldon Book's Preston entry peculiar to *z*: *Adam filius Walteri de Stockton' tenet j. carucatam pro x. s. tantum*: Greenwell, p.14. The enquiries of 1208-1210 confirm that he had bought his holding at Preston from Bishop Hugh, and call him Ada de Prestun': BF i.29.

116 In 1208-1210 Adam's mother, said to be in the king's gift (the see then being vacant) was reported to hold a third of a carucate in Stockton: *BF* i.31. This looks like her widow's portion of Walter's land. But at the same date Adam, for his yearly render of one mark, appears to be holding only two bovates and 13 acres; unfortunately the entry breaks off unfinished, leaving an unresolved problem: *BF* i.29.

117 For his half carucate Robert's obligation for works would be half William's, i.e. half Alan's as set out at Norton, Greenwell, p.13.

jointly, and Richard *rundus*, who has half a carucate. A later and changed situation is witnessed by *z*. For while B shows Walter and Richard as tenants still (the latter's holding now reduced to two bovates), and Orm the son of Toki is brought out of the fog, now holding jointly with Utting's son William, *Waldewini* has been replaced as tenant of the third full carucate by Adam, son of Walter of Stockton, holding by rent alone (10/- a year, *tantum*). *Waldewini* in *x* looks like the genitive of a form of *Baldewinus*. So it turns out to be, for the charter by which Bishop Hugh granted this carucate to Adam states that it was bought by the bishop from William, son and heir of Baldwin.[118] Thus in 1183/4 the five tenants of the four Preston drengages will have been Walter, Baldwin or his son, Orm son of Toki, Utting and Richard *rundus*; they held on the same terms as Alan of Normanton and Walter of Stockton (Richard's rent and services no doubt being proportionate to his holding of only half a carucate). This information is not evident in *x*'s botched version of the entry. By the time the record was amended in *z*, there had been changes: Richard's holding had been halved; William had succeeded his father Utting; Adam of Preston now held the carucate formerly in the hands of Baldwin (or Baldwin's son). Moreover, Adam had come to enjoy more favourable terms than the others. As the *tantum* in *z* indicates and Bishop Hugh's charter makes explicit, he held by rent only, free from predial works.[119]

At this point discussion along these lines can be broken off. Enough has been said to make clear that the text of Boldon Book as vouchsafed by its tradition does not provide an invariably secure data base. The items of information it offers demand individual scrutiny and interpretation. Mention in Boldon Book gives no certain guarantee that a particular situation existed when the survey was made. It cannot without risk be used indiscriminately as a repertory of facts precisely datable to 1183/4. The survey's nature as an administrative instrument exposed it to alteration as time went on; traces of this – partial and fortuitous as the process of amendment may have been – are scattered throughout the document as we now have it.

Of course these considerations do not greatly impair the value of the general view which Boldon Book offers of the legal, economic and social conditions on most of the bishop of Durham's estates in the last decades of the

---

118 Cited in note 106.
119 Probably he secured a similar amelioration in the terms by which his father had held at Stockton; see *Hatfield Survey*, p.166. That his holding at Preston had once lain in drengage appears from *BF* i.31.

Re-reading Boldon Book

twelfth century. If not all its contents come from 1183/4, most of them do. Contrast between the comparatively underdeveloped north-west of Durham and the rest of the county leaps to the eye. The bishop is still largely a rent collector; his direct exploitation of the demesne is recorded explicitly in perhaps no more than a dozen vills;[120] though elsewhere sheep and meadows are kept in hand.[121] As has been seen, at Whickham the direction of change was from direct exploitation towards leasing (unfortunately the date is uncertain). This was a well established system in the twelfth century; it was indeed, as has been remarked, the obvious way to manage big and widely dispersed estates at a time when administrative talent was scarce.[122] If the next half-century or so brought an increase in direct exploitation of the Durham episcopal demesnes, as current doctrine would seem to require, the evidence must be sought outside Boldon Book. At the turn of the twelfth and thirteenth centuries fixed rents continued to contribute about half the bishop's income from his estates; £1259 in the year following du Puiset's death, £1260 in 1208-9, £1259 again in 1209-10. And in 1210-11 and 1211-12, probably driven up by the royal keepers of the vacant bishopric, they reached £1473.[123]

For effective rent collecting properly defined tenurial arrangements were necessary. Inevitably Boldon Book was much concerned with the ubiquitous ancient drengages; as has been seen, it provides considerable evidence of activity, not wholly effective, to find more profitable substitutes for them. In the forest settlements in upper Weardale, at Wolsingham and Stanley, a notable number of men of no high prosperity were esteemed free enough to have their names recorded individually. Among the anonymous villeins elsewhere conditions were far from uniform. There is a sharp contrast between their heavy labour obligations at Boldon and on estates in east Durham following the Boldon pattern[124] – three days' work a week on the demesne for some 47 weeks in the year, together with four boon-works in autumn – and what was

---

120 Newbottle, Houghton-le-Spring, Quarrington, Sedgefield, Middleham, Ricknall, Middridge, Thickley, Great Coundon, Broadwood, Witton Gilbert, a quarter of Gateshead.
121 At Cleadon and Whitburn, Easington and Thorpe, Little Haughton, Redworth, Winlaton and Norham.
122 P.R. Hyams, *Kings, Lords and Peasants in Medieval England*, Oxford, 1980, p.255.
123 These figures are calculated from *Chancellor's Roll 8 Richard I*, pp.253,261; *PR 13 John*, ed. D.M. Stenton, PR Soc. n.s. xxviii (1953), pp.35-6; *PR 14 John*, ed. P.M. Barnes, PR Soc. n.s. xxx (1955), p.46. They include the proceeds from the Yorkshire estates, not surveyed in 1183/4.
124 Listed in note 9 above.

expected from villeins in Heighingtonshire and Aucklandshire. The men of Ryton hold the vill and the demesne at farm for £14; it is difficult to see who they can have been other than the villeins there. At South Biddick, where the villeins themselves hold their township at farm for £5, it seems likely that their reaping and carting services at Houghton-le-Spring amounted to four days of boon work (*precaciones*) with 40 men and 9 carts each day, though the survey simply says that they are to find 160 men to reap and 36 carts to carry corn. But though Boldon Book can tell us much about the varied details of the villeins' services, it is wholly silent about an unpredictable burden to which they were liable: tallage at the lord's will. How often tallage was imposed and how assessed are dark matters. The figures from the vacancies after the deaths of Hugh du Puiset and Philip of Poitou are ominous: £341 levied in 1196, £1359 between 1208 and 1211.[125]

There remains a practical problem: what is the best available means of access to this rich source? The tenor of this paper has been to stress that a perfect reconstruction of the survey's original state is not possible, since the surviving manuscripts betray the effects of deliberate alteration over the years. The two recensions x and z can help to correct each other's errors and omissions, but comparing them will not always lead infallibly back to o. To present effectively in print so multi-layered a text would call for typographical ingenuity of a higher order than any of the three existing editions displays.[126] Of these the most serviceable is the one put out by William Greenwell in 1852, which deservedly superseded Ellis's *editio princeps*, for that followed the youngest and least reputable of all the manuscripts. Modern purists may find distasteful Greenwell's practice of 'classicising' spellings, in accordance with the conventions of his time. But, all considered, he made the right choice in taking B, the historically 'official' version of Boldon Book, as the basis for his text. Though at times B lets him down, he transcribed it carefully and intelligently; the variants which he printed from the Laud manuscript (D) and C occur also, with very few exceptions, in A, so in effect his apparatus offers a nearly complete conspectus of the readings of the x recension. Misreadings and misprints are rare.[127] Dr Austin's recent edition, based on A – in itself a

125 *Chancellor's Roll 8 Richard I*, pp.255-6; *PR 13 John*, pp.35-41; cf. Margaret Howell, *Regalian Right in Medieval England*, London, 1962, p.217. These sums include the Yorkshire estates.
126 Dr Hunnisett's prescriptions about 'process notes', *Editing Records*, pp.44-5, can be applied fully, of course, only when the original manuscript of the document is available.
127 A few have already indicated *passim*. Others are: in the Boldon and Sedgefield entries

Re-reading Boldon Book

questionable decision – is less reliable than Greenwell's. Four false readings on the first page of his text make an unhappy start, after which it is difficult to recover confidence.[128] Even if slips in the press are taken in one's stride, the expansions he offers for the frequent abbreviations shown by the manuscripts, in particular of case and tense endings, often inspire doubt and at times incredulity; they are capable of distorting the sense of the text.[129] Potentially the most helpful item in Dr Austin's edition, the appendix containing a gazetteer of the placenames in Boldon Book, is marred by a number of misidentifications.[130] None of the editors offers much help with two obdurate *cruces* in the Latin text.[131] But Greenwell is the guide to follow.

Greenwell, pp.4,11, seems to have misunderstood B's *quater viginti* or iiii.^{xx} as meaning *xxiv*; at Little Haughton, Stanhope and Lanchester the preferable extension of B's contraction is probably *similiter* rather than Greenwell's *simul* (pp.18,29,31); in the Heighington entry (p.21) *vsque* has been omitted from the phrase *fecit vsque ad lx. acras*; at Escombe B shows *Ranning* rather than Greenwell's *Raning* (p.25); at Hunstanworth *incrementa*, not *nutrimenta* (p.32); in the Bedlingtonshire insertion *cohoperiendo* rather than *co-operiando* (p.39). Possibly Greenwell's *dimidiam j. castlemanni* at Thickley and *dimidiam castelman* at Sheraton (pp.23,36) could be defended, but the *molendinam* at Middleham (p.12) is a misprint.

[128] The correct readings are: *ad festum* in line 1; *assise* in line 4; *domini Episcopi* in line 18; *instauramento* with B in line 30.

[129] For instance, by expanding as *reddit* instead of *reddunt* the first *redd'* in four successive entries he imposes on the individual villein at Heighington, Killerby, Middridge and Thickley an obligation for renders in kind which seems quite impossibly heavy: Austin, pp.64-6. B indeed shows *reddit* at Thickley (see note 98 above), but this must be amended in the light of the other three entries: Greenwell, pp.20-2.

[130] Hedley Hill and Healeyfield, both wrongly identified as Hedleyhope; *Croketun'* by Witton Gilbert as Crookhall; *Twizel* by Easington as the place of that name north of Craghead; Sunderland as the port at Wearmouth; Winston as Westoe. In Norhamshire *Audeham* is *x*'s corruption not for Middle Ord, as Austin supposes, but for Duddo (*Dudehowe* in B), which is linked with the Norhamshire Twizell both in Boldon Book and Book of Fees (*BF* i.27).

[131] The first concerns Odo's 33 acres of ploughland at Darlington: *ubi fagina fuit seminata* B; *nisi sagniter* (*segniter* D) *fuit seminata* ACD. Greenwell, p.16 follows B; Austin, p.58 reads *nisi saginta fuit seminata*. Some sort of sense can be derived from B and D; but what Austin's reading can mean defeats me. The second occurs in the entry for Upsettlington, where the bishop is said to have a source of revenue worth 50/-: *Vadium Episcopi quod de femina Mauberti habet*. Thus B, followed by Greenwell, p.42 and Austin, p.34. Maubert is perhaps the *Malb' vicecomes de Norham* who witnesses an episcopal charter *c*. 1172 X 1174: *FPD* 198n. But 'the bishop's pledge (or gage, as Lapsley translates) which he has from Maubert's wife' makes somewhat uneasy sense. For *femina* in B, A shows *feu'*, CD *fen'*. *Vadium* can be found as an alternative form of *vadum* = a ford. Just possibly 'The bishop's ford which he has from Maubert's fee' may be the answer.

Non-Latinists will be well advised not to rely exclusively on any one of the three available translations of Boldon Book. Lapsley's, the most consciously stylish, on at least twenty occasions prints numerals which, as far as I can see, cannot be justified by the manuscripts of either recension. Like Greenwell's 'cow in milk', his 'milch cow' oversimplifies the technical term *vacca de metride*, which Austin prudently abstains from rendering. But Austin's 'obligatory work' for *precatio* seems too strong in itself and capable of causing confusion with obligatory week work, even if the familiar translation 'boon-work' used by Lapsley may be criticised for evoking more an overtone of jovial voluntarism remote from the facts: perhaps more wisely than either Greenwell prefers the neutral 'precation'. In Durham *commune auxilium* was due from all free men of the bishopric (in contrast to the unfree, who were tallaged), not just from those recognisable as feudatories, so Austin's rendering 'common feudal aid' seems rather too restrictive. A sum of money stated to be *ad plus* was surely, as Greenwell saw, the maximum allowable (thus *i. marca ad plus* = 1 mark at most), not something additional, as Lapsley and Austin would have it. Jordan Escouland or Escolland, member of a well-known Durham family, would hardly have relished being transformed by Dr Austin into 'Jordan of Scotland'. He has produced, with a fine modern ring, a 'coal-miner' at Escombe, where Greenwell and Lapsley settled for 'collier'; against all three it is worth recalling that a primary meaning of *carbonarius* in the late twelfth century was 'charcoal-burner'. All the translators repeatedly state that the bishop stocked his demesnes with ploughs and harrows, rather than with plough-teams and beasts for harrowing (and sometimes with sheep and seed, in typical stock and seed-lease fashion). In fine, approach to the translations of Boldon Book needs to be both eclectic and skeptical. Again it is Greenwell who outdoes his competitors; he had chosen a better text to work from.

Re-reading Boldon Book 37

Appendix I
Bishop Nicholas Farnham grants Butterwick in fee to William son of William of Sadberge. Darlington 28 March 1248.
Duplicate originals: Durham County Record Office, Salvin Deeds, nos. 216, 217.
Copies: Durham D & C Mun. Misc. Chart. 6362; Reg. I, pt.ii, ff.8v-9r.
Here from Salvin Deed no. 216

Omnibus Christi fidelibus presentem cartam visuris uel audituris Nicholaus Dei gratia Dunelmensis episcopus, salutem. Ad universitatis vestre notitiam volumus peruenire nos concessisse, dedisse et hac carta nostra confirmasse Willelmo filio Willelmi de Sadberg' pro homagio et seruicio suo et specialiter pro bono et fideli obsequio nobis et ecclesie nostre diligenter inpenso totam villam de Buterwyk tam in dominicis quam in seruiciis, villanis et eorum sequelis et catallis, in homagiis, wardis, releuiis, redditibus et esschaetis et in omnibus aliis proficuis que aliquo tempore inde poterunt prouenire. Quam villam Rogerus filius Willelmi de Buterwyk de nobis tenuit in drengagio et quam nobis reddidit et de se et heredibus suis in perpetuum quietam clamauit cum predictis pertinenciis suis pro quinquaginta marcis argenti quas ei dedimus pro eadem. Habendam et tenendam eidem Willelmo et heredibus suis de nobis et successoribus nostris in feodo et hereditate libere, quiete, pacifice et integre cum omnibus pertinentiis suis sine aliquo retinemento. Reddendo inde annuatim nobis et successoribus nostris ad scaccarium nostrum Dunelmi decem marcas argenti ad quatuor terminos in episcopatu nostro constitutis in recompensationem seruicii quod nobis et successoribus nostris debebatur dum predicta villa de nobis et predecessoribus nostris in drengagio tenebatur. Et faciendo inde forinsecum seruicium quantum pertinet ad sextam partem feodi unius militis et sectam singulis annis ad tria capitalia placita curie nostre Dunelmensi [*sic*] pro omnibus aliis seruiciis. Volumus etiam et concedimus quod heredes dicti Willelmi qui legitime fuerint etatis dent nobis et successoribus nostris pro certo releuio suo decem marcas argenti, nisi prius in custodia nostra uel successorum nostrorum ratione minoris etatis exstiterint. Nos vero et successores nostri predictam villam de Buterwyk cum omnibus pertinentiis suis prout predictum est dicto Willelmo et heredibus suis contra omnes warantizabimus in perpetuum. In huius rei testimonium presentem cartam sigillo nostro si<n>gnatam eidem Willelmo fieri fecimus. Act' apud Darlington' vicesimo octauo die martii pontificatus nostri anno septimo. Testibus magistris Odone de Kylkenny et Willelmo de Manefeld', dominis Galfrido de Forsete, Willelmo de Blokely, Roberto de sancto Albano, Willelmo de Bromham, Waltero de Eggesclyue, Marmeduco filio Galfridi, Thoma de Herington', Jordano de Daldene, Johanne Gyllet, Waltero de Seleby, Ada de Bradely', Laurencio de Ponthope, Ricardo de Scrutteuill' et aliis.

Appendix II

Conjectural reconstruction of the original state of Boldon Book's entry for Whickham; *cf.* Greenwell, pp. 33-4; Austin, p.48. No attempt has been made to simulate the abbreviations which doubtless occurred in *o*.

In Quicham sunt xxxv. villani quorum unusquisque tenet i. bouatam de xv. acris et reddit xvi.d. et operatur per totum annum iii. diebus in ebdomada. Et preterea faciunt iii. precaciones in autumpno cum omni familia domus excepta husewiua et quartam precacionem cum ii. hominibus. Et in operacione sua falcant prata et leuant et quadrigant fenum. Et metunt et quadrigant totum bladum similiter in operacione sua. Et extra operacionem suam arant de unaquaque caruca ii. acras de auerere et herciant et tunc semel habent corrodium. Et in operacione sua faciunt i. domum longitudinis xl. pedum et latitudinis xv. pedum et faciunt ladas et summagia sicut villani de Boldona. Et quandocumque metent blada et falcabunt prata et faciebunt precaciones eciam habebunt corrodium.

Preterea reddunt ix.[1] s. de cornagio et i. vaccam de metride et de unaquaque bouata i. gallinam et x. oua. Et in operacione sua faciunt iii. piscarias in Tyna.

Prior de Brenkburn'[2] tenet ibidem ii. bouatas et i. piscariam de elemosina Episcopi. Gerardus prepositus tenet xxiiii. acras pro seruicio prepositure[3] et ille xxiiii. acre ante eum solebant reddere iiii. s. Molendinum reddit iii. marcas. Piscarie iii. marcas.[4] Et dominium ii.[5] carucarum est in manu Episcopi.

1 xx ACD
2 Fisseburn' ACD
3 suo ACD
4 iiii li. ACD
5 iiii. ACD

XIII

Fitz Meldred, Neville and Hansard

If asked to discuss what impact the Norman Conquest made on English society, any competent undergraduate in the 1930s would have turned to the writings of J.H. Round and F.M. Stenton. Probably the essay would have laid much weight on the rapid dispossession of the native landlords, fated at the highest level to be almost completely superseded by a new governing class. Its members, drawn from William's French-born followers, sooner rather than later found their life in England organised within the framework of such institutions as the honour, the castlery and the knight's fee; their obligations of military and other services to their superiors took definite shape within the understanding of a general tenurial system. Much of that construction, of course, still remains acceptable. But it does not provide an absolute and exclusive truth. Nowadays we have developed a keen eye for the anomalies, the local peculiarities and divergencies from the normal patterns. The far north of England, at one of the frontiers of the Norman colonial empire, as has long been understood, did not fit comfortably or speedily into this feudal scheme. Landlords with

---

Documents cited with the prefix DC Mun. are at Durham among the muniments of the Dean and Chapter. Unless it is stated otherwise, references to the Pipe Rolls are to the volumes published by the Pipe Roll Society.

The following abbreviations are used for printed works or series frequently cited:

AA	*Archaeologia Aeliana* [a suprascript number for the series]
DEC	*Durham Episcopal Charters 1073-1152*, ed. H.S. Offler, SS clxxix (1964)
EHR	*The English Historical Review*
EYC	*Early Yorkshire Charters*, ed. William Farrer and C.T. Clay (Yorks. Archaeological Soc. Record Series. Extra Series), 12 vols., 1914-65.
FPD	*Feodarium Prioratus Dunelmensis*, ed. W. Greenwell, SS lviii (1872)
HD	R. Surtees, *The History and Antiquities of the County Palatine of Durham*, 4 vols., 1816-40
NCH	*A History of Northumberland*, ed. by the Northumberland County History Committee, 15 vols., 1893-1940
PR	Pipe Roll
RPD	*Registrum Palatinum Dunelmense*, ed. T.D. Hardy, 4 vols., RS, 1873-8
RS	Rolls Series
SS	Publications of the Surtees Society
ST	*Historiae Dunelmensis Scriptores Tres*, ed. J. Raine, SS ix (1839).

native names, sometimes holding by archaic forms of tenure, are to be found persisting in considerable numbers north of the Humber well into the thirteenth century. Barons, knights and knights' fees are there indeed, but also many rather surprising fossils originating in the pre-Conquest social order.[1] This fact did not escape the notice of scholars of such calibre as the two just mentioned. It was Stenton fifty years ago in one of his masterly surveys of the changing feudalism of the English middle ages who stressed one of history's more ironic comments on the doctrine of complete Normanisation of the upper ranks of English society in the aftermath of 1066. Richard Neville, the fifteenth-century earl of Warwick, he pointed out, 'who for a time could dethrone or bring back the Conqueror's descendants at his pleasure, was descended in the male line from an Anglo-Danish Northumbrian thegn, Dolfin son of Uhtred, who received Staindropshire [in co. Durham] from the prior of Durham in the reign of Henry I.'[2] In starting the story with Dolfin son of Uhtred in 1131/2 Stenton was basing himself on Round. The latter had worked out from Dolfin the succession of the native lords of Staindrop and Raby who by marriage with the heiress of Bulmer and Neville were to expand their possessions beyond co. Durham into Yorkshire and Lincolnshire and thus, from their bases at Raby, Brancepeth and Raskelf, lay the foundations of one of the greatest territorial lordships in medieval England.[3] Probably we can be rather less cautious than Round, and trace the family back for at least another two generations, almost to the time of the Conquest itself. For Dolfin's father Uhtred witnesses under Bishop Rannulf Flambard in the second decade of the twelfth century as the son of Meldred, and it is likely that this was the

---

[1] Early milestones in the discussion of these 'archaic' characters are F.W. Maitland, 'Northumbrian Tenures', *EHR* v (1890), 625-33; G.T. Lapsley, 'Cornage and Drengage', *American Hist. Rev.* ix (1904), 670-96; *id.*, 'Boldon Book' in VCH *Durham* i, London, 1905, pp.284-91; J.E.A. Joliffe, 'Northumbrian Institutions', *EHR* xli (1926), 1-42. For more recent treatments, see G.W.S. Barrow, 'Northern English society in the early middle ages', *Northern History* iv (1969), 1-28; William E. Kapelle, *The Norman Conquest of the North*, London, 1979, pp.50-85. To the author of *Havelok* c.1300 it still seemed natural enough (though the demands of rhyme may have played a part) to lump together:
        Erles, barouns drenges, theynes,
        Klerkes, knithes, bu[r]geys, sweynes.
Havelok, ed. G.V. Smithers, Oxford, 1987, lines 2195-6.

[2] F.M. Stenton, 'The Changing Feudalism of the Middle Ages', reprinted from *History* xix (1935) in *id.*, *Preparatory to Anglo-Saxon England*, ed. D.M. Stenton, Oxford, 1970, p.205; see also his 'English Feudalism and the Norman Conquest', reprinted *ib.*, pp.325-34 from *Trans. Royal Hist. Soc.* 4th ser. xxvi (1944).

[3] J.H. Round, 'The origin of the Nevilles', in *Feudal England*, London, 1909, pp.488-90.

Meldred from whom Bishop William of St. Callais had obtained half of Ketton in exchange for Winlaton early in the 1080's.[4]

In the extent of its landed possessions this family, holding on obdurately to native names for a full hundred years after 1066, was pre-eminent among the lay proprietors within the bishopric of Durham during the twelfth century. The famous grant to Dolfin son of Uhtred and his heirs of Staindrop and Staindropshire in March 1131/32 by Prior Algar and the monks of Durham is hardly to be regarded as initiating a wholly new state of affairs.[5] There is good evidence that before that date Dolfin was already holding four librates of land at Staindrop;[6] probably the grant in 1131/2 only gave formal sanction to a situation which had long existed, possibly even from the time when King Canute had first granted to St. Cuthbert *villam quae vocatur Staindropa cum suis appendiciis*.[7] Canute's donation had comprised a swathe of lands and settlements some four miles wide and running about eight miles north-east and east of Staindrop, in all thirty square miles or so of south-west county Durham.[8] This was the core of the estate confirmed to Dolfin by Prior Algar as *Standropam et Standropsciram*, to hold for an annual render of £4. Canute's endowment (or, more precisely, the monks' claim to it all, and consequently the title of Dolfin and his heirs) did not remain wholly intact during the twelfth century. In 1183/4 West Auckland, Luttrington and Thickley were being treated by Boldon Book as parts of the bishop's demesne; Bishop Hugh du Puiset granted Evenwood to Gilbert Hansard I.[9] But Dolfin and his heirs held more in west Durham than a somewhat truncated Staindropshire. They reached northwards to the Tyne and southwards to the Tees. At a date between c.1160 and 1177 Bishop Hugh granted Dolfin's heir Meldred the

---

4   DEC no.12, and *cf.* pp.76-7. The suggestion that the Staindrop family was of the male line of Crinan the Thane, father of Duncan I king of Scots (1034-1040), is canvassed by genealogists; *cf.* A.R. Warner, *English Genealogy*, 2nd ed., Oxford, 1972, pp.26-7; id., *Pedigree and Progress*, London, 1975, p.51. It is too speculative to be pursued here.

5   The grant, surviving only in a cartulary copy, is printed *FPD* 56n. The date is given as *Anno ab incarnacione Domini m.c.xxxi tercio decimo kal.Aprilis*, which can be rendered as 20 March 1131 or 1132. In either case the document was issued while the see was vacant after the death of Bishop Rannulf, though his two archdeacons head the list of witnesses.

6   Durham, DC Mun.2.1.Reg.12 = *FPD* 145n; *cf. DEC* pp.104, 109.

7   *Historia de Sancto Cuthberto*, ed. T. Arnold in *Symeonis Monachi Opera Omnia* i (RS, 1882), p.213.

8   *Cf.* H.H.E. Craster, 'The Patrimony of St. Cuthbert', *EHR* lxx (1954), pp.195-6, 199.

9   *Boldon Buke*, ed. William Greenwell, SS xxv (1852), pp.25-6, 27, 22-3. For the grant of Evenwood, see note 27 below.

vills of Winlaton, *Sunderland* (presumably in the neighbourhood of Sunderland Bridge), Winston and Newsham and part of the episcopal forest, all to be held at fee-farm for a rent of £20.[10] Here again, as with Staindropshire, it is likely that the native line's effective possession of at least some of these vills was older than the recorded grant: as has been pointed out, Meldred's great-grandfather had probably obtained Winlaton eighty or ninety years previously.[11] Both this earlier transaction and later evidence suggest that Bishop Hugh's grant can be regarded as an attempt to regularise matters in places at least some of which were already controlled by the family of Dolfin son of Uhtred.[12] By the modest standards of the bishopric of Durham that family from its centre at Raby near Staindrop commanded in all an imposing estate. When at farm during the episcopal vacancy in 1196 its yield was more than three times greater than that from the lands of the Amundevilles of Witton-le-Wear, who held one of the largest 'baronies' in the bishopric by the service of five knights.[13]

On occasion the lords of Raby witnessed episcopal charters: under Bishops Rannulf Flambard and Geoffrey Rufus, and in the early years of Hugh du Puiset.[14] Yet despite their territorial power their position as lay magnates in county Durham was bound to appear increasingly out-of-date as the world in which they lived became ever more permeated by Norman

10 Bishop Hugh's charter is not extant. Our knowledge of it comes from a confirmation by Prior Germanus and the convent of Durham, to be dated c. 1163 X 1177, which itself survives only in a corrupt eighteenth-century transcript, BL Landsdowne ms.902, f.87v. Mr Martin Snape will include it in his edition of Bishop Hugh's *acta*. Unfortunately the confirmation is not specific about the extent of forest granted.
11 See note 4 above.
12 Robert son of Meldred son of Dolfin held at Winston and Newsham: *FPD* 51-2nn. Robert's brother Gilbert held at Barford (par.Winston, west of Newsham) in the early thirteenth century: *FPD* 53-4nn; this is not the Barforth south of the Tees in Yorks NR, as Dr G.V. Scammell supposed, *Hugh du Puiset*, Cambridge, 1956, pp.232,330. Barford may well have been held by Meldred son of Dolfin. In Boldon Book, *Sunderland*, Winston, Newsham and Barford are given as a consecutive series of entries, of which the basis is clearly thematic rather than geographical: *Boldon Buke*, p.35. They appear to represent vills once held by Meldred son of Dolfin, but now in 1183/4, after Meldred's death and during the minority of his heir Robert, taken back into the bishop's demesne and set out at farms amounting to just over £50 – more than double the farm agreed to with Meldred. Only two other Boldon Book entries are relevant to the family. One mentions a piece of land at Stella near Winlaton *quae fuit Meldredi filii Dolfini* (p.35). The other concerns a single carucate at Whessoe by Darlington held in drengage by Robert son of Meldred (p.20); on this, see note 40 below.
13 Chanc.R 8 Richard I, PR Soc.n.s. vii (1930), p.260.
14 *DEC* nos.12,29,31; DC Mun.3.1.Pont.11 = *FPD* 100n (c.1154-6).

Fitz Meldred, Neville and Hansard

influences. Before the death of Henry I the bishops had established some forty knights' fees on St. Cuthbert's domain north of Tees, intermingled with their own lands and those belonging to the priory.[15] A band of feudatories can be glimpsed emerging as the new class of lay landlords in Durham. They came from families originating in northern France; holding their lands directly from the bishop by the obligation of military service and its incidents they were capable of providing him with the nucleus of a feudal court: Bishop Rannulf's kinsmen, for instance, Conyers, Amundeville, Humez and Bulmer, de Musters, Escolland and the like. Into the conventions of this new society the native lords of Raby did not fit easily. Their style was much more that of the great thegns of pre-Conquest times. To their superior lords they did indeed owe loyalty, but for them this duty was still unfettered by those stipulations about defined quotas of military service and so forth which were now the general currency. When in 1131/2 Dolfin son of Uhtred declared himself the liege vassal (*homo ligius*) of the prior and monks of St. Cuthbert and accepted liability for suit of court, the agreement was that he would pay the monastery a money rent for Staindrop and Staindropshire. At the same time it was made explicit that he owed a superior allegiance not only to the bishop of Durham and the king of England, but also to the king of Scotland. The inclusion of the last named was something more than a gesture to the supranational status of St. Cuthbert. It reflected the political realities of a time when the frontier between the two kingdoms was still uncertain; within a few years David I and his son Earl Henry were to make serious efforts to extend Scottish power southwards to the Tees. During the determined, though ultimately unsuccessful attempt to intrude a partisan of the Scots into the see of Durham after the death of Bishop Geoffrey Rufus, Dolfin son of Uhtred, it seems likely, actively supported the pro-Scottish faction against Bishop William of Ste. Barbe and the Durham monks, Dolfin's nominal overlords.[16] Though Dolfin's son Meldred recognised that he held vills and

---

15 Calculated from *The Red Book of the Exchequer*, ed. Hubert Hall (RS, 1896) i.417 the precise figure is 39 and 11/12ths fees. The suggestion by H.G. Richardson and G.O. Sayles, *The Governance of Mediaeval England*, Edinburgh, 1963, p.86 that the aid levied in 1129 on the knights of the bishopric of Durham was at only 1 mark on the fee seems to be mistaken. The total to be accounted for was £58 6s. 8d., according to PR 31 Henry I, ed. Joseph Hunter, Record Commission, 1833, p.132. By 1135 the total knight service of the bishopric, including the Yorkshire and Lincolnshire fees, was 63 and 2/3rds. The levy on the bishop's fees in 1129 was presumably at the rate of £1 a fee, as elsewhere.

16 Likely, but not quite certain. It depends on whether the *quidam procerus ...... nomine Dolfinus* who made war on William of Ste. Barbe, according to Reginald of Durham,

forest rights from Bishop Hugh, again this was tenure at fee-farm, not by knight service.[17] Thus the lord of Raby does not appear in the *Cartae* returns of 1166 among those holding on St. Cuthbert's demesne either of the old or the new enfeoffment.[18]

Dolfin son of Uhtred hardly, if at all, outlived his putative enemy William of Ste. Barbe, who died in November 1152.[19] The arrival of William's successor as bishop, the ambitious and authoritarian Hugh du Puiset, was bound to raise doubts how much longer Dolfin's heir Meldred would be able to maintain his family's conservative standpoint, so rooted in Anglo-Saxon traditions, so comparatively unassimilated into what was becoming the prevailing Anglo-Norman ordering of society in the bishopric. We do not know who Meldred's mother was.[20] But by *c.*1170 there was an unmistakable token of change. Nearly forty years ago Charles Clay established a high probability that at about that date Meldred son of Dolfin son of Uhtred found (or perhaps was found?) a wife among the Anglo-Norman nobility: one of the two sisters of Roger de Stuteville, son of John de Stuteville, of the branch of that family then holding in Warwickshire.[21] From this marriage Meldred had at least two sons, and probably four, all of whom bore French names. The eldest was Robert fitz Meldred; his brothers were Gilbert and (less certainly) Richard and William.[22] Clearly, Meldred's wife, sister of Roger de Stuteville (Clay did

---

Libellus de vita et miraculis s. Godrici cv, ed. Joseph Stevenson, SS xx (1845), p.220, can be identified as Dolfin son of Uhtred. He is not mentioned by Dr Alan Young in his *William Cumin: border politics and the bishopric of Durham 1141-1144*, Borthwick Papers no.54, York, 1978.

17 See above, notes 10 and 12.

18 *Red Book*, i.417-8. Nor are the twelfth-century holdings by the lords of Staindrop and Raby from the bishop in Co. Durham recorded in the later episcopal feodary dating from c.1250: *HD* I.i.app.xii, p.cxxvii. The attribution there of five fees to *Heres de Brancepeth* refers to what had been inherited from Bulmer in the meantime; *cf. Red Book* i.417.

19 See Reginald of Durham, *Libellus* (as note 16), p.220.

20 Meldred, it would seem, had at least two brothers. Patrick witnesses DC Mun.3.1.Pont.11 a & b = *FPD* 100n, though the wording is just possibly ambiguous: *Meldredo filio Dolphini & Patricio fratre eius*. Robert's witness to DC Mun.3.1.Pont.10 = *Priory of Finchale*, ed. James Raine, SS vi (1837), no.ii, p.2 is clear: *Maldredo filio Dolfini & Roberto fratre suo*. 'Patrick' may point towards the Celtic fringe, but Robert sounds French enough.

21 C.T. Clay, 'A note on a Neville ancestry', *Antiquaries Jnl.* xxxi (1951), 201-4; *cf. EYC* ix (1952), p.26 n.9.

22 If the appearance of *Ric(ardo) filio Meldredi* among the witnesses to DC Mun.1.11.Spec.19 and *Ricardo filio Meldredi. Willelmo fratre eius* to 1.11.Spec.17 = *FPD* 54n will bear this interpretation. At least once Gilbert entitles himself *Gilbertus*

not suggest a name for her), was not over-patient with Anglo-Saxon attitudes when it came to the christening of her children.

If we look a little more closely at the story of this marriage, we run into a puzzle. In a grant made to the monks of Durham *c.* 1208 X 1212 by Robert fitz Roger, lord of Warkworth, there appears among the witnesses the name of Robert fitz Meldred immediately followed by that of Gilbert Hansard 'his brother'.[23] How came Gilbert Hansard to be called Robert's brother? Not surprisingly, attempts have been made to identify him with the Gilbert son of Meldred already mentioned; even Robert Surtees was so uncharacteristically incautious as to adopt the opinion that the ancestor of the Hansard line 'was a cadet of the house of Raby'.[24] This will not do. The father of this Gilbert Hansard II was in fact the feudatory of the same name who was already witnessing for Bishop Hugh *c.* 1158 X 1162.[25] Gilbert Hansard I was holding a fee from the bishop of Durham at Hornby and Ireby in Northallertonshire in 1166;[26] during the next decade and a half he had become a great proprietor. At the time of his death he was holding at South Kelsey in Lincolnshire under Montbegon and the Augustinian canons of Thornton Curtis; at Welbury, Worsall, Landmoth, Blacktoft and Hook in Yorkshire under Ingram, de Vesci and the bishop of Durham; in Northumberland a fragment of the Worcester fee under Hairun. Between Tyne and Tees he had built up two extensive complexes of property: in west Durham the vills of Evenwood, Morley and Walworth, with an outlier at Kimblesworth, all held from the bishop; in east Durham, in the area of the headwaters of the Skerne, lands centring on Hurworth and Embleton, held under Hairun and de Vesci.[27] Everything known about this elder Gilbert Hansard supports Dr Scammell's view of him as one of the most active and acquisitive feudatories to enjoy Bishop Hugh's

---

filius Meldredi filii Dolfini: DC Mun.1.11.Spec.16 = *FPD* 53n, while his son Eudo remembers his own grandfather in the same way: *Eudo filius Gilberti fillii Meldredi*, DC Mun.1.11.Spec.17 = *FPD* 54n.

23 DC Mun.2.4.Spec.8 = *FPD* 113-4n: *Roberto filio Meldredi. Gileberto Hansard fratre suo*. The document is also witnessed by Henry Neville, who took seisin of his deceased mother's northern fees in 1208: *Rot. de oblatis et finibus*, ed. T.D. Hardy, Rec.Comm., 1835, p.423. Robert fitz Roger died c.1212. His grant must be earlier than that by Prior William of Durham printed *FPD* 10n, of which the limits of date are 1213 X 1218.

24 *HD* iii.316; *cf. Antiquaries Jnl.* ii (1922), 216.

25 *AA*[4] xxxiii (1955), 68.

26 *Red Book* i.416.

27 Enumerated in the general confirmation of his father's lands made to Gilbert Hansard II by King John, 22 September 1199: *Rot. Chart.*, ed. T.D. Hardy, Rec.Comm., 1837, p.23.

favour.[28] There is no good reason to doubt that the Gilbert Hansard who witnessed as Robert fitz Meldred's 'brother' c.1208 X 1212 was the son and heir of this Gilbert Hansard I; in the course of the lawsuits in which Gilbert II often became involved no question was ever raised about who was his father.[29] The obvious solution of the difficulty is that Gilbert Hansard II was Robert fitz Meldred's half-brother, witnessing as 'brother' just as naturally as, say, William of Valence witnessed as 'brother' of King Henry III.[30] It may be inferred, then, that Meldred son of Dolfin and Gilbert Hansard I were the successive husbands of the same lady, sister of Roger de Stuteville. By her first marriage she certainly had two, and perhaps four sons: Robert and Gilbert fitz Meldred fitz Dolfin, and Richard and William fitz Meldred. Her known children by her second marriage were Gilbert Hansard II and his sister Alice, who became the wife of Brian fitz Alan.[31]

Perhaps the name of this sister of Roger de Stuteville can be discovered. By the twelfth century the *Liber Vitae* of the cathedral church of Durham was being used as a combined record of benefactors and visitors. On f.23 verso a bold coarse charter hand of the last third of the century has made this entry: *Gilebert Halsart. Iohanna de Stuteuilla. Philipp(us) vicec(omes) Aaliz uxor eius*. The entry extends nearly across the page, with *uxor eius* relegated to the beginning of a second line, under the name *Gilebert*. It is just possible to read the entry in two parts: viz. *Gilebert Halsart et Iohanna de Stuteuilla uxor eius. Philippus vicomes et Aaliz*. If that were permissible, we would know for certain the full name of the mother of Gilbert Hansard II (and of Robert fitz Meldred). Alternatively, as the punctuation of the entry suggests, *uxor eius* may refer only to Alice, who is elsewhere attested as wife of Philip fitz Hamo the sheriff.[32] Or again, the entry may record a joint visit to the cathedral of two wedded or plighted couples. There would be no great oddity in Joanna holding on to her Norman family name. After all, the new man Gilbert seems to have had no more than a nickname, if *Halsart* comes from the O.F. *hausacs, hausart*, a dagger or pruning tool: 'Bert the Knife', as it were. This scrap of evidence from *Liber Vitae* is not absolutely conclusive. But it does

---

28   *Hugh du Puiset*, p.225.
29   For examples, see *Curia Regis Rolls* ii.221 (1203); vi.220, 242 (1212).
30   *Calendar of Greenwell Deeds*, ed. J. Walton, *AA*[4] iii (1927), no.37, p.19.
31   *Curia Regis Rolls* vi,165,170,220,226,242.
32   A collotype facsimile of Liber Vitae Ecclesiae Dunelmensis, now preserved as BL Cotton ms. Domitian vii.2, was published in SS cxxxvi (1923). For Alice as wife of Philip fitz Hamo, see DC Mun.3.7.Spec.20 = *FPD* 126n; for Philip, who served Bishop Hugh as sheriff from c.1180 to 1195, Scammell, *Hugh du Puiset*, p.227.

Fitz Meldred, Neville and Hansard

nothing to weaken the contention that the same lady was the mother both of Robert fitz Meldred and of Gilbert Hansard II. She was a Stuteville; it is highly probable that her name was Joanna, and so she will be called henceforward in this paper.[33]

A plausible chronological scheme for her two marriages can be suggested. Gilbert Hansard the elder, alive in 1183, had died by October 1184.[34] His heir Gilbert II was still under age when Bishop Hugh died in March 1195; *sede vacante* he fell into royal wardship for his Durham fiefs. By Michaelmas 1196 Archbishop Hubert Walter had bought the wardship of Gilbert, his land and marriage from the king for 600 marks.[35] In September 1199 Gilbert received from King John general confirmation of his father's estates.[36] Presumably, then, he came of age in 1198 or 1199, which suggests that he was born in 1177 or 1178. Thus his father must have married Joanna at the latest between 1176 and 1178: she was already the mother of Meldred fitz Dolfin's children.

How long she had been a widow is uncertain. Meldred witnessed an episcopal document on 10 November 1172;[37] no evidence for his survival after that date has been found. Round's assumption on the basis of the Pipe Roll for 7 Richard I that Meldred lived on until or just before 1195 is very wide of the mark,[38] and, of course, wholly incompatible with the remarriage of his widow in 1176 X 1178. Closer examination of the Pipe Roll entry reveals a different story. At the Exchequer at Michaelmas 1195, the see of Durham being vacant and in the king's hands, Robert fitz Meldred

---

33 In 1207 Robert fitz Meldred was involved in questions concerning the inheritance of William de Stuteville: PR 9 John, p.4. Among the tenants-in-chief in Domesday Book French toponymics appear to have enjoyed a notably superior esteem to patronymics and nicknames; *cf.* J.C. Holt, *What's in a name? Family nomenclature and the Norman Conquest*, The Stenton Lectures no.15, Reading, 1981, p.20.

34 Gilbert I was alive at Michaelmas 1182, PR 28 Henry II, p.40, and witnessed Race Engaine's charter for Sherburn Hospital at an undetermined date in 1183, *Second Calendar of Greenwell Deeds*, ed. J. Walton, *AA*[4] vii (1930), no.41, p.98. According to *Rot. de dominabus*, PR Soc. xxxv (1913), p.5, his Lincolnshire holding at South Kelsey was in crown custody from 13 October 1184; at Michaelmas 1188 his heirs and lands were said to be in wardship and at farm, PR 34 Henry II, p.33. *FPD* 142n, where he appears to be alive in March 1185/6, has mistranscribed DC Mun.3.6.Spec.18; the correct reading is *anno Domini m°c°lxxx^{mo} Quinto Nonas martii*, i.e. 3 March 1180/1.

35 Chanc.R 8 Richard I, p.171; Hubert Walter has paid the 600 marks by Michaelmas 1198, PR 10 Richard I, p.33. The farm of the Hansard 'barony' in the bishopric of Durham yielded £178 12s.8d. (including corn sold) during the year accounted for at Michaelmas 1196: Chanc.R 8 Richard I, p.261.

36 See note 27 above.

37 DC Mun. Cart.II, f.82r.

38 J.H. Round, *Feudal England*, p.489.

rendered account for the 600 marks which he owed as a fine in order to have the land which was his father's; computed in this sum were the 300 marks of fine which he had formerly promised the bishop of Durham for the same purpose. Robert had paid 100 marks into the Treasury and still owed the king 500 marks.[39] The Pipe Roll does not tell us when Bishop Hugh had taken over Meldred's lands, only that the latter's heir had arranged to recover them from the bishop by fine. Before this transaction could be completed the bishop's death had lodged his assets in the hands of the king, who proceeded to exploit them further. We do not know how long before March 1195 Robert had fined with the bishop, nor that when he did so he had only just come of age. So we are not entitled to calculate by a simple subtraction from 1195 that Robert was born in 1173/4; his date of birth may well have been somewhat earlier than this. If it be accepted that he had three younger brothers, it would be prudent to set the marriage of Meldred and Joanna a little before 1170, rather than after, as Charles Clay suggested.[40] In any case Robert was less than a decade older than his half-brother Gilbert Hansard II. Each in his nonage became ward of Bishop Hugh du Puiset. That was no enviable situation. For Hugh had a bad reputation as feudal suzerain, according to the Durham monastic chronicler; he failed to abide by the old conventions 'in the treatment of his vassals, whose hereditary rights he sometimes transferred to others, while he drastically changed the ancient laws and customs of the bishopric by his new legal dispositions.'[41]

Despite gaps in the evidence, a fairly coherent story can thus be pieced together. The native exclusiveness of the Raby family had been

---

39 PR 7 Richard I, p.26. In succeeding years Robert gradually reduced the debt: to 300 marks by Michaelmas 1196, Chanc.R 8 Richard I, p.94; to £100 by 1197, PR 9 Richard I, p.10; to £60 in 1198, PR 10 Richard I, p.146; to £40 in 1199, PR 1 John, p.126. He was finally quit in 1200, PR 2 John, pp.2-3.

40 'A note' (cited note 21 above), p.203: 'c.1170 to 1173'. In 1183/4 Boldon Book (Greenwell's edn., p.20) has a *Robertus filius Meldredi* holding a carucate of the bishop's land at Whessoe near Darlington in drengage. If he is our Robert, it might not have been too untoward for a boy of 12 or 14 to have been responsible for such a tenure. This holding had been allowed to escheat to the bishop by 1242: PRO JUST 1/223 m.2d = *Two Thirteenth-Century Assize Rolls for the County of Durham*, ed. K.C. Bayley, SS cxxvii (1916), p.22. But it was still remembered late in the fourteenth century as having once belonged to Robert fitz Meldred: *Bishop Hatfield's Survey*, ed. William Greenwell, SS xxxii (1856), pp.9-10.

41 Geoffrey of Coldingham, *ST* pp.8-9: Episcopus igitur nec erga barones neque clericos, in quibus maxime confidebat, veterum statuta seruabat .... ut quorundam hereditates et iura videretur in extraneos contulisse et nouis institucionibus antiquas episcopatus leges et consuetudines penitus immutasse.

Fitz Meldred, Neville and Hansard

breached c. 1170, when Meldred son of Dolfin married a lady of Norman descent. After a few years he died, leaving her with very young sons and wide estates. The question of wardship arose. Meldred's liege lords for Staindrop and Staindropshire, the prior and convent of Durham, were not much practised in the exercise of the higher feudal suzerainty. When we find Meldred's widow married by c.1176 X 1178 to Gilbert Hansard I, the thrusting vassal of Hugh de Puiset, it is not unreasonable to infer that the bishop had taken a hand. Meldred was the bishop's tenant at fee-farm, though not by military service.[42] Possibly this was pretext enough for the bishop to exercise his claims to prerogative wardship based on his regality, for this allowed the assertion that within the bishopric wardship of all the lands of a minor, from whomever held, fell to the bishop if the heir also held anything from him. Such pretentions were still causing controversy between the bishop of Durham and his feudal community more than a century later.[43] Bishop Hugh could be a rough character, not too scrupulous in pursuit of his own interests.[44] We do not know whether he made Gilbert Hansard pay for his marriage to Meldred's widow, but it seems likely that as Joanna's husband Gilbert controlled the Raby estates. In 1184, however, Joanna was again a widow, now with Gilbert's own considerable 'barony' and his young children on her hands, besides Raby and its brood. What happened on the Hansard side of things seems clear enough. The bishop, as he was entitled, took the Durham lands and Hansard children into wardship, and farmed them out. During the vacancy after Bishop Hugh's death this wardship fell to the king, who sold it for its remaining term to Archbishop Hubert Walter;[45] there is no indication that either Hugh or Hubert exercised the right to marry off Joanna a third time.[46] The situation

42 See note 17 above. The monks' confirmation of Bishop Hugh's charter does not detail the obligations which Meldred may have accepted: *et faciendo alia libera servitia que in predicta carta contine[n]tur*. In Boldon Book the four vills granted to Meldred are listed together, treated as forming part of the bishop's demesne, and reported at farm. Unfortunately we do not know whether Gilbert Hansard I was still alive when Boldon Book was made, 1183/4.
43 In 1303, even under considerable pressure, Bishop Antony Bek was unwilling to renounce this prerogative. Bek conceded that he would not seek wardship over those who held nothing from the bishop by military service. But he maintained his prerogative rights over his own tenants in drengage and also those of the priory. See G.T. Lapsley, *The County Palatine of Durham*, New York, 1900, p.56; C.M. Fraser, *A History of Antony Bek*, Oxford, 1957, pp.85-6, 178-89. The documents are printed *RPD* iii.41-2, 62; *Records of Antony Bek*, ed. C.M. Fraser, SS clxii (1947), no.89, p.94.
44 *Cf.* Scammell, *Hugh du Puiset*, pp.239-44.
45 See note 35.
46 The right had been recorded as belonging to Bishop Hugh in 1184 in *Rot. de dominabus*,

at Raby between c.1184 and the date when the heir Robert fitz Meldred came of age (perhaps c.1192-3) is more obscure. Bishop Hugh, it seems, exercised wardship and set out the estates at farm; so they remained for half a year after his death, though before then Robert had attempted to recover them by fine.[47] But did the bishop during this period dispose of Robert's marriage?

It is irksome to be unable to answer that question. For, of course, it was Robert's marriage to Isabel Neville, the sister and eventual heir of Henry Neville, which was in time to transform the lordship of Raby. Henry and Isabel were children of the marriage of Geoffrey Neville of Burreth in Lincolnshire (ob.1192) and the Bulmer heiress Emma Humez; on his mother's death in 1208[48] Henry thus came into possession of the Bulmer inheritance in Yorkshire as well as of that family's five knights' fees forming the 'barony' of Brancepeth in county Durham.[49] When Henry Neville died, married but without children, in or just before 1227, his sister Isabel inherited; her husband Robert fitz Meldred did homage to the crown for the lands which had been Henry Neville's, fining 200 marks for relief.[50] The materials for the building of the Neville's great territorial power in northern England were thus crucially augmented, as well understood at Durham a century later.[51] But it would be mistaken to suppose that 1227 marked the complete absorption of the old native house of Raby into the Anglo-Norman feudal world. Robert son of Meldred son of Dolfin did not forthwith – nor indeed ever – start calling himself Robert de Neville, though for some time he can be observed acquitting at the Exchequer the financial obligations of the Neville fees in Yorkshire and Lincolnshire with the sister and heir of Henry Neville of Burreth.[52] This, however, was as his wife's

p.5: *Heres est in custodia matris que est de donacione Episcopi Dunelmensis.*
47 Chanc.R 8 Richard I, p.260.
48 See PR 10 John, p.154 and note 23 above.
49 It is not clear why J.H. Round, 'Neville and Bulmer', in *Family Origins*, London, 1930, p.57, was sure that the five Bulmer fees in Durham 'must have included not only Brancepeth, but Sheriff-Hutton in Yorkshire.'
50 *Excerpta e Rotulis Finium 1216-1272*, ed. C. Roberts, Rec.Comm., 1835, i,156: 17 March 1227.
51 In 1331 the Durham monastic chronicler comments wryly on the hauteur of the contemporary Nevilles. Their holdings from the monks 'conferebantur progenitoribus suis quando non erant tanti domini ut mariscallum, pincernam et tales ministros solempnes haberent. Quia solum tunc habebant Raby cum pertinenciis, que tunc non erant tanti valoris quanti nunc. Nam Branspath habent ex maritagio post, et eodem modo Raskelf et alias terras in comitati Ebor' et Richemund': 'Robert Greystanes', *ST* p.112.
52 PR 14 Henry III, pp.33, 292-3, 310. In 1231 Alice, widow of Henry de Neville, was

Fitz Meldred, Neville and Hansard

representative; her heir was not her husband, but their son Geoffrey, and after Geoffrey's death (c.1239 X 1242), Geoffrey's son Robert.[53] Until about 1230 Geoffrey appears as Geoffrey son of Robert, and at least once in the old fashion as Geoffrey son of Robert son of Meldred.[54] Then, as *The Complete Peerage* claims, he did take the name of Neville and was 'put in possession of the whole, or part of the Nevilles' fees in Lincolnshire'.[55] He was called Geoffrey Neville in 1230-1, when together with Alice, widow of Henry Neville, he was defendant at the suit of the abbot of Bardney about boundaries of land in Burreth.[56] It is probably that by this time his mother was dead.[57] By 1242-3 his eldest son, young Robert, had succeeded him in the Lincolnshire estates and was in possession of Burreth; it was young Robert too who at that time made the return for the former Bulmer fees in Yorkshire.[58] As the result of a Yorkshire inquest on 26 May 1248 he was explicitly declared to be the heir of Henry Neville.[59]

Meanwhile his grandfather, Robert fitz Meldred, lived on in control of his patrimony at Raby (possibly of Brancepeth too, at least until the early 1240s, by virtue of 'courtesy') until approaching or past his eightieth year. Contrary to Round's belief, he never 'assumed the surname of Neville';[60] as late as January and February 1252 he was still witnessing as *Robertus filius Meldredi*.[61] Not till 7 May 1254 was it recorded that Robert Neville had done fealty to King Henry III for all the lands which his grandfather Robert son of Meldred, whose heir he is, held in chief from the king. The relief was small, for Robert fitz Meldred had held little directly from the crown.[62] For Robert Neville and his family fortunes the real importance

    taking action at law against Robert fitz Meldred concerning some of the Bulmer manors in Yorkshire: *Curia Regis Rolls* xiv, no.1325; *cf.* xiii, nos. 134,341.

53 Geoffrey was certainly alive in 1239; on 10 September he and his heirs were granted free warren in the demesne lands of his manor of Danby (Wiske): *Cal. Ch. R.* i.246.

54 *EYC* ii, no.785, p.123, dated by Farrer 1227-1228, is witnessed *Galfrido filio Roberti filii Meldr[edi]*. He appears as Geoffrey fitz Robert in Dugdale, *Monasticon* vi.871.

55 [GEC] *Complete Peerage* ix.494.

56 *Close Rolls 1227-31*, p.395.

57 The supposition in *Complete Peerage, ut supra*, that Isabel outlived her husband and married again is based on the untenable assumption that Robert fitz Meldred died between June 1242 and May 1248. See note 61 below.

58 *Book of Fees* ii.1061-2, 1100-1.

59 *Close Rolls 1247-51*, p.53.

60 'Neville and Bulmer', p.55.

61 DC Mun.2.14.Spec.41 is a chirograph dated 21 January 1252. Northumberland County Record Office, North Gosforth, Ravensworth Deed no.16 is a licence by Bishop Walter Kirkham dated 10 February in the third year of his episcopate [i.e. 1252]; *cf. Calendar of Ravensworth Deeds*, ed. H.E. Bell, *AA*[4] xvi (1939), 49.

of Robert fitz Meldred's passing lay elsewhere. By it he acquired as his grandfather's heir the lordship of Raby and Staindrop and the whole of the Durham patrimony, which was henceforward united with Brancepeth and the rest of the inheritance from Bulmer and Neville. By 1254, one dare say, the Norman Conquest had at last come to fruition in western Durham.

Robert fitz Meldred, the priory's greatest tenant, had been a man of consequence for more than fifty years under six bishops and as many priors of Durham. His assiduity in local business often brought him into contact with his half-brother Gilbert Hansard II; until Gilbert's death in the mid-1220s the two of them appear together in a large number of witness-lists, with Robert's name normally coming first.[63] Though direct evidence is lacking, it is difficult to believe that they had no part in the agitation which persuaded King John in 1208 to sell the knights and freeholders of *Haliwarfolc* the protection of the normal legal procedures of the kingdom *secundum communem et rectam assisam regni Anglie.* Whereas for the text of this first charter of Durham liberties we now have to rely on the royal enrolment or cartulary copies, it is probably no mere coincidence that in the early fourteenth century an engrossed original was in the keeping of Robert's direct descendant, Rannulf Neville of Raby.[64] Robert could not hope to escape wholly the national obligations of his position: he was among those granted protection for going overseas on the royal expedition to Brittany and Poitou in April 1230; in August 1241 he was summoned for the king's campaign to Wales.[65] But in general Robert remained prominent on the local scene while steering clear of national politics; there is no indication that he was concerned in the northern resistance to the king in 1215. Nevertheless he was far from being a moss-covered backwoodsman. His recognised capacity for legal affairs brought him to work alongside some of the most competent professional lawyers of the time. He was appointed a royal justice to hear two assizes of novel

---

62   *Close Rolls 1253-4*, pp.55-6; the relief paid was £15 16s. 3d. *Book of Fees* brings little evidence for Robert fitz Meldred's tenures outside co. Durham. In 1224 X 1230 he was holding a fee in Kepwick (Yorks) and elsewhere from Nigel de Mowbray (p.1460); in 1242-3 he was a mesne tenant of a fee at *Cumba* (Kent) under Thomas de la Haye (pp.662,677).

63   An exception is Greenwell Deed no.6; *cf. Calendar of Greenwell Deeds*, p.4.

64   *Rot. Chart.*, p.182a. The charter is entered twice in DC Mun. Cart. Vetus, at ff.63r and 152r. On the first occasion the copy is followed by a note in a different hand in very faded ink: *Ista carta est in custodia domini* [R de almost illegible] *Nevill'*. At f.152r the hand of the copy seems c.1300. Immediately after the text the same hand has added: *Custos istius carte. Dominus Ranulphus de Neuill'*.

65   *Patent Rolls 1225-32*, p.357; *Close Rolls 1237-42*, p.362.

Fitz Meldred, Neville and Hansard

disseisin at York in August 1227.[66] But it is in the courts of the bishopric that most record of his activity is to be found. In 1235-6 he was hearing pleas at the head of a commission of bishop's justices which also included two other local magnates and the highly experienced administrator John Rumsey, steward of the bishopric under Bishop Richard le Poore.[67] On the general eyre of the bishopric in 1242 Robert fitz Meldred again headed the list of justices. Rumsey was there too, and the magnate Geoffrey fitz Geoffrey of Ravensworth and Horden, but also Walter of Merton, Geoffrey Leuknor and Richard Ducket, all three of whom at one time or another made careers for themselves in the king's courts.[68] In 1246 agreement was reached between Peter de Brus III and the convent of Guisborough in the presence of Henry of Bath, justiciar of the lord King, Robert fitz Meldred, Stephen Meynil and John Hansard.[69] The combination on the bench of Robert's ancestral wisdom and deep local knowledge with such trained legal expertise can hardly have failed to produce profitable interactions;[70] it would be interesting to know how Robert behaved when cases touching his personal interests came before the court.[71] It seems quite appropriate that Walter of Merton on his way to becoming chancellor of England and

---

66   *Patent Rolls 1225-32*, p.160.
67   PRO JUST 1/224 m.1 = *Two Thirteenth-Century Assize Rolls*, SS cxxvii (1916), p.75. For the Durham legal records of this period, see David Crook, *Records of the General Eyre*, PRO Handbooks no.20, HMSO 1982, pp.53,85,93,104.
68   PRO JUST 1/223 m.1 = SS cxxvii, p.1. The heading of the roll mentions only Robert fitz Meldred, Ducket *et socii eorum*. The other justices can be identified from records of individual cases; *cf. Priory of Finchale*, SS vi (1837), no.cxviii, pp.108-9; *Guisborough Cartulary* ii, ed. William Brown, SS lxxxix (1894), pp.333-4. Lapsley, *County Palatine*, p.175 has gone somewhat astray here.
69   *Guisborough Cartulary* ii.199-200.
70   For the retaining of royal clerks and justices by the monks of Durham at this period, see J.R. Maddicott, 'Law and Lordship: Royal Justices as retainers in thirteenth and fourteenth-century England', *Past and Present* supplement 4 (1978), pp.6-7. But he says nothing about the bishops. See also C.M. Fraser and K. Emsley, 'Justice in North East England, 1256-1356', *American Jnl. of Legal History* xv (1971), 184-5. More about Robert's expert legal companions can be found conveniently in C.A.F. Meekings, *Studies in Thirteenth-Century Justice and Administration*, London, 1981: for Leuknor, iv.186; Merton, ix.lix-lxxv; Ducket, xi.158-9,179; Henry of Bath, iv.183; viii.14-15; x.134-8; xiii.467. For Walter of Merton and the rectory of Staindrop, see *Cal.Papal Letters* i.301-2.
71   For example, his inconclusive appeal against Robert Trayne for felony came before the eyre of 1242: PRO JUST 1/223 m.4d = SS cxxvii, pp.49-50. So too did his disputes with the burgesses of Durham city: *ib.* m.5 = pp.56-7; 58. Clearly, Robert disliked the monopolistic tendencies of the rising bourgeoisie. Nothing more has been found about his action against John Balliol in the court of Sadberge, respited in February 1238: *Close Rolls 1237-42*, p.29.

bishop of Rochester should have held the rectory of Staindrop, probably within Robert's lifetime.

The views of the Hansard family were less settled and ranged further afield. There was some sense of grievance about the past; in 1211 Gilbert II was proffering £100 to recover lands allegedly lost while he was under age.[72] Though in 1213 he is recorded at Dover leading a troop in the royal service,[73] by 1215 he was among the Durham rebels against King John, perhaps drawn into the movement by connexion with the recalcitrant knights of the honour of Richmond through his sister's husband, Brian fitz Alan.[74] Gilbert's heir and successor, John Hansard I, though by no means inactive in county Durham, also looked outside the bishopric. Married to a Mowbray, he was serving the king at Bamburgh Castle in December 1233 and in Gascony in October 1242; he died in Gascony in the king's service in late December 1253 or January 1254.[75] He had hardly, if at all, outlived his grandfather's step-son.

By now the expansive era for the Hansards in county Durham was past. Sir Gilbert III's long career as head of the family – he was still alive in 1292[76] – escaped disaster in the 1260s, for like other northerners he appears to have resisted the blandishments and the threats of the Montfortians.[77] But he does not seem to have been a prudent or retentive manager of his possessions. 'Bert the Knife's' imposing agglomeration of lands and fees north of the Tees can be seen crumbling. Gilbert III sold off the family interest in West Chirton to Tynemouth Priory for no more than £5.[78] The Durham estates were to be divided between his heir John and a younger son, Robert. By January 1295 John Hansard II had sold his manors of Evenwood, Morley and Fulley to the bishop; he retained Worsall in the North Riding, which he had already held in his father's lifetime.[79] Sir Robert, enfeoffed in 1291 before his father's death, continued to hold Walworth in county Durham and the remnants of the old de Vesci fief at Newton Hansard, with its vills of Swainston and Embleton, as well as

72 PR 13 John, p.34.
73 Praestita R 15 John, PR Soc.n.s. xxxvii (1964), p.97. Robert fitz Meldred may have been there too, *ib*.
74 See J.C. Holt, *The Northerners*, Oxford, 1961, pp.46,48n.
75 *Excerpta e Rotulis Finium 1216-72*, i.251; *Close Rolls 1231-34*, p.357; *Patent Rolls 1232-47*, p.334; *Patent Rolls 1247-58*, pp.232,259,262.
76 *Records of Antony Bek*, SS clxii (1947), nos.30,36, pp.30,34.
77 *Patent Rolls 1258-66*, pp.336,339,343,364,374,397,400,415,507.
78 NCH viii.76 n.1,336.
79 John [II] is described as heir of Gilbert III, *RPD* iii.69. For his alienations, see *ib*. 68-70; *Records of Antony Bek*, no.53, p.49; *Feudal Aids 1284-1431* vi.57.

Blacktoft in Yorkshire and the Lincolnshire base at South Kelsey and Thornton.[80] In April 1303 he was joined with John fitz Marmaduke on a commission of array to select 500 foot soldiers from the bishopric to serve the king in Scotland.[81] But we do not hear of him playing any outstanding part in the Durham commonalty's opposition to Bishop Antony Bek, as we do of John fitz Marmaduke and Rannulf Neville. After Robert's death in 1313 the Hansard interest in Durham faded.[82] Though John Hansard II lived on till 1327, adhesion to John Mowbray against Edward II had cost him imprisonment and forfeiture in 1322.[83] Probably initially more agile than Meldred's line at grasping short-term advantages, the Hansards in Durham displayed nothing like the enormous stamina and genetic vitality of the lords of Raby. After two centuries the intertwined history of these two families with their common ancestor in Joanna de Stuteville found its epilogue in a final concord dated 3 January 1371:[84] the manor of Newton Hansard, comprising forty messuages, six hundred acres of arable and sixty of meadow and rents worth £5 a year, together with its appurtenances in Swainston and Embleton, was quitclaimed to Sir John Neville of Raby – direct descendant in the male line at a remove of six generations from Robert son of Meldred son of Dolfin son of Uhtred.

---

80 *RPD* ii.1234-7.
81 *Patent Rolls 1301-7*, p.132.
82 *RPD* i.347.
83 *Patent Rolls 1321-4*, p.20; *Cal. Inquisit. (Misc.)*, ii, No.527, p.131; *Cal. Inquisit. (P.M.)*, vi, no.456; vii, no.1.
84 Thomas Madox, *Formulare Anglicanum*, London, 1702, no.ccclxxx, pp.229-30.

XIV

MURDER ON FRAMWELLGATE BRIDGE

Attempts are sometimes made to distinguish between happenings and events. A happening, it is argued, which may be in itself wholly trivial, becomes an event only if interpretation of it in its context justifies, as it were, its promotion to a higher status of significance. What this paper tries to ascertain and explore a medieval chronicler denoted by the non-committal Latin word *res*: "a strange and wholly detestable occurrence in the bishopric of Durham."[1] As Sir Richard Marmaduke, the bishop's steward, was riding in to the county court at Durham, he was attacked and killed on Framwellgate bridge. The assailant, rather loosely described as Richard's kinsman, was Sir Robert Neville, who, we are told, asserted that Richard had betrayed both king and realm. The year was 1318; the month December.[2]

In some ways this act of violence was banal. Framwellgate bridge has witnessed countless disorderly incidents since Bishop Rannulf Flambard first caused it to be built. The early decades of the fourteenth century, from the late years of Edward I onwards, were times when lawless and homicidal passions were notably unrestrained and ineffectively punished. The Lincolnshire trailbaston proceedings in 1305 yield almost sickeningly abundant illustration of individual and gang crimes, violent disorder and wanton cruelty.[3] Only a year before Richard Marmaduke's murder the bishopric of Durham had been the scene of the scandalous activities of the Northumbrian freebooter Sir Gilbert Middleton, operating with his armed gang from Mitford. Near Rushyford on the road between Darlington and Durham Middleton had robbed the baggage of two cardinal legates on their way to Scotland and kidnapped the bishop elect of Durham, Louis Beaumont, and his brother Henry. How helpless the local authorities initially were when confronted by this outrageous character appears from a document dated six weeks after the assault at Rushyford:

> "Be it known to all men that I, Gilbert of Middleton, have received 200 marks of silver from the community of the bishopric of Durham by the hand of William of Denum, to ensure as far as I am able that no harm or damage comes to it through me, my men or others, as is contained in an indenture about this between me and the aforesaid William. In witness of which matter I have put my seal on this letter."[4]

Blackmail had been levied and a formal receipt given. Illustrations could be multiplied. At about the same time as Middleton was on the rampage Sir Jocelyn Deyville, we are told, ravaged the Durham manors in Allertonshire with some 200 men, hooded, cowled, sandalled and bearded in the guise of lay brothers from Rievaulx.[5] In the end both Middleton and Deyville suffered the violent deaths their misdeeds had earned. But not all villains did. There comes to mind Dr. Natalie

By permission of The Society of Antiquaries of Newcastle upon Tyne.

Fryde's sketch of Sir John Molyns's career in Buckinghamshire: between 1330 and 1340 Molyns, a respected, loyal servant of the crown, was "concurrently pursuing a life of banditry, murder and dissimulation often between missions on the king's behalf."[6] And yet, from 1352 to 1357, he was serving the "gentle" Queen Philippa as steward of her household.

The question to be addressed is why, even amidst all this contemporary welter of violence, was the killing of Richard Marmaduke thought momentous enough to call for mention by at least some of the northern chroniclers?[7] Three aspects of it may perhaps justify an attempt to answer that query by a more detailed investigation than the scattered and incomplete evidence has hitherto received. First, there is the eminence of the parties concerned; the interests they represented, not negligible in themselves, transcended the limits of a merely local feud and were not without significance in the general history of England at the time. Then there are the effects of the crime in reshaping quite definitely the balance of lay proprietorship within the bishopric of Durham. Finally, as in all good murder stories, there is the puzzle, the intractable mystery of motivation. Writing some forty years after the event, but with an insider's knowledge of the society he was discussing, Thomas Gray of Heaton had no doubts: what moved Robert to kill Richard was anger born of emulation as to which of the two was to be the greater lord.[8] Though the element of truth in Gray's dictum must stand, possibly there was rather more to the murder than that.

The assailant, Sir Robert Neville, the eldest son and heir apparent of Rannulf Neville of Raby, had in prospect a very great inheritance: not just Staindrop and Raby from his ancestor Robert Fitzmeldred and the former Bulmer fiefs at Brancepeth in county Durham and clustered round Raskelf and Sheriff Hutton in Yorkshire, but also eventually the Fitzrandolf lands in the North Riding through his grandmother Mary, daughter and heir of Ralph Fitzrandolf of Middleham, together with some part of the Clavering estates in Northumberland and Essex through his mother Euphemia, daughter of Robert Fitzroger. In 1318 Robert Neville was the effective head of the Nevilles of Raby, for his father Rannulf, formerly so active, had since 1313 been a crushed and discredited man, excommunicated for incest with his daughter Anastasia; withdrawn, we are told, from secular business, he now spent his time frequenting the canons of the family's priories at Coverham and Marton.[9] Robert's victim on Framwellgate bridge was also a man of estate and lineage. But they are less well known than the Nevilles', and so call for more discussion.

The known story of the Fitzmarmaduke line begins in 1127, when Bishop Rannulf Flambard enfeoffed his nephew Richard (some would say his son) with a considerable holding in the Team valley in north-west Durham; centred on Ravensworth, Eighton and Lamesley its terms of tenure were rated beneficially at no more than the service of half a knight.[10] Richard of Ravensworth's son and successor, Geoffrey Fitzrichard, survived until about 1200. In 1166 he had been recorded as holding 1½ knights' fees from the bishop. This increase is to be explained by the family's acquisition of further episcopal fiefs: at Horden on the coast by Easington, at Homildon south of Pallion in modern Sunderland, and probably at Silkesworth (though it is just possible that Silkesworth had come from the monks of Durham, from whom Geoffrey's family certainly held Blakiston in south-east Durham till past the middle of the thirteenth century).[11] By the 1170s Geoffrey had made Horden his main seat.[12] It was lands there and at Silkesworth which provided the matter for an important but difficult lawsuit in the king's court in 1204 between William of Laton and Geoffrey Fitzrichard's son and successor, Geoffrey Fitzgeoffrey. Some of the details of this suit puzzled contemporaries, and have continued to puzzle scholars ever since. But in the upshot, Geoffrey Fitzgeoffrey did more than vindicate his possessions in Horden and Silkesworth against his opponent's challenge. By thwarting William of Laton's attempt to make him do battle for them, he gave conclusive impulse to the demand that cases concerning the Durham lay feudatories arising in the bishop's court should be tried there according to the up-to-date and evolving procedures of the Curia Regis. That success, as Lapsley saw, had much to do with forcing the bishops of Durham to develop for their liberty a genuinely palatine judicial organization, closely patterned on the royal model.[13] In the light of Geoffrey's experience in 1204 it would be difficult to believe that he was not prominent among those knights and freeholders of Durham who a few years later, in 1208, bought from King John what amounted to the first general charter of liberties for the Durham feudal community, guaranteeing its members legal process according to the laws and customs prevailing throughout the kingdom.[14]

For nearly the whole of the first half of the thirteenth century Geoffrey Fitzgeoffrey was an outstanding baron of the bishopric, his only real peer being Robert Fitzmeldred of Raby. He witnessed frequently and prominently in the courts of both bishop and prior. On the eyres of 1235–6 and 1242 he sat as one of the bishop's justices, representing with Robert Fitzmeldred the landed magnate element in company with such administrative and legal professionals as John Romsey, Walter of Merton, Richard Ducket and Geoffrey Leuknor.[15] Busied locally in the affairs of the Haliwaresfolc community and in consolidating his family estates,[16] he does not seem often to have sought a wider field. No firm evidence suggests that he was involved with the rebellion of the northern knights against King John in 1215–16. Nevertheless, there is one aspect of his story which points to contacts beyond the bounds of Tees and Tyne. During the proceedings in the king's court in 1204 offer to wage battle over a particular issue was made on Geoffrey's behalf by Marmaduke Thweng. Son of Robert Thweng, who held fiefs in east Yorkshire from Percy and perhaps from Bruce, Marmaduke may have come by his forename from the family of his mother, Emma, one of three sisters and co-heirs of Duncan Darel of Lund in the East Riding.[17] When Geoffrey Fitzgeoffrey is found naming his son Marmaduke and himself using (the first of his line to do so) an armorial seal showing a fess between three popinjays, which were also the arms of Thweng, a marriage alliance between the two families is a reasonable conjecture, though proof is lacking.[18] By early in 1248 Marmaduke Fitzgeoffrey had succeeded his father.[19] Fashioned on much the same pattern as Geoffrey, if maybe on a slightly reduced scale, Marmaduke's prominence and assiduity in the public business of the bishopric until well into Robert Stichill's episcopate is abundantly attested.[20] With a satellite group of smaller knights and gentry from his neighbourhood—Scrutvilles, Farnacres, de l'Isles, Lumleys, Bassetts—he maintained without difficulty the predominant standing in northern Durham which his family had now enjoyed for three generations. Before April 1281, it seems likely, he had been succeeded by his son John Fitzmarmaduke, who had witnessed as a knight in 1275.[21]

John Fitzmarmaduke had more of the thruster about him than his father; he was alive to the wider opportunities on a national scale which the warlike policies of Edward I were opening up. His first wife was a Bruce, Isabella, daughter of Robert Bruce the Competitor, grandfather of King Robert I; she brought with her in marriage the considerable manor of Stranton in Hertness.[22] By her John certainly had a son, Richard Fitzjohn Fitzmarmaduke, whom contemporaries commonly called Richard Fitzmarmaduke or Richard Marmaduke; it was he who was murdered in 1318. From this marriage there was probably also a daughter, Mary, who became the wife of Robert I of Lumley and, it may be assumed, died before her father.[23] The significance of this alliance between John and Isabella Bruce did not escape Thomas Gray, who rightly described Richard Marmaduke as cousin of that Robert Bruce who in 1306 became king of Scots.[24] Isabella had died long before this; by 1285 John Fitzmarmaduke had married again, in circumstances suggesting that he had already managed to bring himself to the favourable notice of Edward I. John's second wife, Lady Ida, had twice been widowed. Her first husband, Roger Bertram III of Mitford, had died by 1272, leaving Ida dowered in Mitford and Felton. Her second husband had been Sir Robert Neville of Raby, grandson and successor of Robert Fitzmeldred and great grandfather of Robert the murderer in 1318; like Ida Sir Robert had been married before, and as far as is known she bore him no children. After his death in 1282 Ida was snapped up by John Fitzmarmaduke. It is unfortunate that the origins of this obviously attractive lady remain obscure, for she plays a part of consequence in the present enquiry. Possibly she came from a family in south Durham and brought in marriage to John Fitzmarmaduke the two Teesside manors, Ulnaby and Carlbury. John's possession of these manors, of which he undoubtedly died seised, is otherwise difficult to explain.[25] There were no children from John's second and Ida's third marriage.

John had acted precipately in wedding Ida without waiting for the royal licence necessary when the widow of a tenant-in-chief married again. But the sequestration of Ida's dower lands which followed was lifted in May 1285 on the grounds that "the king wishes to show favour to John in consideration of his good service".[26] It is likely that this service had been in the field against the Welsh in 1282, for at the Rhuddlan muster on 2 August Sir John Fitzmarmaduke appears among those performing service due from the bishop of Durham.[27] Probably more details about John's military employments during the next three decades could be brought to light by minute scrutiny of such evidence as the pay rolls, letters of protection and horse valuations have to offer. But the general picture is already clear. Like his close northern associates Marmaduke III of Thweng and Walter of Huntercumbe John was making the transition from obligatory feudal service—direct or indirect—to the king, towards becoming a professional mercenary soldier, regularly organizing paid troops for the royal armies in Wales and Scotland.[28] He was campaigning against the Welsh in 1294–5 and against the Scots in 1296.[29] He avoided the disaster at Stirling Bridge in 1297, perhaps because at the time he was overseas with Bishop Antony Bek's forces in Flanders.[30] Ranking now as banneret,[31] he had earned the reputation of being a very hard man indeed, if we can believe the chronicler's report of how Edward I encouraged him to the ruthless capture of Dirleton on the Falkirk campaign in 1298: "You [John] are a cruel man and at times I have blamed your excessive thirst for blood and the way in which you glory in the death of your enemies."[32] At Falkirk itself John was one of Bishop Bek's bannerets;[33] his prowess at the siege of Caerlaverock in July 1300 earned him repeated mention in the poem celebrating the siege.[34] During the royal sequestration of the bishop's franchise in 1302–3 John in company with Robert Hansard was commissioned to muster the knights and men-at-arms of the bishopric together with 500 foot soldiers for service at the king's wages in Scotland.[35] And as the position of the English in Scotland worsened after Edward I's death, John was esteemed a proper instrument in the efforts to check the rot. Warden of Galloway in 1308, in May 1310 he was appointed to keep Perth for the English king.[36] There he died in the winter of 1310/1311.

He had wished to be buried in the churchyard of the cathedral at Durham. But, defeated by the problem of conveying his corpse through a hostile countryside, his followers at Perth cut the body up and boiled the flesh off the bones, which they preserved: to the scandal of the papal penitentiary at this gross breach of recent canon law.[37] Whether John's bones ever reached Durham is unknown; it is to be hoped that they did. For though he had done the crown good service, John Fitzmarmaduke remained essentially a Durham magnate, one of the two great bulwarks of the bishopric's feudal community. Unlike the Nevilles, his only real peers locally, he held little, if anything, outside the Palatinate; his eight manors all lay within the county. Viewed absolutely that was a modest estate, even taking into reckoning the intangibles of influence and patronage which were undoubtedly exercised through it. In the restricted context of Durham, however, it was quite sufficient to sustain preeminence. The inventory made of John's chattels after his death reveals no great magnificence of household goods at Silkesworth, his chief residence. There he kept his dozen golden spoons, his peacock and two peahens; at St. Leonard's chapel nearby he had endowed masses for himself and his ancestors.[38] Perhaps more interesting are the stock accounts, which indicate a notable degree of specialization: ploughoxen everywhere, of course, but sheep and goats concentrated at Ravenshelme, a ewe flock and pigs at Horden, lambs at Eighton (if that is *Le Spen*) and Wheatley Hill, fatstock at Lamesley and on the Teeside manors, horses at Stranton.[39] The picture is completely framed by Tyne and Tees. Here was the primary field for John Fitzmarmaduke's activities, though his relations with the English crown certainly added to their effectiveness. It was with royal approval that from 1300 onwards Fitzmarmaduke and Rannulf Neville had led the Durham community of knights and freeholders in successful opposition to the authoritarian and at times arbitrary gestures of Bishop Antony Bek. Edward I's support and the active sympathies of a strong faction among the monks of Durham enabled John and Rannulf to secure for the free landowners of the bishopric the important ratification of their privileges which Bek was obliged to concede in May 1303.[40] Though he held no lands directly from the crown, John attended the Lincoln parliament in January 1301. There in company with Rannulf Neville he sealed among the tenants-in-chief of the crown the barons' letter protesting against Pope Boniface VIII's claims to intervene in the dispute with the Scots. That he appeared at Lincoln not under the title of knight or banneret, but with the seemingly baronial style of *Dominus de Hordene* perhaps reflected the ambivalence of his status.[41] His family had long been "barons of the bishopric"; at Lincoln John moved among the barons of the realm.

Thus on his father's death Richard Marmaduke inherited not just lands but also heavy public responsibilities in the bishopric: the heavier because, with the impending moral collapse of Rannulf Neville, the fortunes of the Nevilles of Raby were to suffer temporary eclipse. There is no reason to doubt that Richard was ambitious; he was fated to be the most important layman in Durham at a ghastly period in its history. The years 1311 to 1318 witnessed natural calamities of flood, famine and pestilence beyond ordinary experience. But above all there were the repeated inroads into the northern counties of the Scots under their now triumphant king Robert Bruce, ravaging and burning less with intent to acquire territory than to terrorize, take plunder and exact blackmail.[42] The king of England, Edward II, so often at odds with faction among his own magnates, proved quite incapable of protecting his northern subjects; he tried, indeed, but military fiasco followed military fiasco: Bannockburn (1314), the loss of Berwick (1318), the "Chapter of Myton" (1319), defeat near Byland (1321). For the most part the northern counties were left to fend for themselves, and this they did by raising what money they could to buy temporary truces from the Scots, who of course came again when next the harvest was ripening. On at least eight occasions between 1311 and 1327 Durham made its own terms with the Scots, never with hope of securing more than respite from the imminent worst.[43]

From 1312 until his murder Richard Marmaduke played the chief part for Durham in these transactions. It is difficult to imagine who else could have undertaken the task. He enjoyed the confidence of Bek's successor as bishop of Durham, Richard Kellaw, monk of Durham and member of a local gentry family, who had long been a close friend of his father John;[44] as episcopal councillor he was retained at a higher fee than Robert Neville;[45] it was after much assiduity in the bishop's service that he was appointed steward and keeper of the bishop's royal liberty of Durham in December 1314.[46] Significant too was the fact that Richard Marmaduke was a close kinsman, a cousin, of Robert Bruce; his first known appearance in the historic record is as witness to an *inspeximus* by Bruce, still earl of Carrick, at York in 1304.[47] As far afield from Durham as Berwick Richard could thus be esteemed as peculiarly fitted to negotiate with Bruce.[48] Circumstances had cast Richard in the invidious role of chief broker of Durham's blackmail payments to the Scots; he can be seen occupied in this activity from the summer of 1312 at the latest until shortly before he was killed. It was an arduous and perilous path to tread. Heading the Durham negotiators for the truce bought from the Scots at Hexham in August 1312 he had perforce to accept explicitly the fact of Bruce's kingship.[49] This was a concession the English crown was not prepared to countenance officially till 1328; when Andrew Harclay made it in 1323 it cost him his life as a traitor.

Amidst almost chaotically disordered circumstances Richard Marmaduke managed to keep the cash flowing northwards; at least in part to his efforts it was due that during these years Durham suffered rather less than Cumbria or Northumberland.[50] They had been the salvation of both the monastery and countryside of Durham, Prior

XIV

MURDER ON FRAMWELLGATE BRIDGE

Geoffrey Burdon declared a few years later.[51] Richard's methods will often have been peremptory, although at any rate nominally he acted on behalf of the *communitas episcopatus Dunelmensis*, that is in effect the available free landowners of standing and the well-to-do of the county. Whether this community was formally embodied in meetings of the county court is perhaps uncertain. Nevertheless, to the king's judges in 1320 it appeared as a viable corporate entity, capable of levying money to buy off the Scots, of authorizing emergency procedures for collecting the money, of exacting oaths from its members to observe the ordinances it made for the general safety of the bishopric, and of appointing its own envoys and agents; actions of recovery lay against the community itself, not against the agents personally. How in practice contributions were assessed and the money raised is not wholly clear, though by 1318 there is regular mention of two collectors of the community's money. The means they sometimes used were rough-and-ready: for instance, a house-to-house search along Durham's North Bailey and forcible seizure of any money found, on promise of future repayment.[52] Richard also made free with the mandatory papal tenths levied from the clergy for the king's purposes. These, we are told, he abstracted from the Durham diocesan collectors and paid them over to the Scots, again with promise of reimbursement.[53]

Probably Richard was not particularly scrupulous about the ways in which he handled the monies levied, nor wholly motivated by altruistic concern for the public weal. Again the witness of Prior Geoffrey Burdon throws a little light. Attempting to defend himself against the charge of improperly alienating a jewelled chapelet or coronal belonging to the monastery, which he had given to Richard, he declared:

> "Sir Richard Marmaduke was keeper of the bishopric of Durham and sustained many labours on behalf of the church, both in journeying to Scottish parts to secure truces and in helping in many matters in these parts. And since he [Geoffrey] had no money or other jewels available with which to reward Sir Richard for his efforts, he gave him the chapelet in question to hand over to his wife, who was extremely eager to have it. Which action proved vastly useful to the monastery—and Richard would not have exerted himself to save the monastery if he had not received the chapelet or more."[54]

Geoffrey Burdon was not a thoroughly admirable character;[55] in trying to justify himself he may have been somewhat less than fair to Richard, who by this time was dead and unable to speak in his own defence. No doubt Richard did pocket any advantages which chance offered: he was that sort of man. Even so, it is difficult to believe that the whole explanation of Richard's murder lay in the Nevilles' desire to divert from him to themselves the incidental profits of the blackmail system.[56] It is necessary to probe deeper, into two of Richard's personal predicaments and an associated political complication.

The first factor involved was Richard's relations with his step-mother, John Fitzmarmaduke's second wife, the Lady Ida. After her husband's death she had claimed her customary widow's third of John's lands. About this claim her step-son behaved so irrationally as to suggest that some profound emotional antipathy divided the two. Richard was obstinately determined to frustrate Ida of her seemingly legitimate dues, and to effect this he was prepared to use every possible resource of legal chicanery and even violence. He began by arguing with John's executors that his father had died without leaving a widow at all.[57] When that contention appeared too ridiculous, Richard shifted his ground. Though prepared to accept that John and Ida had once been married, he now claimed that a solemn divorce between them had been pronounced in the Galilee of Durham cathedral in Bishop Bek's time. The Durham consistory court declared that there was no evidence of this;[58] whereupon Richard vainly pursued the matter to York.[59] Lady Ida's rights to her thirds were legally quite inexpugnable, and Bishop Kellaw's secular court gave judgement in her favour. Nevertheless Richard continued to do his utmost to prevent her enjoying the lands to which she had been declared entitled.[60] All this harassment took the affair far beyond the limits of a mere family squabble. After all, for some ten years before the death of Sir Robert Neville in 1282 Ida as his wife had been lady of Raby. The murderer in 1318, Robert, was, so to speak, her great grand step-son; her repute among the Nevilles had remained so good that one of his sisters bore her name. Richard's mistreatment of Lady Ida, construed as injury to the pride and perhaps the affection of her former family, must have exacerbated rancour between the representatives of Neville and Fitzmarmaduke.

At the time of his murder Richard, it seems a reasonable guess, was in his late thirties or early forties. He had a wife, Eleanor, who outlived him by half a century; perhaps she was in some way connected with the family of Clare, though that is no more than inference from the evidence of an armorial seal.[61] By the end of 1313 hope of issue from this marriage seems to have been abandoned, leaving open the question of who would eventually inherit the Fitzmarmaduke possessions. Only this, it may be thought, together with Richard's determination that Lady Ida should not profit from the situation, explains the settlement he made of the major part of his Team valley estates, Ravenshelme and Lamesley, on 2 January 1314, on the very same day that judgement had been given against him in Ida's favour and in the same court. The settlement secured a life interest in these Team valley lands to Richard and Eleanor jointly and severally, with remainder to John, son of Robert of Lumley.[62] Lumley genealogy is treacherous ground on which to venture, and John is a neglected figure in the story of this up-and-coming local family. The best interpretation of the evidence appears to be that he was a younger son of Robert I of Lumley by Robert's marriage with Mary Fitzmarmaduke, Richard's sister. Robert I died *c.* 1308; it must be assumed that his wife predeceased her father John.[63] Her eldest son, Robert II, succeeded his father as head of the Lumley family; a younger son, John, another nephew of Richard Fitzmarmaduke, was the remainderman of the settlement in 1314.

Before January 1314 had ended Richard, no doubt still pursuing the bafflement of Lady Ida, had taken steps to settle the rest of his estates. With licence from Bishop Kellaw he enfeoffed John Kinnersley with Horden, Silksworth, Ulnaby and Carlbury. In this transaction Kinnersley was no more than a nominee for a very great man indeed: none other than Thomas earl of Lancaster, whom Kinnersley served as councillor and eventually as executor; he was the candidate whom Lancaster unsuccessfully supported for the succession to the see of Durham after Kellaw's death in 1316.[64] The naked truth emerged three months later, when Kinnersley returned the estates to Richard to hold for life, with remainder to Thomas of Lancaster and

Lancaster's heirs.[65] That overmighty and obstreperous magnate had acquired the reversion of a considerable landed interest within the palatinate of Durham. Presumably despairing of a future for a family of his own in his native county, Richard was prepared to envisage alienating about half his Fitzmarmaduke inheritance there. In return he secured rent charges on two of Lancaster's manors in Northamptonshire together with a house and land.[66] The grant of the reversion was not a sudden decision. For at least two years before this transaction Richard had been an overt Lancastrian partisan. Bishop Kellaw's steward of Durham was a feed retainer of Thomas of Lancaster for peace and war, esteemed able to serve the earl with a troop of ten men-at-arms. On the list enumerating the adherents of Lancaster granted the king's pardon in October 1313 for complicity in the death of Piers Gaveston sixteen months previously stood the names of Richard Marmaduke and two of his henchmen, the brothers William and Robert of Silkesworth.[67]

Behind the crude act of violence on Framwellgate Bridge in December 1318 thus lay a quite complex story. Thomas Gray's description of it as the outcome of a local struggle for power, though not wrong, is incomplete. More was involved than just who should be the greatest lay lord between Tees and Tyne. Nor can the murder be understood simply as a gesture by the "outs" of disappointed envy at the profits they assumed Richard Marmaduke was making for himself from his brokerage of the blackmail to the Scots; after all, by 1318, with a new bishop in charge, the "outs" had a reasonable prospect of becoming "ins". Family pride was as potent a factor as perceived material interests; the family pride of the Nevilles, already bruised by the disgrace into which Rannulf had fallen, was further injured by Richard Marmaduke's bad behaviour towards Lady Ida. Moreover, the allegation reported by the Bridlington chronicler that Richard was a forsworn betrayer of king and realm cannot be dismissed as wholly implausible. From the point of view of the English crown, Richard's repeated dealings with the king of Scots were bound to arouse suspicion, however explicable they were by the consanguinity between the two, however beneficial, if onerous, they proved for the inhabitants of the bishopric. Hardly less sinister to established authority in England must have seemed Richard's willingness to move closely in the wake of Thomas of Lancaster, with more than a shade of connivance on the part of Bishop Kellaw.[68] The cry of treason against Richard came from an avowed enemy; suspicion is not proof. But it cannot be claimed that on this head there was no case at all for him to answer.

In the short term the murder brought disaster on the Nevilles. In the following summer Robert, seeking perhaps to extenuate his crime and curry royal favour, led his brothers Ralph, John and Alexander with a gang of rough-necks on a freebootring expedition against the Scots in the Marches. At Bewick, about six miles south-east of Wooler, James Douglas, that wily old hand at border warfare, surprised and routed them on 6 June 1319. Robert Neville was killed and his brothers were all captured. Means of paying their heavy ransoms were not found easily.[69] Yet it must be confessed that in the longer term the crime and its consequences turned out very profitably for the Nevilles. It must be reckoned pure gain for them that the erratic, flamboyant Robert was replaced as effective head of the family by his able and long-headed brother Ralph. Above all, the extinction with Richard of the Fitzmarmaduke male line left the Nevilles as indisputably the dominant lay landowners in the bishopric of Durham. The women came out of things comfortably enough. Lady Ida secured her widow's thirds, which she continued to enjoy until perhaps as late as 1340; if so, she may well have been near ninety when she died.[70] Richard's widow, Eleanor, soon married again (an Umfraville from Prudhoe), and yet again (a Mauduit of Eshot in Northumberland); until her death in 1368 she kept control of the Team valley manors according to the settlement of 1314.[71] These two ladies handily confirm the findings of recent demographical expertise about increasing female longevity in the later middle ages. Both seem to have found the same formula: superior feeding (one suspects), three husbands in succession, no children.

The Fitzmarmaduke landed interest, so substantial and coherent at Richard's accession in 1311, broke up when he was killed. Occasionally during the fourteenth century the senior line of the Lumley family tried vainly to establish themselves as Richard's heirs general, on the very dubious argument that Mary Fitzmarmaduke had outlived her brother and inherited from him, passing the inheritance on to her elder son, Robert II of Lumley. Possibly Robert II's marriage to Lucia, daughter and co-heir of Marmaduke III of Thweng, brought hope of asserting a title to the Fitzmarmaduke inheritance along an alternative route, if, as seems likely, one of Richard's thirteenth-century ancestors had married a Thweng. These pretentions of the senior Lumley line had little success. In fact it was a cadet line of the Lumleys, descended from Mary Marmaduke's younger son John, which eventually secured the Team valley manors after Eleanor's death, precisely as envisaged when they had been settled in 1314. By 1406 John's grandson, Sir Marmaduke Lumley of the cadet line, was established in his castle at Ravenshelme.[72] In accordance with the other settlement of 1314, on Richard Marmaduke's death the reversion of Silkesworth, Horden, Carlbury and Ulnaby fell to Thomas of Lancaster. By the summer of 1320 Thomas had conveyed them to his friend, accomplice and man of business, Robert Holland, who granted them back to Lancaster for life, with remainder to Holland and his heirs.[73] "Chicanery and extortion", Dr. Maddicott has assured us, "were characteristic of Lancaster's dealings in land"; this manoeuvre was perhaps designed to frustrate rival claims by other parties alleging themselves to be Richard's heirs.[74] Lancaster's schemes to gain a territorial footing within the palatinate of Durham crashed like all his other ambitions at Boroughbridge and Pontefract in 1322; his estates and those of his supporters were forfeited. But the Hollands were a resilient lot and contrived to salvage some of their remainder rights in the bishopric from the wreck. Silkesworth was lost to them, falling in fee simple by grant from the crown to the royal keeper of rebel lands in Northumberland and Durham, Richard of Emeldon, a powerful urban patrician and office-holder in Newcastle upon Tyne.[75] At Horden, however, the Hollands managed to maintain their hold until the 1340s, when seisin passed by amicable agreement to Ralph Neville and from him to the Menville family with whom it remained despite a challenge from the senior Lumley line.[76] Perhaps it was also through the Hollands that Carlbury and Ulnaby came (or returned) to the Nevilles; at any rate, in 1380 a younger son of Ralph Neville died seised of these two manors.[77] Busily as it hunted for flotsam from the Fitzmarmaduke inheritance, the senior line of Lumley made only one substantial acquisition: Stranton, held under Clifford.[78]

XIV

MURDER ON FRAMWELLGATE BRIDGE

The crime which led to land and lordship being thus dispersed did not lack a certain dramatic irony in its circumstances. It was on the bridge built by Bishop Rannulf Flambard that the male line descended from his kinsman Richard Fitzrannulf came to an end in 1318, shattering the imposing territorial position it had created in northern Durham over five generations. Henceforward, as long as they remained united, the Nevilles could do unopposed much as they pleased in the county. The significance of the murder on Framwellgate bridge, then, was that it produced, or at least hastened, a decisive shift in local power; at the same time potentialities for increased Lancastrian or Scottish influence in the Palatinate were aborted. That much emerges with fair certainty from the sources, imperfect as they are. But the murder was an individual's deed, and on the motives of individuals the records can throw little direct light. The knightly effigy still commemorating Robert Neville in Brancepeth church is in better condition than monuments set up elsewhere for far greater Nevilles. In contrast, Richard Marmaduke has no memorial; his burial place is unknown, though it seems prudent to reject the allegation in a much later source that Robert, not content with killing him, threw his body over the bridge into the Wear.[79] Yet it is the victim of 1318 who provides the deeper mystery. Because of his family tradition, his kinship to the king of Scots, the demands made inescapably on him by the situations of his time, Richard Marmaduke could not be unimportant. But why did he so hate Lady Ida? What did he really think of Robert Bruce, of Thomas of Lancaster, of Edward II? Had failure to produce an heir perhaps bred desperation in this energetic, practical, not very scrupulous man? To such legitimate questions a conscientious historian can give no honest answers.

APPENDIX

Settlement of Ravenshelme and Lamesley

Two copies of this final concord on 2 January 1314 survive. Given by Lord Ravensworth to the Society of Antiquaries of Newcastle upon Tyne, they are now deposited at the Northumberland County Record Office, North Gosforth: Ravensworth Deed no. 31, items ii and vi. The earlier and rather more correct version is 31 (vi), referred to here as *a*. It is now attached to a collection comprising all the documents 31 (i)–31 (v), calendared by H. E. Bell, "A calendar of deeds given to the Society by Lord Ravensworth", *AA*[4] xvi (1939), 53–4. This collection, which cannot have been made before 1387, offers the second copy of the 1314 fine: 31 (ii), here called *b*. The text which follows is based on *a*; variants from *b* are noted.

Hec est finalis concordia facta in curia domini Dunelmensis episcopi apud Dunelmum in crastino circumcisionis Domini anno regni regis Edwardi filii regis Edwardi septimo et pontificatus domini Ricardi Dunelmensis episcopi tercio coram Lamberto de Trikingham,[1] Hugone de Louthre, Adam de Middleton', Thoma de Fyschburn'[2] et Willemo de Denum, justiciariis assignatis, et aliis dicti domini episcopi fidelibus tunc ibi presentibus inter Ricardum filium Johannis filii Marmaduci[3] et Alianoram vxorem

XIV

eius querentes et Willelmum de Silkesworth[4] deforciantem[5] de maneriis[6] de Rauenshelme et Lamesley cum pertinenciis, vnde placitum conuencionis sum(monitum) fuit inter eos in eadem curia: scilicet quod predictus Ricardus recognouit predicta maneria cum pertinenciis esse ius ipsius Willelmi vt[7] illa que idem Willelmus habet de dono predicti[8] Ricardi. Et pro hac recognicione, fine[9] et concordia idem Willelmus concessit predictis Ricardo et Alianore predicta maneria cum pertinenciis et illa eis reddidit in eadem curia habenda et tenenda[10] eisdem Ricardo et Alianore et heredibus ipsius Ricardi de corpore suo procreatis de domino Dunelmensi episcopo et successoribus suis per seruicia que ad illa maneria pertinent imperpetuum. Et si contingat quod predictus Ricardus[11] obierit sine herede[12] de corpore suo procreato,[13] tunc post decessum ipsorum Ricardi et Alianore predicta maneria cum pertinenciis integre remaneant Johanni filio Roberti de Lumeley[14] et heredibus de corpore suo procreatis tenenda de domino episcopo et successoribus suis per seruicia que ad illa maneria pertinent[15] imperpetuum. Et si contingat quod predictus Johannes obierit sine herede[16] de corpore suo procreato,[17] tunc post decessum ipsius Johannis predicta maneria cum pertinenciis integre remaneant rectis heredibus predicti Ricardi tenenda de domino episcopo et successoribus suis per seruicia que ad illa maneria pertinent imperpetuum. Et hec concordia facta fuit per preceptum ipsius domini episcopi.

[1] Trikyngham *b*; [2] Fissheburn' *b*; [3] Marmeduci *b*; [4] Silkysworth *b*; [5] deforc' *b*, de forinc' *a*; [6] manerio *ab*; [7] vt *b*, et *a*; [8] dicti *b*; [9] fine *b*, siue *a*; [10] et tenenda *om. b*; [11] predictus Ricardus *a*, si predictus *b*; [12] hered' *a*; [13] procreat' *a*; [14] Lomley *b*; [15] pertinent *om. b*; [16] hered' *a*; [17] procreat' *a*.

NOTES

Documents cited with the prefix DC Mun. are at Durham among the muniments of the Dean and Chapter. The collection of Ravensworth deeds is now deposited at the Northumberland County Record Office, North Gosforth; references to them are according to the numbers given by H. E. Bell in his calendar. *AA*[4] xvi (1939), 43–70 [=*Cal.*].

The following abbreviations are used for printed works or series frequently cited:

AA   *Archaeologia Aeliana* [a suprascript number denotes the series]
DS   *Durham Seals*, ed. W. Greenwell and C. H. Hunter Blair, *AA*[3] vii–xvi (1911–21)
EHR   *The English Historical Review*
FPD   *Feodarium Prioratus Dunelmensis*, ed. W. Greenwell, SS lviii (1872)
GEC   *The Complete Peerage*, ed. G. E. Cokayne, rev. by Vicary Gibbs and others, 13 vols., 1910–59
HD   R. Surtees, *The History and Antiquities of the County Palatine of Durham*, 4 vols., 1816–40
NCH   *A History of Northumberland*, ed. by the Northumberland County History Committee, 15 vols., 1893–1940
RPD   *Registrum Palatinum Dunelmense*, ed. Thomas Duffus Hardy, RS, 4 vols., 1873–8
RS   Rolls Series
SS   Publications of the Surtees Society
ST   *Historiae Dunelmensis Scriptores Tres*, ed. J. Raine, SS ix (1839)

[1] BL Harley ms. 1808, f. 23v: res mirabilis et omnino detestabilis.

[2] *Gesta Edwardi de Carnavan auctore canonico Bridlingtoniensi*, ed. W. Stubbs, *Chronicles of the reigns of Edward I and Edward II*, ii (RS 1883), p. 57: asserens ipsum esse regis et regni perfidum proditorem. The dating from Bridlington is the most acceptable we have; Harl. 1808, f. 23v confirms the year explicitly, though its description of Robert as Richard's *cognatus* must refer to affinity rather than close blood-relationship. Richard was still active in late June and early July

1318: DC Mun. Misc. Chs. 4399, 4086, 4912. So Mrs. Scammell cannot be right in assigning his death to June, *EHR* lxxiii (1958), 396 n. 1. Robert had at least one accomplice in his crime, his younger brother John, who was granted a royal pardon for the death of Richard Marmaduke on 11 September 1322: *CPR 1321–4*, p. 204; cf. *CCR 1318–23*, p. 428.

[3] Edited by Professor Alan Harding in *Medieval Legal Records in memory of C. A. F. Meekings*, ed. R. F. Hunnisett and J. B. Post, London, 1978, pp. 150–68.

[4] Dated from Mitford, 12 October 1317: DC Mun. Misc. Ch. 5053.

[5] According to the *Historia aurea*, printed from Lambeth Palace Library ms. 12, f. 226rb by V. H. Galbraith, *EHR* lxiii (1928), 208. For a survey of conditions in the north over a longer period, see C. M. Fraser and K. Emsley, "Law and society in Northumberland and Durham, 1290 to 1350", *AA*[4] xlvii (1969), 47–70, in particular pp. 62–3 for violence at Penshaw in 1328.

[6] In *Medieval Legal Records . . .* (as note 3), pp. 198–221.

[7] Though not in *Lanercost* or *Historia aurea*.

[8] Thomas Gray, *Scalacronica*, ed. for the Maitland Club by Joseph Stevenson, Edinburgh, 1836, p. 143: pur coroucesours entre eaux par enuy qui enseroit le plus graunt meistre. This seemed to Surtees, *HD* i.ii. 302, "a very satisfactory reason".

[9] According to a fifteenth-century account of the lords of Middleham, which H. M. Colvin, *The White Canons in England*, Oxford, 1951, p. 298, suggests was probably written by a canon of Coverham; printed by R. H. C. FitzHerbert, "Original pedigree of Tailbois and Neville", in *The Genealogist*, n.s. iii (1886), pp. 31–5, 107–11. It treats Rannulf discreetly (p. 34): nobilis baro fuit, sed quoad regimen temporale non circumspectus erat. Nam maluit inter canonicos de Marton et Couerham quam in castris seu maneriis suis conuersari. For the sordid story of Rannulf's excommunication, see the entries in Bishop Kellaw's register between August and December 1313, *RPD* i, 411, 429, 437, 450, 461, 484. He survived until 1331.

[10] *Durham Episcopal Charters 1071–1152*, ed. H. S. Offler, SS clxxix (1969), nos. 23, 23a, pp. 100–7.

[11] See *FPD* p. 123 n. 1; DC Mun. 2.10. Spec.12=*FPD* p. 146 n.

[12] Geoffrey Fitzrichard's daughter Emma referred to him c. 1170 X 1180 as Gaufridus de Hordene: DC Mun. 3.7.Spec.16=*FPD* p. 124 n. The seal of Geoffrey's son, Geoffrey Fitzgeoffrey, shows the legend [Sigill]vm. Gaufridi. de. Hordene: *DS* no. 1064.

[13] *Curia Regis Rolls* iii.108–10; cf. C. T. Flower, *Introduction to the Curia Regis Rolls*, Selden Society vol. lxii (1943), pp. 94–5; G. T. Lapsley, *The County Palatinate of Durham*, New York, 1900, p. 166–8, 313–6.

[14] *Rot. cart.* 182a: secundum communem et rectam assisam regni Anglie. By the fourteenth century Rannulf Neville had custody of an original of this charter: DC Mun. Cart Vetus, ff. 63r, 152r; Cart. I, f. 114r.

[15] PRO JUST 1/223 m.1d and 1/224 m.1=*Two Thirteenth-Century Assize Rolls of the County of Durham*, ed. K. C. Bayley, SS cxxvii (1916), pp. 11, 75; cf. David Crook, *Records of the General Eyre*, H.M.S.O., 1982, pp. 93, 104. See also Newcastle upon Tyne Central Library, Greenwell Deed no. 25; calendared by J. Walton, *A Calendar of the Greenwell Deeds*, Newcastle upon Tyne, 1927, pp. 12–13. In 1212 Geoffrey headed a jury of Durham knights at the king's court: *Curia Regis Rolls* vi. 220.

[16] By 1208 Geoffrey had moved the capital messuage of the Team valley estates from old Ravensworth to Ravenshelme, after enfeoffing his uncle Robert with the former for the service of a quarter of a knight's fee together with the forinsec service for Hedley; Robert quitclaimed the rest: Ravensworth Deeds nos. 6 and 7 (variant texts of the same document); *Cal.* p. 46. William of Hilton, who witnesses, had died before 20 April 1208: *Rot. cart.* 177a. By June 1223 Geoffrey had enfeoffed Robert de l'Isle, member of a family in the service and favour of Bishop Richard Marsh, with Ravenshelme itself, according to the bishop's confirmation of the grant on 4 June: Ravensworth Deed no. 20; *Cal.* p. 50. The de l'Isles quitclaimed Ravenshelme to Geoffrey's grandson John Fitzmarmaduke at the end of the century: Ravensworth Deeds nos. 21–6, *Cal.* pp. 50–2; cf. nos. 28 and 29, *Cal.* p. 52.

[17] On the Thweng family *GEC* XII.i (1953), 735–44 brings many corrections to the discursive account by W. M. l'Anson, "Kilton Castle", *Yorkshire Archaeological Jnl.* xxii (1913), 55–125. For a Marmaduke Darel in the household of Bishop Hugh du Puiset see G. V. Scammell, *Hugh du Puiset*, Cambridge, 1956, p. 65, n. 5; the bishop of Durham was overlord of Lund.

[18] *DS* no. 1064, attached to DC Mun. 2.10. Spec.13=*FPD* p. 146 n., which is to be dated 1233 X 1244. Seals of John Fitzmarmaduke and Richard Fitzjohn Fitzmarmaduke show the same arms: *DS* nos. 1709, 1711. For Marmaduke I Thweng's seal see *DS* no. 1708. Perhaps Geoffrey married a sister or daughter of Marmaduke; but the latter's known daughter Cecily married William son of Robert of Holderness: *Early Yorkshire Charters* XI (1962), 203–7.

[19] As can be inferred from Durham County Record Office, Salvin Deed no. 216.

[20] He always appears high among the lay witnesses to episcopal *acta*, commonly immediately after the steward. See for example in the bishopric of Walter Kirkham (1249–60) DC Mun. 3.2.Pont. nos. 4–5, 8a–9b, 12–13; 4.3.Pont.1 (duplicated); 4.5.Elemos.1; 4.1.Spec.21; Misc. Chs. 1816, 5150. For Stichill's episcopate, FPD pp. 187 n., 188 n. (1267–8).

[21] J. Raine, *The History and Antiquities of North Durham*, London, 1852, app. no. dccxl, p. 131; DC Mun. 5.1.Elemos.21 (formerly Misc. Ch. 89).

[22] To be inferred from Ralph Lumley's claim to Stranton in 1389: *CCR 1389–92*, p. 428; cf. *Scots Peerage*, ed. J. B. Paul, II, 432, n. 2; *GEC* VIII (1932), 267. On 18 November 1307 John Fitzmarmaduke was ordered to do homage and fealty (for Stranton) to Robert Clifford, to whom Edward I had granted the manor of Hart lately in the tenure of Robert Bruce, earl of Carrick: *CPR 1307–13*, p. 17.

[23] No contemporary evidence about Mary has been found, though she provides the essential link in the claims raised to the Fitzmarmaduke inheritance by the senior line of the Lumley family in the late 1380s: Ravensworth Deeds nos. 31(iii) and 31(v), *Cal.* pp. 53–4; *CCR 1389–92*, pp. 428–9. Against this belated Lumley case, which implied that Mary outlived both her father and her brother and so inherited from them, must be set what Richard declared when arriving at a composition with his father's executors on 16 August 1311. According to Richard, his father at his death *uxorem non habuit nec liberos preter eum*: *RPD* i, 135. While the first part of Richard's statement was blatantly untrue, it is not easy to see why he should have wished to lie about the second.

[24] *Scalacronica*, p. 143: Richard le fitz Marmaduk, que cosyn estoit Robert de Bruys.

[25] See the inventory of John's chattels *post mortem*: *RPD* ii, 675. The early history of these adjoining manors, lying near the Tees between Piercebridge and High Coniscliffe, is obscure. Seemingly Carlbury had once formed part of the early endowments of Tynemouth Priory in the wapentake of Sadberg, perhaps by gift of Robert Mowbray or Guy Balliol; it is said to have been lost by Tynemouth to the bishop of Durham c. 1265 X 1290: H. H. E. Craster, in *NCH* viii (1907), p. 50. In 1307 it was yielding a farm of 10s. 5d. to the bishop: *Boldon Buke*, ed. W. Greenwell, SS xxv (1852), app., p. xxix. In an assize of mort d'ancestor in 1228 it had been held by Alan *Pelerum* against Petronilla daughter of Alexander: *Feet of Fines, Northumberland and Durham*, Newcastle upon Tyne Records Committee Publications x (1931), no. 281.

[26] *CCR 1279–88*, p. 318.

[27] *Parl. Writs*, ed. F. Palgrave, i (Record Commission, 1827), pp. 228, 235.

[28] On Huntercumbe's military career see J. E. Morris, *The Welsh Wars of Edward I*, Oxford, 1901, pp. 70, 159. John, together with his putative kinsmen Robert II and Marmaduke III Thweng, stood surety for a debt of Huntercumbe's in 1282, *CCR 1279–88*, p. 188, while Huntercumbe was among the witnesses of Bishop Antony Bek's grant to John on 1 January 1289 of free warren at Lamesley and Ravenshelme: Ravensworth Deed no. 19; *Cal.* p. 49.

[29] John handled the prests made to Gilbert Umfraville of Prudhoe on 12 December 1294 at Wrexham and on 30 December at Conway: E. B. Fryde, *Book of Prests of the King's Wardrobe for 1294–5*, Oxford, 1962, p. 146. He was among the notable Englishmen styled as *barones* witnessing at Berwick on 28 August 1296, according to Andrew de Tange's "Ragman" rolls: *Instrumenta Publica, sive Processus super Fidelitatibus et Homagiis Scotorum Domino Regi Factis, AD. MCCXCI–MCCXCVI*, Edinburgh, The Bannatyne Club, 1834, pp. 113–14.

[30] Thirty followers of Bek had letters of protection to perform gratuitous service in Flanders in 1297–8; cf. N. B. Lewis, "The English Forces in Flanders, 1297", *Studies in Medieval History presented to F. M. Powicke*, Oxford, 1948, p. 312, n. 4. Whether John was among them might appear from examination of the supplementary Patent Roll for 25 and 26 Edward I. C. H. Hunter Blair, "The Northern Knights at Falkirk, 1298", *AA*[4] xxv (1947), p. 70, n. 11, is mistaken in supposing that John served as a banneret at Stirling Bridge and valorously cut his way to safety. He has confused John with Mar-

maduke III Thweng, who was there with Huntercumbe: Walter of Guisborough, *Chronicle*, ed. H. Rothwell, Camden 3rd series lxxxix (1957), pp. 301-3; Morris, *Welsh Wars*, p. 283.

[31] John Fitzmarmaduke was still called the bishop's bachelor when Bishop Bek granted him the manor of Wheatley [Hill] forfeited *racione guerre* by John de Parco: C. M. Fraser, *Records of Antony Bek*, SS clxii (1953), no. 55, p. 51, suggesting c. 1297 as the date. John del Park Chiualer had done fealty to Edward I on 28 August 1296: *Instrumenta Publica*, p. 150. His forfeiture was for adherence to John Balliol, according to a late fifteenth-century memorandum about the bishop of Durham's right to forfeitures of rebellion, treason and war within his liberty: *ST* app. no. ccclii, p. ccccli. John Fitzmarmaduke kept Wheatley Hill until his death, but his son released it to John de Parco's son, also named John: BL Harley ms. 1985, f. 95v (notes made c. 1580 from Lumley deeds). Between 1318 and 1325 Richard Marmaduke's nephew, Roger II of Lumley, presumably on the (unfounded) assumption that he was Richard's heir, made the following grant, noted by the same source, to John II de Parco and his wife: Ego Robertus de Lumley miles dedi Johanni de Parco et Cecilie vxori sue et heredibus de corpori(bu)s eorum procreatis omnes terras quas habui in villa de Qwetelaw simul cum reuersionibus omnium tenementorum que Ida que fuit vxor domini Johannis filii Marmaducis et Eleonora que fuit vxor domini Ricardi filii Marmaduci tenent in dotem *et cet*. Surtees, *HD* i.ii.100, cites this document as "among the Horden deeds".

[32] Walter of Guisborough, pp. 324-5: Tu autem homo crudelis es et pre nimia crudelitate tua aliquociens redargui te eo quod exultando gaudes in mortem inimicorum tuorum.

[33] John's arms are blazoned Dargent ov ung fesse de gulez et troys papejoys de vert according to the Falkirk Roll. This, as it exists in BL Harley ms. 6589, Dr. N. Denholm-Young suggested, is a copy of a roll made by Henry Percy's herald Wauter le Rey Marchis from a muster or pay roll: *History and Heraldry, 1254-1310*, Oxford, 1965, pp. 103-9.

[34] *The Siege of Caerlaverock*, ed. N. H. Nicolas, London, 1828, pp. 56, 68, 70; on the song, see Denholm-Young, "The Song of Carlaverock and the parliamentary Roll of Arms", *Proceedings of the British Academy* xlvii (1962), 255-7; id., *History and Heraldry*, p. 114.

[35] *CPR 1301-7*, p. 134; *Parl. Writs* i.372.

[36] Jean Scammell, "Robert I and the North", p. 399, n. 7; *CPR 1307-13*, p. 228. Shortly before his appointment to Perth John had been granted vills to the yearly value of 200 marks in the manor of Penrith "for his good service to the late king": *CPR 1307-13*, p. 226.

[37] *RPD* ii.1149-50: letter of Berengar Fredoli, cardinal bishop of Frascati, dated 9 December 1311.

[38] DC Mun. Misc. Ch. 6377.

[39] *RPD* ii, 675. For John's acquisition of Wheatley Hill, see note 31.

[40] Together with Rannulf Neville John took a prominent part in the protests of the knights and free tenants of Durham during 1300 against alleged abuses by Bek's officials: *Gesta Dunelmensia A.D. M° CCC°*, ed. R. K. Richardson, *Camden Miscellany* xiii, Camden 3rd series xxxiv (1924), pp. 13-14. He was summoned to appear before the king on 24 February 1303 with full power from the community of Durham to accept the king's mediation between community and bishop: *Parl. Writs* i.405. The charter of liberties is printed from Bishop Kellaw's register in *RPD* iii, 61-7 and from the Close Roll by C. M. Fraser, *Records of Antony Bek*, no. 89, pp. 93-8; cf. Lapsley, *County Palatine*, pp. 131-4. This important aspect of John's activities is brought out clearly by C. M. Fraser, *A History of Antony Bek*, Oxford, 1957, pp. 176-90.

[41] *Parl. Writs* i.102-4.

[42] The situation in Durham is discussed in detail by Jean Scammell, "Robert I and the North of England", *EHR* lxxiii (1958), 385-403. See also G. W. S. Barrow, *Robert Bruce and the Community of the Realm of Scotland*, London, 1965, pp. 331-69 for a general account of Anglo-Scottish relations from Bannockburn to 1328.

[43] Listed by Jean Scammell, p. 393, n. 2.

[44] At the latest, it may be supposed, from the time when Kellaw as sub-prior of Durham in 1300 had withstood Bek with firmness, good manners and good sense: *Gesta Dunelmensia*, pp. 43-4. On 30 April 1312 Kellaw declared to Archbishop William Greenfield of York: fuit enim prefatus dominus Johannes nobis dum in claustro egimus admodum benevolus et amicus intimus, *RPD* i, 322-3.

[45] Richard's fee was 20 marks a year, Robert's £10: *RPD* i, 9-10; ii, 1169-70.

[46] Richard frequently witnessed Kellaw's *acta* in the latter's early months as bishop: on seven occasions, for example, between 21 October 1311 and 10 January 1312, *RPD* ii, 1127-8, 1130, 1133,

1140, 1142, 1145, 1149. His commission as steward, printed *RPD* ii, 686, would normally have lapsed on Kellaw's death in October 1316. But Bridlington, pp. 56–7, still describes Richard as steward when he was murdered two years later. Possibly Bishop Louis de Beaumont renewed Richard's commission in an act now lost; alternatively, in a situation of uncertainty and disorder, Richard may have continued in office without regard to formalities. It was only on 26 March 1318 that Beaumont achieved consecration (at Westminster); his career in Durham can have overlapped with Richard's by no more than a few months. Nevertheless, in view of Richard's known Lancastrian leanings, Beaumont may have thought it prudent to establish a not very friendly watchdog alongside him. Though a feed member of the episcopal council under Kellaw, Robert Neville had played a much less prominent role in the administration of the bishopric than Richard. But on 31 October 1317 Robert is to be found acknowledging receipt of one hundred marks from the community's collectors on account of what was owed him for the keepership of the bishopric: in partem solucionis trecentum marcarum racione custodie dicte Episcopatus debitarum, DC Mun. Misc. Ch. 3448; cf. Misc. Ch. 3462 (29 January 1318). If *custodia* be taken to mean an office rather than some undefined function of defence, Robert had either supplanted Richard Marmaduke as "keeper" by this date or been made his coadjutor. In either case, here was a situation pregnant with mischief.

[47] 9 November 1304; noted by J. Bain, *Calendar of Documents relating to Scotland* ii, Edinburgh, 1884, no. 1606 (10), pp. 422–3.

[48] In May [1316] the authorities at Berwick informed Edward II that Richard was with them, ready to try to mediate on their behalf with Robert Bruce: Bain, *Calendar* iii, 1887, no. 486, p. 93.

[49] The text of the truce is printed *RPD* i, 244–5 and by E. L. G. Stones, *Anglo-Scottish Relations 1174–1328*, 2nd edn., Oxford, 1970, pp. 288–91. It designates Bruce: le noble prince monsire Robert par la grace de Dieu roi d'Escoce.

[50] As Jean Scammell accepts, "Robert I and the North", pp. 389–90.

[51] DC Mun. Locellus xxvii no. 31, to art. 25: Necnon per suos labores ac industriam et idem monasterium et patria sunt salvata. In what looks like an effort at accounting in late June 1318 Richard records personally making or authorizing payments to Robert Bruce on five occasions, with another envisaged. The total money involved in this account is £1274 3s. 9d.: DC Mun. Misc. Ch. 4339.

[52] See the record of proceedings Coram Rege 14 Edward II, printed *RPD* iv, 159–65. William of London and Master William Kellaw are named in 1318 as *collectores denariorum communitatis*: DC Mun. Misc. Chs. 3462, 4086, 4399. On the harsh methods at times employed, cf. C. M. Fraser, *Northern Petitions*, SS cxciv (1981), no. 130, pp. 175–7.

[53] Clerical tenths were being levied for the king in the diocese of Durham between October 1309 and June 1312, between October 1313 and April 1314 and between June and October 1318; in the second two instances the official local sub-collectors were the prior and convent of Durham: W. E. Lunt, *Financial Relations of the Papacy with England to 1327*, Cambridge, Mass., 1939, pp. 609, 635–7. With Prior Geoffrey's connivance Richard did not hesitate to take some of the money collected, on promise of repayment, in order to buy off the Scots. He was murdered before he could redeem his promise, and Prior Geoffrey in an attempt to recover the money was reduced to suing (or pretending to sue) Richard's executors and the community of Durham. DC Mun. Locellus xxvii no. 31, to art. 37.

[54] DC Mun. Locellus xxvii no. 31, to art. 25.

[55] Jean Scammell, "The case of Geoffrey Burdon", *Revue bénédictine* lxviii (1958), 226–50. But the contemporary Durham monastic chronicler admired Geoffrey: *ST*, pp. 95–7, 102.

[56] As Mrs. Scammell seems to imply, "Robert I and the North", p. 401.

[57] *RPD* i, 133–5 gives a memorandum of the composition reached between Richard and his father's executors (Sir Thomas Whitworth and Sir Henry Fitzhugh) in Bishop Kellaw's presence on 16 August 1311: Item, super hiis que dictus dominus Ricardus de bonis dicti patris sui nititur vendicare, pro eo quod pater suus uxorem non habuit, nec liberos preter eum, consistorii nostri Dunelmensis consideracioni tam secundum leges ecclesiasticas quam secundum consuetudines se apposuerunt partes memorate. Controversy between Richard and the executors about John's chattels was still dragging on in October 1314: *RPD* i, 628–9.

[58] Richard had raised the hare about a divorce between John and Ida by 23 April 1313: fuit divortium inter predictum Johannem filium Marmeduci et ipsam Idam solemniter celebratum, executioni demandatum et factum; on 25 July the

Durham consistory court certified that diligent enquiry had failed to discover evidence of any such divorce: *RPD* ii, 946.

⁵⁹ *RPD* i, 322-3, 435-7.

⁶⁰ Judgement in favour of Ida's claims was given in Bishop Kellaw's secular court on 2 January 1314. Richard's immediate reaction was to allege error in the plea and record. When the Durham court refused to budge, he took the matter to the king's court, though without effect. Meanwhile he frustrated, presumably by force, an attempt on 23 February to give Ida livery of seisin of her third of Horden. Only after Ida's complaint on 11 April to the bishop presiding over his own court (*seant en baunke*) was she assigned and given livery through her attorney John Menville of her widow's rights in Silkesworth, Horden, Ravenshelme, Lamesley and Eighton by the sheriff of Durham: DC Mun. Misc. Ch. 6262. For Richard's attempts to get the king's court to intervene, see *RPD* ii, 998, 1008-9. Richard's harassment of Ida, perhaps not without suspicion of covert complicity on the part of Bishop Kellaw, continued after April 1314; she was still making representations to the king in *1315*: *RPD* ii, 1086; iv, 526-7.

⁶¹ *DS* no. 1728, from the year 1332. Of the four shields on the seal three, Fitzmarmaduke, Umfraville and Mauduit, refer to Eleanor's successive husbands. The fourth, three chevrons and a label of three points, may suggest Clare; cf. W. P. Hedley, *Northumberland Families* i, Newcastle upon Tyne, 1968, p. 212.

⁶² See appendix. This records a final concord in an action of covenant between Richard Marmaduke and his wife, plaintiffs, and William of Silkesworth, defendant, concerning the manors of Lamesley and Ravenshelme. Made with the bishop's concurrence, this transaction by way of feoffment and refeoffment in effect allowed Richard to exchange his estate in fee simple in the two manors for a life estate for himself and his wife with remainder to a designated third party. The defendant in this collusive action, William of Silkesworth, witnesses as steward in the hall of Ravenshelme: Ravensworth Deed no. 33, *Cal.* p. 54; his seal is described *DS* no. 2249a. William was a man of some standing, named with his brother Robert immediately after Richard Marmaduke on the list of those pardoned by Edward II on 18 October 1313 for complicity in the death of Gaveston: *Parl. Writs* ii.ii. (1830), app. p. 66. He may be the Willelmus de Silkesworthe recorded as doing fealty to Edward I in Scotland on 10 July 1296: *Instrumenta Publica*, pp. 89-90. Surtees' suggestion that William was perhaps a Lumley cadet will hardly do: *HD* ii.211; cf. *Notes & Queries* clxxvi (1939), 88-9. As appears from documents referred to at *HD* i.ii.306 William's father was named Philip and his mother Agnes. William's daughter and heir Agnes married John Menville of Whittonstall, and their son Sir William married Isabella daughter of Sir Marmaduke Lumley of the senior line: see J. C. Hodgson in *NCH* vi, 1902, p. 192. William must have died long before the Inq.p.m. recorded 23 Hatfield, which shows him dying seised of the manors of Lamesley and Ravensworth held from the bishop: transcript in PRO Durham 3/2, f. 79d, calendared in app. i to *45th Report of the Deputy Keeper of the Public Records*, 1885, p. 260. He was still living in 1325: DC Mun. Misc. Ch. 6597.

⁶³ The senior Lumley line from Robert I is best traced by *GEC* VIII (1932), 267-9, despite the objections by L. G. H. Horton-Smith, *The ancient northern family of Lumley and its Northamptonshire branch*, St Albans, 1948, pp. 2-6; cf. *Notes & Queries* cxcii (1947), 340-1. But *GEC* does not concern itself with the younger branch from Robert. This paper assumes that John Fitzmarmaduke did indeed have a daughter named Mary, who predeceased him, and that she, as the Lumleys later claimed, became the wife of Robert I of Lumley. To him she bore at least two male children: the heir Robert II, who succeeded his father c. 1308, and John, the remainderman of the 1314 transaction. On the other hand, the claim raised by the senior Lumley line that Mary outlived both John Fitzmarmaduke and her brother Richard, inherited from the latter, and thus established a right to the Fitzmarmaduke lands in her elder son Robert II Lumley, is unacceptable; see note 23 above. John Lumley is found witnessing in 1315: Ravensworth Deeds nos. 28, 29; *Cal.* p. 52. It is the seal of this John Lumley of the younger line which shows a fess between three popinjays in 1353, a dozen years before the earliest known instance of this device being used by a member of the senior line. John's seal, *DS* no. 1657, probably looks back through Mary Lumley to John Fitzmarmaduke; his nephew Marmaduke's *DS* no. 1662, possibly to the marriage of Marmaduke's father, Robert II of the senior line, with Lucia daughter and eventually co-heir of Marmaduke III Thweng.

⁶⁴ Bishop Kellaw's licence to Richard dated 13 January 1314 mentions only Horden and Carl-

bury: *RPD* ii.1246–7; DC. Mun. Misc. Ch. 6261 (badly worn and in part illegible) appears solely concerned with Horden. But that Silkesworth and Ulnaby were also involved can be inferred from Thomas of Lancaster's later grant of them together with Horden and Carlbury to Robert Holland: DC Mun. Misc. Ch. 6379; see note 73 below. Richard Marmaduke enfeoffed Kinnersley by charter with Horden (and presumably the other three manors) on 21 January: cf. DC Mun. Misc. Ch. 6262. For Kinnersley's activities as a member of Lancaster's council and executor, and his relations as canon of Lichfield with the Coterel gang, see J. G. Bellamy, "The Coterel Gang", *EHR* lxxix (1964), 703; for his candidature at Durham, *ST*, p. 98.

[65] DC Mun. Misc. Ch. 6262: Le jeody en le sismaigne de Pask' le xiii iour daurill' prochein suyant le dit sire Johan de Kynnardesley rendist le dite maner entier par fyne a Richard fitz Marmaduk' pur terme de sa vie le remayandre a Thomas count de Langcastre et as ses heires. Though only Horden is mentioned in this document, there can be little doubt that the other three manors were also involved in this transaction; see note 64 above. If the day of the week is given correctly, the date is 11 rather than 13 April 1314.

[66] At Raunds and Higham Ferrers: A monsieur Richard Marmaduke pur son seruice ... et pur la reuersion daucunes terres queles il granta al dit Conte en leuesche de Duresme; printed by G. A. Holmes, *The Estates of the Higher Nobility in fourteenth-century England*, Cambridge, 1957, p. 137.

[67] At one time or another Richard also held from Lancaster for service in peace and war rents from the Lancastrian manors of Easingwold (Yorks.), Hoby (Leics.), and Rushden (Northants.). For these and his troop see Holmes, *Estates*, pp. 136, 141, 142; J. R. Maddicott, *Thomas of Lancaster, 1307–1322*, Oxford, 1970, pp. 42, 54–5, 61, 65. For his pardon in 1313, see note 62 above. He had not figured on the roll of the Dunstable tournament of 1309, which throws light on Lancaster's retinue at that date; see the edition of the roll by C. E. Long in *Collectanea Topographica et Genealogica* iv (1839), 63–72, esp. pp. 67–8; A. Tomkinson, "Retinues at the Tournament of Dunstable, 1309", *EHR* lxxiv (1959), 79.

[68] The Durham chronicler hints that, at least until Bannockburn, Kellaw inclined more to the magnate opposition than to Edward II: *ST*, pp. 94–5.

[69] The date given by Bridlington is acceptable, and is confirmed as to the year by Harley ms. 1808 and "Original pedigree", p. 108; see note 2 above. The rout is put too early by Lord Hailes, *Annals of Scotland* ii, 73, Barrow, *Robert Bruce*, p. 340 and R. Nicholson, *Scotland in the later middle ages*, Edinburgh, 1974, p. 96. There is some uncertainty about the place. Bridlington says Berwick, as does Barbour, *The Bruce* xv, 402, 435, ed. W. W. Skeat, Scottish Text Society, 1st series, xxxii (1894), 41–6. But Harley 1808 f. 23v gives *ad parcum de Bewyk* and this placename is corroborated by "Original pedigree" and seems also to have been the original reading of the sole surviving manuscript of *Scalacronica* (perhaps mistakenly altered by the editor on p. 143 to Be[re]wyk). Bewick in Northumberland (par. Eglingham) was on the northward route from Alnwick towards Wooler and Roxburgh. It cannot be ascertained whether the extensive forest rights enjoyed at Bewick by Tynemouth Priory were called a park at this time; parks there certainly were at Chatton and Chillingham close by: *NCH* xiv (1935), pp. 205–6, 424–32. The chronicle fragment in Harley 1808, f. 23v has reasonably good authority. It seems likely that it came from Kirkham Priory in Yorkshire, for it gives accurately the date of Edward II's stay there at Easter 1319: cf. *CPR 1317–21*, p. 326; *CCR 1318–23*, p. 133. Kirkham had been endowed at Titlington in Eglingham parish by Walter Espec and may have received news of the skirmish from its connexions there. Though the fragment survives only in a copy made at least a century after 1319, its testimony is not to be disregarded. It cost Ralph Neville 2000 marks to gain his freedom (from Patrick of Dunbar, according to Harley 1808 and "Original pedigree", p. 107), and well into 1320 his brothers John and Alexander were still prisoners of the Scots; see Ralph's petition to Edward II for licence for his father to enfeoff him with the manor of Houghton in Norfolk (which had belonged to Ralph's grandmother, Mary of Middleham): printed by C. M. Fraser, *Northern Petitions*, no. 132, p. 179; calendared (with a false date) by J. Bain, *Calendar of Documents relating to Scotland* iii, no. 527. The date of the petition must lie between Mary's death in April 1320 and the grant of the royal licence on 28 October 1320: *Calendar of Inquisitions* vi, no. 232; *CPR 1317–21*, p. 514.

[70] The arrangement Ida reached on 2 November 1320 with Richard Marmaduke's widow and her new husband did not include Horden among

the properties where Ida was to enjoy her widow's portion: Ravensworth Deed no. 35, *Cal.* p. 55. But *CCR 1318–23*, p. 600 makes clear that she also held her thirds at Horden and Silkesworth. On 31 May 1340 Thomas Holland could order livery of seisin to Ralph Neville of only two-thirds of Horden, which suggests that Ida was still alive: DC Mun. Misc. Ch. 6263. On 13 December 1340, however, Ralph Neville granted the whole of Horden to John and Agnes Menville: DC Mun. Misc. Ch. 6264. The inference is that Ida died between these two dates. She had brought her writ of dower after the death of her first husband as long ago as Trinity Term 1272: W. P. Hedley, *Northumberland Families*, i, 27.

[71] Ravensworth Deeds nos. 36, 38, 39; *Cal.* pp. 55–6. *GEC* I (1910), 150.

[72] See notes 23 and 63 above. Sir John Lumley's son and heir Robert witnesses in 1356, when John was still alive: Ravensworth Deed no. 38; *Cal.* p. 56. Robert's son and heir Sir Marmaduke Lumley was called lord of Ravenshelme on 17 April 1388: Ravensworth Deed no. 42; *Cal.* p. 57. To him Sir John Lumley of the senior line quitclaimed on 20 February 1406 that line's dubious pretensions to the castle of Ravenshelme, Lamesley and Eighton, formerly belonging to Richard Fitzmarmaduke: Ravensworth Deed no. 46; *Cal.* p. 58.

[73] DC Mun. Misc. Ch. 6379 (this document is badly damaged, the month of the date and the names of some of the witnesses being lost); cf. Surtees, *HD* i.ii.26. Holland's grant to Lancaster is calendared by A. M. Oliver, *Northumberland and Durham Deeds*, Newcastle upon Tyne Records Committee Publications vii (1929), no. 8, p. 287.

[74] J. R. Maddicott, "Thomas of Lancaster and Sir Robert Holland: a study in noble patronage", *EHR* lxxxvi (1971), 453–5. Dr. Maddicott, p. 462, reminds us that Holland "as companion and friend, estate steward, political agent and general factotum . . . had no rival in Lancaster's entourage."

[75] *CPR 1321–4*, p. 398; see also C. M. Fraser, *Northern Petitions*, nos. 135, 191, 192, pp. 182, 256–9. For Emeldon's almost continuous service as chief bailiff or mayor of Newcastle from 1306 to 1332, see A. M. Oliver, *Early Deeds relating to Newcastle upon Tyne*, SS cxxxvii (1924), pp. 209–12.

[76] Robert Holland had been restored to his lands by December 1327: *CCR 1327–30*, pp. 192, 286–7; *Rot. Parl.* ii.18, 29. He succeeded in founding the fortunes of a notable dynasty, his grandson being the half-brother of King Richard II. His second son, Thomas, granted Horden to Ralph Neville who passed it on in 1340 to John Menville, husband of Agnes, daughter of William of Silkesworth; it remained with the Menvilles after it had been confirmed by Thomas Holland in 1343: DC Mun. Misc. Chs. 6263–8; cf. note 70 above. A memorandum dated 28 April 1365 shows William Menville giving two parts of the manor of Horden to Sir Marmaduke Lumley of the senior line, son and heir of Robert II by Lucia Thweng: DC Mun. Misc. Ch. 6980. But there seems no evidence that this grant took effect.

[77] According to the Inq.p.m. taken 30 March 1380 on Ralph Neville, fourth son of the great Ralph, he died seised of the manors of Ulnaby and Carlbury held of the bishop of Durham: transcript in PRO Durham 3/2, f. 102, calendared in app. i to *45th Report of the Deputy Keeper of the Public Records*, 1885, p. 243.

[78] See Surtees, *HD* iii. 121; C. M. Fraser, *Northern Petitions*, no. 182, pp. 246–7; *CCR 1389–92*, p. 428. For the abandonment by Robert II of Lumley of John Fitzmarmaduke's acquisition of Wheatley Hill, see note 31 above.

[79] "Original pedigree", p. 108.

XV

A Note on the Northern Franciscan Chronicle

Historians concerned with the first half of the fourteenth century, especially those interested in Anglo-Scottish affairs, have cause to be grateful to a lost northern Franciscan chronicle [NFC]. A version of it has come down to us in the 'Chronicle of Lanercost' [L], which was printed by Joseph Stevenson in 1839 from the only surviving manuscript, BL Cotton Claudius D.VII. A. G. Little could be quite definite in 1916 about the authorship of L: 'the chronicle as we have it is a Franciscan chronicle adapted and interpolated by a canon or canons of Lanercost.'[1] NFC, the original basis for L, still 'existed at the beginning of the sixteenth century, and was known among the London Grey Friars as the chronicles of Friar Richard of Durham', though Friar Richard's own contribution probably ended in 1297, after which date the chronicle was continued by another Franciscan hand.[2] In 1927 V. H. Galbraith showed that it was this later part of NFC, either in its original form or in some version not identical with L, which the anonymous compiler of the French chronicle of York [AC] used as a source for his account of the years 1334-46, for the most part translating literally an existing Latin text. Galbraith was careful to point out that no closer relationship could be traced between AC and L than that 'both are ultimately derived from a common original'.[3] It would be unsafe to assume that the text of NFC could be recovered exactly by collating AC with L, for possibly (at any rate, for its narrative after 1338) AC was combining its Franciscan basis with an additional source. That raised the question which Galbraith termed 'the most insoluble of all the Lanercost problems': to what date had NFC extended?[4] L ends in 1346, a few lines after its account of the battle of Neville's Cross. AC, however, carries on the discussion of border affairs into 1347, with an account of the English expedition to aid Edward Balliol in Scotland, and then continues this section of its narrative without noticeable break, though with a markedly decreased interest in northern happenings, till 1356. So Galbraith

---

[1] *Chronicon de Lanercost 1201-1346*, ed. Joseph Stevenson (Bannatyne Club, Edinburgh, 1839). Translation by Sir Herbert Maxwell in vols.vi-x of the *Scottish Hist. Rev.*, 1908-13, collected with an introduction by Canon James Wilson, Glasgow, 1913. A. G. Little, 'The authorship of the Lanercost Chronicle', *English Hist. Rev.*, xxxi (1916), 269-79, and xxxii (1917), 28-9; reprinted in *Franciscan Papers, Lists and Documents* (Manchester, 1943) (which I cite), p.42.
[2] Little, pp.44-5.
[3] *The Anonimalle Chronicle 1333-1381*, ed. V. H. Galbraith (Manchester, 1927), p.xxviii.
[4] *Ibid*.

did not rule out the possibility that NFC might have extended to 1356. But he thought the more likely hypothesis was that it ended with the account of the Balliol expedition in 1347.[5]

Further light is thrown on these conclusions by some evidence which was known to neither Little nor Galbraith. Manuscript B.ii.35 in the Dean and Chapter Library at Durham contains at ff.1-35 a Latin Brut chronicle continued down to 1347 [B]; since the fifteenth century the chronicle has remained bound up with some much more illustrious companions.[6]. The little the compiler of B tells us about himself is not illuminating. Identifying Edward III as the *sextus Hibernie* of Merlin's prophecies, he claims to have acquired prophetic verses about the king at Paris in 1332.[7] He relates the great slaughter of the Scots at Dupplin Moor on 12 (*rectius* 11) August 1332 as personal hearsay from those present at the battle, but rather undermines his own credibility about this by using language which seems in fact to derive from a written source.[8] Almost certainly a northerner, he may have been a Durham monk, though I have met no proof that this was so.

---

[5] p.xxix.

[6] R. A. B. Mynors, *Durham Cathedral Manuscripts* (Oxford, 1939), pp.41-2. The section containing the *Brut* appears to have been bound in with the other contents of the book (Bishop St Calais's gift of Bede, *Hist. ecclesiast.* and important twelfth-century MSS. of Nennius and Gilbert of Limerick) after 1395 and before the end of the fifteenth century. On the Nennius text, see D. M. Dumville, 'The Corpus Christi "Nennius"', *Bull. Board of Celtic Studies*, xxv (1974), 372-3.

[7] B, f.31ra Edwardus vero de Karnaruan genuit istum Edwardum qui est sextus linealiter descendens ab Henrico filio imperatricis qui fuit primus Hibernie. De sexto autem Hibernie recepi versus Parisius anno domini m°.ccc^{mo}.xxxii°. cuiusdam Normanni sic dicentis: Anglia transmutet leopardum. lilia galli / Qui pede calcabit cancrum cum fratre superbo *etc*. There follow another 11 lines of this 'Prophecia de mutacione armorum Regis Anglie scilicet leopardi', as they appear in Bodley, Rawlinson B.214, f.121; for other manuscripts of these 'versus Northmannie' see H. L. D. Ward, *Catalogue of the Romances in the Department of MSS. in the British Museum*, i (1883), pp.308, 317, 319. B continues with another set of 6 lines: Item versus eiusdem Normani de tempore et modo regnandi eiusdem sexti: Ter circa lustra tenent cum semi tempora sexti *etc*. For 'sextus Hibernie' see Geoffrey of Monmouth, *Hist. reg. Britann*. vii.3, ed. Acton Griscom (London, 1929), p.388. As Paul Meyvaert, 'John Erghome and the *Vaticinium Roberti Bridlington*', *Speculum*, xli (1966), 659, n.20 points out, there is still much work to be done in sorting out the 'prophecy' literature of the later middle ages.

[8] B, f.31va: Audiui enim a pluribus valentibus qui in predicto bello fuerant quod Scottorum cadauera in altitudine unius lancie corpora super corpora iacentia fuerunt eleuata et quod plures sine ictu gladii corporibus interfectorum compressi fuerant suffocati. *Cf. Historia aurea*, Lambeth Palace Library ms.12, f.229rb: Cadauera enim Scotorum altitudine unius lance, ut ferebatur, fuerant eleuata, et multi plures corporibus oppressi quam in ore gladii interfecti fuerant suffocati. This is copied in *Cont. of Walter of Hemingburgh*, ed. H. C. Hamilton (Eng. Hist. Soc., 1849), ii. 304-5.

There is little if anything original about his compilation; he gathered other men's flowers. From 1328 until Edward III's crossing to Brabant in July 1338 B's main source is akin to that of the continuator of the Guisborough chronicle. Its short entry about the Weardale campaign in 1327 is not obviously related to the continuator's, nor is its account of Archibald Douglas's surprise attack on Edward Balliol at Annan on 17 December 1332. Nevertheless from 1328 to the end of 1333 on a number of occasions it is clear that the two works were drawing upon the same source; even if B's account of the battle on Dupplin Moor has some distinctive features, its end is almost verbally the same as that in the Guisborough continuation.[9] In the narrative of the next four years these resemblances become much more striking; verbally identical passages are now frequent.[10] Though B's tendency is to select, there is no indication that for these years it had any source which was not available to the continuation. But, as Galbraith pointed out, the text of the Guisborough continuator as printed by Hamilton can 'be regarded as a rough-and-ready text of John of Tynemouth's *Historia aurea*'.[11] From 1328 until the summer of 1338, then, B's principal source appears to be *Historia aurea*—'the mother of all histories' in the eyes of a fourteenth-century Durham scribe.[12] Comparison of B with the text of *Historia aurea* as it survives in Lambeth Palace MS.12 fully corroborates this suggestion.[13]

---

[9] See note 8. B, f.31vb names John Neville as the only English knight killed at Halidon Hill in 1333; *Historia aurea*, f.229vb and *Cont. Guisborough* (i.e. *Cont. Hemingburgh*, ed. Hamilton, as in note 8), p.309 lack the name. Presumably this was John Neville of Raby, brother of Ralph, rather than John Neville of Hornby, the earliest writs for whose inquests *post mortem* are 1 and 16 December 1335: *Cal. of Inquisitions Post Mortem*, vii, no.682.

[10] For example, the account of Balliol's fealty to Edward III in June 1334 in *Cont. Guisborough*, ed. Hamilton, p.309 = B, f.31vb; the capture and imprisonment of the earl of Moray in 1335, Hamilton, p.311 = B, f.32ra; Edward III's raid as far as Inverness in 1336, with the deaths at Perth of John of Eltham and Sir Hugh de Frene, called earl of Lincoln, Hamilton, pp.311-12 = B, f.32ra; the embassy of the bishop of Lincoln and earls of Salisbury and Huntingdon to France after Corpus Christi 1337, Hamilton, p.313 = B, f.32ra; the capture and death at sea of Bishop John Wischard of Glasgow, Hamilton, p.314 = B, f.32rb; Salisbury's siege of Dunbar from January to July 1338, Hamilton, p.315 = B, f.32rb; the raid on Portsmouth on 23 March 1338, Hamilton, p.315 = B, f.32rb.

[11] V. H. Galbraith, 'The *Historia aurea* of John, vicar of Tynemouth, and the sources of the St Albans Chronicle (1327-77)', in *Essays in History presented to R. L. Poole*, ed. H. W. C. Davis (Oxford, 1927), p.389.

[12] Jesus College, Cambridge, MS Q.B.7, f.111: Excerpciones quedam breues siue notule ex historia aurea omnium historiarum matre collecte. On the Durham provenance of this manuscript, see M. R. James, *Cat. of MSS. in the Library of Jesus College, Cambridge* (Cambridge, 1895), pp.28-9.

[13] All the passages in B indicated in note 10 occur more or less verbally in Lambeth Palace Library, MS.12, between ff.229vb and 230va. The full text of *Historia aurea* from 1327 to 1342

In 1338, however, B changes horses. Its accounts of the siege of Dunbar begun by the English on 28 January and of the French raid on Portsmouth on 23 March are still ultimately based upon *Historia aurea*.[14] But from this point onwards, until it ends in 1347, B relies exclusively on NFC, either in its original form or in a version of it very close to that used by L. A comparison of the entries in L and B for 1338 makes this transition clear. The passage in L, p.304 describing Edward III's arrival in Brabant during July, his search for an effective German alliance and reception of the imperial vicariate and the consequent reproaches of Pope Benedict XII appears quite literally in B, f.32rb down to: 'cum inimicis ecclesie fedus contraxit'—just as it does, in a French rendering, in AC, p.13. B then omits Benedict's three letters to Edward which at this point L somewhat clumsily inserts in full,[15] and continues immediately:

> et Rex Anglie eidem pape litteram excusatoriam sue confederacionis et declaratoriam sue iusticie in regno Francie per suos ambassiatores transmisit.

This sentence is picked up by L at the end of its interpolation of the papal letters (p.317); it appears, in French, in AC p.13 exactly as in B, for AC too lacks the text of Benedict's letters. Here, there can be little doubt, B and AC remain more faithful to NFC than does L. B's next entry for 1338, describing the negotiations of Archbishop Stratford and Bishop Richard de Bury with the two cardinals sent to mediate between Edward and Philip of France, appears in the same slightly corrupted form in L; both can be amended by aid of the French version in AC.[16]

The transition accomplished, from the end of 1338 until the end of the narrative of the Crécy campaign in 1346 the texts of B and L are almost identical, except that B continues to omit official documents reproduced in full by L. Such is the case s.a. 1339 with the three royal letters, *Amabilium Deo patrum, Reverenter et devote recepimus* and *Universorum Dominus Rex excelsus* which, together with a pedigree and declaration in French of Edward's right to the throne

---

is also preserved in the St Albans *Historia anglicana*, ed. H. T. Riley (Rolls Ser., 1863-4, 2 vols), i.191-221.

[14] B, f.32rb; cf. Lambeth MS 12, f.230va; *Cont. Guisborough*, p.315. Though L lacks these passages, they occur in AC, p.13.

[15] L, pp.304-17: *Dudum te*, 13 November 1338; *Dum diligenter*, 23 December 1339; *Recentem habemus*, 12 October 1339.

[16] B, f.32rb (cf. L, p.317): Qui quamuis multa grauamina et pericula eciam sub protexione cardinalium predictorum Parisius et apud Atrabatum vsque ad mensem Nouembr. insimul commorantes sustinuerant, tamen [famem BL] sine re [siue spe *om*. BL] pacis regum et regnorum ad regem Anglie in Brabanciam redierunt. AC, p.14, puts them both right.

of France, appear in L presumably as additions made to NFC at Lanercost or elsewhere; they are not to be found in AC.[17] B lacks too, as does AC, the full text of the truces at Malestroit given by L, and also that of Edward III's French newsletter to the archbishop of York dated from Caen 30 July 1346, which AC does know and cite.[18] Undoubtedly due to the compiler of B is the interpolation of one short passage missing from L.[19] With these exceptions L and B agree so closely that it seems reasonable to suppose that they relied either on the same copy of NFC or on two nearly identical copies. Though B is not immaculate, on the whole it offers a rather more accurate version than does Claudius D.VII as printed by Stevenson, and would be helpful if his text were ever to be revised. For example, L's defective entry about van Artevelde's murder in 1345 becomes intelligible only when its omission is corrected from B.[20] On the other hand L offers a rather longer list than B of the French magnates killed at Crécy.[21]

---

[17] L, pp.319-32. Though the text of AC lacks the royal letters, pedigree and declaration of right, the pedigree and declaration are to be found elsewhere in the Ingilby MS in which AC survives, as Galbraith pointed out, AC, pp.xx, 158. The royal letters, dated Antwerp, 16 July 1339, Ghent, undated (? January 1340), and Ghent, 8 February 1340, are printed in Rymer, *Foedera*, ii. 1086-7, 1108-9.

[18] L, pp.335-40, *cf.* B, f.33va L, pp.342-3, AC pp.19-20, *cf.* B, f.33vb.

[19] L, p.332 and B, f.32vb read: Et literas [eciam *om.* L] excusatorias de ingressu et inuasione regni Francie summo pontifici demandauit. To this B adds: Unde de eo sic metrice quidam scripsit: Rex sum regnorum bina racione duorum *etc.*, followed by the remaining 5 lines of the epigram printed from Bodley, Rawlinson B.214, f.121^v by Thomas Wright, *Political Poems and Songs relating to English History from the accession of Edward III to that of Richard II* (Rolls Ser., 1859-61, 2 vols), i.26. 'Unde ... scripsit' has perhaps been added later.

[20] L, p.341, lines 15-16; B, f.33vb: fuisse Jacobum de Nardfeld qui vices regis Anglie tenebat in Flandria. A few errors are common to both: L, p.335, line 5 and B, f.33va show 'qui', where 'quia' might be expected (and as Stevenson amended); both L, p.343, line 23 and B, f.33vb have 'in pulsu leui' for 'inpulsu leui'; in B, f.34rb a missing 'laborans' after 'infirmitate' has been supplied later, and L, p.351, line 31 exhibits the same fault, which Stevenson amended by reading '[propter] infirmitate[m]''. But a few lines earlier the word missing from L, rightly indicated by Stevenson though Claudius D.VII, f.242^v here shows no lacuna, can be supplied without hesitation from B as 'multitudine'. B's reading at f.33ra, 'quantum ad dominia, successiones', makes better sense than L, p.333, line 13, 'quantum ad divina successores'; and it is clearly right with 'nimium' instead of L's 'minimi' at p.334, line 3. The unintelligible passage at L, p.334, line 5, can be resolved by following B, f.33rb: 'Ad regem vero anglie et francie in flandria existentem', and B's 'fuerat' is to be preferred to L's 'fuerit' ten lines later. Stevenson's conjectural addition '[incarceravit]' at L, p.335, line 3 can be replaced by 'cepit' from B. B, f.33va, 'elegerat in omnibus periculis est protectus' seems superior to L, p.340, lines 28-9, 'eligerat in omnibus periculis est protractus'. So does B, f.33vb, 'Eo autem existente super mare' to L, p.341, line 14, 'Eodem anno [rege] existente super mare'.

[21] The lists in AC, p.23 and B, f.34ra, though not quite the same, are closer to each other than to that in L, p.344. They may both come wholly from NFC, while L may have added something from elsewhere.

When one turns to compare B with AC for these same years 1338-1346, again the most prominent feature is their reliance on the common source NFC, sometimes at variance with L, though there are also examples of agreement between L and B against AC which suggest that AC has diverged from the Franciscan chronicle.[22] At the beginning of 1338 AC, p.13, shows the two passages which occur in B but are lacking from L; possibly they were to be found in NFC, though their ultimate source was *Historia aurea*.[23] The textual corruption in AC s.a. 1339, noted by Galbraith, is made as clear by B as it is by L;[24] like B, AC omits Edward III's letters from its entry for this year, and so supports the view that L has interpolated them into NFC. On the other hand, the account of the capture of William Montague by the French, basically the same in L and B, has been rehandled and expanded in AC: Robert Ufford is reported as having been taken too, and AC's story of the mocking reception of the two prisoners at Paris finds no parallel in L or B.[25] AC's confusions about dates for the obituaries in 1340 of Henry de Beaumont[26] and Archbishop Melton[27] can be helped by resort to L and B, while its account of the parliamentary proceedings in the spring of 1340 (printed distinctively by Galbraith) is revealed as a clumsy and not wholly intelligible paraphrase of an entry common to L and B, though rather corrupt in the former.[28] The substance of the two short passages indicated by Galbraith s.a. 1340 on p.17 as peculiar to AC does in fact appear in both L and B; it comes from NFC.[29] But L and B lack AC's truncated notices of the death of Pope Benedict XII and succession of Clement VI (mistakenly s.a. 1343), and also AC's chronologically confused account of Henry of Lancaster's Gascon expedition in 1345-6;[30] clearly

---

[22] L, p.333 and B, f.33ra agree that Edward III at Sluys in 1340 had 147 ships, while AC, p.16 gives him an improbable 412. L, p.341 and B, f.33rb correctly date the beginning of the English reprisals in Dumfrieshire as 15 December 1345; AC, p.19 has 24 December.
[23] See note 14 above.
[24] AC, p.14, note 10; B, f.32ra; L, p.318.
[25] AC, p.15; B, f.32rb; L, p.332.
[26] AC, p.15 lacks the date of burial, 13 March, which B, f.32rb gives incorrectly as 'in crastino sancti Georgii martiris' [= 24 April]. L, p.332 rightly reads 'Gregorii', but retains 'martiris'.
[27] AC, p.15 and L, p.332 appear to have confused the date of Melton's burial (24 April) with that of his death (5 April). L now reads 'Gregorii' improperly, instead of 'Georgii', while B, f.32rb seems to have the whole matter right: Quo tempore ... obiit dominus Willelmus de Melton' archiepiscopus Ebor. qui apud Ebor. in crastino sancti Georgii traditur sepulture. Cui successit dominus Willelmus de la Souche.
[28] B, f.33ra gives the preferable reading (see note 20): quod regnum Anglie in nullo regno Francie subiceretur nec pro eo nec pro quocumque successore suo, sed quantum ad dominia, successiones et libertates remanerent libere et totaliter separata.
[29] L, p.334; B, f.33rb.
[30] AC, p.18.

NFC is not the source here. It is doubtful whether AC's entry s.a. 1345 about the murder of James van Artevelde elaborates what is found in B (and corruptly in L) to an extent which makes it necessary to suppose that it was not based on NFC.[31] The story of Duncan Macdowell's capture by William Ufford in 1345, however, is found only in AC; neither L nor B shows any trace of it. For the Crécy campaign in 1346 AC begins by incorporating into its narrative Edward III's letter from Caen, which, as we have seen, L includes and B omits. Then AC goes on to depend on a source or sources which neither L nor B used; at the end its list of French casualties in the battle may again derive, though corruptly, from NFC.[32]

Thus far, a pretty clear pattern emerges from these detailed comparisons. They indicate that L, AC and B all drew by far the most part of their information about events between the summer of 1338 and August 1346 independently of each other either from the original of NFC or from some version or versions of it closely resembling the original.[33] Possibly L and B used the same copy of NFC; as a translation into French, AC does not lend itself so readily to exact verbal comparison, and it would be hazardous to attempt to define closely a textual relationship between it, L and B. To NFC L made rather clumsy additions of official documents reproduced *in extenso*. AC's additions, though shorter, are more numerous;[34] no single source can be identified for them all, though it is likely enough that for the Gascon and Crécy campaigns AC used military newsletters of

---

[31] AC, p.19. B, f.33vb: Eoque existente super mare Flandrenses, qui tunc ad fidelitatem regis Anglie credebantur fuisse, Jacobum de Nardfeld, qui vices regis Anglie tenebat in Flandria, peremerunt. For L's corruption of this passage, see note 20 above.
[32] See note 21.
[33] The small differences between AC and L in their entries between 1333 and 1337, which Galbraith indicates by distinctive type, pp.4-13, could all have been derived by AC from *Historia aurea*; *cf.* Lambeth MS.12, f.230^{ra-b}; *Cont. Guisborough*, pp.311-5. The one apparent exception can be explained by slight variation in the textual tradition of *Historia aurea*. S.a. 1337 AC, p.9, when reporting Edward of Woodstock's creation as duke of Cornwall, adds: 'Et le roi commaunda as touz issi estre nome et appelle'. Like L, the text of *Historia aurea* in Lambeth MS 12 and *Cont. Guisborough* lacks this sentence. But it is given both by *Hist. anglicana*, i.197 and by B, f.32ra: 'Edwardum tunc comitem Cestrie ducem Cornubie fecit et sic precepit ab omnibus nominari.' It is not surprising that in all these slight discrepancies between AC and L, with one exception (the notice of the death of Sir William Keith s.a. 1337: AC, p.10 and Lambeth MS 12, f.230ra) AC is supported by B, f.32^{ra-b}, since at this stage B's principal source is *Historia aurea*. An alternative, but perhaps less likely explanation of the discrepancies would be that these additional scraps from *Historia aurea* shown by AC had already been taken into NFC, whence they were faithfully rendered in AC, but omitted by L. For the two early entries for 1338, common to B and AC, but missing from L, see note 14.
[34] To those already mentioned should be added the naming of Sir Robert Morley as admiral in 1340, AC, p.16; L and B lack this.

the kind which was not uncommon at this time and of which Edward's letter from Caen (which AC, like L, certainly did use) is an example. Among the progeny of NFC it is B which seems to have preserved most accurately the lineaments of its parent. It makes a small decorative addition s.a. 1339, and omits Edward's letter from Caen—if that was indeed included by NFC, which, though likely, is not quite certain, for L and AC could have acquired it independently. Otherwise B appears to have followed its source from 1338 to September 1346 precisely; it offers the most faithful reflection of NFC which we have for that period.

After Crécy matters become more complicated. L, AC and B all bring Edward to the siege of Calais with essentially the same sentence, which presumably all took from NFC.[35] Then their ways diverge. After inserting a proleptic statement about the surrender of Calais on 4 August 1347, B turns back to give a short, bald account of the campaign and battle of Neville's Cross in October 1346, with lists of the Scottish notables killed and taken prisoner. It goes on to report the subsequent expedition of Ralph Neville and the earl of Angus into the Lowlands. Next are recounted the siege and capture of Hermitage (co. Roxburgh) by William Heron and John Coupland in April-May 1347. B's final entry tells of the combined English expeditions into Scotland to aid Edward Balliol in mid-May 1347, which ended with the establishment of Balliol in the peel at Hestan.[36]

In contrast, L adds nothing to its single sentence about the beginning of the siege of Calais before passing on to an elaborate and flamboyant account of the battle of Neville's Cross, stuffed with Old Testament imagery and other biblical reminiscences, 'fine' writing, with crass alliterative effects and a couple of almost impenetrable puns. The whole is pervaded by a coarse jocosity at the expense of the defeated Scots, and what look like bits of local folklore are worked in to add an extra edge of hatred and despite.[37] This is certainly not the voice of the northern

---

[35] B, f.34ra and L, p.344: Post hec ad obsidendum villam de Kalays anglicis ab olim infestissimam rex Anglie profectus est; *cf.* AC, p.23.
[36] See Appendix.
[37] L, pp.344-52; *cf.* p.349: sunt varii validi viri, veniunt cito; p.350: victus vecordia votum violavit Domino; and of Ralph Neville: vir verax et validus, audax et astutus et multum metuendus. Of the puns, that on p.350 can perhaps be understood by punctuating thus: In tertio exercitu erat comes Patrik, sed melius vocaretur 'de patria non hic'. But that on p.351 defeats me, unless John Mowbray had a loud voice or talked like an ass: In tertio exercitu dominus Johannes de Moubrai, qui habet nomen a re. The stout activity on the English side of a Franciscan suffragan bishop (pp.350-1) is elsewhere reported, as far as I know, only in verses from Durham: Dom David Knowles, *The Religious Orders in England*, ii (Cambridge, 1961), p.375, identified him as Matthew *Manchensis* O.F.M., but unfortunately gave no authority. The story of the infant David's mishap at the font (pp.346, 349) appears too in

Franciscan chronicler; its tone betrays it as a blatant piece of tendentious rewriting. The question is: what was being rewritten? For most of its length L's account has almost nothing in common with B's story of the battle; despite all its errors of taste and judgement it shows itself much more fully informed about details than does B. Then, some twenty lines before it ends, L's tone changes completely; it gives calm, factual accounts of the Scottish casualties at Neville's Cross and of the Neville-Angus expedition into the Lowlands, which are verbally the same as those in B. The 'Chronicle of Lanercost' in Claudius D.VII ends at this point.

Whether AC relied on the same source as B for the progress of the siege of Calais is uncertain: if so, its compiler was careless, for the dates are wrong.[38] At any rate, hereabouts agreement between AC and B is interrupted. Though factually much fuller than L and eschewing L's rhetorical excesses, despite discrepancies in detail there can be no doubt that AC's long account of the Neville's Cross campaign follows the same main source as L. All the basic structure of the narrative is common to AC and L: King David's attack on Liddell peel, the execution of Walter of Selby, the Scots' march through Naworth, Ridpath and the Tyne valley to Hexham, then veering south-east through Ebchester across the river Derwent to Bearpark, the Yorkshire mobilisation under Archbishop Zouche at Richmond, the English concentration at Barnard Castle on 15 October and the mustering and ordering of the English forces at Auckland on 16 October, the skirmish with William Douglas's raiders early on the morning of 17 October, David's interview with the Durham monks and their narrow escape, the battle itself. With this narrative B's short treatment of the campaign shows no relation. Not till AC comes to tell of the sending of David and his fellow prisoners to London after the battle does it rejoin B. But from that point, save for the interpolation by AC of three lines about Edward III's jubilation at the news of the victory, AC and B keep exactly in step until the latter ends with the establishment of Balliol at Hestan in 1347.[39]

These close but intermittent relationships between B, L and AC from the autumn of 1346 onwards call for explanation. The obvious reason for the verbal agreement between AC and B from late in the Neville's Cross entry until B ends in

---

Geoffrey le Baker, *Chronicon*, ed. E. M. Thompson (Oxford, 1889), p.40; it is exploited at tedious length in the verses *Dux Valeys hinnit* printed by Thomas Wright, *Political Poems and Songs*, i.46-7.

[38] AC, p.23: 'un an entier et pluis'. As Galbraith, p.161 points out, in fact the siege lasted from 4 September 1346 to 3 August 1347.

[39] AC, pp.28-9.

1347 is that both were here continuing to follow NFC, AC's main source from 1333 and B's only source from mid-1338. That B does not continue beyond 1347, while AC has little northern material for the years 1347-56, reinforces Galbraith's suggestion that NFC itself may have ended in 1347. If this is so, only a few sentences of it have been lost in L, and these B can supply in their original Latin form.[40]

But was NFC the common source of L and AC for the campaign of Neville's Cross? If so, it is odd that, though B also had access to NFC, its short account is so different from the two others until towards its end, when L comes in to match its casualty list and, even later, AC rejoins to parallel what B has to say about the fate of the Scottish prisoners. Any attempt to resolve this difficulty is bound to be speculative. Perhaps the most simple supposition is that NFC attached to its own brief report of the battle a contemporary newsletter.[41] This B, in its concern for brevity, excluded, as it had already excluded Edward III's newsletter of 30 July, which NFC is likely, though not certain, to have purveyed. L rehandled the Neville's Cross letter to suit its polemical purposes, but truncated its lengthy casualty list, preferring at that point to return to NFC's concise account. AC remained more faithful to the newsletter, though adapting it for its narrative, as it had done previously with Edward's letter; it returned to NFC only for its information about the Scottish prisoners in London, which would have been lacking from a letter written before the disposal of the prisoners was known.

What this explanation postulates—the existence of a newsletter now lost, probably transmitted by NFC and certainly known to both L and AC—does not seem at all unreasonable. At least two contemporary letters about Neville's Cross, Thomas Sampson's[42] and Prior John Fossor's, have survived. Though it is necessary to remember that AC's narrative of Neville's Cross was written down

---

[40] Galbraith, p.xxix; see Appendix.
[41] For the practice of communicating information about the fourteenth-century campaigns by newsletter, see A. E. Prince, 'A letter of Edward the Black Prince describing the Battle of Nájera in 1367', *EHR*, xli (1926), 417, with examples for Halidon Hill, Sluys, Crécy, etc.
[42] Not, I think, the Thomas Sampson to whom the letter is often attributed, i.e. the Oxford teacher of business methods and compiler of treatises on letter writing, who flourished c.1350-1409; on him see H. G. Richardson, 'An Oxford teacher of the fifteenth century', *Bull. John Rylands Library*, xxiii (1939), 452-5; idem, 'Business training in medieval Oxford', *American Hist. Rev.*, xlvi (1941), 259-80; A.B. Emden, *A Biographical Register of the University of Oxford to A.D. 1500* (Oxford, 1957-9, 3 vols), iii.1636-7. A much more likely author is an older Thomas Sampson, D.C.L. of Oxford, king's clerk, official of York 1331-43 and experienced in the financial business of the northern wars. He was canon and prebendary of York and Beverley, made his will in June 1348 and was dead by July 1349. See Emden, c.1636.

A NOTE ON THE NORTHERN FRANCISCAN CHRONICLE

thirty years after the battle,[43] in much of it can still be discerned the staple ingredients of fourteenth-century military newsletters: the approach marches, the numbers of the combatants, the rival battle orders, the duration of the conflict, the knightings and casualties among the notables. Even errors in AC's casualty lists strengthen the impression that it was basing itself on a document reflecting immediate experience of the battle.[44] Names of participants who do not appear in other sources are by no means incredible; indeed, if the postulate of an underlying contemporary newsletter is legitimate, they may give a hint about where the letter originated. AC's account brings into the picture Cumbrians like Sir Hugh Moresby and John Huddleston of Millom; it gives detailed attention to the Scots' approach through the west march and to the truces bought from the Scots by the men of the Carlisle area.[45] If newsletter there were, it seems reasonable to suggest that it came from west rather than east of the Pennines. We know that it was by a letter of this kind that Edward III kept the Cumbrian Thomas de Lucy informed about the progress of his French campaign in 1346.[46] A reciprocal newsletter from Cumbria about the English victory at Neville's Cross seems a quite plausible hypothesis.

Along this line of argument L can give no help; its reworking of the same prime source as AC's for Neville's Cross was so drastic that it disguises the source's original form. It would not be safe to assume that the reworking took place at Lanercost. As Little pointed out, the last obvious Lanercost insertion in Claudius D.VII is that relating to the death of Prior Henry de Burgh in 1315.[47] It seems strange that a member of that house should have been content to describe the Scots' depredations at the priory in October 1346 in no more than a single

---

[43] Twice Gilbert Umfraville, the 'English' earl of Angus, is miscalled Thomas, perhaps by confusion with the Scottish earl, Thomas Stewart; AC, pp.25-6. The claim that Ralph Neville's son John, who fought at Neville's Cross, had been present at Crécy two months before (p.26) is improbable. The only John Neville to feature in Wrottesley's lists is Sir John Neville of Essex: *Crécy and Calais* (London, 1898), p.117.

[44] 'Instant' casualty reports are rarely completely accurate. AC's list of 22 Scottish notables killed (pp.27-8) includes the names of 6 elsewhere recorded as prisoners (William Ramsey, Thomas Boyd, John Stewart *le frère*, William More, Patoun Heryng and Patrick of Dunbar); 2 I have not found recorded elsewhere at all (Alexander del Rathe and William Wyseman). Of the 15 prisoners named, there is corroborative evidence for 12; Thomas Charteris and Adam Nickson (or Nicholson) were in fact killed; only William de Conyngstoun remains uncertain.

[45] AC, pp.24, 27.

[46] Francisque Michel, *Le Prince Noir, poème du héraut d'armes Chandos* (London, 1883), p.307.

[47] 'Authorship', p.45, note 1.

sentence, much of it borrowed from I Machab. 1.23.[48] Strange too, perhaps, that a Lanercost writer should have thought it necessary to explain who the inhabitants of Lanercost were, and that the priory of Hexham was held by black canons, while not bothering to note that Bearpark belonged to the prior of Durham.[49] The piece of writing which comes nearest to L's account of Neville's Cross, both in its narrative progress and by occasional verbal echoes, is undoubtedly of Durham provenance: the verses 'O miranda bonitas Jhesu Salvatoris'.[50] The significance of that relationship merits further enquiry.

As to B, it is in itself, at any rate for the first twenty years of Edward III's reign, a more limited and less interesting work than either L or AC. The value of this modest compilation is to serve, as it were, as a third trigonometrical point, by aid of which we can conduct a more precise survey of the probable contents of the lost northern Franciscan chronicle between 1338 and 1347 than a merely two-handed comparison between L and AC permits. Other than a number of textual corrections in detail, B's direct contribution amounts to no more than a jejune (though not inaccurate) report of the battle of Neville's Cross, which may well come from NFC, together with the Latin text of two of NFC's entries for 1347, known previously only in AC's French rendering. B was probably written at or near Durham not long after the middle of the fourteenth century. Perhaps there is another indication of NFC's presence at Durham. When John Wessington, apparently in the years just before he became prior in 1416, set to work on his history of the church of Durham, what he found to say about Neville's Cross was for the most part verbally identical with B's account.[51] But small variations between the two texts suggest that Wessington did not draw directly on B, for his version is a shade the more accurate of the two.[52] Possibly then, he made use of a

---

[48] L, p.346. But Canon J. Wilson could esteem the account of the ravaging of Lanercost 'as certainly that of an eyewitness', *VCH Cumberland*, ii.158, note 7.
[49] L, p.346 on Lanercost: ubi manent canonici, viri venerabiles et Domino devoti; on Hexham: ubi nigri canonici morantur. AC, p.24 omits these descriptions, but does identify Bearpark: le quele boys est le bois del priour de Durrem.
[50] Surviving only in BL Harley MS 4843, ff.243-6. This is an early sixteenth-century manuscript containing the collections of the Durham monk William Tode. It has not, I think, been firmly established when the poem was composed. Printed by William Hutchinson, *History of Durham* (Newcastle, 1787-94, 3 vols), ii.342-5; by Joseph Stevenson, *Illustrations of Scottish History* (Maitland Club, Edinburgh, 1834), pp.63-72; and by Joseph Hall, *The Poems of Laurence Minot* (2nd edn, Oxford, 1897), App.iv, pp.112-20.
[51] Bodley, Laud misc. MS 748 f.66ʳ. For the date of compilation, see R. B. Dobson, *Durham Priory 1400-1450* (Cambridge, 1973), p.381.
[52] Wessington's history shows a necessary 'obsessa' omitted by B from its account of the siege of Calais (see Appendix). Among the list of English captains at Neville's Cross Wessington gives '*Willelmus Dayncourt*'—a more familiar form of this midland magnate's name than the

copy of NFC itself. If so, we could identify as in the possession of Durham priory by the early fifteenth century the two works on which B drew almost exclusively for its narrative of English history between 1328 and 1347. To set beside *Historia aurea*, now in Lambeth Palace Library (as well as its abbreviation, now at Jesus College, Cambridge),[53] we would be entitled to suppose at Durham a copy, now lost, of the northern Franciscan chronicle.

APPENDIX

Durham, Dean & Chapter Library, MS B.ii.35, f.34[ra]:

[1346] [a] Post hec ad obsidendum villam de Kaleys Anglicis ab olim infestissimam rex Anglie profectus est.[a] Que villa a fine mensis Augusti anno quo supra vsque ad principium eiusdem mensis anno sequenti [   ].[b] Nam anno Domini m°.ccc.moxlvii.° iiii.to die mensis Augusti, deficientibus victualibus et Philippo rege Francie presidium, quia non potuit, non prebente, incole ville de Kalays cum predicta villa nimia fame afflicti se voluntati regis Anglie dediderunt.

Anno Domino m°.ccc.mo xlvi.to nonis Octobris Dauid dictus rex Scottorum cum exercitu maximo Angliam ingressus fortalicium de Ledell' obsedit, cuius custos tunc erat dominus Walterus de Selby miles strenuus in rebus bellicis et probatus. Qui / f.34rb Dauid predictus quinto id. eiusdem mensis dictum fortalicium expugnando cepit ac militem antedictum cum plurimis viris fortissimis capitis obtrunccacione peremit. Et exinde versus Episcopatum Dunelmensem procedens vsque ad parcum de Bewerpay[r] peruenit. Contra quem domini et principes incliti Willelmus de la Sowche Archiepiscopus Ebor., Gilbertus de

---

Willelmus de Danchour' in B.
[53] Lambeth Palace Library, MSS 10,11 and 12, formerly Durham books, on which see M. R. James and C. Jenkins, *Descriptive Catalogue of the MSS. in the Library of Lambeth Palace* (Cambridge, 1932), pp.22-6; for the Jesus College MS see note 12 above.

Oumfrauille comes Dangous, Henricus de Percy, Johannes de Moubray, Radulfus de Neuil, Henricus de Scroppe, Willelmus de Danchour' cum aliis nobilibus, militibus et populo numeroso Anglicorum in vigilia sancti Luce Ewangeliste vsque Dunelmum peruenerunt, et ibidem iuxta crucem que wlgo vocatur Neuill' Cros contra Dauid dictum regem Scocie cum suis prelium commiserunt. ᶜUbi paucis Anglicorum interfectis, Domino protegente, pene tota milicia Scocie capta fuerat uel occisa. Nam in illo prelio Robertus comes Morauie et Mauricius comes de Stretherne cum meliori milicia Scocie pariter ceciderunt, Dauid autem dictus rex Scocie cum comitibus de Fyfe et de Menteth ac de Wygton' et domino Willelmo de Douglas ac insuper armatorum copiosa multitudine captus fuit. Et non multo post ⟨se⟩ ᵈpredictus Dauid rex Scottorum cum multis nobilioribus captiuis vsque London' est perductus et carceri mancipatus, vbi comes de Menteth tractus fuit et suspensus, quarterizatus et eius membra ad diuersa loca Anglie et Scocie sunt transmissa. Unus autem predictorum captiuorum, scilicet dominus Malcolmus Flemyng comes de Wygton', infirmitate laboransᵉ London' cum aliis captiuis nullatenus transmissus sed apud Bothale proth dolor dimissus, prodicione cuiusdam armigeri custodis sui dicti Roberti de la Vale in Scociam sine redempcione aliqua est reuersus.

Post predictum autem bellum Dunelm' domini comes Dangouse et Radulfus de Neuil, domino Henrico de Percy egrotante, in Scociam profecti castrum Rokesburgie certis condicionibus receperunt, et marchiam Scocie peruagantes, tributum aliquibus hominibus citra mare Scoticanum imponentes et aliquos homines ad suam fidelitatem recipientes non sine sui exercitus aliquali detrimento in Angliam redierunt.ᶠ

Anno Domini m°.ccc.ᵐᵒ xlvii.° quarto id. Aprilis dominus Willelmus Heroune et Johannes de Coupeland castrum del Hermitage obsederunt, quod eis pridie id. / f.34va Maii redditum fuerat pactis interpositis obseruatis.

Anno Domini m°.ccc.ᵐᵒ x[l]vii.° ᶠ tercio id. Maii dominus Edwardus de Baliol' rex Scocie assistentibus sibi dominis Johanne de Mowbray, Thoma de Lucy, Thoma de Rokeby et Anglicorum milicia copiosa iuxta Karlioll' Scociam intrauit ad recuperandum regnum Scocie sibi iure hereditario debitum, et eodem tempore magnifici viri domini Gilbertus de Vmfrauill' comes de Angous, Henricus de Percy, Radulphus de Neuill' cum aliis nobilibus Anglie in subsidium predicti Edwardi regis Scocie iuxta Rokesburgiam Scociam intrauerunt. Qui insimul conuenientes, Scociam citra mare Scoticanum pro maiori parte pervagantes, sine aliquo notabili facto, cum tamen suorum aliquali [   ]ᵍ et animalium preda numerosa, paucis exceptis in Angliam redierunt. Nam domini comes Dangous,

Henricus de Percy, Radulphus de Neuill' et alii armati de Anglia cum domino Edwardo rege Scocie permanentes, ipsum cum armatorum multitudine dimiserunt, et sic in Angliam cum honore et gloria redierunt.*d*

---

a-a   As in *Chron. Lanercost*, p.344.
b   Something like *obsessa fuit* is needed.
c-c   As in *Chron. Lanercost*, pp.351-2.
d-d   In a French rendering in *Anon. Chron.*, pp.28-9.
e   *laborans* is added by a later hand. *Chron. Lanercost* has *[propter] infirmitatem*
f   Corrected from *xvii°* by a later hand.
g   B shows a lacuna. Something like *detrimento* or *dampno* is needed.

XVI

Reason in Politics, 1363-4: A *Quaestio* from Scotland*

The meeting of the three estates at Scone on 4 March 1364 was an event of no small significance in the history of medieval Scotland and its parliament.[1] The assembly's unequivocal rejection of proposals which would have led to a personal union of the English and Scottish crowns confirmed an attitude which was to have a long future; it was to be justified by the history of Scottish national independence for the rest of the middle ages and beyond. The scanty records printed among *The Acts of the Parliaments of Scotland* offer little information about the details and circumstances of this crucial occasion.[2] One collateral piece of written evidence, however, is in my view capable of providing additional help, even though in a fashion rather different from that which has previously been supposed. The nature and status of that document are the chief concerns of this essay.

At a date after 1397 and possibly, though not certainly, before 1406, a Scottish churchman, unnamed but known to have been a member of or closely connected to the chapter at Aberdeen at some time between 1388 and 1397, set out to compile an account of happenings during the reign of David II, for the information and warning of David's successors. After touching briefly on David's upbringing, his return from France and his capture by the English at Neville's Cross in 1346, the account turns to the negotiations for restoring David to his own country. It refers specifically

---

* My warm thanks are due to Professor Lionel Stones and Mr Bruce Webster for the encouragement they gave me to complete this paper.

1 Ranald Nicholson, *Scotland: the later middle ages*, Edinburgh, 1974, pp.170-2; W. Croft Dickinson, *Scotland from the earliest times to 1603*, 3rd edn. revised and edited by A.A.M. Duncan, Oxford, 1977, pp.182-3, where the tone differs somewhat from Croft Dickinson's exposition in the 1st edn., London and Edinburgh, 1961, pp.183-4.

2 Ed. T. Thomson and C. Innes, Record Commission, 12 vols., 1814-75 [= *APS*], i, 492-5.

to conditions proposed by the English and transmitted to the Scots through Sir William Douglas of Liddesdale; no date is given, but it probably lies between 1350 and 1352.[3] According to the anonymous compiler these conditions were brought before a council-general meeting at Scone under the presidency of Robert the Steward, then acting as keeper of the realm of Scotland in David's absence. Opinions in this council, he tells us, were much divided: some arguing for acceptance, others for refusal of the English terms. He adduces – confusedly, as will appear – as evidence for this statement a certain *libellus antiquus* in the hand of Master William de Spyny, who, he claims, was present at this council as one of the secretaries (*clericus commensalis*) of William Laundels, bishop of St. Andrews. William de Spyny, while dean of Aberdeen, the compiler relates, had often discussed this matter with him. This must have been between 1388 and 1397, for in the latter year William, already an old man, became bishop of Moray.[4] He lived on till 1406, and it is not wholly clear whether he was still alive when the compiler set to work; but he is referred to as *venerabilis vir*, not *bone memorie*.

While it is wholly possible that William de Spyny did indeed have intimate knowledge of the Douglas negotiations in 1350-2 as a member of Bishop Laundels' *familia*,[5] the compiler seems mistaken in claiming that William's *antiquus libellus* was primarily concerned with them. For he proceeds to offer what appears to be a complete text of the *libellus*, and this makes no more than a single incidental reference to the Douglas negotiations [lines 226-31 below]. It addresses itself in fact to problems arising after David's release from captivity in 1357 and consequent upon his failure to meet the financial obligations for his ransom which the Scots had then accepted. The contents of the *libellus*, as transmitted by the anonymous compiler, obviously refer to Anglo-Scottish negotiations in the winter of 1363-4.

This was recognised by the late Dr E.W.M. Balfour-Melville twenty-five years ago. But the true nature of the *libellus* has so far been

---

3   E.W.M. Balfour-Melville, *Edward III and David II*, London, 1954, pp.15-16; Nicholson, *Scotland*, pp.157-9.
4   D.E.R. Watt, *Fasti Ecclesiae Scoticanae Medii Aevi*, 2nd draft, St. Andrews, 1969, pp.7, 215, 222; A.B. Emden, *Biographical Register of the University of Oxford to A.D. 1500* [=*BRUO*] iii, Oxford, 1959, 1747-8; D.E.R. Watt, *A biographical dictionary of Scottish graduates to A.D. 1410* [=*BDSG*], Oxford, 1977, 503-6. Watt, *BDSG* 503 does not think that the compiler necessarily implies that William was an octogenarian by 1397; as William's probable date of birth he suggests a year or so before 1327.
5   Watt, *BDSG*, 505.

obscured by the weak and defective tradition of its text. The sole version known is that given by the anonymous compiler. All that we have of his compilation (his introduction, followed by the *libellus*) survives only in a single copy made, to judge by the script, late in the fifteenth century and now preserved in BL Cotton Vespasian C.XVI, a miscellaneous collection of Scottish historical materials written in a number of different hands. The compilation occurs at folios 34-40, with the *libellus* beginning on f.35r; each of the paper folios is now mounted separately. All the text is in a single 'pre-secretary' hand, small, niggling, frequently difficult and on occasion almost impossible to decipher; the scribe seems to have used an ill-cut pen on paper of indifferent quality. A later reader, who writes in a neat early modern hand, has done good service by systematically explicating in the margin some of the scribe's worst written and more impenetrable words and phrases; at times other pens have joined in this work. But none of the annotators appears to have had access to any other version of the compilation. The scribe's own knowledge of Latin was very shaky; he produced or reproduced constructions and spellings which are clearly incorrect. Whether he used the compiler's holograph or depended on some intermediate version is uncertain; the gloss at line 46 possibly suggests the latter. The *libellus*, composed in 1363-4, had appeared *antiquus* to the compiler when he was at work with it only four or five decades after its composition; this may indicate that he himself had trouble with the original hand. Probably, though not necessarily, it was the compiler who added to his transcription of the *libellus* (presumably in the margins) a significant number of comments and glosses. By the time that the scribe of Vespasian C.XVI, ff.34-40, had completed his work these marginalia had become incorporated into the text and are now not distinguishable by merely physical inspection.

To Dr Balfour-Melville was due the credit for recognising the interest of this compilation and publishing it for the Scottish Historical Society in 1958.[6] Unfortunately he confined himself for the most part to printing a painstaking and on the whole accurate transcription of the highly corrupt Vespasian text. No one who has wrestled with this manuscript is likely to underrate the value of Dr Balfour-Melville's pioneering effort. But the limitations he imposed on his approach have left difficulties. Above all, what is the real nature of the *libellus*? As he showed by his choice of a running headline, Dr Balfour-Melville thought of it as an account of 'Debate in Council-General' at Scone in March 1364. In 1960 Professor

6   E.W.M. Balfour-Melville, 'Papers relating to the Captivity and Release of David II', in S.H.S. *Misc.* ix (1958), pp.36-50 (text); pp.51-6 (abstract in English).

Ranald Nicholson moved cautiously towards endorsing that view. Though proposing an entirely acceptable emendation to the text of the compiler's introduction, he described the *libellus* itself as embodying 'recollections of two arguments reputedly advanced in a Scottish general council which discussed the English proposals' of 1363 to secure the Scottish succession in favour of Edward III or one of his sons.[7] Returning to this matter in 1966 and 1974, he maintained much the same opinion about the *libellus*.[8] More recently, Professor D.E.R. Watt has continued rather further along this line. He has been prepared to attribute to William de Spyny some of the material he thinks reported in the *libellus*: 'he [William] certainly kept an account of some debates, which was used for a memorandum on the subject drawn up in the early 15th century .....; at least part of this debate was probably at Scone in March 1363/4, when Spyny would have been present.'[9] Only Dr James Campbell (though preferring not to commit himself about the date) has been willing to consider the *libellus* less as a report about public debate than as a treatise in its own right.[10]

Perhaps revision of the text of the *libellus* can help us to a more precise appreciation of the work than those just mentioned. It seems possible to detect with reasonable certainty the later material now incorporated, and exclude it. This, together with conjectural emendation of some of the readings exhibited by Vespasian C.XVI and printed by Dr Balfour-Melville can, I believe, throw new light on the general character as well as on the details of the *libellus*. No doubt such a procedure involves risks, and it is only fair to state the two assumptions on which it has been applied. The first, that Vespasian C.XVI gives a corrupt version of the original text, I take to be self-evident. The second assumption, though it seems likely enough, is obviously less certain: it is that the author of the *libellus*, though perhaps no great stylist, was capable of expressing himself with tolerable correctness in the scholastic Latin of the 1360s.

When the text has been reviewed in this fashion, some interesting results emerge. It becomes clear that the *libellus* was not the record of any sort of public, multilateral debate at Scone in March 1364 or elsewhere. On the contrary: it is a political opinion or *consilium* composed by a single author, who often refers to himself in the first person [lines 125, 173,

---

7 'Miscellanea Scotica', *SHR* xxxix, 48-9.
8 'David II, the historians and the chroniclers', *SHR* xlv, 688; *Scotland: the later middle ages*, p.171, where he uses the phrase 'unofficial jottings'.
9 *BDSG*, 505.
10 'England, Scotland and the Hundred Years War', in *Europe in the Later Middle Ages*, ed. J.R. Hale, R. Highfield and Beryl Smalley, London, 1966, p.202.

212-13, 302, 303, 343, 389]. The problem he considers is whether the Scots should accept a specific set of English proposals designed to end the imbroglio caused by the arrears in the agreed payments for David II's ransom. The contents of the *libellus* allow these proposals to be identified with certainty. They are those which had been recorded at a meeting of the two kings and their councillors at Westminster on 27 November 1363; the most important stipulation was that, in return for the abandonment of the English ransom demands, the Scots, if David died childless, should accept as their king Edward III and his English successors. The wishes of the people of Scotland about these proposals – which were recorded in a carefully noncommittal manner – were to be certified to Edward before the quinzaine of Easter 1364.[11] To discuss the problem for the Scots represented by these proposals the author of the *libellus* resorted to the scholastic device of the *quaestio*, natural to any theologian or jurist trained in the schools. He justifies this proceeding in a short prologue: human nature is naturally inclined to give intellectual assent to a true conclusion (that is, one properly arrived at as the end result of the formal exercise of reason). Then the question is propounded: *An oblatis per Anglicos expediat consentire?*

First, in the established tradition of the form, are produced the *argumenta quod sic* [lines 10-102]: 15 in all, comprising 10 from the point of view of Scottish advantage, 2 from the English point of view and 3 from that of the *finis* or end to be achieved (i.e. peace). These are counterbalanced, as might be expected in any *quaestio*, by the *argumenta in contrarium* [lines 103-262], under the heading *[O]ppositum*: again 15 arguments, subsumed under two main heads. Under the first it is contended that the acceptance of the English proposals would be unlawful, as trenching on papal rights. Under the second head it is maintained that agreement arrived at on such terms would be a dishonourable sham: this is shown by 7 arguments considering matters in the light of how the English would probably behave later and another 7 claiming that it would be wholly

---

11 The record of the proposals was drawn up in the form of an indentured instrument. What is presumably the English copy survives in London, PRO Diplomatic Documents Exchequer, Scottish Docs. 2(22) = *APS* i.493-4; Rymer, *Foedera* (Record Commission edn.) III.ii.715-6; *cf.* J. Bain, *Cal. Docs. Scot.* iv. no.91. Discussion in the *libellus* matches the details of these proposals exactly, except in one instance. At lines 363-74 the author considers a suggestion that the successor to a childless David should not be Edward III himself but his eldest son, Edward prince of Wales. No such suggestion was recorded on 27 November, and there is no independent evidence that it was put forward on the English side at all. More probably the author of the *Libellus* thought up this unwelcome possibility for himself, in order to argue against it – as he did.

unfitting for the Scots to accept. There follows, as again is to be expected, the short and definite *conclusio* or *decisio quaestionis* [lines 261-69]: it is not lawful, decent or expedient for the Scots to accept the English proposals. To complete the scholastic model it only remains for the author to add his *responsa ad argumenta quod sic*: these are to be found at lines 270-77. Only at this last stage are there indications that the author's adherence to the formal pattern of the *quaestio* is beginning to falter. For while all 8 replies given do refer to arguments adduced *quod sic*, there is not that systematic and comprehensive refutation of the latter which the form ideally demands.[12]

Nevertheless, thus far the nature of the *libellus* is unmistakable: it is an attempt at rational discussion of an urgent political problem thrown into the form of a *quaestio*. What follows to the end of the *libellus* is a kind of coda or appendix [lines 377-427]. Despite his firm conclusion that English proposals envisaging the eventual succession to the Scottish crown of Edward III or his eldest son are unacceptable, the author now warns against breaking off the negotiations completely and so provoking the English to war. As an alternative to the current English proposals he supports the suggestion that the succession to Scotland should be secured definitely to Edward's third son, John of Gaunt, rather than to any other English prince. I do not wholly understand what he means by saying that the Scots have already in some fashion chosen and assumed John as the successor to a childless David [lines 384-5].[13] His contention [lines 407-11] that a son of John of Gaunt and Blanche of Lancaster, if he eventually became king of Scots, would be half a Scot, because of Blanche's Scottish maternal grandparents,[14] seems a pretty desperate piece of special pleading. But it was on the succession to David of John that the author of

---

12 In effect, of the 15 arguments *quod sic* only nos. 5, 6, 8, 12 and 13 are refuted.

13 The undated indenture, London, PRO Diplomatic Documents Exchequer, Scottish Docs. 2(2) [= *APS* i.494-5; *cf.* Bain, *Cal. Docs. Scot.* iv. no.92], which is often associated with the negotiations in November 1363, contains the suggestion that, if childless, David should be succeeded by one of the sons of Edward III who was not heir apparent of England. Possibly this represents a proposal put forward by the Scots at an earlier stage of the negotiations than the dated indenture of 27 November; a somewhat similar scheme seems to have been canvassed by Sir William Douglas of Liddesdale in 1350-2, as the *libellus* indicates [lines 227-32 below]. By the time the *libellus* was written Edward III had already ruled out any such solution [lines 386-7 below]. That did not prevent the author in his coda reverting to a particular form of it, in relation to Edward's third son, John of Gaunt. According to Bower's chronologically confused account of these matters, David's own preferred candidate for the succession was Edward's second son, Lionel of Clarence: *Scotichronicon* xiv.25, ed. Goodall, ii.366.

14 Henry Beaumont, designated earl of Buchan, and Alice Comyn.

the *libellus* pinned his faith for preserving the independence of Scotland from the English.

The author knew the contents of the Westminster indenture of 27 November 1363 by something more substantial than hearsay; presumably they had become available to him *via* the Scottish counterpart. This cannot have reached Scotland until December, and perhaps late in that month, for the first evidence for renewed governmental activity by David after his return from England seems to be on 1 January 1364.[15] The *quaestio* gives no indication that the English proposals had already been considered and rejected by the Scottish estates meeting at Scone on 4 March. So, unless its author was a member of the Scottish delegation to Westminster, it must have been composed between December 1363 and late February 1364. Just possibly the coda was written slightly later than the main *quaestio* – in answer, one might imagine, to some reader's comment: 'You say we must reject the English proposals. But what then is the next step?' We do not really know.

The author had been trained in the schools; he had an accurate knowledge of the English proposals before they could have been widely known in Scotland. It seems reasonable to suppose that he was a *peritus* in the household of a member of the Scottish royal council – probably an ecclesiastical member, for the *quaestio* stresses the danger to Scottish prelates inherent in the proposals [lines 116-25]. As might be expected, his writing abounds in scriptural quotations and echoes. He shows some, if not very profound, knowledge of the concepts and *exceptiones* of Roman civil law; he understands too the significance of the decretal *Intellecto* for the problem of the inalienability of sovereign rights [lines 24, 83-4, 87-8, 172-4, 217, 219-20]. He is not devoid of more general literary culture, as his quotations from Ovid and Cicero and the *Speculum stultorum* show. He took some pleasure in word-play, even venturing into adaptations from the Greek;[16] he knows when he is employing a neologism [lines 388-9]. A sententious creature, he salts his discussion with proverbial wisdoms and expressions [lines 66-7, 282-3]; his characterisation of Edward III's offer to return the four castles as *dulce nichilum* [line 240] is pleasantly resonant of the vernacular. Perhaps not an outstandingly clever man, he is yet a genuine patriot, vastly suspicious of the English threat to Scottish national independence. His feeling for and understanding of Scotland's past are deep and heartfelt. If he knew about Arthur and Angusel from a late

15 See *The Acts of David II, King of Scots 1329-1371*, ed. Bruce Webster (Regesta Regum Scottorum VI, Edinburgh, 1982), nos.312, 313.
16 For the *utupeus* in line 96 and *acephalus* in line 354 see the notes to the text.

thirteenth-century source rather than from Geoffrey of Monmouth [line 209], he was able to quote at some length from Boniface VIII's letter *Scimus fili* [lines 109-14]. He had reflected on weighty episodes like the treaty of Birgham [lines 89-91] and the failure of the hopes raised by the treaty of Northampton [lines 253-4]. He was not happy about David's attitude towards the possibility of bartering the succession for freedom from the demands for ransom; as his information about this presumably came from his patron and employer, a royal councillor, his view cannot be wholly discounted [lines 51-4].[17] But he does not despair of David, and clearly wants to believe the best of him [lines 284-94], though he has harsh things to say about the evil effects on the royal revenue of David's grants [lines 308-11; *cf.* 165-68]. He gives no overt support to any claim to the succession by the Steward [lines 301-5], though it seems to be the underlying and unspoken assumption of all the arguments in the *libellus* that David — still only 39 years old — will never beget an heir.

Can a name be put to this author? Not with absolute certainty at present. But it is quite likely that he was that same Master William de Spyny whom the anonymous compiler identifies as the source of his knowledge of the *antiquus libellus*.[18] William had studied arts at Oxford and Paris in the 1350s; by November 1362 he was bachelor of decrees at Paris; his career as secretary to that important prelate and royal councillor, William Laundels, bishop of St. Andrews, may well have begun before 1351.[19] Even intermittent activity in that sort of capacity could have brought him into contact with the Douglas negotiations in 1350-2 and given him the impulse and the knowledge to compose the *quaestio* in 1363-4. The case for his authorship is thus tolerably strong, though it would be rash to rule out the possibility of some more convincing candidate emerging.

Revision of the text of the *libellus*, then, shows that what survives of it is in fact a *quaestio*, a discussion of a problem according to the convention of the schools. There is no hope of finding in it, in however muddled and incoherent a form, reports or even echoes of debates which may actually have taken place at the Scone parliament in March 1364; the

---

17 In the light of the *libellus* possibly Mr Bruce Webster's claim that 'nothing definitely suggests that David wished any other decision' than that reached at the Scone parliament in March 1364 may need further consideration: 'David II and the Government of Scotland', *Trans. Royal Hist. Soc.* 5th series, xvi (1966), 123.

18 Unfortunately the compiler's language is ambiguous: 'prout in quodam libello antiquo manu venerabilis viri Magistri Willelmi de Spineto ..... scriptum reperi', Balfour-Melville, 'Papers', pp.37-8. Did he regard William as the composer or merely as the scribe of the *libellus*?

19 See Watt and Emden, as in note 4 above.

quaestio was written before the assembly met. In compensation, the revision offers us a document of uncommon interest for the history of culture in Scotland among the learned and official class. The *quaestio*, it should be emphasised, reveals the opinions of no more than a single individual, neither ill-educated nor uninformed, intent on applying rational considerations and techniques in the search for an answer to an urgent political question. Obviously it cannot safely be assumed to represent the views of any large part of the Scottish political community in 1363-4. Indeed, in its failure to come fully to terms with the national sentiments of the time it illustrates the limitations not seldom shown by the educated official mentality in the face of intractable realities.[20]

In revising the text I have not felt it necessary to abide exactly by the punctuation or orthography of the scribe of Vespasian C.XVI. There is no certainty that the idiosyncratic forms which he often shows were those used by the author of the *quaestio*. Possibly the latter did write *nuncquam, marcatores, discisio, volimus* and the like. But we cannot be sure of this, and it has seemed convenient to prefer more conventional spellings throughout. In the textual apparatus V denotes the scribe of Vespasian C.XVI; a the systematic explicator; a^2 marginal notes in other hands.

---

20 *Cf.* Harmut Boockmann, 'Zur Mentalität spätmittelalterlicher Gelehrter Räte', *Historische Zeitschrift* ccxxxiii (1981), 295-316.

CUM casus[21] inopinabiles emergunt[22], quos antiquitas non agnouit, maturioris deliberacionis opus est, presertim cum ab hiis proponuntur,[23] qui secum contrahentes in precipium conantur inurgere,[24] cum ea offerant, que tantum cum audiuntur oblectant et considerata vere acucius vilescunt[25] et intus gustata [ad ventrem][26] amarescunt. Et cum humane nature sagax condicio per intellectum assentire conclusioni vere naturaliter inclinetur, per modum questionis proponitur: AN OBLATIS PER ANGLICOS EXPEDIAT CONSENTIRE?

ET PROBATUR QUOD SIC, persuasione et examine videlicet, primo ex parte nostra:

Quia cum populus semper uni principi habeat parere necesse, parum[27] refert de mutacione persone principantis[28] et, dummodo laudabiliter suum officium exequatur, frustra requiretur sic nocio nacionis, iuxta illud apostoli: *Non enim est distinctio Iudei et Greci*, et cotidie dominia et regna de gente in gentem et de uno[29] ad populum alterum multimodis[30] transferuntur[31].

Secundo, quia, cum regnum debeat manere integrum, non diuisum nec mutilatum in suis iuribus, libertatibus et consuetudinibus, per Scotos officiis et ministeriis omnibus proficiendos gubernandum, regnum semper plena integritate letabitur. Nec poterit dici sine rege proprio, cui tantus princeps sicut rex Anglie imperabit.

Tercio, hinc est plena libertas et nulla seruitus, cum iuxta legistarum sentenciam *res sua nemini seruit*, nec ex ista regnorum unione tollitur spes promocionis secularibus oriundis de patria, cum ipsi et non alii sint ad singula officia regenda assumendi.

21 *before* Cum casus: Proposicio multum dampnosa et periculosa regno Scocie et omnino prodiciosa, eneruans et destruens totam libertatum regni et annullans, et non solum libertatem sed omnes magnates et populum processu temporis V; *omitted as later comment*
22 emergant V*a*
23 proponantur V
24 inurgere: mergere *a*
25 vilescant V
26 ad ventrem *doubtful reading*
27 parum: istud V
28 principantis: principatus V
29 uno: regno V
30 multimode V
31 transferantur V

Quarto, quia ex ista unione videtur in nullo minui honor regni aut noster, cum ipse rex sicut in regem Anglie ita in regem Scocie debeat in Scocie per deputatos ab antiquo[32] coronari et rex Scocie et Anglie nominari, parliamenta et consilia tenere in Scocia et iusticiam ministrare.

Quinto, quia ita sumus inbecilles in potencia et viribus quod eis resistere nequeamus in bello. Nec inter nos hiis diebus est nobilis aliquis de sanguine regio vel magnus dominus, qui sit expertus aut aptus ducere populum, nec est spes verisimilis[33] de aliquo propinquo.

Sexto, quia ita nostri nobiles sunt obstupefacti et pene exanimes facti ex diuersis bellis, in quibus contra Anglicos iam plures corruerunt, et aduersarii adeo animati, et nostrates sunt nulli vel pauci, iuuenes et inexperti, alii sagaces et ad bellum doctissimi, quod ipsis in potencia nequeamus[34] resistere aut in bello.

Item septimo, quia ex eo non minus a talibus bellis est cauendum, quia si aliqui ex nostris caperentur inpugnando in terra vel in mari, non possunt sperare redimi, cum simus cum omnibus bonis nostris pro redempcione regis generaliter obligati. Nec aliquos obsides pro captiuis admittere[nt],[35] eo quod de obsidibus nostris ultimo eis pro rege datis nos indebite habuimus, nec iuramentis[36] est credendum, quia talia hacentus seruauimus negligenter.

Octauo, quia ipsi Anglici videntur iustam causam fouere, guerram mouendo pro redempcione regis, eo quod defecimus in promissis solucionis terminis et multis aliis, non ex necessitate sed voluntate.

Nono, quia dominus noster rex videtur vel saltem presumitur velle petitis consentire, cuius opinioni multi innitentur. Et ipse loca forcia omnia habet, et sic non est locus tutus pro volentibus resistere, si qui essent.

Decimo, quia confederati nostri, ut Gallici, per composicionem cum aduersariis sunt de nobis ammoti, ita quod oppressis non possint[37] succurrere nec exules receptare. [Et][38] affines nostri, ut quondam Noruici, nobis erunt infesti, eo quod inita[m][39] cum eis fidem non seruamus.

32 antiquo V: *but the author may have written* apostolico
33 veresimilis V
34 nequimus V
35 admitere V
36 *after* iuramentis: aliter fidei add.V; *omitted as gloss*
37 possunt V
38 Et *om.*V

Item, ad idem ex parte petencium:
Quia[40] ipsi nos exsuperant in multitudine bellatorum, usu et experiencia bellandi, in armaturis et in audacia sumpta, et fortuna semper est eis solita arridere, ita quod fugere sint obliti, et in castris nostris et villis muratis, quas[41] habent, nos possunt expugnare et ad ipsas[42] reuerti secure et nobis inuitis terram occupare. Et ideo verisimiliter videretur caute factum si de necessitate faceremus virtutem et illud, quod non possumus eis denegare et quod nobis inuitis poterunt habere nullis condicionibus placidis vel gratis nobis datis, sub istis bonis condicionibus iam concessis et pluribus aliis petendis et optinendis dare, transferre et concedere voluntarie, quasi simus potentes eis resistere, et sic grates et gracias ac amicicias bonas reportare, id est bonos et tollerabiles ipsos postea inuenire.

Secundo, quia tollerabilius et gracius est uni domino et regi seruire quam quemlibet eciam vilissimum et potenciorem tyrannum et predonem sentire, secundum quod fuit tempore captiuitatus principis nostri et ita eo cessante presumitur in futurum, presertim cum rex Anglie sit satis potens latrunculos comprimere et hostes alios repellere.

Item, ex parte finis idem probatur euidenter, scilicet quod populus debeat assentire oblatis:
Quia sic erit plena concordia, quia cum ipsi habeant regnum, rem scilicet quam petebant, pinguius quam unquam petierant, nosque iuri nostro renunciemus libere cum populo, voluntarie, nulla coactione precedente nec metu aut dolo, et sic efficaciter, inconuertibiliter et irreuocabiliter ius nostrum transferatur, non est nec erit locus ulterius discordie, cum non sit de quo questio moueatur. Et sic erimus *in pacis pulchritudine* et *iusticia* habitabit in terra nostra, et quod *suum* est *cuique tribue*tur.

Item, multum gauderemus, si per maritagium primogeniti Anglie cum filia nostra et herede e contra nos et ipsi unus populus fueramus. Et cum idem finis ex oblatis resultet, sequitur quod nunc sicut et tunc consentire et applaudare debeamus.[43]

---

39   inita V
40   Quia: quod V
41   quas: quos V
42   ipsos V
43   *after* debeamus: Sed forsan non est eadem nec equa nunc sicut tunc racio *add*.V; *omitted as gloss*

Reason in Politics, 1363-4: A Quaestio from Scotland

93 Item, ex ista pace multa alia commoda subsequentur. Quia terre
94 vaste et inculte per aduenas inhabitabuntur, ville vacue inhabitabuntur
95 et vaste reedificabuntur, et terre ad antiquam statum et taxacionem
96 ascendent, et per communicaciones aduen[arum][44] et mercatorum
97 regnicoli ditabuntur, et mundus erit quasi *utupeus*. Et multe utilitates
98 alie accrescent, quas prudens animus poterit preuidere[45] iuxta illud
99 [Tullii][46]: *Nomen certe pacis dulce est et ipsa res salutaris, nec est*
100 *aliud quam tranquilla libertas;*[47] et iuxta vaticinium Ysaye: *Habitabit*
101 *lupus cum agno*[48] *et pardus cum [h]edo accubabit: vitulus, leo et ouis*
102 *simul morabuntur, et puer paruulus minabit eos.*

103 [O]PPOSITUM[49], videtur scilicet quod populus non debeat
104 consentire oblatis, ymmo non est licitum hoc nobis facere:
105 Quia, cum regnum Scocie sit immediate subiectum sancte
106 Romane ecclesie tam in personis ecclesiasticis quam secularibus –
107 prout patet in sentencia domini Bonifacii pape octaui super iure
108 libertatis regni Scocie promulgata et regi Anglie Edwardo directa, in
109 qua dicitur: *Sane ad celsitudinem tuam potuit peruenisse et in libro*
110 *tue memorie nequaquam ambigimus contineri qualiter ab antiquis*
111 *temporibus regnum Scocie pleno iure pertinuit et adhuc pertinere*
112 *dinoscitur ad ecclesiam supradictam,* et in fine omnes *lites* et causas
113 de iure regni ipsius mouendas ad suam decisionem[50] *reducit* et
114 *reseruat, decernens irritum et inane* etc. – , submittere vel unire
115 regnum regno vel iura successionis transferre in alium non possumus
116 superiore domino ignorante, quia ipse omnia reuocaret forsan. Eciam
117 aduertant caute domini nostri prelati supremi, scilicet episcopi et alii,
118 ne fiant eorum ecclesie suffraganee archiepiscopi Anglie per istam
119 unionem, sicut contigit ecclesie Sanctii Dauid in Vallia. Que quondam
120 fuit metroplitana sex ecclesias suffraganeas sub se habens, et
121 tamen, postquam Vallia Anglie est unita, ipsa metropolis et omnes
122 alie Cantuariensi archiepiscopo sunt suffraganee et subiecte et in
123 tanta vilipensione[51] habentur prelati Vallie in Anglia quod patent

44 aduene V
45 prouidere V
46 Tullii *om.* V*a*
47 *after* libertas: Tull. *add.* V; Tullius *a*
48 *after* agno: et Anglicus cum Scoto *add.* V; *omitted as gloss*
49 *in margin* Fidelis opinio *a*²
    [..]ppositum V
50 decisionem *a*; discisionem V
51 vilipensa V

124 contemptui et opprobrio toti populo: quod[52] sic fuere cum episcopis
125 Vallie Londonii ego vidi.
126   Secundo, quia nunquam est illud incohandum a fideli populo
127 vel promittendum, quod non presumitur verisimiliter duraturum. Sed
128 ita est de ista concordia. Igitur eciam hoc probatur, primo ex parte
129 promittencium:
130   Quia cum ipsi soleant in promissis bonam fidem non agnoscere,
131 ut patet in concordia et confederacione tempore affinitatis nostre cum
132 eis inite[53] et in pecunia non modica tunc eis soluta pro pace perpetua,
133 quam statim exquisitis occasionibus fregerunt: unde non mirandum si
134 de malo iam eciam presumamus iuxta illud:
135   *Qui semel est* captus *fallaci piscis ab hamo*
136   *omnibus era cibis unca subesse putat.*
137   Item, quia ipsi Vallicos per totum et Ybernicos quantum[54]
138 possunt ita inhumaniter[55] et seruiliter[56] tractant quod iam Vallicorum
139 nomen et nobilitas in toto euanuerit, cum non sit aliquis de gente illa
140 vel populo secularis dominus vel prelatus, et idem de Ybernicis prout
141 possunt subtiliter suo more faciunt,[57] presumitur quod nos inhumanius
142 et crudelius tractarent, quos senserunt hactenus grauius aduersantes
143 et de quibus vix securos se fore putabunt quamdiu unus de nobis
144 supererit, ex inimicicia ab olim radicata. Et sic[ut][58] nos pro modulo
145 nostro capitibus Scoticis et stolidis innitentes repulsam vel
146 vilipensionem[59] inauditam reportabimus, maximam et vindictam
147 volemus,[60] eciam si mori oporteat, cum puerum, cuius ad fletum
148 dependent labia, ad plorandum facile sit mouere. Et ideo, dum licet,
149 videtur cautius abstinere, cum *melius* [sit][61] *viam* Domini *non*
150 *cognoscere quam post agnicionem retro*ire.

52   quod: quia V
53   initae *a*
54   quantum: quibus V
55   inhumaniter *expunct.* V
56   seruiliter *expunct.* V
57   faciant V
58   sicut: sic V
59   vilipensam ineditam reputabimus V
60   volimus V
61   sit om. V; add. *a*

Item, cum banniti terras suas non rehabeant, semper erit remanens seminarium discordie inter ipsos et nostrates, qui ipsas terras habebunt. Et cum banniti sint verisimiliter specialiores futuri apud principem, sequitur quod vel subtili ingenio vel premeditata malicia ipsi occupantes spoliabuntur terris ipsis ex causa satis leui, presertim cum rex Anglie promittat eis bannitis remuneracionem pro ipsis terris. Et ut referunt experti sequentes curiam Anglie, tales promissiones[62] longos[63] et difficiles tractatus[64] habent, ymmo communiter respondet rex Anglie talia petentibus quod prius habet filiis propriis prouidere, quia *ordinata caritas incipit a seipso*. Et cum ipsis ad votum per suas terras in Scocia poterit satisfieri, non est hereticum sapere regem Anglie et suum consilium occasiones querere, faciendo – tamen de non causa – ut nostrates morti eciam turpi condempnentur, ut alii rehabeant quod est suum.

Item, quia, cum ipse promittat seruare et non reuocare donaciones regum Roberti et Dauid et custumam lane ad sex solidos et octo denarios pro sacco[65] perpetuo reducere, sequitur quod viuet ex rapina, cum nichil de suo habeat, et populum predabit vel interpretabit[ur] donaciones illorum regum non debere reuocari, que facte sunt sine dampno corone et iuste fieri potuerunt[66] sine periurio donantis, ceteras vero reuocabit, ymmo reuocare necesse est tales donaciones sub pena periurii, ut in ca[pitulo][67] *Intellecto*, Extra, *de iureiurando*. Et isto modo sencio ego, quicquid dicant alii vel pretendant.

Item, alieni tollent locum nostrum et gentem, cum maritagia[68] nobilium mulierum Anglicis concedentur et warda et maritagia puerorum et adolescencium nobilium de Scocia. Sequitur quod infra paucos annos dominia multa et quasi omnia Scocie venient et transferentur per maritagia et aliter in Anglicos, dato adhuc quod rex Anglie seruet inuiolabiliter omnia promissa, et sic maiorum nostrorum nomina et cognomina deperibunt.

62 promociones V
63 longas V
64 tractus V
65 sacco: suo V
66 poterunt V
67 capitulo: c' V; causa *a*
68 maritagio V

182 Item, illud regnum et regnicoli Scoti adeo attenuabuntur et ad
183 tantam exinanicionem[69] deuenient quod ipsorum miseria futura non
184 poterit breui sermone exprimi, eo quod redditus uniuersi,[70]
185 custume,[71] exitus itinerum iusticiarie et camerarie contribuciones et
186 emolumenta alia ad regem spectancia deferentur in Angliam et
187 redditus terrarum, que ad dominia Anglicorum per wardas, maritagia
188 vel alias deuenient, eo quod preeligent morari in sue natiuitatis terra
189 et prope dominum regem quam in ista. Et sic diuicie auferentur in
190 terram alienam et pauci, qui remanebunt de natiuis, erunt coloni
191 subseruitute perpetua et erumpna.

192 Item, caueant sibi nobiles nostri, et eo caucius, quo domino
193 nostro regi Dauid attinent propinquius. Quia non obstantibus promissis
194 quibuscunque ad eorum exterminium rex Anglie ultra citra[que][72]
195 conabitur nec unquam se reputabit securus quamdiu supererit unus de
196 semine regio viuens, eo quod semper suspicabitur tales questionem
197 super iure regni moturos, licet ipsi nunquam meditentur talia.
198 Exemplo Herodis, qui credens Christum de semine et stirpe
199 antiquorum regum Iude sibi regnum Iudee et Ierusalem erepturum
200 finxit se prius adorare velle eum, ut interficeret, et postea adeo ipsum
201 persecutus est ut coetaneos necaret, putans quod ex quo ipsum
202 specialiter inuenire non poterat, sub generali saltem clade faceret
203 deperire. Aliud exemplum habemus Iudicum ix° capitulo. Et
204 familiarius exemplum est magis ad propositum in Vallia et Hybernia,
205 ubi Anglici principantur.

206 Item, oblatis consentire [nos][73] non decet:
207 Cum breuis vita nobis sit data a natura et memoria bene acte
208 vite sempiterna sit, istudque regnum semper eciam in tempore regis
209 Arthuri regem proprium nomine Anguselem[74] habuerit et semper
210 distinctum fuerit, nos pro breui vita nostra et in nostre dampnacionem
211 memorie ipsius statum antiquum, pro quo tuendo maiores nostri
212 aliquando gloriosum triumphum et aliqui, ut erat fides ipsorum et
213 opinio et est mea, victoriosum marthirium de hostibus reportauerunt,
214 interuertere <nos> non decet.[75]

69 exaninmacionem V; *corr.a*
70 universos V
71 custumas V
72 citraque: citra V
73 nos *om.* V
74 Anguselum: augurelum V

Reason in Politics, 1363-4: A Quaestio from Scotland

215 Quia si isto modo, nulla coactione precedente, consenciat
216 populus, irreuocabilis est consensus et nunquam poterit permutari,[76]
217 cum nec metus, nisi vanus, dolus malus aut coactio intercedat. Et si
218 nitatur postea resilire, erit in dominum insurgere et tanquam
219 proditores in dominum proprium punientur. Et idcirco dum res est
220 integra bonum est a talibus abstinere.

221 Item, quia consenciendo petitis cessaret unctio nostra et per
222 consequens insignia celebriora regalia: quia quilibet rex eciam
223 pedaneus, ut in Hybernia, est coronatus. Quia, cum unctio regis iterari
224 non debeat et rex Anglie inungeretur in Anglia, sequitur quod apud
225 nos postea inungi non potest.

226 Item, quia dominus Willelmus de Douglas miles tales quondam
227 habuit condiciones, quod dominus rex noster pro .xl. milibus librarum
228 redimeretur et castra nostra in termino prime solucionis nobis
229 redderentur, dummodo concederetur a populo quod unus de iunioribus
230 filiis regis Anglie domino nostro regi, si sine liberis decederet, deberet
231 succedere: non videtur quod, cum non simus debiliores nunc quam tunc
232 extitimus, pro defectu solucionis in terminis tocius regni dominium et
233 successionem debeamus a nobis et nostris successoribus abdicare.

234 Item, quia multi nobiles nostri et maiores de regno casualiter
235 exheredarentur perpetuo, rege Anglie seruante omnia. Quia ipsi
236 nunquam sufficerent suas terras releuare, et sic semper in manu
237 superioris domini remanerent: quod non solet hic fieri, cum
238 consueuerimus habere regem proprium propicium et benignum.

239 Item, reddicio castrorum et remissio custume ad antiquum statum
240 sunt unum dulce nichilum. Quia vult quatuor castra reddere et sibi
241 finaliter [cedi],[77] ut totum regnum habeat. Et cum per nos magis meliorari
242 possint quam per ipsum, ad hoc [ea][78] offert nobis ad tempus, ut ipse
243 totum habeat regnum perpetuo et ut ipse ea meliorata recipiat et ut ipse
244 interim exoneretur a sumptibus quos facit circa ipsa. Que stantibus
245 condicionibus inter nos et ipsos, ad modicum commodum nobis cedent
246 et, si resiliamus, non erunt qui ea pro nobis tueantur contra dominum
247 proprium insurgendo, presertim cum a nobis sperare non poterunt de
248 succursu. Reducere autem custumam ad statum solitum tenebitur per
249 iuramentum, cum eciam domino nostro regi non sit concessa ad tantam
250 summam nisi ad tempus et ex causa sue redempcionis.

75 nos non decet V
76 permutari: prutere V
77 cedi *om.* V
78 ea *om.* V

Quod autem dominus noster rex et sui heredes terras suas habeant et alii domini in Anglia, bonum esset si nichil aliud latitaret. Sed quia regi Roberto viro tam sapienti, strenuo et experto non placuit in hoc articulo, circa premissa notandum est quod mercatores[79] Anglie rem venalem[80] ad duplum veri precii et pro quo eam vendere volunt solent appreciare, ut si institorem incautum inueniant, ipsum illequeant, sed antequam rem venalem reportent, pro medio petiti precii, si sit qui offerat, ipsam vendunt. Et forsitan ita est in proposito, quia domini in hoc casu a mercatorum moribus non sunt penitus alieni. Dummodo sit cautus institor, quam[81] offerat racionem:

Ex premissis CONCLUDENDUM[82] quod non licet nec decet nec expedit petitis vel oblatis consentire. Probatur quod non licet per racionem immediate post oppositum, quia subsumus immediate domino pape. Nec decet, quia insignia nostra cessarent, puta unctio, et quia memoriam nostram dampnaremus,[83] et quia maiores nostri, viri sapientissimi Anglicorum magis experti astuciam, nunquam voluerunt talibus consentire. Nec eciam expedit propter multa inconueniencia et intollerabilia enarrabilia,[84] que post oppositum iam sunt dicta.

Ad raciones prime partis RESPONDETUR:
Quod sicut nos sumus attenuati in viribus per moralitates et guerras, ita sunt ipsi, quia licet in Francia eis prospere successerit sepe in victoriis, hoc tamen non contigit sine dispendio sue gentis. Et semper ipsi fuerunt plures quam nos, et tamen aliquando contendabamus cum eis de pari et eos vicimus diuersis vicibus successiue. Nec *in multitudine* bellancium consistit semper *victoria*, et ipsi hodie multum sunt dispersi in Britannia, in Ybernia et versus Terram Sanctam. Et qui sunt, non habent cor ardens ad inuadendum nos, cum sint emolumenta[85] modica habituri si, quod absit, preualeant et non sine tediosis laboribus et suarum personarum periculis, sicut alias sunt experti. Et sciunt quia nos habemus aptos ad bellandum,

---

79 marcatores V
80 venalem: venditam V
81 quam: qui V
82 concludendo V
83 dampneremus V
84 enarrabilia V; inenarrabilia *a*
85 emolimenta V

licet aliquos inexpertos, et iuxta vulgare prouerbium 'catuli mordent acerbius[86] et minus lupos verentur quam canes alii seniores.'

Ducem eciam habemus et principem, dominum nostrum regem, pro quo et eius statu populus hactenus multa sustinuit. Qui dominus noster rex ita difficilia et ardua facit proponere, ut probet an si *spiritus fortitudinis* vel vite scintilla illuceat in aliquo, in quo *spiritus* et animus *domini* nostri regis possit *acquiescere*, cum videat eum velle stare pro libertate populi et confouenda iusticia, et ut possit infallibiliter percipere quod *spiritus vite* sit *in rotis*, id est in suis nobilibus et aliis. Nec est aliter senciendum de domino nostro, <quia>[87] cum ipse tot humanitatis beneficia a populo isto receperit,[88] qui[89] se et sua pro ipso exposuerit et adhuc exponere sit paratus, quod ipse tot beneficiorum oblitus populum velit inducere ut subsit et seruiat suo hosti. Quia inter ista ambigua, nodosa et difficilia videretur eligibilius censum vel recognicionem in signum subiectionis soluere quod solum solent petere inimici − et regem proprium habere, quam totum regnum subdere et antiquos hostes constituere voluntarie dominos, cum in uno spes future libertatis semper vigeat, in alio spes recuperacionis omnimoda sit sublata.

Plures eciam nobiles Dei gracia habemus aptos ad duces assumi, quos nominare omitto, ne forsan eque digni et maioris meriti inuideant. Et licet nullum nominarem, *suscitabit Dominus spiritum fortitudinis* in *puero iuniori*, et mille modis Dominus sue plebi prouidebit.

Nec fouebunt Anglici more insolito iustam causam. Quia non est iustum pro quodam pecuniario debito petere totum regnum, de quo debito, modo quo possumus meliori, volumus[90] satisfacere. Et hoc bene possumus, dummodo rex donaciones ineptas factas in preiudicium corone regis reuocet et de suo habeat unde viuat, et soluat cum aliis notabiliter suam partem et colat iusticiam. Et banniti nostri ad rehabendum terras suas condiciones bonas in prorogacione terminorum solucionis et in remissione penarum pro suis viribus[91] procurabunt, et contribuent libenter cum aliis in redempcionem. De quibus omnibus bonum est quod temptentur.

---

86 acerbius: acribius V; acrius vel acerbius a^2
87 quia V
88 reciperit V
89 qui: quid V
90 volumus: volimus V
91 viribus: iuribus V

Ad racionem ubi dicitur quod bonum est facere de necessitate virtutem et eis concedere voluntarie quod possunt nobis inuitis habere, respondetur quod melius est quod talia inconueniencia habeant[ur]⁹² nobis inuitis – quia tunc licitum est semper et qualibet hora reluctari, sicut pluries nostris fiebat temporibus – , quam quod semel de consensu populi haberent[ur],⁹³ quia tunc nunquam posse populus resilire.

Et ad hoc quod fortuna eis arridet, dicitur quod quando magis applaudit tunc tendit cicius ad ruinam, et *que tota* nobis iam *enotuit eis se velat* et insidias secus⁹⁴ parat iuxta illud:

Impetus euertit, quicquid fortuna ministrat
prospera: nil stabile, cui dedit illa omina.⁹⁵
Casibus in letis quam sit propinqua⁹⁶ *ruina*
et lapsus facilis, nemo videre potest.

Et quando dicitur quod melius est uni subesse quam quemlibet sentire tyrannum, respondetur quod illi faciliter in fide et fidelitate terre et populi perseuerantes reuertuntur ad suum dominum et per eum stabilita terra in pace cito castigantur, et modicum deberet cuilibet videri si, quamdiu pugnent pro libertate, viuant de communi. Et talis tyrannis⁹⁷ cito finitur, sed crudelitas Anglorum, si semel approbati fuerint, de peiori in pessimum perseuerabit perpetuo, acrius semper solito inualescens. Et ideo videtur eligibilius pati ad tempus aspera quam sine redempcionis spe aliqua subici perpetue seruituti.

Ad racionem ex parte finis, quia tunc plena erit concordia, quia non erit de quo litigetur etc., respondetur quod verum est, si renunciamus iuri nostro, non habebimus super iure illo materiam ulterius murmurandi, ex quo renunciauimus non coacti: sed an ipsi nobis ministrabunt materiam insurgendi, ego non dubito, sed dubitet ipse si quis careat racione. Sed si quis velit sagaciter et acute futura prospicere, poterit euidenter et ineuitabiliter colligere regem Anglie et ipsius consilium ista persuadens et petens, ad delecionem, euulsionem et exterminium totale populi istius conari.⁹⁸ Quia cum sit naturale cuilibet ut suorum, maxime filiorum, promocionem

---

92 habeant V
93 haberent V
94 secus: secas V; caecas *a²*
95 illa omina V; illa statum *Spec. stult.*
96 propinqua V; vicina *Spec. stult.*
97 tyrannides V
98 conari: coronari V

Reason in Politics, 1363-4: A Quaestio from Scotland

349 desideret seniorique filio regis per successionem hereditariam
350 sufficienter et ultra sit prouisum regnumque Scocie videretur
351 sufficiens promocio pro aliquo de iunioribus, quod iam oblatum contra
352 paternam pietatem erga filium rex renuit et recusat, non videtur alia
353 subesse racio, nisi quod in detestacionem et odium istius populi et ut
354 sit non solum acephalus sed ut tollatur et euanescat penitus et quod de
355 ipso de cetero non habeatur memoria, istud fiat, cum tamen magnum
356 sibi videri debeat quod, exheredatis quodam modo nostris heredibus,
357 in suum filium successionem regiam transferamus. Et debet sibi ad
358 magnum gaudium et gloriam crescere quod duos filios reges posset
359 dimittere et maxime sic vicinos, et iuniorem prouehi [ad][99]
360 excellenciam sine preiudicio vel diminucione aliqua senioris. Sed ipse
361 tante gracitudinis ingratus, non [in][100] odium filii sed in detestacionem
362 gentis nostre, non vult super nos regem regnare, qui nos tueri debeat,
363 sed ut ipse nos deuoret, deleat penitus et euellat, annullet et nullos
364 faciat, et ut finaliter ad nichilum redigamur.

365 Et hec omnia, que mouent dissentire in regem Anglie, vetant
366 in principem Anglie et Vallie consentire, cum eadem sit racio de
367 utroque. Quia cum ipse sit futurus rex, consentire in ipsum est in
368 regem consentire Anglie. Et si dicas non, quia filius eius habebit,
369 nichil est: quia talis pater, talis filius sunt eadem persona, et postquam
370 res per directum dominium est mea, possum de ea disponere prout
371 placet. Et certe, si consenciamus in principem Vallie, equa erit nostra
372 condicio cum Vallicis, quorum quam debilis sit condicio fide cernimus
373 oculata, quia sic lesi sunt ut *corru*ant, sic persecuti quod ulterius non
374 *resurg*ent. Et est felicius[101] de aliis et aliorum ruinis exemplum sumere
375 quam, quod absit, simus toti mundo in fabulam proprie miserie et
376 exemplum.

377 Et quia magni ingenii est cogitacione futura percipere et ante
378 constituere quid faciendum sit cum euenerint, et ignaue gentis et
379 desperate mentisque deiecte absurditates predictas et inconueniencias
380 innumeras inde secuturas concedere, petulantisque tamen sit et
381 precipitis petita nimium mordaciter interimere et sic ad guerram
382 aduersarios prouocare, idcirco per litteras vel nuncios informentur:

99   ad *om*.V
100 in *om*.V
101 filicius V

Primo quod populus iste inconstancie et variacionis notam effugiens, cum unum et certum de filiis Anglie, scilicet dominum Iohannem de Gandauo, quodam modo elegerit[102] et assumpserit, in regem Anglie vel principem nunquam volumus consenciendo variare, et quod, si tempora preterita vel eciam presencia bene considerarent, circumstancionando[103] debite deberet eis videri magnum, ymmo, ut ita dicam, maximissimum, quod uni[104] de eorum filiis ex tanta causa nobis offerimus in regem succedere. Quod cum ipsi refutent, cum sciamus hoc non esse in odium filii, sequitur quod in annullacionem nostram redundare cogitent, ut eciam antedictum est.

Et si ipse filius domino nostro regi succederet, sequeretur pacis eternitas: que racio in aliis filiis Anglie cessat. Quia, cum ipse habeat multas terras in Anglia, pro quibus semper tenebitur homagium et fidelitatem facere regi Anglie, verisimiliter et indubie potest colligi quod nunquam aliquid faceret aut temptaret unde posset terras suas perdere – que racio cessat in aliis, cum non habeant quid perdant – et rex Anglie semper illo modo ipsum punire poterit, quod nequibit fieri in filio minori.

Et nuncii informantes Anglicos loquantur audacter et palam, non meticulose et pauide, quoniam iuxta Tullium sapienti nullum incommodum pro republica est vitandum. Et cum pro ea maiores nostri mortui sint[105] pugnantes in bello, nos degeneramus a patribus, qui nec verbum asperum in ipsius subsidium proponere volumus[106] aut audire.

Secunda racio, que mouere nos debet ad petendum istum magis quam alium filium, est quia, cum uxor sua sit de domo Scocie et familia, puta neptis comitis Buchanie, filius suus nobis futurus rex et dominus pro parte media foret Scotus, nec videretur penitus translata successio, cum sic in nostris quodam modo remaneret.

Tercia racio est quia, cum ipse sit potens in Anglia, eo plures habere poterit in consilio Anglie promotores, et tanto magis pater, rex Anglie, verebitur suam promocionem impedire – que eciam racio cessat in aliis filiis –; et si pater palam et aperte impediat promocionem filii, presumi poterit de scismate inter ipsos; et si filius volente patre consenciat, nobis patris beneuolenciam et aliorum assensum

---

102 eligerit V
103 circumstancionando: certum stancionando V
104 uni: unus V
105 sint: sunt V
106 volimus V

procurabit; et si [pro]¹⁰⁷ deuitanda¹⁰⁸ patris displicencia filius dissenciat, populo isti de sua beneuolencia grates reddet¹⁰⁹ et de duro hoste fiet micior inimicus.

    Vel modo isto satisfiat voluntati regis Anglie: ut in eum transferatur successio sub tali condicione, ut ipse totum ius suum et nostrum in illum filium transferat, de quo supra est dictum, ita libere et integre sicut unquam fuit liberius, nullis reliquiis aut vestigiis superioritatis aut directi dominii in eo remanentibus, id est quod de eo non teneatur in capite [nec] signo quocumque aut censu aliquo teneatur.

---

107 pro *om.* V
108 de vitanda V
109 reddit V

XVI

24   Reason in Politics, 1363-4: A Quaestio from Scotland

Notes to text
line(s)

15   Rom.x.12.
24   *Digest* 8.2.26; *cf. Gl. ord. ad Inst.*2.4 pr. *s.v.* 'alienis'.
43-4   According to the terms of the treaty of Berwick in 1357: prelates chapitres seignures et marchaundes descoce se sount reconuz et chescun de eux est deuenu principale debitour de la somme entier appaier as termes et lieux susditez, in *Acts of David II*, ed. Bruce Webster, no.148, p.178.
66-7   de necessitate faceremus virtutem: *cf.* for example Jerome, *Ep.* liv.6, in Migne, *PL* 22,352.
83-4   For these *exceptiones* in Roman law, see *Inst.*4.13.1; *Dig.*44.4; and line 217 below.
86-7   *cf.* Is. xxxii.18.
88   *cf. Inst.*1.1.1.
89-91   Presumably a reference to the treaty of Birgham in 1290.
97   *utupeus*: perhaps the result of scribal corruption of some form of *eutyches*. Evrard of Béthune, *Graecismus* vii.3, ed. Wroebel, Corpus grammaticorum medii aevi I, Breslau, 1887, p.23 offers *Euterpe:* 'bona delectatio'; and Euterpe had been rendered as 'bene delectans' by Sedulius Scottus, *In Donati Artem maiorem*, ed. Bengt Löfstedt, in *Corpus Christianorum* cont.med. xIB, 1977, p.127. But it would be hardy to conjecture a Latin adjectival construction *euterpeus* from the name of the Muse.
99-100 Cicero, *Philipp.*ii.113: Et nomen pacis dulce est et ipsa res salutarius. sed inter pacem et seruitutem plurimum interest: pax est tranquilla libertas.
100-2   Is.xi.6.
109-14 Boniface VIII, *Scimus fili* (27 June 1299), best printed by E.L.G. Stones, *Anglo-Scottish Relations 1174- 1328*, rev.edn. Oxford, 1970, pp.162,174.
130-3   In October 1327 Robert Bruce had agreed to pay £20,000 within three years after the confirmation of the peace, and the whole sum had been paid by January 1331; see Stones, pp.318,337,n.4. David Bruce was married to Edward III's sister Joanna on 17 July 1328.
135-6   Ovid, *Epp. ex Ponto* 2.7.9-10: Qui semel est laesus fallaci piscis ab hamo / omnibus unca cibis aera subesse putat.
147-8   cum .... mouere: perhaps an echo from a grammar book. For the difference between *flere* and *plorare*, see Isidorus Hispal., *Differ.* 1.227, in Migne, *PL* 83.34: Flere est ubertim lacrymas fundere, quasi fluere; plorare est quasi cum voce flere, plangere, cum lacrymis pectus aut faciem tundere.
149-50 *cf.* II Petr.ii.21.
151   banniti: specified in the indentures of 27 November 1363 as the earl of Atholl (David de Strathbogie), lords Beaumont, Percy and Ferrars and the heirs of Talbot; *APS* i.493; Rymer, *Foedera*, III. ii.715.
160   *Gl.ord.ad Decretum Gratiani*, c.35, C.7, q.1 *s.v.* 'praeferenda est'; *cf.* Jesselin de Cassagnes, *Gl.ord.ad. Extrav.Ioann.XXII*, V, c.unic. *s.v.* 'multo fortius'.
172-4   *X* II.24.33. For the pivotal importance of this decretal in the canonists' discussion of inalienability, see P.N. Riesenberg, *Inalienability of Sovereignty in Medieval Political Thought*, New York, 1956, *passim*; Ludwig Buisson, *Potestas und Caritas*, Cologne, 1958 (repr. 1982), pp.273-98); Hartmut Hoffman, 'Die Unveräusserlichkeit der Kronrechte im Mittelalter', *Deutsches Archiv für*

Erforschung des Mittelalters xx (1964), 389-474; J.R. Sweeney, 'The problem of inalienability in Innocent III's correspondence with Hungary: a contribution to the study of the historical genesis of *Intellecto*', *Mediaeval Studies* xxxvii (1975), 235-51.

198-203   *cf.* Matth.ii.8-16.

203   *cf.* Iudic.ix.1-6 (the story of Abimelech).

209   For king Angusel(us), see Geoffrey of Monmouth, *Hist.Brit.*i.16 *et seqq.* and the insertion in Edward I's letter to Boniface VIII dated 7 May 1301, in Stones, *Anglo-Saxon Relations*, p.196. Fordun was to present an account of the *origio* of the Scottish people and kingdom differing markedly from Geoffrey's history; see Hans Utz, 'Erste Spuren van Nationalismus im spätmittelalterlichen Schottland: Forduns *Chronica gentis Scotorum*', *Schweizerische Zeitschrift für Geschichte* xix (1979), 311-4.

226   quondam: on Douglas's attempts in 1350-2 to secure David's liberation, see E.W.M. Balfour-Melville, *Edward III and David II*, London, 1954, pp.15-16; Nicholson, *Scotland: the later middle ages*, pp.157-9.

240   quatuor castra: Berwick, Roxburgh, Jedburgh and Lochmaben, according to the indentures of 27 November 1363; *APS* i.493; Rymer, *Foedera* III.ii.715.

253-4   *cf.* Robert's demands dated 18 October 1327, in Stones, *Anglo-Scottish Relations*, p.318, and the editor's n.1 on p.342.

261-2   non licet ... expedit: the three criteria of just action had been defined by Bernard of Clairvaux, *de Consid.*iii.4.15, in *Opp.omnia* III, ed. J. Leclercq and H.M. Rochais, Rome 1963, p.442. They had gained currency among the canonists from Innocent III's decretal *Magna devotionis*, X III.34.7: tria praecipue duximus in hoc negotio attendenda: quid liceat secundum aequitatem, quid deceat secundum honestatem, et quid expediat secundum utilitatem. *Cf.* Hostiensis, *Lectura in X* III.34.7. § *Illa s.v.* 'et quid expediat': Igitur quando id de quo queritur licet, decet, expedit, tunc omnino recte et sine reprobacione agitur. Alioquin si unum ex his deficiat, vituperari potest.

271   On the second great outbreak of plague, in 1362, see Fordun, *Chron.gentis.Scotorum*, ed. Skene, i.380-1.

276   *cf.* I Machab.iii.19.

282-3   *cf.* Jakob Werner, *Lateinische Sprichwörter und Sinnsprüche des Mittelalters*, Heidelberg, 1912, p.87: 'sepe fit, it catulus det maxima vulnera parvus'.

286-8   *cf.* Is.xi.2.

289-90   *cf.* Ezech.i.20-1.

303-4   *cf.* Dan.xiii.45.

324-5   A combination of echoes from Boethius, *Philos.Cons.*ii.1.ii, ed. Bieler, *Corpus Christianorum* ser.lat. xciv, 1957, p.18: Quae sese adhuc uelat aliis, tota tibi prorsus innotuit, and Geoffrey de Vinsauf, *Poetria nova* lines 181-4, ed. E. Gallo, The Hague, 1971, p.22:
> Quod magis optatur, magis effluit. Omnia lapsum
> Spondent et citius sunt prospera prompta ruinae.
> Insidias semper ponit sors aspera blande
> Anticipatque fugam melior fortuna repente.

326-9   Nigel de Longchamp (Wireker), *Speculum stultorum*, ed. John H. Mozley and Robert R. Raymo, Berkeley, 1960, lines 581-2, 827-8.

354   acephalus: Boniface VIII had used this word in *Scimus fili* (1299); Stones, *Anglo-Scottish Relations*, p.168. But it was not uncommon; *cf.* for example Geoffrey de Vinsauf, *Poetria nova* line 2, ed. Gallo, p.14.

373-4   *cf.* Is.xxiv.20.
388   circumstancionando: this verb was used by Duns Scotus; *cf. Ordinatio* I, d.17, n.60, in *Opp.omnia* V, cura C. Balic, Rome, 1959, p.163.
402-3   iuxta Tullium: if this is a verbal quotation, I have not identified it. For the sentiment, see Cicero, *De offic.*i.21.70; i.25.85; *De fin.*iii.19.64; iii.21.69.

GENERAL INDEX

In the articles reprinted in this volume the spelling of the names of places and persons is not entirely consistent; the entries below follow the spellings used by the Ordnance Survey and *Handbook of British Chronology*, ed. E. B. Fryde et al., third edn (London, Royal Historical Society, 1986). Cross-references to medieval historical writings are given under Chronicles, etc.

Aberdeen, Dean Spyny: XVI 1–9
Abernethy (Perthshire): V 263
Abetot, Urse d': VI 337
Absalon, prior of Durham: III 204; VIII 185 n.11
Acca, St, bishop of Hexham: IV 592; X 52–3, 60 n.29
Aclea, synod: II 165 n.7
Adelwald, prior of Nostell: IX 177
Ælfwald II, king of Northumbria: II 167–8
Æthelberht, king of West Saxons: X 54
Æthelric, bishop of Durham: IV 592
Æthelwald, bishop of Lindisfarne: IV 592
Æthelwine, bishop of Durham: IV 592, 593 n.10
Æthelwulf, king of West Saxons: X 60 n.19
Aidan, St, bishop of Lindisfarne: I 12; IV 591–2
Ailred of Rievaulx: IV 592–3; VII 20; *De sanctis ecclesiae Haugustaldensis*: X 53, 61 n.43
Aimery, archdeacon of Durham: III 207
Alan, archdeacon of Durham/Northumberland: III 207 n.90
Albini, Nigel *al.* Nele de: VI 337; William de: VIII 182–3
Alchmund, bishop of Hexham: X 52–3
Aldhun, bishop of Durham: IV 591; V 274; X 61 n.46; XII 12
Aldwin, monk of Winchcombe: V 266; abbot (?) of Jarrow: III 192 n.11; monk of Durham: III 195 n.22; prior of Durham: III 191
Alexander III, pope: XI 155–6
Alexander I, king of Scotland: VI 336
Alfred, dreng: XII 25
Alfred, king of West Saxons: X 60 n.19
Alfred son of Westou, sacristan of Durham: IV 592–4; X 53
Algar, prior of Durham: III 195 nn.21–2, 196, 199; XIII 3
Alhmund, St: IV 592
Allan, George: I 4
Allerton, North (N. Yorks.): VII 17
Allertonshire: XIII 7; XIV 193
Alnwick (Northumb.): XIV 210 n.69; Castle: VIII 181, 184–7
Alton (Hants.): VII 15
Ambrose, St: V 278
Amundeville, family: VII 22; XIII 4–5
Ancroft (Northumb.): III 199 n.41
Anglo-Saxon Chronicle: I 9; II 165–7; V 271, 273 n.46, 276 n.61; VI 325–7
Angulsel(us), king: XVI 7, 25
Angus, earl (Stewart, Umfraville): XV 52–3, 55 n.43
Anjou: VII 22
Annales Lindisfarnenses et Dunelmenses: I 11, 21 n.21; II 167–9
Anonimalle Chronicle: IX 176; XV 45, 48–56
Anselm, St, archbishop of Canterbury: III 196, 198 n.36, 207 n.90; V 275–7, 279; VI 335, 339–40; VII 14–18; X 55
Antwerp: XV 49 n.17
Arnold, Thomas: I 7
Artevelde, James van: XV 49, 51
Arthur 'Finboga' (?), Scottish rebel (1154): XI 154, 156
Arthur, king: XVI 7
Ascelina, mother of Bishop William of St Calais: V 261
Ashburnham, fourth earl: XII 7
Ask, John de: XII 17
Asser, *Life of Alfred*: X 51, 56, 61 n.41
Atholl, earl (Strathbogie): XVI 24
Aubigny: *see* Albini
Auckland, Bishop, (Co. Durham): XII 5, 26; XV 53; North: XII 6 n.12, 25; West: XII 4 n.8, 10, 19 n.69, 29; XIII 3
Aucklandshire: XII 4, 23, 34

GENERAL INDEX

Audre, Roger d', lord of Croxdale, Butterby and Coxhoe: XII 11
Augustine, St, of Hippo: V 278
Aumale, Stephen of: V 276
Aycliffe (Co. Durham): I 15; XII 15
Aycliffe, Thomas of: XII 20, 26, 29

Baard, Ralph: VIII 188
Baker, Geoffrey le, *Chronicon*: XV 53 n.37
—, Thomas, of Crook Hall: I 4
Baldwin, dreng: XII 31
Balliol, family: XII 12.;Edward: XV 45–7, 52–3; Guy: XIV 206 n.25; John: XIII 15 n.71; XIV 207 n.31
Bamburgh (Northumb.), castle: VII 20–21; XIII 16
—, earls: V 264
Bannockburn (Stirlingshire): XIV 198, 207 n.42, 210 n.68
Bardney, abbot: XIII 13
Barford (Co. Durham): XII 11–13; XIII 4 n.12
Barforth (N. Yorks.): XII 12 n.37
Barnard Castle (Co. Durham): XV 53
Bartholomew of Farne, St, *Vita*: I 14
Bassett, family: XIV 195
Bath & Wells, bishop: *see* Villula
Bath, Henry of: XIII 15
Battle (Sussex), abbey: V 280
Bayeux: V 260; VII 14
Bayeux, Odo of: V 264, 271, 272 n.45; VI 326–7, 334–5
Bearpark (Co. Durham): XV 53, 56
Beaumont, lords: XVI 24
—, Henry de, earl of Warwick: VI 338
—, Henry, earl of Buchan: XIV 193; XV 50; XVI 6 n.14
—, Hugh de: in the *De iniusta vexacione Willelmi episcopi primi*: VI 333–4, 337–8
—, Hugh de, 'le Poer', earl of Bedford, son of Robert of Meulan: VI 338
—, Louis de, bishop of Durham: I 14; XII 18 n.65; XI V 193, 208 n.46
Bec, abbey: V 280
Becket, Thomas, archbishop of Canterbury: XI 156
Bede: I 4, 8; X 56; writings: X 51; *Historia ecclesiatica*: I 6; II 164; V 267–8, 278; X 57, 60 n.29; XV 46 n.6; death song: I 20 n.8; translation of relics to Durham: IV 591–4
Bedford, Thomas: I 4, 20 n.4, 22 n.23
Bedlington (Northumb.): XII 5 n.9, 9 n.25, 18, 24
Bedlingtonshire: VII 22; XII 2, 4, 9–10, 18–20, 22, 24, 35 n.127

Bek, Anthony, bishop of Durham: I 16; VI 325 n.3; VII 20; XII 19; XIII 11 n.43, 17; XIV 196–7, 200, 206–7 nn.28, 30–1, 40 & 44
Belmeis, Richard II de, bishop of London: XI 153 n.2
Benedict XII, pope: XV 48, 50
Benedict, abbot of Whitby: X 61 n.33
Bernard, Roger: XII 19 n.69
Bernard, St, of Clairvaux: III 203; XVI 25
Bernicia: V 264, 267
Bertram, Roger III, of Mitford: XIV 196
Berwick-on-Tweed: I 5; XI 157 n.3; XIV 198, 206 n.29, 208 n.48, 210 n.69; XVI 24–5
Berwickshire: VII 20
Bessin (France): V 261
Béthune, Evrard of: XVI 24
Beverley, Alfred of, *Annales*: X 61 nn.41 & 43
Bewick (Northumb.): XIV 201, 210 n.69
Biddick (Co. Durham); North: XII 19; South: XII 34
Bigod, Roger: VI 337
Binchester (Co. Durham): XII 10, 14 n.47, 16
Birgham, treaty (1290): XVI 8, 24
Birtley (Co. Durham): XII 21, 23
Bishop Auckland: *see above* Auckland
Bishop Middleham: *see below* Middleham
Blacktoft (E. Yorks.): XIII 7, 17
Blackwell (Co. Durham): XII 24
Blakiston (Co. Durham): III 200; VII 22; XIV 194
Blanchland (Northumb.): XI 157 n.3
Bloet, Robert, bishop of Lincoln: VII 25
Blois, family: III 203; Henry, bishop of Winchester, papal legate: III 202, 204; *see also* Le Puiset
Blyborough (Lincs.): III 202 n.63
Blythe, river, (Northumb.): XII 2
Boie, William: XII 26
Boisil, St: IV 591
Boldon Book: XIII 3, 4 n.12, 10–11 nn.40 & 42; XII 2; comparison with Domesday Book: XII 2–3, 6; compilation: XII 3–6; organization: XII 11–14; tenurial system described: XII 13–17, 33, 36; official version: XII 21–2, 25, 27, 29, 31–2, 34; recensions: XII 5–6, 8, 9–11, 17–23, 25–32, 34; later additions: XII 18–21, 25–7, 29–32; editions: XII 7, 11, 17–18, 34–5; manuscript transmission: XII 6–11, 21–8; *see also* Index of Manuscripts: Durham, Dean and Chapter Muniments, Register I; London, BL, Stowe 930; London, PRO SC/12/21/28; Oxford, Bodl. Lib., Laud misc. 542

GENERAL INDEX

Boldon (Co. Durham): XII 5, 25 n.94, 28, 33
Boniface VIII, pope: XIV 198; letter Scimus fili: XVI 8, 24–5
Bonne Ame, William de, archbishop of Rouen: V 280
Bonnville, family: VII 22
Book of Fees: IX 177, 179; XII 30 nn.112–13, 35 n.130; XIII 14 n.62
Boroughbridge (W. Yorks.): XIV 202
Boso, knight of Durham, vision: V 279 n.73; VI 328 n.1
Boulogne, Eustace count of, son of King Stephen: III 203
Boutflower, D. S., *Fasti Dunelmenses*: III 190
Bower, Walter, abbot of Inchcolm, chronicle: IX 177, 179
Boyd, Thomas: XV 55 n.44
Brabant: XV 48
Brafferton (Co. Durham): XII 10, 13–14, 17, 23
Brancepeth (Co. Durham), barony: XIII 2, 12–14; XIV 194, 203
Breteville, Gilbert de: VI 337
Bridlington chronicle: XIV 201, 210 n.69
Brihtric, king of West Saxons: XI 152
Brinkburn (Northumb.): XII 24
Brittany: VII 22; XIII 14
Brittany, Alan count of: VI 331–2, 337
Brittany, Odo of: VI 331, 333
Broadwood (Co. Durham): XII 33 n.120
Brown, Hugh: XII 25
Bruce, Isabella, daughter of Robert 'the Competitor': XIV 196; Robert, king of Scotland: XIV 194–6, 203, 206 nn.22 & 24, 208 nn.48–9 & 51; XVI 24
Brus, Peter III de: XIII 15. Robert de: VIII 182–3
Brut Chronicle: I 22 n.29; XV 46–57
Buchan, earl: XVI 6 n.14
Buckinghamshire: XIV 194
Bulmer (N. Yorks.): XIII 2, 5, 6 n.18, 12–14; XIV 194
Bulmer, Robert: VIII 188
Burdon (Co. Durham): XII 5 n.10; Little: XII 11 n.30, 15
Burdon, Geoffrey, prior of Durham: I 16; XIV 199, 208 nn.53 & 55
Burgh, Henry de, prior of Lanercost: XV 55
Burghersh, Henry, bishop of Lincoln: XV 47 n.10
Buron, Erneis de: VI 337
Burreth (Lincs.): XIII 12–13
Bury, Richard de, bishop of Durham: I 15–16; *Vita*: I 24 n.40; XV 48
Bushblades (Co. Durham): XII 24 n.88

Butterby (Co. Durham): XII 11
Butterwick (Co. Durham): XII 10, 14, 16, 37
Butterwick, William of, dreng: XII 14–16
Byermoor (Co. Durham): XII 21, 23
Byland (N. Yorks.): XIV 198

Caen: XV 49, 51–2
Caen, Walter son of Hugh of, nephew of Simon the Chamberlain: XII 20
Caerlaverock (Dumfriesshire): XIV 197, 207 n.34
Calais, siege: XV 52–3, 56 n.52
Calatria (Stirlingshire): XI 156 n.5
Calatria, Dufoter of: XI 156 n.5. Ness of: XI 154 n.5, 156
Calixtus II, pope: III 196; X 55
Callidus (the Crafty, le Cu<i>nte), Ralph: XII 24
Calzmonte, Robert of: III 197
Cambois (Northumb.): XII 18–19
Cambois, Adam of: XII 18; Stephen of: XII 18 n.65
Canterbury: VI 339; VII 17–18, 22
—, archbishops: *see* Anselm; Becket; Corbeil; Escures; Lanfranc; Stratford; Theobald; Walter; dispute with York over primacy; VI 336; X 55
—, Christ Church cathedral priory: III 198 n.36, 207 n.90; V 268, 275–6; St Augustine's abbey: III 201 n.55; VI 330; VII 19; St Gregory's priory: III 198 n.36, 207 n.90
Carham (Northumb.), battle: X 56–7, 61–2 nn.46 & 47; XI 154
Carlbury (Co. Durham): XIV 196, 200, 202, 206 n.25, 209–10 nn.64–5, 211 n.77
Carleton (Cumb.): IX 177–9
Carlisle: III 194; V 274; VII 17, 20–21; XI 152 n.2; XV 55
—, bishopric founded: VI 336; IX 180–81 Bishop: *see* Strickland
—, priory, early history: IX 176–81
Carmen de situ Dunelmi: IV 591, 593
Carrington (Northumb.): XI 157 n.3
Cassop (Co. Durham): XII 5 n.10
Castell, Thomas, prior of Durham: I 18
Ceolwulf, king of Northumbria: I 11–12; X 51
Cerdic, king of West Saxons: XI 152
Cettingaham: II 165 n.9
Chambre, William de: I 16, 18
Champagne, Odo count of: VI 337
Charteris, Thomas: XV 55 n.44
Chartres, Fulcher of, *Gesta Francorum Jherusalem peregrinantium*: XI 151 n.2
Chatton (Northumb.): XIV 210 n.69

GENERAL INDEX

Chester-le-Street (Co. Durham): I 2, 7; IV 591; VII 22; XII 4, 5 n.9, 14 n.47, 19
—, Bishop: see Cutheard; community: see Cuthbert
—, ward: XII 4, 11 n.33
Chillingham (Northumb.): XIV 210 n.69
Chirton, West (Northumb.): XIII 16
Choppington (Northumb.): XII 18–19
Christchurch (Hants.), collegiate church: VII 18
chronicles, etc.: see Anglo-Saxon Chronicle; *Anonimalle*; Annales; Asser; Baker; Bede; Bower; Bridlington; *Brut*; Beverley; Chambre; Chartres, Fulcher of; Coldingham; *Cronica*...; *De obsessione Dunelmi*; *De primo Saxonum adventu*; Devizies; Diceto; Durham; Durham, Richard of; Durham, Symeon of; *Dux Valeys hinnit* verses; Eadmer; Eddius; Flete; *Flores*; Gray; Graystanes; Guisborough; Hexham; *Historia*...; Holyrood; Howden; Hugh the Chanter; Huntingdon; Jumièges; Lancercost; *Liber de gestis Anglorum*; Malmesbury; Marianus Scottus; Melrose; Monmouth; Northern Franciscan; Northumbria – annals; Ordericus; Paris; Phrygius; *Rites of Durham*; St Calais – *De iniusta vexacione*; *Scotichronicon*; Swalwell; Tynemouth; Wendover; Wessington; Worcester
Cicero: XVI 7
Cistercians: III 203; IV 592; X 51, 55
Clare, family: XIV 200, 209 n.61
Clarence, Lionel duke of, son of King Edward III: XVI 6 n.13
Clavering estates: XIV 194
Cleadon (Co. Durham): XII 5 n.10, 33 n.121
Cleatlam (Co. Durham): XII 12 n.37
Clement III, anti-pope: VI 335
Clement VI, pope: XV 50
Clifford, Robert: XIV 202, 206 n.22
Clinton, Wiliam de, earl of Huntingdon: XV 47 n.10
Cnut, king of England: X 56, 61 n.45; XIII 3
Cogesall, Robert of: XII 21
Coldingham, Geoffrey of, monk of Durham, *Liber de statu ecclesiae Dunelmensis*: I 14–15, 20 n.4, 23 nn.32 & 39; III 203; VI 324–5; *Vita* of Bartholomew of Farne: I 14
Columbanus, St: III 195
Comines, Robert de: V 264
Comtisvilla, Robert de: VI 337
Comyn, Alice: XVI 6 n.14
Coningstoun, William de: XV 55 n.44
Coniscliffe, High (Co. Durham): XIV 206 n.25

Consett (Co. Durham): XII 5
Conway (Caernarvonshire): XIV 206 n.29
Conyers, family: VII 22; XIII 5; Roger: III 197
Cook, Monk: XII 26, 27 n.103
Copsi, deputy to Earl Tostig: VII 17
Corbeil, William of, archbishop of Canterbury: III 197–8, 207 n.90; VII 16, 24
Cornforth (Co. Durham): XII 5 n.10
Cornhill (Northumb.): XII 26
Cornsay (Co. Durham): XII 20
Cornwall: XV 51 n.33
Cornwall, duke: see Woodstock
Corvei, Widukind of: I 6
Cosin, John, bishop of Durham, I 4
Cospatric: see Gospatrick
Coterel gang: XIV 210 n.64
Coucy, Aubrey de, earl of Northumbria: V 264
Coundon (Co. Durham): XII 14 n.47. Little: XII 6 n.12
Coupar-Angus (Perthshire): XI 156
Coupland, John: XV 52
Courcy, Richard de: VI 337 n.1
Coutances, Geoffrey of: V 264, 271, 274; VI 327, 337
Covenham, priory: V 261 n.10; XIV 194, 205 n.9
Cramlington (Northumb.): VIII 183, 185–6
Crawcrook (Co. Durham): XII 15
Crecy, campaign: XV 48–9, 51–2, 54–5 nn.41 & 43
Crema, John of, papal legate: VII 23; X 61 n.42
Crinan the Thane: XIII 3 n.4
Cronica regum Anglie post Conquestum: I 13
Crookhall (Co. Durham): XII 35 n.130
Croxdale (Co. Durham): XII 11
Coundon (Co. Durham), Great: XII 33 n.120
Coxhoe (Co. Durham): XII 11
Cuinte: see Callidus
Cultura, Richard de: VI 337
Cumba (Kent): XIII 14 n.62
Cumba, Robert of: XII 30–1
Cumberland: V 274
Cumbria: XIV 198; XV 55
Cumin, William, soi–disant bishop of Durham: I 12–13, 22 n.30; III 199–201, 203–04; VII 21
Curia Regis: VI 321, 329, 333, 336–7, 340; XIV 195
Curthose, Robert, duke of Normandy: I 11; V 262–4, 280; VI 323, 327, 335, 338 n.3; VII 15–16; relations with Bishop William of St Calais: V 271–4, 279

Cuthbert, St, bishop of Lindisfarne, cult: I 3, 7, 18, 24; IV 591; V 266, 277; VII 20; X 53; XII 3; translation of relics, in 875: I 7–8; IV 592, 593 n.l2; in 1104: I 8; III 194, 195 n.21; IV 591, 593; VII 24; *De miraculis et translationibus*: I 23–4 n.39; III 194, 195 n.2 1; IV 593 n.12; V 273 n.49; VII 16 n.8; *Historia de S. Cuthberto*: XII 12 n.37; *Miracles of St Cuthbert at Farne*: I 24 n.46; *see also* Durham, Reginald of; Todd
—, community of, at Lindisfarne, Chester–le–Street and Durham, up to 1083: I 7, 11, 16–17, 20 n.11; II 163; III 191, 199 n.43, 200; IV 593; V 269; VII 14, 22; IX 180; XII 11 n.33, 12; Dean: *see* Leofwine
Cuthbert, letter to Cuthwine on the death of Bede: I 7
Cutheard, bishop of Chester–le–Street: XII 12
Cuthwine: letter from Cuthbert on the death of Bede: I 7

Dalton (Co. Durham): I 15
Danby Wiske (N. Yorks.): XIII 13 n.53
Danelaw: III 191
Darel, Duncan, of Lund: XIV 195. Marmaduke: XIV 205 n.17
Darlington (Co. Durham): XII 4–5, 11 n.33, 14 n.47, 24–5, 35 n.l31; XIII 4 n.12, 10 n.40; XIV 193
Darlington, Odo of: XII 35 n.131
David I, king of Scotland: III 199, 203; VI 336; VII 20–21; VIII 186; X 60 n.8; XI 156 n.5, 157; XIII 5; XV 53
David II, king of Scotland: XVI 1, 5–8, 24–5
De iniusta vexacione Willelmi episcopi primi: *see* St Calais, William of
De obsessione Dunelmi: I 10; X 57, 62 n.47; V 263–4
De primo Saxonum adventu: I 11–12, 21 n.21
Denifle, H.: I 4
Denmark: XIII 2
Denum, William de: XIV 193
Derwent, river (Co. Durham/Northumb.): XV 53
Devizies, Richard of, monk of Winchester: VII 23
Deyville, Jocelyn: XIV 193
Diceto, Ralph de, *Opuscula*: XI 156, 159 n.9; *Ymagines Historiarum*: XI 156
Dilston (Northumb.): XI 157 n.3
Dirleton (E. Lothian): XIV 197
Dolfin son of Uhtred son of Meldred: III 199; XIII 2–6; *see also* Meldred
Domesday Book: V 261, 265, 280; VI 329, 337, 339; XII 1–2, 3 n.5, 6–7, 27; XIII 9 n.33
Dorward, Simon: XII 21, 27
Douglas, Archibald: XV 47. James: XIV 201; William, of Liddesdale: XV 53; XVI 2, 6 n.13, 8, 25
Dover (Kent): XIII 16; St Martin's collegiate church: III 207 n.90; VII 18
Doxford (Northumb.): VIII 182–4, 186–7
drengage: XII 13–15
Ducket, Richard: XIII 15; XIV 195
Duddo (Northumb.): XII 23, 35 n.130
Dufoter of Calatria: XI 156 n.5
Dumfriesshire: XV 50 n.22
Dunawal, Owen son of: X 61 n.45
Dunbar (E. Lothian): XV 47 n.10, 48
Dunbar, Patrick of: XIV 210 n.69; XV 55 n.44
Duncan I, king of Scotland: XIII 3 n.4
Duns Scotus, John, *Ordinatio*: XVI 26
Dunstable (Beds.), tournament: XIV 210 n.67
Dupplin Moor, battle: XV 46–7
Durham, castle: VI 326–31, 334.
—, cathedral, Galilee: XIV 200; *see also* Rites of Durham
—, cathedral priory: I 4–7; II 163; III 190, 193, 196, 205; V 258–60, 266–9; VII 17–18; XII 2, 12–13, 22; XIII 3; XIV 197; *see also* Cuthbert – community; Confraternity: *see Liber Vitae*; Foundation: V 259–60, 266–70; VI 323, 327; Grants: VIII 185–6, 188; Jurisdiction: XIII 5–6, 11; *Liber Vitae*: III 190–3, 195, 198 n.36, 201 n.54; V 261 n.11; VI 328 n.1; XIII 8; library: V 278; X 54; martyrology (MS B.IV.24): III 195, 200; V 261, 269 n.35; monks: *see* Aldwin; Durham, Reginald of; Durham, Symeon of; Godwine; Gosfridus; Greystanes; Kellawe; Lawrence; Leofwine; Osbern; Papa; Swalwell; Todd; Wikin; prior: I 13; III 193, 195–7; V 260, 269; VII 17; XII 2, 22; XIII 2, 14; XIV 195; XV 56; *and see* Absalon; Aldwin; Algar; Burdon; Castell; Fossor; Germanus; Lawrence; Melsonby; Roger; Thomas; Turgot; Wessington; Whitehead; William
—, chronicles: I 3–19, 20 n.4, 22 n.28; II 163, 165; V 267; VI 325, 327; The corpus styled by HSO *Gesta episcoporum Dunelmensium*: I 14–17, 22–4 nn.29, 31 & 38–9; VI 324; its components: *see* Durham, Symeon of, with anonymous continuations; Coldingham; Graystanes; Chambre; *Liber magni altaris*: V 267 n.28; *Red Book of Durham*: V 267 n.28; *see also*: *Brut*; *Historia post Bedam*; *Historia regum*;

Howden; Huntingdon; Wessington
—, city: I 8–9; XII 4, 5 n.9, 9–10, 25–6; XIII 15 n.71; XIV 193, 197, 202; XV 47 n.12, 56; Framwellgate Bridge: VII 20; XIV 193, 201, 203; North Bailey: XIV 199; St Giles' church and hospital: VII 24; School: I 4; *see also* Neville's Cross
—, county (*Haliwerfolk*): XII 2, 4, 9, 11, 13; XIII 14; XIV 195; Barons: VII 22; Palatinate: XIV 201–03.;Sheriff: XIV 209 n.60; *see also* FitzHamo; Osbert
—, diocese: VI 336; VII 14, 17; XII 1, 4, 20; Bishops: I 11, 13, 22 n.23; II 163; III 193–4; V 260; VIII 183; IX 180; XII 12; XIII 5, 7, 14, 16; XIV 195–6, 200, 206–7 nn.25 & 31, 211 n.77; *and see* Æthelric; Æthelwine; Aldhun; Bek; Bury; Cosin; Cumin; Edmund; Farnham; Flambard; Fordham; Greystanes; Hatfield; Kellawe; Kirkham; Le Puiset; Marsh; Poitou; Poore; Rufus; St Calais; Ste Barbe; Stichill; Tunstall; Walcher; Wolsey; jurisdiction and income: IX 180–1; XII 33; *and see* Boldon Book; archdeacons: III 189–207; V 269; VII 19; IX 180; *and see* Aimery; 'Havegrim'; Henry; Le Puiset; Michael; Robert; Thurstan; Turgot; Wazo; *and for* Durham/Northumberland *see* Alan; John; Pertico; Ranulf; Simon; William. Archdeaconries: III 189–90, 205–6
Durham, Gilbert son of Humphrey of: XII 19 n.69
—, Reginald of, monk of Durham, *Libellus de admirandis virtutibus S. Cuthberti*: III 194–5; IV 593; *Libellus de vita et miraculis S. Godrici*: XIII 5 n.16, 6 n.19
—, Richard of, O.F.M., chronicle: I 13; IX 177, 179; XV 45
—, Symeon of: III 195 n.22; Writings: I 20–23 nn.6, 14 & 31; and the *Historia regum* (*q.v.*): X 51, 54, 56–7, 61 n.40; XI 152; *Historia Dunelmensis Ecclesiae* (*Libellus de exordio* . . .): I 6–8, 20–21 nn.4, 6–7 & 21; II 167; III 190–91, 193–4; IV 591–2, 593–4 nn.12 & 14; V 258; VI 321–5, 339; VII 14 n.2; sources: I 7–8; manuscript tradition: 200–1 nn.47 & 54, *and see* Index of Manuscripts: Durham University Library, Cosin V.II.6; on the foundation of the Durham cathedral priory: V 267, 268 n.34, 269–70; on Bishop William of St Calais: V 260, 264–5, 270, 274; VI 324, 327–8; anonymous continuations: I 12, 22–3 nn.30 & 39; *Continuatio prima*: VI 324–5; VII 14 n.2, 19–20; attributed continuations: *see* Coldingham, Graystanes, Chambre
Dux Valeys hinnit verses: XV 53 n.37

Eadberht, bishop of Lindisfarne: IV 592
Eadferth, bishop of Lindisfarne: IV 592
Eadmer, *Historia Novorum*: V 275 nn.58–9, 276, 278 n.69; VI 328 n.2, 335, 339–40; VII 18 n.24; X 54–5, 57, 59
Eadulf Cudel, earl of Northumbria: X 56, 61 n.47
Eanberht, bishop of Hexham: II 163–9
Eardwulf, king of Northumbria: II 166
Easington (Co. Durham): VII 22; XII 4, 5 nn.9–10, 11 n.33, 23, 33 n.121, 35 n.130; XIV 194
Easingwold (N. Yorks.): XIV 210 n.67
Ebchester (Co. Durham): XV 53
Ecgred, bishop of Lindisfarne: XII 12
Edderacres (Co. Durham): XII 23
Eddius Stephanus: *Life* of St Wilfred: II 164
Edgar, king of Scotland: VII 20
Edgar the Ætheling: V 263
Edmund, bishop of Durham: IV 592
Edward I, king of England: XIV 193, 196–7, 206–7 nn.22 & 31, 209 n.62; XVI 25
Edward II, king of England: XIII 17; XIV 198, 203, 208–10 nn.48, 62 & 68–9; his son: *see* Eltham
Edward III, king: XV 46–56; XVI 4–7, 24; his wife: *see* Philippa; his sister: *see* Jeanne; his sons: *see* Clarence, Gaunt, Woodstock
Eglingham (Northumb.): XIV 210 n.69
Eighton (Co. Durham): III 200; VII 22; XIV 194, 197, 209 n.60, 211 n.72
Eleanor, wife and widow of Richard Marmaduke, Robert de Umfraville and Roger Mauduit: XIV 200, 202, 209–10 nn.61 & 70
Elias, son of Bishop Flambard: VII 22, 25
Ellingham (Northumb.), barony: VIII 182–8; *and see* Jesmond; church of St Maurice: VIII 186
Ellington, Hugh de: VIII 183 n.6, 187–8; his wife Alice de Gaugy: VIII 184, 187–8
Elstan, dreng: XII 26, 29–30
Elstob, Elizabeth: I 4
Eltham, John of, earl of Cornwall: XV 47 n.10
Ely, Bishop Longchamp: XI 156
Embleton (Co. Durham): XIII 7, 16–17
Emeldon, Richard of: XIV 202, 211 n.75
Engaine, Race: XIII 9 n.34
Erkembald, son: *see* William the moneyer; grandson: *see* William son of William

Escolland, family: VII 22; XIII 5; Jordan: XII 36
Escomb (Co. Durham): XII 35 n.127, 36
Escures, Ralph d', archbishop of Canterbury: III 198 n.36; VII 16
Espec, Walter: VII 20, 21 n.42; XIV 210 n.69
Essex: XII 4 n.6; XIV 194; XV 55 n.43
Ethingaham: II 165
Eudo son of Gilbert son of Meldred: XIII 7 n.22
Eugenius III, pope: VIII 185
Evenwood (Co. Durham): XIII 3, 7, 16
Exeter, bishops: V 265 n.19; VI 336 n.1
Eyncourt, Walter d': VI 337

Falkirk (Stirlingshire): XIV 197
Farnacres (Co. Durham): XII 24 n.90
Farnacres, family: XIV 195
Farne Island (Northumb.): I 23 n.34
Farnham, Nicholas, bishop of Durham: XII 16, 23 n.82, 37
Felton (Northumb.): XIV 196
Ferrars, Lord: XVI 24
'Finboga', Arthur (?), Scottish rebel (1154): XI 154, 156; Gilbert: XI 156 n.5
Finchale (Co. Durham): III 197–8
FitzAlan, Brian: XIII 8, 16; his wife Alice: XIII 8
FitzGeoffrey, Geoffrey, of Ravensworth and Horden: XIII 15; XIV 195, 205–6 nn.12, 15–16 & 18; his wife a Thweng (?): 195: his son Marmaduke: XIV 195–6; his uncle Robert: XIV 205 n.16
FitzHamo, Philip, sheriff of Durham: XIII 8
FitzHugh, Henry: XIV 208 n.57
FitzJohn, Eustace, lord of Alnwick: VII 20; VIII 184, 186–7
FitzMarmaduke, John: XIII 17; XIV 196–7, 199–200, 205–11 nn.16, 18, 22, 25, 28–30, 31, 33, 36, 57–8, 63 & 78; his family and forbears: XIV 194–5, 200–2, 209 nn.61 & 63; his daughter (?): *see* Lumley, Mary wife of Robert I; his son: *see* Marmaduke, Richard; his wives: *see* Bruce, Isabella; Ida
FitzMeldred: *see* Meldred, *and* Neville
FitzRandolf of Middleham, Ralph: XIV 194; his daughter Mary: *see* Neville, Robert (d. 1271)
FitzRanulf, William, son of Archdeacon Ranulf: III 201; VII 22
FitzRichard, Geoffrey: XIV 194–5, 205 n.12; his brother Robert: XIV 205 n.16; his daughter Emma: XIV 205 n.12; his son: *see* FitzGeoffrey
FitzRoger, of Warkworth, Robert (d. c. 1212):

XIII 7; Robert (d. 1310): XIV 194
—, Robert, nephew of Simon the Chamberlain: XII 20
FitzTurstin, Robert, royal dispenser: VII 17 n.19
Flambard, Ranulf, bishop of Durham: I 7–8, 11, 13, 16, 22 n.30; III 189, 194, 196–201, 204–5; VII 14; VIII 183; XII 1–2; XIII 2, 4–5; XIV 193–4, 203; character: VII 23–5; trial, imprisonment and exile: VII 15–17; IX 180; relations with Archbishop Anselm: VII 17–18; with Durham monks: VII 19–20; with King Henry I: VII 15–16; with Robert Curthose: VII 15–16; with Scotland: VII 20–21; with King William II: VII 14–16; IX 180; his brothers: *see* Fulcher, (?) Osbern; his father: *see* Thurstan; his nephews: *see* Osbert, Paganus, Ranulf, Richard, Robert; his sons: *see* Elias, Ralph, Thomas; *see also* FitzRanulf, Paganus, Papa, Wibert
Flanders: XIV 196, 206 n.30
Flete, John, *History of Westminster Abbey*: III 193 n.14
Flores Historiarum: I 10
Fordham, John, bishop of Durham: VI 323
Fossor, John, prior of Durham: I 24 n.40; XV 54
Fothadh, bishop of St Andrews: VI 336
Fountains, abbey: X 52
France, kings: *see* Philip I & VI
Franciscans: I 13; XV 45
Fredoli, Berengar, cardinal bishop of Frascati: XIV 207 n.37
Frene, Sir Hugh de: XV 47 n.10
Frosterley (Co. Durham): XII 5–6, 9 n.26, 24 n.88
Fulcher, bishop of Lisieux, brother of Bishop Flambard: VII 16
Fulk, count of Anjou: V 262
Fulley: XIII 16

Gainford (Co. Durham): XII 12
Galloway: XIV 197
Galo, knight: VIII 187 n.21
Gascony, expedition (1345–46): XV 50–51; service (1242 and 1253/4): XIII 16
Gateshead (Co. Durham): III 191–2; V 263; XII 9, 14 n.47, 24, 28, 33 n.120
Gaugy, family: VIII 185–7; Alice de, sister of Mabilia, wife of Hugh de Ellington: VIII 184, 187–8; Mabilia de, niece of Nicholas de Grenville: VIII 183–5, 187–8; Ralph I de: VIII 187; charter from Henry I: VIII 182, 184–6; Ralph II de: VIII 185–8;

(Gaugy, family continued) charter: VIII 183 n.6
Gaunt, John of, duke of Lancaster: XVI 5; his wife Blanche: XVI 6
Gaveston, Piers: XIV 209 n.62
Geoffrey, abbot of St Mary's, York: I 21 n.22, 26; X 61 n.33
Geoffrey, monk: VI 328 n.1
Gerard, archbishop of York: VII 16 n.13, 17; X 55
Germanus, prior of Durham: XII 12 n.39; XIII 4 n.10
Ghent: XV 49 n.17
Gildeford, Philip de: XII 21
Gilbert 'Fimboga': XI 156 n.5
Gilbert son of Meldred son of Uhtred: XII 12 n.38, 15; XIII 4 n.l2, 6, 8. His son: *see* Eudo
Gillingham (Kent): VI 335
Glasgow, bishops: IX 181; *see also* John; Wischard
Glastonbury (Soms.), abbey, survey of estates: XII 4 n.6
Gloucester: V 264, 274; VI 322
Godric, St, of Finchale: III 198; VII 22, 24; *see also* Durham, Reginald of
Godwine, monk of Durham: III 195 n.22
Gosfridus, monk of Durham: VI 328 n.1
Gospatrick, earl of Northumbria: V 264
Gournay, Gundred de: VI 337
Gowland, Ralph: XII 12 n.39
Grantmesnil, Hugh de: V 271
Gray, Thomas, of Heaton, *Scalacronica*: XIV 194, 196, 201, 205 n.8
Graystanes, Robert, monk of Durham, bishop: VI 324–5; VII 14; continuator of *Gesta episcoporum*: I 14–17, 20 n.4, 23–4 nn.34 & 39
Greenfield, William, archbishop of York: XIV 207 n.44
Greenwell, Revd William: I 4
Greenwood, Thomas, *Cathedra Petri*: I 5–6
Gregory the Great, pope: V 278
Gregory VII, pope: V 266, 268, 269 n.36; VI 335
Grenville, family: VIII 184, 187. Nicholas de: VIII 182–8; Ralph III de: VIII 188; Walter de: VIII 183; William de: VIII 184, 187
Grindon (Co. Durham): XII 28 n.107
Guisborough (N. Yorks.), priory: XII 24; XIII 15
Guisborough, Walter of, chronicle: I 10; XIV 207 n.32; its continuations: XV 46 n.8, 47

Hadrian IV, pope: VIII 185 n.11

Hairun: XIII 7
Halfdan, Viking leader: II 163
Halidon Hill, battle: XV 47 n.9, 54 n.41
Haliwerfolk: see Durham – county
Hallowstell, fishery (R. Tweed): III 200
Hansard, family: XIII 16–17; Gilbert I: XIII 3, 7–9, 11; Gilbert II: XIII 7–10, 14, 16; Gilbert III: XIII 16; John I: XIII 15–16; John II: XIII 16–17; Robert: XIII 16–17; XIV 197
Harclay, Andrew: XIV 198
Hardwick, Gilbert of: XII 25
Hardy, Duffus: III 190
Harlsey, William of, and his son William: XII 26
Harold, king of England: VII 17
Harraton (Co. Durham): III 201; VII 22
Hart (Co. Durham): XIV 206 n.22
Hartburn (Co. Durham): XII 5 n.10, 11 n.30, 24 n.91
Hartburn, William of: XII 15
Hartlepool (Co. Durham): VII 22
Hartley (Northumb.): VIII 183, 187 n.21
Hastings (Sussex): V 280
Hatfield, Thomas, bishop of Durham: I 16–17, 24 n.40; VII 16; *Survey*: XII 10, 15–17, 22, 27–8, 32 n.119
Haughton–le–Skerne (Co. Durham), Great and Little: XII 3, 25–6, 33 n.121, 35 n.127
'Havegrim', William, archdeacon of Durham: III 194–6
Havelok: XIII 2 n.1
Hawthorn (Co. Durham): III 201; VII 22
Healeyfield (Co. Durham): XII 35 n.130
Heardred, bishop of Hexham: II 163, 165
Heaton (Northumb.): VIII 183–4
Hectona: see Eighton
Hedley (Co. Durham): XIV 205 n.16
Hedley Hill (Co. Durham): XII 20, 35 n.130
Hedleyhope (Co. Durham): XII 35 n.130
Heighington (Co. Durham): XII 5, 6 n.l2, 21, 24–6, 28 n.107, 35 nn.127 & 129
Heighingtonshire: XII 4, 34
Helmington (Co. Durham): XII 19 n.69
Hemingbrough, Walter of: *see* Guisborough
Henry I, king of England: I 11, 21 n.22; III 194, 201; VII 15–16, 20–22, 24; VIII 181; X 60 n.8; XI 153; XIII 2, 5; Charter to Ralph de Gaugy: VIII 181; edition and translation: VIII 182; relations with Carlisle: IX 177–81; his wife, *see* Matilda; his daughter, *see* Matilda
Henry II, king of England: I 10; VII 20; VIII 183–4; XI 155; XII 26
Henry III, king of England: XIII 8, 13

GENERAL INDEX

Henry, archdeacon of Durham: III 194–6
Henry, earl of Northumberland, son of King David I of Scotland: VIII 186; XIII 5
Heppo *balistarius*: VI 329, 337
Heptarchy, regnal lists: I 11
Hereford, bishops: V 265 n.19; VI 336 n.1
Herinas, Hugh de, tenant: XII 14
Herleva: VI 337 n.1
Hermitage (Roxburghshire): XV 52
Heron, William: XV 52
Herrington (Co. Durham): III 201; XII 13–14; East and West: VII 22
Heryng, Patoun: XV 55 n.44
Hestan: XV 52–3
Heworth (Co. Durham, par. Aycliffe): XII 15
Hexham (Northumb.): I 8, 12; IV 592; VII 17; X 52–7; XIV 198; Bishops: II 163; *and see* Acca, Alchmund, Eanberht, Heardred, Tidferth
—, Priory: XV 53, 56; Priors: *see* Hexham, John of; Hexham, Richard of; relations with York: X 55, 57
Hexham, John of, *Historia XXV Annorum*: III 202–3; IX 176; X 52–5, 57, 60 n.20; XI 152–4, 157
—, Richard of, *De gestis regis Stephani*: II 164; *De statu et episcopis ecclesiae Haugustaldensis*: I 23 n.31; II 163 n.2, 164–7; IV 592 n.8; X 53, 55, 60–61 nn.20 & 43; sources: II 164–5, 167–8
Higham Ferrers (Northants.): XIV 210 n.66
Hildebert: *see* Lavardin
Hilton, William of: XIV 205 n.16
Historia anglicana of St Albans: XV 48 n.13
Historia Danorum: XI 157
Historia de S. Cuthberto: XII 12 n.37
Historia post Bedam (*Chronica regum Northumbrie*): I 10, 21 n.16; II 163 n.2, 165; VI 326; X 54–9, 61 nn.33 & 36; XI 157
Historia regum: I 20–23 nn.9, 11, 16, 20, 22 & 32; II 163–4, 167; III 192; IV 592 n.8, 594 n.14; V 272–3 nn.45 & 49; VI 322–3, 325–8, 339; VII 18 n.24; IX 176; X 51; XI 152; attributed to Symeon of Durham: I 8–9, 21 n.14; X 51; XI 152; sources: I 9, 21 n.13; X 55; divisions: X 51, 59 n.4; interpolations: X 52–4, 62 n.47; manuscript transmission: X 51–7, 60 n.32; XI 153; later use and continuations: I 9–12, 20–21 nn.4 & 21; X 54–5, 61 n.41; XI 152–4; *see also* Henry of Huntingdon, John of Hexham's *Historia XXV Annorum*
Hoby (Leics.): XIV 210 n.67
Holderness, William son of Robert of, and his wife Cecily Thweng: XIV 206 n.18

Holland, family: XIV 202; Robert: XIV 202, 210–11 nn.64, 73–4 & 76; Thomas: XIV 211 nn.70 & 76
Holy Island: *see* Lindisfarne
Holyrood chronicle: XI 154–5
Homildon: *see* Humbleton
Hook (W. Yorks.): XIII 7
Horden (Co. Durham): VII 22; XIII 15; XIV 194–5, 197, 200, 202, 207 n.31, 209–11 nn.60, 64–5, 70 & 76
Horley (Oxon.): VII 25
Hornby (N. Yorks.): XIII 7; XV 47 n.9
Horncliffe (Northumb.): XII 10, 26
Houghall (Co. Durham): III 201; VII 22
Houghton (Norfolk): XIV 210 n.69
Houghton-le-Spring (Co. Durham): VII 22; XII 4, 5 n.9, 33 n.120, 34
Howden (E. Yorks.): VII 17
Howdenshire: I 23 n.38
Howden, Roger of, *Chronica*: I 10; VI 326; X 54, 59 n.4; XI 154
Huddleston, John, of Millom: XV 55
Hugh the Chanter, *History of the Church of York*: III 198 n.36
Hugh son of Pinceon, steward of Bishop Flambard: VII 21
Hulam (Co. Durham): XII 13, 14 n.47, 23
Humbleton (Co. Durham): XIV 194
Humber, river: XIII 2
Humez, family: VII 22; XIII 5; Emma: XIII 12
Hunstanworth (Co. Durham): XII 35 n.127
Hunter, Christopher: I 4
Huntercumbe, Walter of: XIV 196, 206–7 nn.28 & 30
Huntingdon: VII 23
Huntingdon, earl: *see* Clinton
Huntingdon, Henry of, *Historia Anglorum*: I 10, VII 23–4; X 54
Hunwick (Co. Durham): XII 25
Hurworth (Co. Durham): XIII 7
Hutchinson, William: I 4; III 190
Hutton Henry (Co. Durham): XII 13, 14 n.47, 23
Hyde, abbey: VII 19
Hyfpherlea, Richard de: XII 23

Ida, king of Northumbria: X 51
Ida, wife and widow of Roger Bertram, Robert Neville (d. 1282) and John FitzMarmaduke: XIV 196, 199–203, 208–11 nn.58, 60 & 70
Ingram, family: XIII 7
Innocent II, pope: III 202
Innocent III, pope: I 5; III 207 n.88; decretal *Magna devotionis*: XVI 25; decretal

(Innocent III, pope continued)
  Intellecto: XVI 7, 24
Inverness: XV 47 n.10
Ireby (N. Yorks.): XIII 7
Ireland: XI 155
Isidore, Pseudo-: *Decretales*: VI 321, 332–3, 336
Islandshire: VII 20; XII 2
Italy: XI 155 n.3

Jarrow, monastic community : I 8; III 192 n.11, 193; IV 592; V 266, 269
Jeanne of the Tower, wife of David II of Scotland: XVI 24
Jedburgh: XI 157; XVI 25
Jerome, St: V 278
Jesmond (Northumb.), barony: VIII 183; *and see* Ellingham
Jesuits: I 5
John, king of England: XIII 7 n.27, 9, 14, 16; XIV 195
John, archdeacon of Durham/Northumberland: III 204–6; VIII 188 n.24
John, bishop of Glasgow: XI 157
Julius Caesar: I 10
Jumièges, William of: I 21 n.13

Keith, William: XV 51 n.33
Kellawe, Richard, monk of Durham, bishop of Durham: I 16; XIV 198, 200–1, 205 n.9, 207–10 nn.40, 44, 46, 52, 57, 60, 64 & 68
Kelsey, South (Lincs.): XIII 7, 9 n.34, 17
Kelso (Roxburghshire): X 61 n.42; XI 157
Kent, earldom: VI 333. Saints: X 51
Kepwick (N. Yorks): XIII 14 n.62
Ketton (Co. Durham): XII 3; XIII 3
Killerby (Co. Durham): XII 26–7, 35 n.129
Kimblesworth (Co. Durham): XIII 7
King's Norton (Northants.): VII 25
Kinnersley, John: XIV 200–1, 210 nn.64–5
Kirkham, priory: XIV 210 n.69
Kirkham, Walter, bishop of Durham: XII 18–19, 22, 24; XIII 13 n.61; XIV 206 n.20
Kirkstead, abbey: V 261 n.10

La Haye, Thomas de: XIII 14 n.62
La Ley, Gilbert de: XII 26
Lamesley (Co. Durham): XIV 194, 197, 200, 203, 206 n.28, 209 nn.60 & 62, 211 n.72
Lancaster: XIV 203, 208 n.46
Lancaster, Henry earl of (d. 1361): XV 50; Thomas, earl of: XIV 200–3, 210–11 nn.64, 67, 72 & 74; *see also* Gaunt
Lanchester (Co. Durham): XII 5, 26, 35 n.127
Landmoth (N. Yorks.): XIII 7

Lanercost (Cumb.): XV 49, 55–6
Lanercost, prior: *see* Burgh
Lanercost Chronicle: I 13; IX 176, 179; XIV 205 n.7; XV 45, 48–56, 59; *see also* Durham, Richard of
Lanfranc, archbishop of Canterbury: V 264–5, 265 n.19, 268, 275; VI 328–9, 332, 334–7, 340; *Constitutions*: V 268, 269 n.35, 278
Langley (Co. Durham): XII 9 n.25
Laon: III 197–8 nn.32 & 36, 207 n.90
Lapsley, G. T: XII 7–8
Laundels, William de, bishop of St Andrews: XVI 2, 8
Lavardin, Hildebert of: VII 24
law-codes: *see* Northumbria – Priests' Law
Lawrence, abbot of Westminster: III 203
Lawrence, episcopal chamberlain: XII 15
Lawrence, monk and prior of Durham: III 203; VII 20
Lawrence son of Odard: XII 23
Layton, William of: XIV 195
Layton, Mr William, notary: VII 26
Le Mans: V 261–2; St Vincent's abbey: V 262–4; abbots: *see* Reginald; St Calais
Le Neve: III 190, 193 n.15
Le Puiset, Burchard of, archdeacon of Durham: III 204–5, 204 n.76, 206 n.83; VIII 188 n.24; Hugh of, bishop of Durham: I 16, 22 n.30, 24 n.44; III 190, 203–4, 206; XII 12, 13 n.40, 15, 20–21, 23, 26–7, 31 n.115, 32, 34; XIII 3–4, 6–12; XIV 205 n.17; and *Boldon Book*: XII 2–3, 22
Lee, Edward, archbishop of York: X 55
Leland, John: IX 179
Leobwine, chaplain: III 192
Leofwine, dean of Durham: III 192
Leofwine, monk of Durham: III 195 n.22
Leuknor, Geoffrey: XIII 15; XIV 195
Liber de gestis Anglorum: IX 176; X 52; XI 151–2, 154; sources: XI 152–3; place of compilation: XI 152, 156–7; continuations: XI 154–6; edited extracts: XI 158–9
Liber magni altaris: V 267 n.28
Lichfield (Staffs.): XIV 210 n.64
Liddell peel: XV 53
Liddesdale: XVI 2, 6 n.13
Ligulf: III 192
Limerick, Gilbert of: XV 46 n.6
Lincoln: VII 18, 25; XIV 197; bishops: *see* Bloet, Burghersh
Lincolnshire: V 261; VI 338; VII 21–2; XIII 2, 5 n.15
Lindisfarne *al.* Holy Island (Northumb.): I 7, 11; bishops: II 166; IV 591–2; *and see* Æthelwald; Aidan; Cuthbert; Eadberht;

GENERAL INDEX

(Lindisfarne al. Holy Island continued)
  Eadferth; Ecgred; community: see Cuthbert;
  Gospels: I 8
Linstock (Cumb.): IX 177-9
Lisieux, bishops: VII 16
Lisle, Robert de (fl. 1087): VI 337
—, de, family: XIV 195; Robert (fl. c. 1220):
  XIV 205 n.16
Lochmaben (Dumfriesshire): XVI 25
London: I 5; XV 53, 54; Bishop Belmeis II:
  XI 153 n.2; Council (March 1143): III 202;
  Grey Friars: XV 45; St Paul's, chapter:
  III 196, 200; VII 18; survey of estates:
  XII 4 n.6; Osbern prebendary of
  Consumpta: III 198 n.35; Tottenham:
  VII 18
London, William of: XIV 28 n.51
Longchamp, Nigel de: *Speculum stultorum*:
  XVI 25
—, Robert, abbot of St Mary's, York: XI 156
—, William, bishop of Ely: XI 156
Lorraine: see Lotharingia
Losinga, Robert: XII 3 n.5
Lotharingia: III 191, 192 n.11; see also
  Walcher bishop of Durham
Lothian: X 56
Lowther, river (Westmorland): IX 180
Lucy, Thomas de: XV 55
Lumley, family: XIV 195-6, 202, 206-7
  nn.23 & 31, 209 n.62. Isabella, daughter of
  Marmaduke: XIV 209 n.62; John, son of
  Robert I: XIV 200; John, son of Robert II:
  XIV 200, 209 n.63, 211 n.72; Lucia,
  daughter of Robert II: XIV 209 n.63;
  Marmaduke: XIV 202, 209 n.62, 211 nn.72,
  76; Mary, daughter (?) of John
  FitzMarmaduke, wife of Robert I: XIV 196,
  200, 202, 206 n.23, 209 n.63; Ralph: XIV
  206 n.22; Robert I: XIV 196, 200, 209 n.63,
  211 n.72; Robert II: XIV 200, 202, 209
  n.63, 211 nn.76 & 78; Roger II: XIV 207
  n.31
Lund (E. Yorks.): XIV 195, 205 n.17
Luttrington (Co. Durham): XIII 3

Macdowell, Duncan: XV 51
Maine (France): V 261-3, 265
Mainsforth (Co. Durham): XII 25
Mainz: I 9
Malcolm II, king of Scotland: X 56
Malcolm III Canmore, king of Scotland:
  V 263, 273; VI 323; X 53, 62 n.47; XI 157
  n.1; his wife, see Margaret
Malcolm IV, king of Scotland: XI 155 n.2
Malestroit, truce: XV 49

Malmesbury, William of: I 6; *Gesta
  pontificum*: III 196; V 277-8 nn.62 & 69;
  Gesta regum: VI 327, 340
Marches, Middle: XI 157 n.3
Margaret, queen of King Malcolm III of
  Scotland: V 263
Marianus Scottus, *Chronicon*: I 9, 21 nn.13 &
  21
Markyate, Christina of: VII 23
Marley (Co. Durham): XII 20
Marmaduke, Richard, bishop's steward:
  XIV 193-4, 196, 198-203, 204-10 nn.2, 18,
  23-4, 31, 45-6, 48, 51, 53, 57-8, 60, 62-7,
  70, 72; his family and forbears: XIV 194-8;
  his sister (?): see Lumley, Mary, wife of
  Robert I; his wife: see Eleanor
Marsh, Richard, archdeacon of
  Northumberland: III 207; bishop of
  Durham: I 15; XII 21; XIV 205 n.16
Marske-by-the-Sea (N. Yorks.): VII 17
Marton, priory: XIV 194
Matilda, empress: III 199, 203
Matilda, queen of Henry I: IX 177, 179
Matthew *Manchensis*, O.F.M.: XV 52 n.37
Maubert: XII 35 n.131
Mauduit of Eshott (Northumb.), Roger III:
  XIV 202, 209 n.61; his wife: see Eleanor
Meldred, thegn: VII 22; XIII 2-3, 10, 17; his
  descendants: see Uhtred son of Meldred;
  Dolfin son of Uhtred; Meldred, Patrick (?)
  and Robert (?), sons of Dolfin; Robert
  Neville, Gilbert, Richard (?) and William
  (?), sons of Meldred son of Dolfin; Eudo
  son of Gilbert son of Meldred; see also
  Neville
Meldred son of Dolfin: XII 12, 13 n.40;
  XIII 2-6, 8-11; Patrick, brother (?) of
  Meldred son of Dolfin: XIII 6 n.20
Melrose (Roxburghshire): V 266; XI 156
Melrose Chronicle: I 10; X 54, 56-7, 60-61
  nn.32 & 36; XI 154-5; II 163n, 165
Melsonby, Thomas of, prior of Durham: I 23
  n.34
Melton, William, archbishop of York: I 14, 23
  n.38; XV 50
Menville, family: XIV 202, 211 n.76; Agnes:
  XIV 211 n.70; John, of Whittonstall:
  XIV 209 nn.60 & 62, 211 nn.70 & 76;
  William son of John: XIV 209 n.62
Mercia, episcopal list: II 166
Merlin: I 14; XV 46
Merton, Walter of, chancellor of England,
  bishop of Rochester: XIII 15-16; XIV 195
Meulan, Robert of: VI 338. Roger of: V 275
Meynil, Stephen: XIII 15

Michael, archdeacon of Durham: III 197–9, 205
Mickletons, antiquaries: I 4
Middle Marches: XI 157 n.3
Middleham: *see* FitzRandolf
Middleham, Bishop, (Co. Durham): VII 22; XII 5 nn.9–10, 24, 33 n.120, 35 n.127; XIV 194, 205 n.9
Middleton, Gilbert: XII 18 n.65; XIV 193
Middridge (Co. Durham): XII 9 n.25, 26, 33 n.120, 35 n.129
Migley (Co. Durham): XII 23
Milman, Henry, dean of St Paul's, *History of Latin Christianity*: I 5
Mitford (Northumb.): XIV 193, 196
Molyns, John: XIV 194
Monmouth, Geoffrey of: *Historia regum Britanniae*: XV 46 n.7; XVI 8
Mont St Michel, abbey: VI 338 n.3
Montague, William de, earl of Salisbury: XV 47 n.10, 50
Montbegon, family: XIII 7
Montford, family: XIII 16
Montgomery, Roger of: V 271; VI 327
Moray, bishops: *see* Spyny, William
Moray, earl: XV 47 n.10
More, William: XV 55 n.44
Moresby, Hugh: XV 55
Morley, (Co. Durham): XIII 7, 16
Morley, Robert: XV 51 n.33
Mowbray, family: XIII 16; John de: XIII 17; XV 52 n.37; Nigel de: XIII 14 n.62; Robert de, earl of Northumberland: V 264, 271, 276; VI 327, 337; VII 19 n.35; XII 12; XIV 206 n.25; Roger de, father of Robert: VI 337 n.3; Roger de, son of Nigel de Albini: VI 337
Murdac, Henry, archbishop of York: III 203
Musters, de: XIII 5
Myton, Chapter: XIV 198

Naworth (Cumb.): XV 53
Nennius: XV 46 n.6
Netherton (Northumb.): XII 18–19
Neville's Cross, battle (1346): I 13, 22 n.29; XV 45, 52–6; XVI 1
Neville, family: VII 22; XII 15, 17; XIII 12, 14; XIV 194, 197–203; forbears: *see* Meldred. Alexander, son of Ranulf: XIV 201, 210 n.69; Anastasia, daughter of Ranulf: XIV 194; Euphemia, wife of Ranulf: XIV 194; Geoffrey (d. 1192), of Burreth: XIII 12; his wife: *see* Humez, Emma; Geoffrey (d. *c.* 1240), son of Robert son of Meldred (*q.v.*): XIII 13; Henry (d. *c.* 1227): XIII 7 n.23, 12–13; his wife Alice: XIII 13; Isabel, wife of Robert son of Meldred: XIII 12; John (d. 1333), son of Ranulf: XIV 201, 205 n.2, 210 n.69; XV 47 n.9; John, of Hornby: XV 47 n.9; John (d. 1389), son of Ralph, of Raby: XIII 17; XV 55 n.43; Mary, wife of Robert (d. 1271): XIV 194, 210 n.69; Ralph (d. 1367), son of Ranulf, of Raby: XIV 201–2, 210–11 nn.69–70 & 76–7; XV 47 n.9, 52–3, 55 n.43; Ralph (d. by 1380), fourth son of Ralph: XIV 211 n. 77; Ranulf (d. 1331): XIII 14, 17; XIV 194, 197–8, 201, 205 nn.9 & 14, 207 n.40; Richard (d. 1471), earl of Warwick: XIII 2; Robert (d. 1252 x 1254), of Raby: *see* Robert son of Meldred son of Dolfin; Robert (d. 1282), of Raby: XIII 13; XIV 196; his wife: *see* Ida; Robert (d. 1319): XIII 13–14; XIV 193–4, 196, 198, 200–1, 203, 204–5 n.2, 207–8 nn.45–6.
New Forest (Hants.): VII 21
Newbiggin (Co. Durham): XII 11 n.30
Newbottle (Co. Durham): XII 11 n.30, 14 n.47, 19 n.69, 25 n.94, 33 n.120
Newburn (Northumb.): VIII 187 n.21
Newcastle-upon-Tyne: I 4; VII 22; XIV 202, 211 n.75
Newminster, abbey: X 52; abbot, *see* Robert
Newsham (Co. Durham): XII 11–12, 13 n.40; XIII 4. Little: XII 12 n.37
Newstead (Northumb.): VIII 182–4, 186–7
Newton Cap (Co. Durham): XII 10
Newton Hansard (Co. Durham): XIII 16, 17
Nicholas, chamberlain to Henry II: XI 155
Nigel: XII 23
Norham (Northumb.): I 8; III 200; VII 20–21; XII 33 n.121; Castle: III 199 n.41
Norhamshire: VII 20; XII 2, 4, 9, 10, 26, 28 n.107, 35 n.130; Sheriff: *see* Papedy
Norman Conquest: III 191; V 263–4; VII 17, 21–2; XII 2, 12; XIII 1–2, 5, 14
Normandy: V 265, 271–2, 273 n.46, 274; VI 326, 334–5, 338; VII 15–16, 18, 22; VIII 183
Normandy, Robert of: VI 321
Normanton, Alan of, dreng: XII 30–2
Northallerton: *see* Allerton
Northampton, treaty: XVI 8
Northamptonshire: XIV 201
Northern Franciscan Chronicle: XV 45–6, 48–54, 56–7
Northumberland: VII 21; VIII 181; IX 180; XII 2; XIII 7; XIV 194, 198, 202; archdeaconry: III 190; archdeacons: III 205–7; VII 19; *see also* Marsh *and*

Durham/ Northumberland
Northumbria: I 7, 11; II 163; IV 591; V 264;
  XI 154; XIII 2; annals: II 163–4, 166, 167;
  X I 9; 51, 53; kings: II 166–7; X 51; *and
  see* Ælfwald II; Ceolwulf; Eardwulf; Ida;
  Oswald; priests' Law: III 191; shire custom:
  XII 4, 14
Northumbria/Northumberland, earls: V 263;
  X 56, 61 n.41; XII 12; *see also* Gospatrick;
  Coucy; Eadulf; Henry; Waltheof; Siward;
  Tostig; Uhtred
Norton (Co. Durham): VII 21; XII 5 n.10, 10,
  25, 30–31
Nostell, prior: *see* Adelwald
Nowell, Laurence: I 23
—, Ralph, titular bishop of Orkney: VII 18

Odard: XII 23
Old English Chronicle: *see* Anglo-Saxon
  Chronicle
Ord, Middle (Northumb.): XII 35 n.130
Ordericus Vitalis, *Historia Ecclesiastica*: I 6,
  12; V 274 n.51; VI 327 n.2, 337 n.3; VII 17
  n.19, 24 nn.61–2 & 64
Origen: V 278
Orkney: VII 18
Orm son of Toki, dreng: XII 23, 25, 31
Orval, Richard d', chaplain to King Henry I:
  IX 179–80
Osbern, monk of Durham: III 195 n.22, 197–8
Osbern, royal chaplain, canon of St Paul's,
  brother (?) of Bishop Flambard: III 198
  n.35
Osbert, bishop of Hexham: *see* Eanberht
Osbert, nephew of Bishop Flambard, sheriff of
  Durham: III 198 n.35, 201, 204; VII 21–2;
  and see Osbern; his brother: *see* Robert
Osburwic: *see* Newstead
Osmund, bishop of Salisbury: VI 337
Oswald, St, king of Northumbria: IV 591–2,
  593 n.12
Ovid: XVI 7
Owen the Bald, king of Strathclyde: X 56–7
Owen son of Dunawal: X 61 n.45
Oxenhall (Co. Durham): XII 14 n.46, 15, 16
  n.57
Oxford: X 61 n.46; XVI 8; Durham College:
  I 14

Paganel, Ralph: VI 329
Paganus, nephew of Archdeacon Ranulf:
  III 201
Pakenham, John, official of the court of York:
  VII 26
Pallion (Co. Durham): XIV 194

Papa, monk of Durham: III 201
Papedy, sheriff of Norhamshire/Islandshire:
  III 199 n.41, 200; VII 20
Parco/del Park, John I and II: XIV 207 n.31
Paris: XV 46, 50; XVI 8
Paris, Matthew: I 6
Paschal II, pope: VII 15 n.3, 17
Patrick, brother of Meldred: XIII 6 n.20
Paynel, Ralf: VI 337–8
Pelerum, Alan: XIV 206 n.25
Pemme, Thomas de: XII 25
Pennines: XV 55
Penrith (Cumb.): XIV 207 n.36
Penshaw (Co. Durham): XII 11 n.30; XIV 205
  n.5
Percy, family: XIV 195, 207 n.33; XVI 24;
  Henry's herald, *see* Rey Marchis
Perth: XIV 197, 207 n.36; XV 47 n.10
Pertico/Perche, Theobald de, archdeacon of
  Durham/Northumberland: III 206, 207 n.88
Petronilla daughter of Alexander: XIV 206
  n.25
Peverell, Ranulf: VI 337
Philip I, king of France: V 273
Philip VI, king of France: XV 48–9
Philippa, queen of King Edward III: XV 194
Phrygius, Dares: *De excidio Troiae*: XI 151
Piercebridge (Co. Durham): XIV 206 n.25
Pinceon: VII 21
Pipe Rolls: III 201; VIII 185; IX 178; XIII 9,
  10
Pittington (Co. Durham): I 15
Poitou: XIII 14
Poitou, Roger count of: VI 331–2, 337, 341
Poitou, Philip of, bishop of Durham:
  III 206–7; XII 15 n.48, 20, 21 n.74, 26, 27
  n.103, 29, 34
Pontefract (W. Yorks.): XIV 202
Poore, Richard, bishop of Durham: XII 23
  n.82; XIII 15
Port, Hugh de: VI 329, 337
Portsmouth (Hants.): XV 47 n.10, 48
Powell, Richard: I 18
Preston-on-Tees (Co. Durham): XII 5, 11
  n.30, 23, 25, 30–31
Preston, Adam of, son of Walter of Stockton:
  XII 30–2
Prudhoe (Northumb.): XIV 202, 206 n.29
Pyrford (Surrey) writ: V 280

Quarrington (Co. Durham): XII 33 n.120
Quarringtonshire: XII 4, 24 n.91, 25 n.94

Rabanus Maurus: V 278
Raby (Co. Durham), lordship: XII 12; XIII 2,

(Raby continued) 4–7, 10–14, 17; XIV 194–6, 200; XV 47 n.9; *see also* Meldred, Neville
Radcliffe, Cuthbert, of Carrington and Dilston (d. 1545); Cuthbert, son of Anthony, of Blanchland; Cuthbert, son of Sir Francis, (d. 1644): XI 157 n.3
Raine, James, the elder, ed. *Historiae Dunelmensis Scriptores Tres*: I 4, 20 n.4; James, the younger: I 4, 22 n.23; II 164
Ralph, abbot of Sées: III 195 n.21
Ralph, prior of Tynemouth: XI 157 n.1
Ralph, son of Bishop Flambard: VII 22
Ramsey, William: XV 55 n.44
Ranulf, nephew of Bishop Flambard, archdeacon of Durham/Northumberland III 197, 200–4, 206–7; VII 21–2; his nephews: *see* Paganus, Wibert; his son: *see* FitzRanulf
Ranulf, royal tax-gatherer: VII 21 n.44; *see also* Flambard
Rashdall, Hastings, *The Universities of Medieval Europe*: I 4
Raskelf (N. Yorks.): XIII 2; XIV 194
Rathe, Alexander del: XV 55 n.44
Raunds (Northants.): XIV 210 n.66
Ravenshelme (Co. Durham): XIV 197 200, 202–3, 205–6 nn.16 & 28, 209 nn.60 & 62, 211 n.72
Ravensworth (Co. Durham): III 200; VII 22; XIII 15; XIV 194, 205 n.16, 209 n.62
Red Book of Durham: V 267 n.28
Redpath (Northumb.): XV 53
Redworth (Co. Durham): XII 6 n.12, 11 n.30, 33 n.121
Reginald, abbot of St Vincent's: V 262 n.13
Rey Marchis, Wauter le, Henry Percy's herald: XIV 207 n.33
Rheims, Council (1119): X 55
Rhuddlan, battle: XIV 196
Richard I, king of England: XII 26
Richard II, king of England: XIV 211 n.76
Richard, abbot of St Albans: VII 19
Richard, abbot of St Mary's York: I 21 n.22
Richard, nephew of Bishop Flambard, of Ravensworth: III 200–1; VII 22; and his descendants: XIV 194 *seq.*
Richard *rundus*, dreng: XII 31
Richard son (?) of Meldred son of Uhtred: XIII 6, 8
Richmond (N. Yorks.): XIII 16; XV 53
Ricknall (Co. Durham): XII 33 n.120; New: XII 5–6
Ridpath: *see* Redpath
Rievaulx, looters disguised as lay brothers: XIV 193

Rievaulx, William of: III 203
Rites of Durham: I 3
Robert I, king of Scotland: *see* Bruce
Robert II, king of Scotland, the Steward: XVI 2, 8
Robert, abbot of Newminster: III 198 n.37
Robert, archdeacon of Durham: III 197–202, 204–5, 207
Robert, bishop of St Andrews: XI 156 n.5
Robert, brother of Meldred: XIII 6 n.20
Robert, nephew of Bishop Flambard, brother of Osbert: III 201; VII 22
Robert son of G(u)alo: VIII 187 n.21
Robert son of Meldred son of Dolfin: XII 12–13, 15, 27 n.103; XIII 6–17; XIV 194–6; his half-brother (?): *see* Hansard, Gilbert II; his wife: *see* Neville, Isabel
Rochester: V 275; VI 326; bishops: XIII 16; monastic community: V 268
Rockingham, council (1095): V 275 n.58, 276; VI 339
Roger, bishop of Salisbury: VII 15–16, 25
Roger, prior of Durham: III 198, 200, 202, 204
Roger son of William, dreng, of Butterwick: XII 16
Rogerley (Co. Durham): XII 3
Rome: I 5, 14; III 203–4; V 265, 272; VI 333, 335; XI 155; XVI 7
Rouen, archbishop: *see* Bonne Ame
Rouen, council (1091): V 280
Roxburgh: XIV 210 n.69; XV 52; XVI 25
Rud, Thomas: I 4
Rufus, Geoffrey, bishop of Durham: I 12–13, 22 n.30; III 189, 199, 201–2; VII 20–1; VIII 183; XIII 4–5
Rumsey, John, steward of the bishopric of Durham: XIII 15; XIV 195
Rushden (Northants.): XIV 210 n.67
Rushyford (Co. Durham): XII 18 n.65; XIV 193
Ryhope (Co. Durham: XII 5 n.10
Ryton (Co. Durham): XII 34

Sadberge (Co. Durham): XII 4, 5 n.9, 20; XIII 15 n.71; XIV 206 n.25
Sadberge, William of, and his son William: XII 16, 37
St Albans, abbey: VII 24–5; chapel of St Alexis: VII 19; abbot: *see* Richard; Historical writing: I 10; XV 48 n.13
St Andrews (Fife): III 189, 194, 196. Bishop: XI 155; and see Fothadh; Laundels; Robert; Turgot; diocese: VI 336

St Barbara: *see* Ste Barbe
St Calais: V 261
St Calais, William of, bishop of Durham:
I 6–7, 10, 13, 15; III 189, 192–4, 197;
V *passim*; VII 18–20, 22; IX 180; XII 1, 19;
XIII 3; XV 46 n.6; his mother Ascelina:
V 261; early career: V 260–5; foundation of
the monastic community at Durham (1083):
V 258–60, 268–70; VI 327; Trial at
Salisbury (1088) recounted, with other
matter, in *De iniusta vexacione Willelmi
episcopi primi*: I 10, 24 n.39; V 258–60,
267 n.30, 271; VI *passim*; authenticity:
VI 321–2, 328–9, 334–41; two parts:
VI 321–3; *libellus* in: VI 323, 326–8; date:
VI 328, 339–41; manuscript history:
VI 323–5; exile: V 271–4; VI 322, 323 n.2,
327–8, 331, 334, 336, 339–41; Council of
Rockingham (1095): VI 339–40; books
given to Durham: V 278
St Longis, mill-site: V 262
St Osyth, Prior William of Corbeil: III 198 n.36
Ste Barbe, William of, bishop of Durham:
I 13, 16, 22 n.30; III 198, 200, 202–4;
XII 19; XIII 5–6
Salisbury: V 271; VI 321–2, 325–8, 332, 336;
VII 18; bishops: *see* Osmund; Roger, earl:
see Montague
Salton, prebend in York Minster: X 55
Sampson, Thomas: XV 54
Sawley, abbey: X 51–3, 55–6; XI 153 n.2
Scone (Perthshire), estates meeting (1364):
XVI 1–4, 7–8
Scotichronicon: IX 177, 179
Scotland: III 194, 202; V 263–4; VII 19–20;
IX 176, 179; X 56; XI 152, 154–6; XIII 5,
17; XIV 193, 196–9, 201, 203; XV 45–6,
52–3; XVI 2; kings: *see* Alexander I; Bruce;
David I–II; Duncan I; Edgar; Malcolm
II–IV; Robert II; William the Lion;
metropolitical jurisdiction of York: VI 336;
X 152, 156; *Quaestio* concerning King
David II's ransom and the succession to
him: XVI *passim*
Scott, William: XII 26
Scrutville, family: XIV 195
Seaham (Co. Durham): VII 22
Sedgefield (Co. Durham): XII 5, 14 n.47, 25
n.94, 28, 33 n.120
Sedulius Scottus: XVI 24
Sées, John of, bishop of Lisieux: VII 16
Selby, Walter of: XV 53
Selkirk: X 61 n.42
Severinus, abbot of St Mary's, York: X 61 n.33

Shadforth (Co. Durham): XII 5 n.10
Shaftesbury, nunnery, survey of estates: XII 4 n.6
Sheraton (Co. Durham): XII 10, 13–17, 35 n.127
Sherburn (Co. Durham), hospital: XIII 9 n.34;
North: XII 5 n.10
Sheriff Hutton (N. Yorks.): XIII 12 n.49;
XIV 194
Shotton (Co. Durham): XII 5 n.10, 14 n.47
Silksworth (Co. Durham): VII 22; XIV 194–5,
197, 200, 202, 209–11 nn.60, 64–5 & 70;
St Leonard's chapel: XIV 197
Silksworth, Robert of, brother of William:
XIV 201, 209 n.62; William of: XIV 201,
209 n.62, 211 n.76; his daughter Agnes:
XIV 209 n.62, 211 n.76; his mother
Agnes and his father Philip: XIV 209 n.62
Simon, archdeacon of Durham/
Northumberland: III 207 n.90
Simon, chamberlain to Bishop Le Puiset:
XII 20; his nephews: *see* Caen; FitzRoger
Siward, earl of Northumbria: V 264
Skerne, river (Co. Durham): XIII 7
Sleekburn (Northumb.), East: XII 18, 23;
West: XII 18–19
Sluys: XV 50 n.22, 54 n.41
Smalleia (Co. Durham): XII 21
Smith, John: I 4
Southampton (Hants.): VI 323 n.2
Spearmans, antiquaries: I 4
Speculum stultorum: XVI 7
Spyny, William de, dean of Aberdeen, bishop
of Moray, *antiquus libellus* incorporating
quaestio on Scottish affairs in 1363–64:
XVI *passim*
Staindrop (Co. Durham): VII 22; XII 12;
XIII 3–5, 6 n.18, 11, 14, 15 n.70, 16;
XIV 194
Staindropshire: III 199; XIII 2–5, 11
Stainmore: V 263
Stanhope (Co. Durham): XII 9 n.25, 23–4, 28
n.107, 35 n.127
Stanley (Co. Durham): XII 33
Stella (Co. Durham): XII 21; XIII 4 n.12
Stephen, king of England: III 202–3;
III 181, 186–7; XI 154; his son Eustace: *see*
Boulogne
Stevenson, Joseph: I 5
Stewart, John *le frere*: XV 55 n.44
—, Thomas, earl of Angus: XV 55 n.43
Stichill, Robert, bishop of Durham: XII 19;
XIV 195, 206 n.20
Stirling Bridge: XIV 196, 206 n.30

Stockton (Co. Durham): XII 4–5, 10, 11 n.30, 11 n.33, 24 n.91, 25, 30–31
Stockton, Walter of, dreng, and his son Adam of Preston: XII 30–32
Stonyhurst Gospel: I 8; VII 24
Stranton in Hartness (Co. Durham): XIV 196–7, 202, 206 n.22
Stratford, John, archbishop of Canterbury: XV 48–9
Strathbogie, David de, earl of Atholl: XVI 24
Strathclyde, king: see Owen
Strickland, William, bishop of Carlisle: IX 179
Stuteville, family: XIII 9. Joanna: XIII 9–11, 17; John: XIII 6. Roger: XIII 6, 8; William: XIII 9 n.33
Sunderland (Co. Durham): XII 11, 35 n.130; XIV 194
Sunderland Bridge (Co. Durham): XII 11–13, 35 n.130; XIII 4
Swainston (Co. Durham): XIII 16–17
Swalwell, Thomas, monk of Durham: I 18; X 54

Taillebois, Ivo : VI 337
Talbot, family: XVI 24
Tange, Andrew de: XIV 206 n.29
Team, valley (Co. Durham): XIV 194, 200, 202, 205 n.16
Tees, river: V 263; VII 20, 22; X 55; XII 4, 9, 11 n.33; XIII 3, 4 n.12, 5, 7; XIV 195, 197, 201, 206 n.25
Templars, survey of estates in Essex: XII 4 n.6
Teviotdale: III 194; VII 17
Theobald, archbishop of Canterbury: III 203; VII 22
Thickley (Co. Durham): XII 11 n.30, 26, 28 n.107, 33 n.120, 35 nn.127 & 129; XIII 3
Thierry, W. son of: IX 180
Thomas I, archbishop of York: V 264, 265 n.19, 277; VI 332, 336; VII 26; IX 180; X 55
Thomas II, archbishop of York: VII 18; X 55, 61 n.43
Thomas I, prior of Durham: I 23 n.34
Thomas, son of Bishop Flambard: VII 16, 22
Thorney, abbey: VII 19
Thornton (Lincs.): XII 24; XIII 17
Thornton Curtis, priory: XIII 7
Thorpe (Co. Durham): XII 5 n.10, 33 n.121
Thurstan, archbishop of York: VII 18; X 55; XI 152
Thurstan, archdeacon of Durham: III 192–3
Thurstan, father of Bishop Flambard: III 201 n.55

Thweng, family: XIV 196, 202, 205 n.17; Marmaduke I: XIV 195–6, 206 nn.18, 20; his daughter Cecily: XIV 206 n.18; Marmaduke III: XIV 196, 202, 206 nn.28 & 30, 209 n.63; his daughter Lucia: XIV 202, 211 n.76; Robert, father of Marmaduke I, and his wife Emma: XIV 195; Robert (d. 1282 x 1284): XIV 206 n.28
Tidferth, bishop of Hexham: II 163–6, 168–9
Tillmouth (Northumb.): XII 23
Tinchebrai, battle: VII 15
Tiron: X 61 n.42
Titlington (Northumb.): XIV 210 n.69
Todd, William, monk of Durham: I 18; VI 324; XV 56 n.50
Toki: XII 23, 25, 31
Tostig, earl of Northumbria: VII 17
Trailli, Geoffrey de: VI 337
Trayne, Robert: XIII 15 n.71
Tunstall, Cuthbert, bishop of Durham: I 18; X 55; XII 5 n.10, 22
Turgot, prior/archdeacon of Durham, bishop of St Andrews: I 8; III 189–90, 193–7, 205; V 274; VI 328 n.1; VII 19–20
Tursdale (Co. Durham): XII 11 n.33
Tweed, river: V 263; VII 20; XII 2
Twizel (Co. Durham): XII 23, 35 n.130
Twysden, Roger, *Historiae Anglicanae Scriptores Decem*: I 20
Tyne, river: III 206; V 264; VII 20, 22; VIII 185–6; XII 2, 4, 9, 11; XIII 3, 7; XIV 195, 197, 201
Tynemouth (Northumb.): III 192 n.11; VII 19 n.36; XI 157 n.1. Priory: XIII 16; XIV 206 n.25, 210 n.69; prior: see Ralph
Tynemouth, John of, *Historia Aurea*: I 13, 22 n.29; XIV 205 nn.5, 7; XV 46 n.8, 47–8, 50–51, 57

Ufford, Robert: XV 50. William: XV 51
Uhtred, earl of Northumbria: V 264; X 56
Uhtred son of Meldred: XIII 2–3; *see also* Dolfin, son of Uhtred
Ulnaby (Co. Durham): XIV 196, 200, 202, 210–11 nn.64–5 & 77
Umfraville of Prudhoe, earls of Angus, family: XIV 202, 209 n.61; Gilbert de (d. 1307): XIV 206 n.29; Gilbert de (d. 1381): XV 55 n.43; Robert de (d. 1325), wife: *see* Eleanor
Upsettlington (Northumb. ?): XII 35 n.131
Urban II, pope: V 272, 276; VI 335–6, 340
Urpeth (Co. Durham): XII 10, 13, 14 n.47, 16
Usworth (Co. Durham), Great: XII 13, 14 n.47, 17

GENERAL INDEX

Utting, dreng: XII 23, 25, 31

Valence, William of: XIII 8
Vesci, William de, lord of Alnwick:
  VIII 184–7; XIII 7, 16
Vikings: II 163; V 264, 266
Villula, John de, bishop of Bath and Wells:
  V 277
Vinsauf, Geoffrey de, *Poetria nova*: XVI 25
Vitalis, abbot of Westminster: III 192–3

Walcher, bishop of Durham: III 191–2;
  V 263–4, 266–8; VII 17
Wales: XIII 14; XIV 196
Walkelin, bishop of Winchester: V 277;
  VI 337
Walpole, Horace: I 4
Walter, chaplain of Henry I, and Carlisle
  priory: IX 177–81
Walter, Hubert, archbishop of Canterbury:
  XIII 9, 11
Waltham (Essex): VII 17
Waltheof, earl of Northumbria: III 192 n.11;
  V 264
Walworth (Co. Durham): XIII 7, 16
Wansbeck, river (Northumb.): XII 2
Wark-on-Tweed (Northumb.): VII 20–21;
  XI 155
Warkworth (Northumb.): I 11; XIII 7
Warwick: XIII 2
Warwickshire: XIII 6
Washington (Co. Durham): XII 15
Watson, Christopher, *History of Duresme*: I 3
Wazo, archdeacon of Durham: III 198–9,
  200–1, 203–5
Wear, river (Co. Durham): VII 20; XII 11;
  XIV 203
Weardale: XII 33; XV 47
Wearmouth, monastic community: III 193;
  V 266, 269; VII 22; XII 5 n.10, 9 n.25, 11
  n.32, 28, 35 n.130
Welbury (N. Yorks.): XIII 7
Wells, bishops: V 265 n, 19; VI 336 n.1
Welton (E. Yorks.): VII 17
Wendover, Roger of: II 167
Wessington, John, prior of Durham,
  Chronicle: I 17; VI 323–5; VII 14 n.2, 17;
  XV 56
West Saxons, kings: X 54; XI 152; *see also*
  Æthelberht; Æthelwulf; Alfred; Brihtric;
  Cerdic
Westminster: III 192, 203; VII 23; XIV 208
  n.46; council (1102): VII 18 n.24; abbots:
  see Lawrence, Vitalis
Westmorland: V 274

Westoe (Co. Durham): XII 35 n.130
Westou: *see* Alfred
Wharton, Henry: I 15, 18, 20
Wheatley Hill (Co. Durham): XIV 197, 207
  n.31, 211 n.78
Whessoe (Co. Durham): XII 14 n.46, 15, 16
  n.57; XIII 4 n.12, 10 n.40
Whickham (Co. Durham): XII 5, 19–20, 24,
  29, 33, 38
Whitburn (Co. Durham): XII 5 n.10, 33 n.121
Whitby (N. Yorks.): V 266; X 61 n.33;
  Abbots: X 56; *see also* Benedict
Whitehead, Hugh, prior and then dean of
  Durham: I 18
Whitworth (Co. Durham): XII 15, 20, 26, 29
Whitworth, Thomas: XIV 208 n.57
Wido, abbot of St Augustine's, Canterbury:
  VI 330
Wiking, monk of Durham: III 195 n.22
Wilbert *miles*, nephew of Archdeacon Ranulf:
  III 201 n.53
Wilfrid, St, cult: X 53; *Vita*: II 164
William I, king of England: III 191; V 260,
  262–5, 267 n.29, 270; VI 324 n.5, 335;
  VII 17 & n.19, 21 n.44; IX 177; XII 12, 14
  n.45
William II, king of England: V 258, 280;
  VI 335, 338, 340; VII 14, 17 n.19, 20 &
  n.38; IX 180; relations with Bishop
  Flambard: VII 14–15;—with Bishop
  William of St Calais: V 270–77, 279; over
  the trial (1088) of: VI 321–3, 327–36, 340
William the Lion, king of Scotland: XI 155
William 'Havegrim', archdeacon of Durham:
  III 194–6
William, archdeacon of Durham/
  Northumberland: III 205–6
William, bishop of Moray: XI 155
William, chamberlain to Bishop Flambard:
  VII 21
William, the moneyer: XII 21; son: *see*
  William son of William son of Erkembald
William, prior of Durham: XIII 7 n.23
William son (?) of Meldred son of Uhtred:
  XIII 6, 8
William son of Thole, archdeacon of York/
  West Riding: III 195
William son of Utting: XII 25, 31
William son of William son of Erkembald:
  XII 21; father: *see* William the moneyer
Willington (Co. Durham): XII 19 n.69
Winchester: III 202; VII 23; VIII 182–3;
  annals: *see* Devizies; bishops: *see* Blois;
  Walkelin
Winchester, Ralph of: VII 22

Windsor (Berks.): V 277; VII 17 n.20
Winlaton (Co. Durham): VII 22; XII 10, 12–13, 24 n.90, 33 n.121; XIII 3–4
Winston (Co. Durham): XII 11–12, 13 n.40, 23, 35 n.130; XIII 4
Wintringham: III 202
Wischard, John, bishop of Glasgow: XV 47 n.10
Wiseman (Wyseman), William: XV 55 n.44
Witeker, Nigel; *see* Longchamp, Nigel de
Witton Gilbert (Co. Durham): XII 24, 26, 33 n.120, 35 n.130
Witton-le-Wear (Co. Durham): XIII 4
Wolsey, Thomas, bishop of Durham: VII 14
Wolsingham (Co. Durham): XII 3, 5, 23, 26, 33
Woodstock, Edward of, the 'Black Prince', duke of Cornwall: XV 51 n.33; prince of Wales: XVI 5 n.11, 6
Wooler (Northumb.): XIV 201, 210 n.69
Worcester: XIII 7. Bishops: V 265 n.19; VI 336 n.1; X 55
Worcester, John of, *Chronicon*, formerly attributed to Florence: I 9, 21 n.13, 25; II 166; III 191–2; V 273 n.48; VI 322 n.3, 325, 327, 335 n.1; VII 15 n.5; X 54–9; XI 152, 153 n.4
Worsall (N. Yorks.): XIII 7, 16
Wrexham (Denbighshire): XIV 206 n.29

Yarm (N. Yorks.): VII 22
York: III 202–3; V 263; XIII 15; XIV 200; XV 54 n.41; and *Historia Regum*: I 9; archbishops: I 11, 14, 22 n.23; VII 18, 26; IX 181; X 55, 57; XV 53; *and see* Gerard; Greenfield; Lee; Melton; Murdac; Thomas I–II; Thurstan; Zouche; their dispute with Canterbury: VI 336; their jurisdiction in Scotland: VI 336; XI 152, 156; archdeaconries: III 205; French chronicle: *see* Anonimalle; Minster, prebend: *see* Salton; St Mary's abbey: I 21 n.22; V 266; IX 176; X 61 n.33; XI 156; abbots: X 56; *and see* Geoffrey; Longchamp; Richard; Severinus
Yorkshire: I 10; VII 21; X 55; XII 2; XIII 2, 5 n.15

Zouche, William, archbishop of York: XV 53

INDEX OF MANUSCRIPTS

Alnwick, Alnwick Castle
  X.II.1 (2): VIII 181

Cambridge, Corpus Christi College
  66: I 20 n.8, 25; X 51
  100 (1): I 23 n.32
  138: I 24 n.40; II 166
  139: I 20–1 nn.9 & 14, 25; III 192 n.11;
    X 51–8, 60–1 nn.32 & 36; XI 152 n.6,
    153–4, 157
Cambridge, Jesus College
  24 (Q.B.7): XV 47 n.12, 57
Cambridge, Peterhouse
  74: V 278 n.72; VI 332 n.3, 341
Cambridge, Trinity College
  1227 (O.3.55): XI 157 n.3
Cambridge, University Library
  Ff.1.27: I 20 n.8, 22–3 nn.30 & 39, 25;
    II 165 n.10; IV 591 n.4; X 51

Durham, County Record Office,
  D/Bo/D/37: III 208
  Salvin Deeds no. 216: XII 37; XIV 206
    n.19 217: XII 37
Durham, Dean and Chapter Library
  A.II.4: V 278 n.70
  A.II.16: V 269 n.36
  A.IV.36 (formerly Phillipps 9374): I 23
    nn.32 & 39; VI 325 n.3
  B.II.13: V 277
  B.II.24: V 268 n.35
  B.II.35: I 22 nn. 23–4 & 29; II 166; III 196
    n.29; V 268 n.31; VII 18 n.29; XV 46,
    57
  B.IV.24: III 192 n.13, 195 n.23, 200–1
    nn.47 & 55, 204–05 nn.70 & 77;
    V 261–2 nn.8 & 11
  Hunter 100: I 21 n.21
Durham, Dean and Chapter Muniments
  1.1.Archidiac.Dunelm.2: III 199 n.38
  4.3.Ebor.4: III 208
  5.1.Elemos.21: XIV 206 n.21
  4.5.Elemos.1: XIV 206 n.20
  1.1.Pont.1–4b: V 259 n.4
  2.1.Pont.1 and 1*: III 199 n.43
  2.1.Pont.2: III 199 nn.39–40, 200 n.50

  2.1.Pont.3: III 199 nn.39–40
  2.1.Pont.3*: III 199 n.39
  2.1.Pont.5: III 199 n.39
  2.1.Pont.6–7*: III 201 n.52
  2.1.Pont.8: III 197 n.32
  2.1.Pont.10: III 199 n.39
  2.1.Pont.11: III 200 n.49
  3.1.Pont.10: XIII 6 n.20
  3.1.Pont.11: III 204 n.75; VIII 186 n.17;
    XIII 4 n.14, 6 n.20
  3.1.Pont.12: III 204 n.76
  3.1.Pont.17: XII 23 n.83
  3.1.Pont.21: XII 26 n.100
  4.1.Pont.3: XII 15 n.48, 24 n.88
  4.1.Pont.7: XII 27 n.103
  4.1.Pont.8: III 204 n.76
  4.1.Pont.15: III 199 n.43, 201 n.58
  4.1.Pont.17: III 199 n.43
  1.2.Pont.1: III 202 n.63
  1.2.Pont.4: III 202 n.63
  2.2.Pont.1: I 23 n.37; III 207 n.90
  2.2.Pont.2: I 23 n.37
  2.2.Pont.5: I 23 n.37; III 207 n.90
  3.2.Pont.4–5: XIV 206 n.20
  3.2.Pont.8a–9b: XIV 206 n.20
  3.2.Pont.12–13: XIV 206 n.20
  4.3.Pont.1: XIV 206 n.20
  2.4.Pont.8: XII 19 n.69
  1.1.Reg.8: VI 328 n.1
  1.1.Reg.17: XII 12 n.36
  2.1.Reg.12: XIII 3 n.6
  3.3.Sacr.7: XII 21 n.76
  4.1.Spec.21: XIV 206 n.20
  3.2.Spec.9: III 206 nn.82 & 84
  4.2.Spec.1: III 204 n.76; VIII 188 n.24
  4.2.Spec.2: VIII 185 n.11
  4.2.Spec.3: VIII 186 n.18
  4.2.Spec.46: VIII 186 n.16
  2.4.Spec.8: XIII 7 n.23
  2.6.Spec.3–4: XII 21 n.76
  3.6.Spec.4: XII 21 n.77
  3.6.Spec.18: XIII 9 n.34
  3.7.Spec.7: XII 24 n.88
  3.7.Spec.16: XIV 205 n.12
  3.7.Spec.20: XIII 8 n.32
  3.7.Spec.21: III 206 n.86

INDEX OF MANUSCRIPTS

(Durham, Dean and Chapter Muniments continued)
3.8.Spec.9: III 202 n.63
2.10.Spec.12: XIV 205 n.11
2.10.Spec.13: XIV 206 n.18
1.11.Spec.16: XIII 7 n.22
1.11.Spec.17: XIII 6 n.22, 7 n.22
1.11.Spec.19: XIII 6 n.22
2.14.Spec.23: XII 21 n.75
2.14.Spec.41: XIII 13 n.61
Cart. I: III 199 n.39, 200 n.50; XIV 205 n.14
Cart. II: III 199 n. 42, 206 n.83; XIII 9 n.37
Cart. III: III 197 n.32
Cart. Elemos: XII 26
Cart. Vet.: XIII 14 n.64; XIV 205 n.14
Loc.XXVII.31: XIV 208 nn.51, 53–4
Misc. Ch. 1354: III 206 n.82
1816: XIV 206 n.20
3448: XIV 208 n.46
3462: XIV 208 n.52
4086: XIV 205 n.2, 208 n.52
4339: XIV 208 n.51
4399: XIV 205 n.2, 208 n.52
4912: XIV 205 n.2
5053: XIV 205 n.4
5150: XIV 206 n.20
5155: XII 23 n.82
6157: XII 23 n.82
6261: XIV 210 n.64
6262: XIV 209–10 nn.60 & 64–5
6263–64: XIV 211 nn.70 & 76
6265–68: XIV 211 n.76
6362: XII 37
6377: XIV 207 n.38
6379: XIV 210–11 nn.64 & 72
6597: XIV 209 n.62
6980: XIV 211 n.76
7243: XII 21 n.74, 27 n.104
Register I: XII 6–11, 19, 22, 25, 29, 30 n.115, 34
Durham, University Library
Cosin V.II.6: I 20 n.5, 22 n.30, 24 n.39; V 269 n.36; VI 324–5, 328 n.1; VII 20 n.37

Glasgow, University Library
Hunterian 85 (T.4.2): I 21 n.21; II 168

Holkham Hall
468: now Oxford, Bodleian Library, Holkham misc. 25

Liège, University Library

369C: I 22 n.22, 26
London, British Library
Add. 24059: I 22–4 nn.28, 38 & 40
39943: IV 592 n.6
40000: VII 19 n.35
40007: XI 156 n.4, 157
Cotton Caligula A.viii: I 21–2 nn.22–3
Claudius D.iv: I 24 n.44; VI 323, 324, 325
Claudius D.vii: IX 176, 177; XV 45, 49, 53, 55
Domitian vii (Durham *Liber Vitae*): XIII 8 n.32
Domitian viii: I 22 n.23
Faustina A.v: I 20 n.5; VI 325 n.2
Julius D.iv: I 15, 20 n.4
Nero D.iv (Lindisfarne Gospels): I 8
Otho A.xii: X 59 n.5
Titus A.ii: I 20 n.1, 23–4 nn. 31, 33 & 39–40; VI 325 n.3
Vespasian A.v: I 23 n.32
Vespasian A.vi: I 24 n.39
Vespasian B.vi: II 166, 168
Vespasian C.xvi: XVI 2–4, 6, 9
Vitellius A.xx: XI 157 n.1
Vitellius D.xx: IV 591 n.4
Harley 433: VII 26
533: I 22 n.30
1804: V 261 n.8
1808: XIV 204 nn.1–2, 210 n.69
1985: XIV 207 n.31
3289: V 262 n.12
4843: I 24 n.46; VI 324; XV 56 n.50
6589: XIV 207 n.33
Lansdowne 902: XII 12 n.39, 15 n.54; XIII 4 n.10
Loan 74 (Stonyhurst Gospel): I 8; VII 24
Royal 13 A.vi: VI 326 n.4
Stowe 930: XII 6–11, 18–19, 22–3, 25, 29, 34
London, Inner Temple Library
Petyt 511.2: I 21 n.16
London, Lambeth Palace Library
10–11: XV 57 n.53
12: I 22 n.29; XIV 205 n.5; XV 46 n.8, 47, 57
London, Lincolns Inn Library
Hale 114: III 197 n.32; VI 323, 324, 325; VII 17 n.14
London *al.* Kew, Public Record Office.
Domesday Book: V 280
Durham 3/2: XIV 209 n.62, 211 n.77
Durham 3/12 (1349–62): XII n.9
E/39/2(2): XVI 6 n.13
E/39/2(22): XVI 5 n.11

INDEX OF MANUSCRIPTS

(London *al.* Kew, Public Record Office, continued)
E/326/11535: III 202 n.63
JUST/1/132: IX 179 n.10
JUST/1/223: XIII 15 nn.68 & 71; XIV 205 n.15
JUST/1/224: XIII 15 n.67; XIV 205 n.15
SC/12/21/28: XII 6–10, 17, 19, 21–2, 24–5, 27–30, 32, 34
London, Westminster Abbey
XXIV(3): V 280

Newcastle–upon–Tyne, Central Library
Greenwell Deeds, no. 3: III 203 n.64
25: XIV 205 n.15
Newcastle–upon–Tyne, Society of Antiquaries,
Ravensworth Deeds, no. 1: III 201 n.51
2: VIII 181 n.1
6–7: XIV 205 n.16
16: XIII 13 n.61
20: XII 21 n.75; XIV 205 n.16
21–6: XIV 205 n.16
28–9: XIV 205 n.16, 209 n.63
31: XIV 203
31(iii): XIV 206 n.23
31(v): XIV 206 n.23
33: XIV 209 n.62
35: XIV 211 n.70
36: XIV 211 n.71
38: XIV 211 nn. 71–2
39: XIV 211 n.71
42: XIV 211 n.72
46: XIV 211 n.72

Oxford, Bodleian Library
Dodsworth 7: XII 15 n.48
Fairfax 6: I 23–4 nn.31 & 38–9; VI 323, 324, 325
Holkham misc. 25: I 20 n.8, 22–3 nn.31, 33 & 39, 25–6; III 203 n.69
Laud misc. 542: XII 6–11, 19, 25, 29, 34
700: I 23–4 nn.31 & 38–9; VI 323–5
748: I 24 n.44; III 197 n.32; VI 323 n.5, 324; XV 56 n. 51
Rawlinson B.214: XV 46 n.7, 49 n.19
Oxford, Magdalen College
53: I 22 n.23
Oxford, St John's College
97: I 21 n.16; X 54

Paris, Bibliothèque Nationale
lat. 5444: V 262 n.13
nouv. acq. lat. 692: I 20–1 nn.9 & 14; IX 176–9; X 52, 54–6; XI 151, 153–4, 157–9

Stonyhurst College
55 (Stonyhurst Gospel): I 8; VII 24

York Minster Library
Reg. Mag. Album: III 202 n.63
XVI.A.1 (St Mary's cartulary): III 202 n.63
XVI.I.12: I 12, 20 n.8, 23 nn. 31 & 33, 23–4 nn.39–40 & 46; II 165 n. 10; VI 325 n. 3